Permanent Liminality and Modernity

This book offers a comprehensive sociological study of the nature and dynamics of the modern world, through the use of a series of anthropological concepts, including the trickster, schismogenesis, imitation and liminality. Developing the view that with the theatre playing a central role, the modern world is conditioned as much by cultural processes as it is by economic, technological or scientific ones, the author contends the world is, to a considerable extent, theatrical – a phenomenon experienced as inauthenticity or a loss of direction and meaning. As such the novel is revealed as a means for studying our theatricalised reality, not simply because novels can be understood to be likening the world to theatre, but because they effectively capture and present the reality of a world that has been thoroughly 'theatricalised' – and they do so more effectively than the main instruments usually employed to analyse reality: philosophy and sociology. With analyses of some of the most important novelists and novels of modern culture, including Rilke, Hofmannsthal, Kafka, Mann, Blixen, Broch and Bulgakov, and focusing on fin-de-siècle Vienna as a crucial 'threshold' chronotope of modernity, *Permanent Liminality and Modernity* demonstrates that all seek to investigate and unmask the theatricalisation of modern life, with its progressive loss of meaning and our deteriorating capacity to distinguish between what is meaningful and what is artificial. Drawing on the work of Nietzsche, Bakhtin and Girard to examine the ways in which novels explore the reduction of human existence to a state of permanent liminality, in the form of a sacrificial carnival, this book will appeal to scholars of social, anthropological and literary theory.

Arpad Szakolczai is Professor of Sociology at University College Cork, Ireland. He is the author of *Max Weber and Michel Foucault: Parallel Life-Works*, *Reflexive Historical Sociology*, *The Genesis of Modernity*, *Sociology, Religion and Grace: A Quest for the Renaissance*, and *Comedy and the Public Sphere: The Re-birth of Theatre as Comedy and the Genealogy of the Modern Public Arena*, and co-author of *The Dissolution of Communist Power: The Case of Hungary*.

Contemporary Liminality

Series editor: *Arpad Szakolczai,*
University College Cork, Ireland

Series advisory board:
Agnes Horvath, University College Cork, Ireland
Bjørn Thomassen, Roskilde University, Denmark
Harald Wydra, University of Cambridge, UK

This series constitutes a forum for works that make use of concepts such as 'imitation', 'trickster' or 'schismogenesis', but which chiefly deploy the notion of 'liminality', as the basis of a new, anthropologically-focused paradigm in social theory. With its versatility and range of possible uses rivalling and even going beyond mainstream concepts such as 'system', 'structure' or 'institution', liminality is increasingly considered a new master concept that promises to spark a renewal in social thought.

In spite of the fact that charges of Eurocentrism or even 'moderno-centrism' are widely discussed in sociology and anthropology, it remains the case that most theoretical tools in the social sciences continue to rely on taken-for-granted approaches developed from within the modern Western intellectual tradition, whilst concepts developed on the basis of extensive anthropological evidence and which challenged commonplaces of modernist thinking have been either marginalised and ignored, or trivialised. By challenging the assumed neo-Kantian and neo-Hegelian foundations of modern social theory, and by helping to shed new light on the fundamental ideas of major figures in social theory, such as Nietzsche, Dilthey, Weber, Elias, Voegelin, Foucault and Koselleck, whilst also establishing connections between the perspectives gained through modern social and cultural anthropology and the central concerns of classical philosophical anthropology *Contemporary Liminality* offers a new direction in social thought.

Titles in this series

1. **Permanent Liminality and Modernity**
   Analysing the sacrificial carnival through novels
   Arpad Szakolczai

Permanent Liminality and Modernity

Analysing the sacrificial carnival through novels

Arpad Szakolczai

LONDON AND NEW YORK

First published 2017
by Routledge
2 Park Square, Milton Park, Abingdon, Oxon OX14 4RN

and by Routledge
711 Third Avenue, New York, NY 10017

Routledge is an imprint of the Taylor & Francis Group, an informa business

© 2017 Arpad Szakolczai

The right of Arpad Szakolczai to be identified as author of this work has been asserted by him in accordance with sections 77 and 78 of the Copyright, Designs and Patents Act 1988.

All rights reserved. No part of this book may be reprinted or reproduced or utilised in any form or by any electronic, mechanical, or other means, now known or hereafter invented, including photocopying and recording, or in any information storage or retrieval system, without permission in writing from the publishers.

Trademark notice: Product or corporate names may be trademarks or registered trademarks, and are used only for identification and explanation without intent to infringe.

British Library Cataloguing in Publication Data
A catalogue record for this book is available from the British Library

Library of Congress Cataloging in Publication Data
A catalog record for this book has been requested

ISBN: 978-1-4724-7388-2 (hbk)
ISBN: 978-1-315-60005-5 (ebk)

Typeset in Times New Roman
by Keystroke, Neville Lodge, Tettenhall, Wolverhampton

Printed and bound by CPI Group (UK) Ltd, Croydon, CR0 4YY

Contents

Preface   vii

Introduction   1

PART I
Before World War I: waiting for the storm   3

1 Empires and their collapse: fin-de-siècle Vienna in context   5

2 Hugo von Hofmannsthal: promises and realities   23

3 Novel origins: Rilke's *Notebooks of Malte* and Hofmannsthal's *Andreas*   37

PART II
Suspended in the In-Between: Franz Kafka   61

4 Kafka's sources and insights: theatre and other modes of distorted communication   63

5 Kafka's novels: in between theatre, theology and prophecy   85

6 The Zürau Notebooks: the indestructible and the way   102

PART III
After World War I: hypermodernity as sacrificial carnival   123

7 Thomas Mann: *Death in Venice* and *Magic Mountain*   125

8 Karen Blixen: 'Carnival' and *Angelic Avengers*   151

9 Hermann Broch: *Sleepwalkers* 165

10 Mikhail Bulgakov: *Master and Margarita* 180

11 Heimito von Doderer: *Demons* 194

12 Béla Hamvas: *Carnival* 209

Conclusion 234
Bibliography 240
Name index 250
Subject index 255

Preface

> There is more freedom within the narrowest bounds, within the most specific task, than in that boundless non-place which modern consciousness imagines to be the playground of freedom
>
> Hofmannsthal, *Book of Friends*

> Count it the worst disgrace to prefer survival to honour;
> And, for the sake of life, lose the point of living.
>
> Juvenal, *Satires*

> Where no gods are, spectres rule
>
> Novalis

Talking about the ambivalence or ambiguity of modernity is a major intellectual fashion. As always, the pioneering ideas (Bauman 1991) were refreshing, even insightful. They offered a way to go jointly beyond the dualism of promoting modernity or endorsing critical theory: schismogenic doubles. However, by our days, the term has lost all its charm, become a facile manner to deflect any serious questioning. The ambivalence of modernity came to mean that the modern world, as all things in life, has many aspects: some good, others less so. Nothing is perfect, there are no beds of roses, so we should rather get on with our daily business. Such a position, however, is clearly unhelpful in understanding what is going on today with all of us in the planet, as what is increasingly rendered impossible to do, in and by the modern world, is just to proceed with normal daily existence.

As so often, Max Weber offers a perspective that is still more fresh today than most sociological works written over the last decades. In a recent article Iván Szelényi argued that in contrast to Habermas Weber is the sociologist of the twenty-first century, having digested the insights of Nietzsche and pointing forward to Foucault (Szelényi 2015: 5).

Taking up his insights, such lasting relevance could be due to Weber's recognition of the disruptive tensions that animate the dynamics of the modern world. What Weber perceived, with singular and almost unique clarity, is that modernity was not simply 'ambivalent', but can be characterised by two sets of radically opposed categories. On the one hand, the modern world seems to spread almost freely – though with the full ambiguity of the term, recognised already by Marx – a series of benefits around the world: unprecedented economic prosperity and well-being, scientific and technological knowledge, legal security and the universality of human rights, a care for the suffering and the weak, tolerance for reasonable difference. On the other, however, it is also evidently the source of some of the most atrocious sufferings that were ever inflicted in the planet, and in a similarly striking and unprecedented manner, including two world worlds, a number of totalitarian states, a series of genocides, including the Holocaust, the disempowering of most human beings, the destruction of cultures and ways of life, and the spread of a single, dominant and particularly repulsive form of technologised mass culture and way of living. Understanding modernity, through Weber, means to take up the task of confronting the nature of the forces animating the increasing, and increasingly intolerable, tensions driving the project of modernity.

This book is part of a long-term effort at understanding the nature and dynamics of the contemporary global modern world. From one perspective, it is the seventh and final volume of a series of books, all published by Routledge, offering elements towards a genealogy of modernity, being particularly close to *Novels and the Sociology of the Contemporary*, which deals with the classical modern novel. From another, it is the first volume of the Routledge (formerly Ashgate) series on 'Contemporary Liminality' that proposes the use of anthropological concepts for analysing our world (see also Boland 2013; Horvath 2013a; Horvath and Thomassen 2008; Horvath et al. 2015; Thomassen 2014; Thomassen and Wydra forthcoming; Wydra 2015). Thus, while part of a long-term project, the book aims at coming to terms with the here and now, jointly relying on historical and anthropological perspectives, exploring the idea that the modern condition can be best characterised as a paradoxical state of 'permanent liminality' (on 'liminality', see van Gennep 1981; Turner 1967, 1969; Szakolczai 2009, Thomassen 2009; on 'permanent liminality', Szakolczai 2000).

Being the concluding volume of a twenty-some-years-long project, this book evidently owes a lot to many people, all of whom cannot be possibly named here. I must focus only on those whose contribution in bringing this book to completion was particularly special.

These include first of all the founding editors of *International Political Anthropology*, Harald Wydra, Bjørn Thomassen and especially Ágnes Horváth, animating spirit of all the intellectual ventures of the journal, including the book series, the Socratic Symposia, the various conferences, and in particular the yearly summer schools; the associate and assistant editors of the journal, Tom Boland, John O'Brien, James Cuffe, Julian Davis, Brian Finucane and Sam Boland; and all the various participants of the past IPA summer schools.

I express warm thanks to my colleagues at University College Cork, in particular Kieran Keohane and Colin Sumner, fellow directors of the *Centre for the Study of the Moral Foundations of Economy & Society*, founded under the President of Ireland Ethics Initiative; the vital, persistent support of Caroline Fennell (Head of College), Colin Sumner (Head of School), Kieran Keohane and Niamh Hourigan (successive Heads of Department) and Anne Gannon; the students attending my postgraduate seminars, especially my PhD students; and the UCC Strategic Fund, which offered a vital help to complete the book more or less in time. As always, it is a special pleasure to recall here the numerous discussions I had with James Fairhead; and also Tony O'Connor.

My sincere gratitude is expressed to the librarians of the Boole Library, University College Cork, the Biblioteca Nazionale Centrale di Firenze, the Library of the European University Institute in Florence and Cambridge University Library; and to my editor, first at Ashgate and then Routledge, Neil Jordan.

I recall those who did not see the completion of the project: my mother, Klára Osztroluczky; my academic mentor in Hungary, Elemér Hankiss; my close colleague and friend in Cork, Paddy O'Carroll; and Martin Riesebrodt, all of whom passed away during the winter of 2014/15.

This is the place to mention my sons, Dániel, Péter, János, Tommaso and Stefano, who all grew up during and under this long-term project, by now more or less completely, rendering the work not only easier, but particularly meaningful.

As it is only right, these acknowledgements start and end with Ágnes. Nobody has, and can have, even an inkling about the depths of my debts, as this is impossible to express, and when expressed, cannot be taken seriously.

Florence, 25 March 2016

Introduction

The modern novel, with Goethe but also *Tristram Shandy* and *Hyperion*, even back to Rabelais and Cervantes, started not by endorsing the promises of modernity, rather by rendering evident its inherent problems. From this perspective it is not surprising that in the second part of the nineteenth century the novel culminated, through Dickens and Dostoevsky, in reasserting the Resurrection in contrast to the Revolution, confirmed in an at once most concrete and symbolic manner by the last great novel of the last great novelist of the century, Tolstoy's *Resurrection*, published in 1899.

Yet, modernity or modernism was by no means finished with this, rather in a truly extraordinary manner got a further boost through another collapse of an eastern Empire, this time Austria, showing most striking parallels with the collapse of the Byzantine Empire and the transmogrification of the Renaissance into early modernity. While the growth of an empire is itself stimulated by an inner void (for details, see Szakolczai forthcoming2), the collapse of an empire proliferates void exponentially. Thus, to mark a new stage within modernity, and following a suggestion by Agnes Horvath, modelled on Ortega's 'hyper-democracy' and Augé's *surmodernité*, the era starting with the twentieth century and immediately marked by the most devastating wars and totalitarian regimes ever inflicted on mankind will be termed as the age of hypermodernity.

At one level, these wars, revolutions and totalitarian regimes follow a sacrificial logic, even technically resurrecting, in the sense of Girard, the sacrificial mechanism. Their sacrificial character was first recognised by Marcel Mauss, reason for his withdrawing from the promises of both Durkheimian sociology, which placed rituals of sacrifice as the origin of culture, and socialism, marked by his two key sets of essays on Bolshevism and on gift relations first published around 1924 (Mauss 1992, 2002); a discovery followed by Borkenau's pioneering recognition of the close similarities between communism and fascism. Yet, at the same time, the modern sacrificial logic is also carnivalesque, celebrating the destruction of traditions, supposedly liberating mankind from the bondage of nature and tyranny, promising to inaugurate a new age of unprecedented freedom and well-being. Liberal and socialist, capitalist or communist dreams converge in the vision of a permanent carnival.

2   Introduction

The two sides, sacrifice and carnival, are not contradictory, rather – part of modern bipolarism – constitute two states that permanently metamorphose into each other, as if alongside a Möbius strip, helped by the progress of theatrical forms of conduct, which explains while the re-birth of the theatre, ignored in the sociology of modernity, played a role comparable in importance to Puritanism, the court or the disciplinary network in the genesis of the modern world. The carnivalesque promises are absurd, unrealisable, and the eventual disillusion inexorably brings in a new set of sacrificial measures and techniques, spinning ever forward into the void, animating the progress of globalisation, which is both a global carnival and the globalisation of the resurrected sacrificial mechanism.

This book will not offer a historically and anthropologically based genealogy of the global modern world, only present the manner in which the visionary recognition of its endgame in the form of hypermodernity was perceived in some visionary novels of the first half of the twentieth century, in the footsteps of three quasi-novels written coincidentally in 1911–2, 'Death in Venice' by Thomas Mann, *Andreas* by Hugo von Hofmannsthal and 'The Verdict' by Franz Kafka, the three most emblematic figures of Central-European culture in the period, based on the pioneering effort of Rilke, a poet, *The Notebooks of Malte Laurids Brigge*, playing an initiatory role both in hypermodern culture and in its (self-) overcoming.

Part One presents the rise of the hypermodern novel in context. Chapter 1 reconstructs the spirit the Austrian (literally 'Eastern') Empire unleashed on to the world by its collapse. Chapter 2 is devoted to Hofmannsthal, representative figure of this Austrian culture, while Chapter 3 to the origins of the hypermodern novel, focusing on the works of Rilke and Hofmannsthal. For reasons of economy and structure, 'The Verdict' and 'Death in Venice' will be discussed at the start of the respective chapters on Kafka and Mann.

Part Two discusses Kafka through his three novels, all unfinished, focusing on their conditions of emergence in Kafka's encounter with East-European Yiddish theatre, and considering Kafka's work, among others in the footsteps of Roberto Calasso and Pietro Citati, as an anti-theological theology, culminating in the unpublished Zürau Notebooks, which strikingly share the formal characteristics of Rilke's *Malte*. Part Three discusses six major hypermodern novels or novelists of the past century. Chapter 7, a threshold chapter, is devoted to Thomas Mann's *Magic Mountain*, itself playing a threshold role in the history of the modern novel, only comparable to its exact contemporary, *Ulysses* by James Joyce. The remaining chapters of the book document, through novels, the epidemic spread of the sacrificial carnival in Europe and then the world, with the two world wars, the various totalitarian regimes and the propagandistic systems of mass communication technology, having as their engine the self-sustaining but mutually reinforcing systems for the alchemical proliferation of the void, technologised science and finance economy.

Part I
Before World War I
Waiting for the storm

1 Empires and their collapse
Fin-de-siècle Vienna in context

Following hints from Bakhtin (1981), *Novels and the Sociology of the Contemporary* presented the rise of the modern novel as a progress across certain 'chronotopes', or concrete times and places central for the rise of modernity which at the same time were birthplaces of the modern novel, through the intermediary of the theatre, as – here following hints from Agnew (1986) – the theatre was considered as not simply 'reflecting' such changes, rather a crucial operator in them as a social practice. The rise of the hypermodern novel is also connected to a new chronotope, and a particularly intriguing one, given that Austria never before or after played a major role in modern or European culture, except for the music of Beethoven, Mozart and Haydn at the end of the eighteenth century,[1] while in the few decades before World War I it suddenly catapulted itself into the incubator of modernism.

Every single element of this crucial chronotope is profoundly shrouded in paradoxes and ambivalence. It starts at the most elementary level, its name. As it has been emphasised by two of its most famous writers, Robert Musil and Joseph Roth, a unique feature of the Habsburg Empire was that it 'had *no accepted name!*' (*sic*.; Janik and Toulmin 1973: 36–7). The political entity is usually called 'Austro-Hungarian' Empire, but Hungary had little to do with its features, entering the name as Pilate entered the credo, the only reason for the name being to please Hungarians who wanted to be *outside* the Empire. Even the expression 'fin-de-siècle Vienna' is misleading, as Prague was not simply part of the Empire, but played a major role both in its political and cultural life, much more than Budapest. Several of the most famous figures of the period were formed in Prague, like Mach, Husserl, Rilke or Kafka. In his speech delivered on the occasion of his Noble prize Elias Canetti described Kafka as an Austrian (Janik 2001: 1, 247), while Prague was often considered as the true capital of Austria.

Taking paradoxes further, members of the Vienna/Prague cultural elite were certainly self-conscious about being in the vanguard, while also keenly aware that such leadership position implied to be ahead of the others in terms of losing sense and direction, a fading of values and a growing sense of vagueness (Francis 1985: 1–2). The presumed vanguard status of Vienna was also combined with a keen sense of imitativity: Vienna followed London in economic terms, while Paris in culture: the famed theatre, poetry, opera, operetta, coffee-house and cabaret cultures of Vienna each imitated Paris models. Thus, far from being an independent centre of cultural flourishing, Vienna was rather the 'seismograph' or 'weather station' of Europe which 'registered inexorably the signs, even the most imperceptible ones, of the catastrophe' (according to Karl Kraus; see Magris 1986: 21), the 'crucible' of modernity (Steinberg 1984: 3); using the remarkable expression of Hermann Broch, it was 'the centre of the European void of values [*Wert-Vakuum*]' (Broch 1974: 47). Even further, this void soon assumed apocalyptic proportions, with the Viennese literary avant-garde, these vagabonds of the coffee tables even offering apologies for an apocalypse (Magris 1986: 21). Yet, in another striking expression of Broch, this apocalypse seemed, at least to some, even 'joyful' (*Die fröhliche Apokalypse*, title of section 4 of the first essay, a clear allusion to Nietzsche's 'gay science', *Die Fröhliche Wissenschaft*).

Yet, again, a joyful apocalypse – meaning not the Second Coming but a genuine collapse and end-of-the-world-as-we-know-it – is simply absurd and unreal, and such unreality was indeed a central feature of fin-de-siècle Vienna. The great Viennese culture of the period only unmasked the 'increasing abstraction and unreality of life', which was 'ever more absorbed by mechanisms of collective information and transformed by its own *mise en scène*', the reality of the world perceived as being 'identical to the spectacle it gave about it' (Magris 1986: 21). Masks and unmasking assumed each other, producing a permanent game of illusion, where existence became inseparable from its images that were reproduced in innumerable copies; where everything was artificial, and therefore staged representation captured the true untruth of reality, with masks hiding not reality but the void. It is in this sense that the representative forms of art in fin-de-siècle Vienna literally represented, and in every possible sense, the void, and in an ever-increasing scale and magnitude. The flagship venue of Vienna was theatre, most closely related to Vienna modernism, a modernism 'officially' inaugurated by the Ibsen week of April 1891 (Yates 1992: 1–2). Theatre again offered a perfect 'representation' of Vienna modernism, where 'in the truest sense of the term, or rather in its double sense, theatre represented the misery of the epoch masqueraded as wealth' (Broch 1974: 16). Due to the centrality of its theatre, the world in Vienna genuinely felt as a stage (Yates 1992: 66); though, at the same time, already by the 1880s, recalling mid-eighteenth century England, theatrical life reached the nadir of intellectual vacuity, though – or, again, rather because of it – theatre remained the heart of Vienna (Ibid.: 68, 72). Still, an even more representative genre of the epoch was opera, which managed to transform the 'non-style' of the epoch itself into style (Broch used the term 'non-style' in the title of his first chapter), to be superseded by the operetta, which was a genuine decoration of the void (*Vakuum-Dekoration*; Broch 1974: 47).

Such decorated void as lying at the heart of the Empire had an unsurpassable symbol, the empty box seat of the Emperor vacated at every single theatrical show of the Empire, waiting for the Emperor to arrive, an event that never took place, and taken by Broch as the true image of Austria (Magris 1986: 24). The theatre expressed this not only representatively but endlessly, staging a prolonged repetition of the apocalypse (Ibid.: 21–2), captured by Hofmannsthal in the *Rosenkavalier*, another representative work of art at the point of intersection between theatre, opera and operetta, where at its end the protagonist, the Marschallin – another par excellent Viennese hero, not a military general but his wife – just cannot ever end saying her goodbyes.

Vienna suddenly came to play a representative role in European culture at the end of the nineteenth century because this was a period of decadence, decay, void and nihilism, and this had a certain affinity with the kind of spirit that was evidently already present in Austria. It was this specific kind of (nihilist) spirit that Viennese modernism managed to stamp on Europe, and so, with a bit of rhetorical excess, evoking Shakespeare it can be claimed that 'We are the stuff of Viennese dreams, we moderns' (Whalen 2007: 1).

Yet, it was not simply the spirit of decay, but the decay of a very specific kind of spirit. We need now to reconstruct this 'Austrian' spirit, starting from its sources, and focusing especially on its affinities with the 'Byzantine spirit', a spirit particularly present in the unique and quite non-Prussian bureaucracy of the 'Monarchy'.[2]

The Austrian spirit

In trying to capture this spirit the first problem we encounter is that it is difficult even to pin down its name. The spirit of what? This spirit is not of Vienna, a city, and certainly not of Austria as a nation state, but of the monarchy, or rather the Empire, connected to the Habsburgs as a dynasty – each element playing its role, yet none identifying the entity. Opting for the adjective 'Austrian' was guided not so much by the contemporary country name, rather its etymological origin: 'Austrian' means Eastern, originally designating the Eastern part of the Carolingian Empire. The 'Eastern', even 'Asiatic' character of Vienna was much bemoaned by visitors even before World War I (Whalen 2007: 148), while Rilke loathed Vienna even more than Paris (Pizer 2003: 117). Such adjectives have their precise meaning, connected to terms like 'Byzantine' and 'Ottoman', whose links to the Austrian court bureaucracy are evident – and which was also connected by Kafka to the Chinese imperial court, stressing further the fruitfulness of such metaphors. The most important link, however, concerns the 'Byzantine spirit'.

The central feature of fin-de-siècle Vienna is decadence (Borkenau 1938: 155).[3] Vienna in its Golden Age (1890–1918) was certainly decadent, and in an extreme manner, which immediately raises some question marks about the value and meaning of such a 'golden age', in contrast to similar periods in Athens or Florence, which certainly were not decadent – at least, until the end. The term also evokes the Paris of Baudelaire and the thinking of Nietzsche, much influenced by Baudelaire's vision of modern decadence. But the 'Austrian spirit' can be traced before fin-de-siècle decadence – and here parallels with the Byzantine Empire become particularly close. This is because a central feature of this spirit was its paradoxical, dualistic, even schismatic character – thus directly recalling the similar Byzantine spirit (Szakolczai 2013a, Chapter 4).

Beyond mere analogy, the connections are historical.

The rise of the Habsburg Empire: a genealogical sketch of its spirit

By coincidence, if not by direct succession, the rise of the Habsburgs followed upon the demise of the Byzantium. While the 1437–38 Ferrara-Florence council marks the last, ultimately unsuccessful attempt to unify the Eastern and Western Churches, and 1453 the sack of Constantinople and the collapse of the Empire, it was in 1437–38 that the Habsburgs finally managed to get hold of the Holy Roman Empire, with its seat shifting from Prague to Vienna, while in 1453 Frederick III was crowned as Holy Emperor in Rome. Within half a century, through successful marriages – just when Henry VIII and Matthias Corvinus had no success with their Aragonian wives to secure an heir – the Habsburgs inherited first Burgundy (1477) and then Spain (1507). The Burgundy court for centuries had close connection with the Byzantine world, while the Eastern connections of Spain, through centuries of Islamic presence, thus an indirect link to the Byzantium are well known.

Growth based not on inner strength, rather clever goal-oriented strategic thinking follows a long Habsburg tradition. The central instance in the growth of the Habsburgs from merely local potentates towards major power players was provided by a forgery, the forging of the Privilegium Maius (1358/59), to promote the claims of Rudolf IV. The forgery was immediately recognised, and by none other than Petrarch, central figure of the Italian Renaissance, yet it eventually became used to support the increasing Habsburg claims for legitimate rule, and in the sixteenth–seventeenth centuries the Habsburgs formally ruled over most of Europe, excepting England, France, small sections of Italy and Poland.

An Empire gained by such means, without any clear human qualities and driving forces, could not be effective, and it wasn't. The Habsburgs lived under the shadow of the Holy Roman Empire, since long little more than a name; and yet, such names and titles mattered much in a Europe increasingly oriented towards theatrical representativeness. In the late eighteenth century Vienna was little more than a medieval city, with effective rule being divided with Prague.

As a result, and especially with the rise of Prussia, challenging the supremacy of Habsburg Austria in the German-speaking areas, the question of 'reform' – the big slogan of all Enlightenments – was increasingly on the agenda. It had two aspects marking the stamp Habsburg Austria would leave through its fin-de-siècle decadence on the modern world: the build-up of imperial bureaucracy and the reconstruction of Vienna. Both turned out to produce extremely paradoxical results, culminating in the schismatic 'Austrian spirit', caught between rigid formalism and decadent sensualism.

Bureaucracy

The emergence of modern bureaucracy is usually identified with the rise of Prussia, closely related to the modern military, legal and industrial machines, and even the modern university system, with consequences that – due to the smokescreen exerted by the World Wars – are still not fully visible. Austria for long lagged behind in following this road of 'progress', so the imitation of the Prussian model was central for the reforms started by Joseph II, shortly after acceding to the throne in 1780. However, Joseph died in 1790, his heir Leopold in 1792, and then the throne was inherited by the extremely conservative Francis, the last Holy Roman Emperor, who – indirectly, through Metternich, until 1848, scared by the developments of the French Revolution and the loss of the Holy Roman Empire – inaugurated an extremely reactionary mode of government.

This modality of reactionary conservatism had two major paradoxes. To begin with, in contrast to England or France, or practically any other European countries, there was no real tradition to preserve. The Habsburg Empire was an artificial construct, gained by tricks and ruse, not by any significant valour or merit, and so it could only survive by mimicking values, including local traditions and Catholicism. While such traditions merited to be preserved, the Habsburg Empire as a political centre never had sufficient inner strength to care for them genuinely; it could only fake. The second, just as glaring paradox is that the main instrument of such reaction came to be the very bureaucracy that was put into place in the service of reform. The Austrian Empire thus ended up with a unique and particularly repulsive combination of Byzantine and Prussian bureaucracy, rendered even more lethal by the importance of Austria as a South-German Catholic stronghold, helping to justify the unjustifiable as bulwark against both the North (Protestantism) and the East (barbarism).[4]

Modernising Vienna

After 1848 changes delayed for long decades started to be implemented, resulting in feverish construction and a quick population explosion in the city. The crucial moment, with evident symbolic significance, was the 1857 demolition of medieval city walls, replaced by Paris-style boulevards, the *Ringstrasse*. These were the years of Manchester liberalism, and a largely speculative economic boom was particularly rampant in Austria, helped by the fact that the previous government even opposed the setting up of railways. Due to such feverish economic activity the period is called *Gründerzeit*, or time of (economic) foundations, when it was possible to make a fortune almost overnight, prompting even Jacob Burckhardt to say that soon Vienna will overshadow Paris (Riedl 2005: 25).

Faithful to the long tradition of make-believe central to Habsburg rule, developments in the entertainment industry were even more spectacular. The first major building completed on the *Ringstrasse* was the Opera house, and the constructions represented an enormous boom for the theatre world, with the launching of a series of private theatrical companies as well as the new, mixed genres of operettas and then cabarets (Springer 2006a: 309; Traubner 2003), taken over from Paris but developed with even more energy. As a result, the new main street of the city became '"a theater of costumes and masks, an art of façade"' (Ann Tizia Leitich, as quoted in Whalen 2007). An overheated economic boom in tandem with a similarly escalated entertainment scene in an Empire historically obsessed with representation and maintaining a reality check only through endemic ruse and behind the scene manipulation was recipe for disaster – and indeed became the incubator of hypermodernism.

This again happened in the most appropriate, at once real and symbolic manner, with the Vienna World Fair, scheduled to open on 1 May 1873. As feverish construction in the city was much sparked by the experiences of the Austrian delegation at the 1851 first World Fair in London, many expected to reap the benefits of their investment through this crowning event. Due to spiralling expectations the economic situation became precarious even before the start of the Fair, with hopes that a success of the event would redeem matters. However, hit by bad weather and general overpricing the Fair turned out to be an economic disaster, generating one of the biggest stock-market disasters, the crash of 1873. This event, together with the Franco-Prussian war of 1870–1 cast the shadow under which fin-de-siècle decadence, breeding ground of hypermodernism, was nurtured – not only in Vienna, but particularly virulent there.

Features of the schismatic spirit

In the title of a central chapter in their classic *Wittgenstein's Vienna* Allan Janik and Stephen Toulmin (1973: 33) characterise 'Habsburg Vienna' as a 'city of paradoxes'.[5] Before World War I Vienna was a city full of radically contradictory qualities. It was the city of glamour, to satisfy every whim and desire, but also a city of dire poverty. It had the lavish new buildings featuring the Ring, but housing conditions for the lower classes were particularly desperate. Still, important as these features are, they were not unique to Vienna, and are only offering a first approximation to its paradoxes. Vienna was not simply the city of wealth and poverty, but first and foremost 'the capital of illusion' (Whalen 2007: 48) where everything was staged for what it looked, and yet for this very reason nothing was as it looked. In the words of its most famous architect, Adolf Loos, it was a 'Potemkin City', shocking with this programmatic 1898 article the inhabitants of a city that tried to overpass Paris and yet became compared to a most lurid aspect of Russian absolutism. The extreme and even absurd anti-ornamentalism of Loos, father of modern architecture, with its – aesthetically untenable – search for the truth and nothing but the truth was thus an Austrian solution to an Austrian problem. Schismatic dualism in Vienna, however, antedated Loos: 'No European city was as famous for hidden passageways as Vienna, so notorious for its subtle deceptions, deceitful half-truths, facades and false fronts, multiple languages and secret codes' (Ibid.: 132). Quoting Hans Weigel, Whalen adds that '"in Vienna, everything is around the corner"', meaning that 'nothing in Vienna was what it seemed' (Ibid.).

Such a dualism between empty forms and utter formlessness, between the search for naked truth and the omnipresence of sheer lies was not limited to art and architecture:

> The sensuous worldly splendor and glory apparent on its surface were, at a deeper level, the very same things that were its misery. The stability of its

society, with its delight in pomp and circumstance, was one expression of a petrified formality which was barely capable of disguising the cultural chaos that lay beneath it. On closer scrutiny, all its surface glories turned to their opposite; this is the fundamental truth about all aspects of life in the Dual Monarchy. These same paradoxes were reflected equally in its politics and its mores, its music and its press, its Imperial aristocracy and its workers.
(Janik and Toulmin 1973: 37)

Joseph Roth captures the absurdities of the Austrian Empire in its 'unwritten and impenetrable rules, the aimlessness and hollow laughter, the Prater and masquerades, the military maneuvres and opera boxes' (as paraphrased in McClatchy 2008: 1).

A city of paradoxes and schismatic tendencies is bound to be a city of extremes. These extremes, following the hints of Janik and Toulmin, can be followed through every level of social life. In politics and ideology, it is present in the extremes of its liberalism, both economic and political, in its socialism, where even the ordinary social-democratic worker's movement had clear totalitarian tendencies (Borkenau 1938: 172–3), and in its conservatism, where – to counteract both its liberals but also the Monarchy which for centuries promoted equal rights to the Jewish population – village priests instigated campaigns which eventually led to the election of the repulsively anti-Semitic Lueger as mayor of Vienna,[6] against the explicit disapproval of the Emperor. Nothing demonstrates so well the coexistence of opposite extremes in Vienna than Wittgenstein and Hitler were not only both born in Austria in the same year, just a few days apart, but for a time attending the same school.

The same dualisms apply to entertainment, where in the Prater many danced until they fell unconscious, yet a certain melancholy sadness was not far from anyone. Whether in politics or social life, in art, economics or entertainment, the dualism and a certain 'magic of the extremes' (Voegelin 1990a) ruled,[7] where time and again 'all proportion between appearances and realities had disappeared' (Janik and Toulmin 1973: 64). The city of Beethoven, Mozart and Haydn eventually became birthplace of modern musical disharmony as well, inaugurated by Schönberg's 1926 essay about the 'Emancipation of Dissonance' (Riedl 2005: 32).

The 'special proclivity for double standards' generally characteristic of the Empire was particularly omnipresent and devastating in the field of Eros (Metzger 2006: 28–9). Sexuality was omnipresent, much catered for, central theme of never-ending theatre, cabaret and operetta performances not simply saturated with hidden sexual meanings but often approaching pornography. Fin-de-siècle Vienna was probably the first city ever – certainly unique since the collapse of Antiquity – where sexuality was over-stimulated to becoming the single overriding thought behind every moment of life for a vast part of the population. At the same time the theme was surrounded with a 'conspiracy of silence' (Janik and Toulmin 1973: 35, 47). Young men, surrounded by a culture where they were supposed to search for entertainment and where such entertainment was all but limited to the stimulation of sexual desire, were supposed to abstain from sexual activity until marriage, which was deferred until their 30s, further spinning overwhelming unease, bad consciousness and pervasive cynicism.

Such silence, *given the conditions*, was all the more absurd as Vienna was not just the city of – artificially incited – sexual pleasures, but also of sexual diseases. Syphilis was particularly rampant, with about 10–20 per cent of young men being infected, and the city being literally littered with specialists in skin and venereal diseases (Decker 1991: 42–3). It is no surprise that sex, pleasure and death thus become intimately and morbidly associated (Whalen 2007: 59, 72–3). By 1900 Vienna became 'marked by the interconnected antipodes of voluptuousness and decay' (Pizer 2003: 117).

Nothing is more recognisably Viennese than the waltz; and nothing captures, at another coincidence of the most real and symbolic, the heart of fin-de-siècle Vienna's schismatism than a few stories about waltzes. Black Friday, the day when the stock-market crashed in Vienna, was 9 May 1873; and 5 April 1874 was the premier of *Die Fledermaus*, the still most popular operetta of the king of waltzes, Johann Strauss. As the first public performance of its famous Polka was already given in October 1873, one can guess that Johann Strauss must have been at work on the operetta practically since the days of the crash. One is again caught between the extremes of whether to deplore this fact as the height of illusion-mongering or congratulate Strauss for his effort at restoring the *joie de vivre* of his fellow citizens under conditions of extreme duress.

The ambivalence of the waltz as genre was recognised by contemporaries. In his poem 'A Waltz Dream', source of a famous 1907 operetta libretto by Oscar Straus, Felix Dörmann characterised the waltz as sick (Riedl 2005: 31) – another par excellence Viennese paradox. A contemporary German visitor described waltzes 'as providing an escape into the demonic', offering a form of ' "modern exorcism [which is . . .] capturing our senses in a sweet trance" ', offering a ' "dangerous power" ' all the more irresistible as it cannot be censored in any way, given that it ' "stimulates our emotions directly" ', without any intervention of thought (as in Janik and Toulmin 1973: 34). The dissolving power of the dancing masters of the court of Ferrara gained new momentum in another incubator (Horvath 2015; Szakolczai 2013a: 147–57).

The conclusions were drawn by Maurice Ravel who composed 'La Valse' at the close of World War I where the music, in explicitly apocalyptic tones, became a 'frantic *danse macabre*', offering a 'grotesque memorial' to the Empire (Schorske 1981: 3). The music was written for the Ballets Russes by the request of Diaghilev, though was not accepted by him, due to which Ravel and Diaghilev almost went to a duel.

Experiencing fin-de-siècle Vienna

How was such a world, such a schismatic and unreal reality experienced? Human beings cannot face for long situations in which they are exposed to widely divergent impressions and impulses without serious consequences. Those who faced only one segment could ignore the flagrant contradictions, while those following established beliefs might have tried to work out ways of justification. But the situation generated 'widespread uneasiness and feeling of decay' (Borkenau 1938: 157); even utter bewilderment. A central means to bring to the surface conflicts between appearance and reality, revealing a deep-seated chaos under apparent stability, are scandals. Few scandals are as revealing as the case of Alfred Redl, high-ranking official of the Secret Service, who in May 1913 was disclosed as a Russian spy, living a double public life so that he could continue with his double private life, filled with homosexual orgies (Janik and Toulmin 1973: 61–2). The case is telling not simply due to its joint political and sexual aspects, but because it perfectly exposed the heart of Austrian fake reality: Redl was considered a model officer exactly because he was a nobody: he had no values, opinions and morals whatsoever, possessing only a single distinguishing feature: he could perfectly anticipate what his superior wanted of him; he was 'a man who had succeeded precisely because he could assume a mask that completely veiled his' non-being (Ibid.: 62). The 'case illustrated the deceptive aspect of everything in the monarchy' where 'artificiality and pretense were by now the rule rather than the exception, and in every aspect of life the proper appearances and adornments were all that mattered' (Ibid.).

In such a world stabilities are dissolved, replaced by liquid formlessness and boundarilessness (McClatchy 2008: 1; Whalen 2007: 105), leading to a cult of transience (Riedl 2005: 30). Eyewitnesses of 1915 gave a striking description of Austria as a country '"more Eastern than Western in character"', whose '"atmosphere is Asiatic"', having a '"baffling air"', where '"[o]n the inside it is quite different from what it seems to be from the outside. Everything is elusive. There is nothing to take hold of, nothing solid to stand on"' (as in Whalen 2007: 148). Once forms are liquefied, the core experience of nihilism, beyond decadence, the encounter with the void is not far. The empty eyes staring at us from Kokoschka's paintings reflect the spiritual vacuum that he perceived on the face of those around him (Janik and Toulmin 1973: 101), an infinity that only belongs to the world of the mind, but which renders human beings a 'helpless subject in a world of mind' (Bonfiglio 2003: 92).[8] In Broch's retrospective, the key term of pre-war Vienna was the void (*Vakuum*).

Yet, the spread of the void in any society, even in such a deeply schismatic society, cannot be simply taken for granted. Humans have an inbuilt horror of the void (Nietzsche 1967: 97). The void can only be spread if it finds a suitable instrument, one that manages to erase the traces of its own operation, rendering it invisible or necessary. The modern world knows three such major instruments for spreading invisibly the void: Newtonian technologised science, Kantian critical philosophy and the theatre.

The main instrument for spreading the void in Vienna before World War I was the theatre. Habsburg Vienna, as recognised by Georg Trakl, was inherently theatrical (Janik 2001: 242). Its theatricality, especially at the end of the century, was part of its main appeal and attraction: 'No one in Europe had the celebrations, the mania for dances and parties and balls that Vienna had', with its reputation for gaiety, with its waltzes and masked festivities, a 'city of splendid, glorious, mid-winter balls', where festivities became almost permanent, as '[t]he ball season began after Christmas and stretched all through the dead of winter to Ash Wednesday' (Whalen 2007: 39). Such characterisation of fin-de-siècle Vienna fits into a series started with late-Renaissance Venice and continued with early modern London and modern Paris, here gestating the spirit of hypermodernity.

Regularly meeting at the level of ordinary daily life situations which are radically and irresolvably contradictory takes away meaning and undermines not simply moral standards as an abstract category but personal integrity which is the basis for decent human existence. Forced to face situations that cannot be resolved implies that instead of facing them people will look the other way. It means that life as a search for meaning – which is already a fall from a life which simply *is*, naturally and in a taken for granted manner meaningful, as most lives most human beings lived most of the times had been, and indeed should be – will be transformed into forms of escapism. Vienna the 'City of Dreams' offered ample such opportunities (Janik and Toulmin 1973: 34), but at the price of losing all weight and any seriousness. In a semiautobiographical account formulated at a particularly liminal moment Franz Borkenau claims that '[r]eading the literature of those years one is struck by the feeling that nothing is serious, and nothing worth while', adding the corollary that 'in fact nothing *was* worth while' (Borkenau 1938: 156). Such life is dominated by resignation, a paradoxically logical consequence of the inconsequentiality of daily existence (Riedl 2005: 31–2). In such weightlessness and inconsequentiality, where life and death came identified through mere sexuality, any previous solidity and values were dissolved and transmogrified into mere phantasms. One lived surrounded by the ghosts of a dead civilisation (Borkenau 1938: 324), while fascination with spiritism became a social epidemic. As Theodor Herzl remarked in 1897, during his time as a journalist of the *Neue Freie Press*: ' "we manufacture ghosts. It's a sort of a comfort to have them around; they are far less terrifying than Nothingness" ' (as in Whalen 2007: 57). This mode of experiencing the world and the altered hearts it produced is expressed with the force of a personal confession by Joseph Roth:

> 'I lived in the cheerful, carefree company of young aristocrats [. . . and] artists [. . . with whom] I shared a sceptical frivolity, a melancholy curiosity, a wicked insouciance, and the pride of the doomed, all signs of the disintegration which at that time we still did not see coming. [. . .] Our wit and our frivolity came from hearts that were heavy with the feeling that we were dedicated to death, from a foolish pleasure in everything that asserted life.'
> (as in McClatchy 2008: 1–2)

Coffee-houses: ambivalence vs. glorification

Apart from the theatre and its modalities like opera or operetta, the other key place for Viennese social life was the coffee-house. Strangely enough, in his glorification of the link between coffee-house culture and the spirit of democracy Habermas makes no mention of the coffee-houses of Vienna. Yet, the connection between fin-de-siècle decadence and the coffee-house in Vienna was central.

Given the major role coffee plays in contemporary everyday diet, it is striking to note that the discovery of coffee drinking is quite recent. First notices go back to about the fourteenth century, with legal documents about coffee drinking only dating to the fifteenth, European notices first appearing in the sixteenth, while the first coffee-houses only emerged in London in the 1650s, spreading quickly in Europe, in particular in Paris, Venice and Vienna (Bradshaw 1978; Ellis 2004; Lemaire 1997). The rise of coffee culture coincided with the rise of not simply modernity, but revolutionary fervour (Ellis 2004: xi). The origins of coffee were Eastern, the importance being not so much the connection with Islam or the Arabs, rather the specific connection with the Sufis and Yemen (Ellis 2004: 14, 18–19; Haine 2013: 3);[9] and also with Istanbul, heir to Constantinople, thus becoming impregnated with 'post-Byzantine' spirit.

The consumption of coffee is associated with a few features that are best visible at its early stages. To begin with, coffee is a stimulant, but a special kind that does not create dizziness, the loss of reasoning power and sleep, rather the opposite, an excessive mental activity, even a spirit of discussion and debate, thus an artificial state of wakefulness. This establishes a connection to entertainment, but also the reading of journals, something quite different either from pubs and taverns, or theatres and opera houses. Finally, through the peculiarities of Eastern, especially Istanbul coffee-houses, with its young male waiters offering sexual services in a culture where women had no place in public life, it also contributed to the spread of a particular sexual culture, present in the Italian word *bardascia* (catamite), a version of the Arabic term for waiter, *bardash*, with a root in *bardaj* 'slave' (Ellis 2004: 7–9).

Apart from such sexual and revolutionary associations, coffee-house culture since its earliest times had two further major connections. One concerned financial activities, especially the stock-market. The first list of stock prices was offered in January 1698 at Jonathan's Coffee-house, to be followed by other similar efforts from coffee-house 'offices', all alongside a twisting road near the stock-market populated with coffee-houses that came to be called the 'Change Alley' and became synonymous to Stock Exchange (Hennessy 2001: 6–10). Furthermore, beyond the mysteries of financial transactions and the 'free and open' public sphere, the coffee-house was also meeting place for avant-garde intellectual circles, gathering in its dark rooms and informed by its 'cabalistic spirit' (Bradshaw 1978: 1).[10]

The specific feature of the Viennese coffee culture was a particularly close connection with cultural life, with various sections of the literary elite gathering in the main coffee-houses, constituting as many clubs, with tables of rival groups being 'rigidly demarcated from each other' even in the same coffee-house (Segel 1995: 22).

A crucial feature of fin-de-siècle decadence, in close connection with coffee-houses, was the cabaret.

Cabaret

While in its contemporary version the cabaret is very recent, being closely linked to fin-de-siècle decadence and gaining its fame from other similarly decadent periods like Weimar Germany, its origins go further than the coffee-house. Cabarets as taverns with performances can be traced back to the times of François Villon in the Middle Ages. The main feature of such taverns was that patrons could sing, just as it allowed the performance of strolling players or jugglers, or 'the whole retinue of out-of-season carnival personalities' (Appignanesi 1975: 9).

The rise of the modern cabaret in the nineteenth century was closely connected both to coffee-houses and journals. It was in Paris cafés that solitary performances were transformed into concerts; the singing of chansons, central feature of such concerts, could be best conceived of as a performed alternative to newspapers, less controlled by the money classes (Ibid.: 9, 11). It was one such venture that in 1881 became turned into the first modern cabaret, the legendary *Le Chat Noir* ('The Black Cat'), the cabaret thus becoming 'the most innovative connection between cafés and the world of the theater' (Haine 2013: 8), eventually leading to a 'veritable cabaret mania throughout Europe' around 1890–1910 (Segel 1987: xiii). The place, founded by a strange crossing between avant-garde literati and money-making entertainers, became animated by a particular spirit of irreverence and cynicism, repudiating any moral and religious values, while taking the logic of social justice to the extreme, having both populist and left-wing anarchist sympathisers, and much catering for the fashionable Pierrot theme (Segel 1987: 16–41). The most popular singer of 'The Black Cat' became Aristide Bruant, who combined a real compassion for and first-hand knowledge of marginalised lives with attacking established values through a style of 'mocking cynicism', showing up the 'polite society' a reality it refused to acknowledge, including prostitution, alcoholism, mugging, even murder, but at the same time not offering any release and specifically aiming at destroying romance and the idyll (Ibid.: 49–61). According to Arthur Symons, a keen observer of the Paris scene, the songs focused on the dark sides of anyway dark lives, but had something real inside them.

This irreverent spirit in moving from Paris to Vienna gained an inflexion in Germany, especially through the peculiar figure of Frank Wedekind. The main German cabaret, founded in Munich, was *Die Elf Scharfrichter* ('The Eleven Executioners'), parading a morbid style of humour and having as their lead singer Marya Delvard who had an electrifying presence as *femme fatale* though – a decade later – Kafka would find her simply ridiculous (Segel 1987: 149–51). Wedekind brought specific skills and perspectives and an even more particular spirit to performances. In 1887–8 in Zürich he encountered a circus clown, Willie Morgenstern, thus incorporated into his theatre and cabaret performances circus elements of grotesque physicality, recognising the artistic possibilities of circus, pantomime, variety theatre and music hall (Ibid.: 166–7). This became a particularly effective vehicle through the spirit it transmitted: Wedekind came to Munich after his plays were consistently rejected by theatre directors, thus in 'a mood of bitter frustration and resentment' (Ibid.: 155), using contemporary cabaret mania as a vehicle, though by no means convinced of its value, believing that ' "sooner or later a serious crisis will befall all this junk" ' (as in Ibid.: 156–7). Yet, as long as the fashion was alive and well, he did promote it, both by writing songs to Marya Delvard and by performing them. Delvard was particularly effective in transmitting the chill of Wedekind's and similar songs, combining a morbid and death-fixated imagery with an 'unspeakably effective melody', thus having a kind of shock-effect close to the eighteenth century sublime (Ibid.: 152–4; see Szakolczai 2016a, Chapter 4), calculated to shock and thrill through titles like 'I murdered my dear old auntie' (Segel 1987: 158). These songs were very far from Aristide Bruant's attention to marginal lives, though only gaining effectiveness through the mechanical-sublime impact. Wedekind's performances were just as effective. Bertold Brecht became one of his early admirers, evoking the stage magnetism of Wedekind in his obituary: whenever Wedekind entered a room, with his close-cropped red hair, everyone fell silent; for Brecht ' "[n]o singer ever gave such a shock, such a thrill" ' (as in Ibid.: 159). The obituary by Heinrich Lautensack, a fellow 'executioner' and songwriter for Delvard, compared his appearance jointly to Pierrot and Lulu (Ibid.: 159–60). The subversive power of this cabaret spirit was tremendous and instantaneous, effective within a few years, yet nobody realised that the end could only be a universal ethical and aesthetical deterioration, promoting literally a jungle (Ibid.: 181).

It was this spirit that was transmitted to the Vienna cabaret, which appeared surprisingly late and took quite some time to become established (Segel 1987, Chapter 4). The first cabaret, arranged in 1901 by Felix Salten, Hofmannsthal's coffee-house-mate, folded after seven spectacles, while the next, 1906 effort, involving Wedekind, ended up in a scandal with Kraus. Only the third venture, organised by the same people and named *Fledermaus,* proved successful, running 1907–13 and rhyming particularly well with the Viennese mood of imminent collapse. The main attraction were the readings of Altenberg, the 'homeless poet' (Magris 1986: 20), producing a thrilling, confusing combination of cheerfulness and tragedy (Segel 1987: 199). The cabaret performed mask plays by Kokoschka, who also had a particular interest in circus and variety and incorporated clown routines, transmitting the message that without masks we are only masks (Ibid.: 203–5, 211–13, 352–5). The most popular show was a mock examination of Goethe from the subject matter of Goethe, resulting in a failing grade, as the great poet could not name the husband of his second niece, just as he did not remember whether a particular poem was written in 1796 or 1797, ridiculising an educational system choking on its Byzantine positivism and formalism. Here again, just as in the case of the coffee-house, the specific aspect of Viennese cabaret was the particularly tight connection with the works of indigenous artists.

Vienna's coffee-house and cabaret culture, far from pioneering a stand against the overwhelming spirit of resignation and decadence, with its heightened theatricality and sophistry only promoted it. This was the stamp it left on modern culture, whether in architecture, painting, music, philosophy or literature.

The contribution of Austrian intellectual life to modern social theory focused around five main, highly intertwined concerns: the existence and integrity of the self, or the person; the importance of sexuality for human existence; the role of language and the possibility of an authentic communication; the role played by illusion, fantasy and in particular dreams in human life; and the search for truth and being truthful as ethical maxims. While these concerns move way beyond the specific topic of this book, a few general considerations must be added here.

Freud and Wittgenstein

The two best-known social theorists coming out of fin-de-siècle Vienna are Freud and Wittgenstein. Their works almost perfectly cover the five areas described above, with Freud's focusing on sexuality and dreams, Wittgenstein's on language and ethics, the problematisation of the self providing the common links between the two. This also means that it is difficult to understand their works without taking into account the context defining the character of their questions, or 'their original *Problemstellung*' (see Janik and Toulmin 1973: 32). For this book the questions concern the extent to which this was shaped by the theatricality of Habsburg Vienna, the relations of their work to this theatricality and the extent to which they thus stamped this Austrian 'spirit' unto the world at large.

Two figures loom large on this intellectual horizon, two exact contemporaries: Ernst Mach (1838–1916), and Carl Menger (1840–1921). Mach was one of the founders of modern physics, professor in Prague, moving to Vienna in 1901, recognised by Einstein as his predecessor, who even has a crater on the Moon named after him. Still, the 'preponderant impact' (Kobry 1986: 124) he exerted on the intellectual life of his time is not due to his virtues as a physicist, rather the – quite unwarranted – inferences he drew from his work, based on the extreme version of positivism and empiricism he came to profess. He was not only a staunch socialist and vehement atheist, but he denied the existence of an 'I' or person, man being merely a complex of elements, guided by an economy of thinking (Ibid.: 125). A human being for him is only a bundle of sensations, not having any specific substance behind it, so any talk about personal integrity is sheer 'idealism'. His position was best expressed in a 1908 letter to Bahr, which claimed that the self is 'unsaveable', being dissolved in sensations, while 'reality is in perpetual movement' (Ibid.: 126).

His ideas were extremely popular: Hermann Bahr was his intimate friend, while Hofmannsthal and Altenberg followed his lectures (Kobry 1986: 125). Musil (1982) wrote his dissertation on Mach, and his famous unfinished novel, the *Man Without Qualities*, far from being a novel of truth in the manner of Bakhtin or Girard, was rather a homage to the relativism and sensualism of Mach, with its hero Ulrich embodying the 'fluid subject' (Kobry 1986: 129). Lenin composed one of his most famous invectives against his ideas in 1908, following the old Sophist maxim of gaining fame by attacking the famous. Mach's influence only increased after his death, as the main figures of the Vienna School formed an 'Ernst Mach Society', which published in 1926 the famous programmatic pamphlet *The Scientific Conception of the World*. Its impact can be pursued in the singular and yet unperceived extremism of Viennese thought – unperceived as identical to modernist empiricism, positivism and philosophical logicism. It was on the basis of Mach's ideas that Carnap famously proclaimed that philosophy is concerned only with statements of fact and logic, expurgating any question of meaning. Thus, the two dominant intellectual tendencies of fin-de-siècle Viennese intellectual life, formalism and sensualism, have their common foundation in the work of Mach, focusing on the alchemic dissolution of the self and the loss of individuality, this being one of the secrets of hypermodernity (Ibid.: 129).

Carl Menger, on the other hand, was pioneer of the theory of marginal utility, thus founder of neoclassical economics. As was only proper for an Austrian civil servant, he took his ideas from the work of Hermann Heinrich Gossen (1810–58), a Prussian bureaucrat who in 1854 first wrote about marginal utility. Menger published his book in 1882, which drew violent reactions from the then ruling German Historical School in economics, in particular its leader, Gustave Schmoller, sparking the famous *Methodenstreit*, at the centre of German academic life when Max Weber attended university. While not being convinced by Schmoller's arguments, Weber had an intuitive hostility to Menger's perspective, though he could not formulate a proper counter-argument. Menger's ideas, with their neo-positivistic and neo-Kantian character, had a huge impact on those Viennese economists and philosophers who made a major contribution towards neo-liberal economics and analytical philosophy, like Friedrich von Hayek, Ludwig von Mises, Rudolf Carnap and Karl Popper.

While his ideas were less a coffee-house topic than Mach's, Menger also made his contribution to Austrian public life. In 1876 he was appointed as tutor of Prince Rudolf, heir to the throne, and stayed in touch with him until the end of the latter's life. It was only once he got a chair in 1878 at Vienna University as a reward that he dared to finish and publish his indeed 'revolutionary' work on economic theory. Whatever the effectiveness of Menger as teacher, his educating the Prince certainly ended up with unmitigated disaster. In late January 1889 Rudolf killed his lover and himself as part of a suicide pact. Holding Menger 'responsible' for this act in any legalistic-moralising sense is meaningless. Yet, the symbolic charge of the fact is evident, coming out best if comparing it to Aristotle, similarly problematic tutor of the future Alexander the Great. The connections between the ideas of Mach and Menger are tight and vital; neoclassical economic theory is not a champion of human individuality, rather a main instrument of its destruction.

Dreams and sex in Fin-de-siècle Vienna

Freud was keenly aware of the revolutionary implications of his work, even played with it. Though published in November 1899, he negotiated a publication date of 1900, to mark it as heralding the new century. It also had a Latin epitaph, from Virgil's *Aeneid*, '*flectere si nequeo superos, Acheronta movebo*' (If I cannot prevail upon heaven, I will stir up hell) (VII: 312; see Freud 1965: 647). If a 'revolution from below' that explicitly plays on the lower, demonic aspects of human life is problematic enough, even more so is its context, which was certainly brought into the game. The words were uttered by Juno, consort of Jupiter – thus appending a gender dimension to the revolt – and as part of her furious efforts – the emotional charge of Juno is characterised by expressions like bitter resentment and vengeful hatred – to prevent Aeneas from founding Rome. It is important that the context is marked by excessive, limitless, raging vengeance: Freud sides here with mad resentment against the very foundation of Rome. The message is crystal-clear and most disturbing: *Interpretation of Dreams* is written to nullify Rome.[11]

Any intellectual revolution takes time to reach its fruits. Freud was evidently impatient. In his recollections he asserts that his work had a negative reception, insinuating the image of an ignored outsider, but this is incorrect: the book was reviewed, and praised, already on 6 January 1900 (Bonfiglio 2003: 90, 94), strikingly, the day of the Epiphany. What rather happened is that the novelty of the central ideas were not recognised simply because they were *not so new*. The idea that human life turns around nothing else but sex by 1900 was rather a commonplace in Vienna – except that it was formulated in cabarets and operettas, and not with the heavy academic jargon used by Freud. The central issue is whether Freud simply elevated a certain mode of human emotionality and behaviour, propagated and thus invested by light entertainment into the unsurpassable horizon of human existence.

A comparison of Freud's ideas with those of Arthur Schnitzler might bring out the point with particular clarity. Schnitzler was a central figure in Viennese modernism, decadence and avant-garde, recognised by Freud as his *Doppelgänger*, whose understanding of sexuality was all but identical to his (Schorske 1981: 11). Yet, such compliments were not returned by Schnitzler, simply because he found nothing that interesting in Freud, given that he was also trained as a doctor and practised hypnosis (Janik and Toulmin 1973: 62). His plays explore the 'compulsiveness of Eros', in particular 'its terrible power to dissolve all social hierarchy' (Schorske 1981: 11) – a feature already captured in Shakespeare's *Troilus and Cressida*. In his play *La Ronde*, written 1897, first circulated privately 1900, published 1903 and finally performed, provoking extreme reactions, in 1920, presented the image of a society in which all human relations were 'reduced to a single common denominator, in the desire for immediate sexual gratification', so the play, with its sequence of character scenes, starting and ending with 'The Whore', 'unfolds like a dance of death' (Janik and Toulmin 1973: 63). In the following year he presented his perhaps most famous play, 'The Green Cockatoo', where characters in the French Revolution become dominated by their instincts (Schorske 1981: 11–12). While presented in the *Burgtheater*, or the Imperial Court Theatre, thus the most prestigious theatre hall in the city, the scene of the play was actually a Cabaret Theatre, 'where the performances aim at obliterating for the patrons the distinction between play and reality, mask and man' (Ibid.: 12). The play can even be taken as an extremely sharp analysis of the dangers of liminality, as its central message is that while such a play in normal times could be considered as mere entertainment, 'in the revolutionary situation this game proves fatal to its devotees' (Ibid.) The play was not merely historical, rather it carried a vital contemporary message: 'Too much dedication to the life of the sense has destroyed in the upper class the power to distinguish politics from play, sexual aggression from social revolution, art from reality' (Ibid.). The stage of 'History' was indeed set for large-scale rule by trickster figures.

Even further, due to his dual background in medicine and literature Schnitzler managed to capture the heart of the problem of communication in a certain kind of egoism, characteristic of humans who 'encapsulate themselves hopelessly within social roles which satisfy their immediate desires, and thereby rob themselves of all hope of more lasting fulfillment' (Janik and Toulmin 1973: 63). Yet, in spite of all this, the works of Schnitzler, especially in placing them into their context, leaves one with the lingering doubt that after all these plays very much enjoyed playing with the demonic forces and took pleasure in inciting the desire of their audiences. Schnitzler was no Beckett; Beckett did not take pleasure in serving the self-hatred of its audience. The diagnosis offered by Schnitzler thus became an occasion to re-inject the venom into the social body. The blending of 'the corruption of art and the art of corruption' (Schorske 1981: 12) in such plays could easily be applied from the theme of the play to the effect mechanism of the play itself, mixing sharp diagnosis with brutally re-infecting the disease.

While Schnitzler was the closest to Freud, complementing Freud's 'science' with an aesthetic of dreams (Bonfiglio 2003: 96), the obsession with dreams was central to the Viennese intellectual landscape (Whalen 2007: 132–3). Hermann Bahr, leader of the 'Young Vienna' literary avant-garde, argued that the 'spirit of the times' can be captured through the joint concerns with self and dream, and sex and death – emblematic themes of the new aestheticism and art of nerves (Springer 2006b: 375). The most telling, and truly striking such formulation, in the spirit of Freud's motto, however, was Hofmannsthal's allusion, in his 1894 poem 'Terzinen III', through Shakespeare's *Tempest*, to a new 'trinity' of Man, Thing and Dream being one (Bonfiglio 2003: 92–3). Apart from plays with the number three up to the point of saturation, the poem also evokes the Kantian dichotomy of object (thing) and subject (man), only to supposedly overcome this dualism through the dream. Instead of moving forward, the maniacal search for the new only resulted in a backward regression, to Jean-Paul and especially Tieck – a good match for Hofmannsthal's similar precocity.

Language and truth in fin-de-siècle Vienna

As Foucault explored it extensively in *Les mots et les choses*, modern thought extended to its limits the capacities of language, captivating it in an irresolvable paradox. Language in the 'classical age' (c. 1650–1800) was on the one hand reduced to the role of merely representing things, so that they would be accessible for proper scientific classification. On the other, through discourses that were supposed to move beyond any reasonable doubt, philosophy was to provide a coherent and reasoned foundation for human existence. Theatricalisation plays a fundamental role in this development, as a theatrical play offers the most evident case of 're-presentation', though the origins of the word move way back into the Middle Ages – even if by no means in the sense of theatrical play. Rather it was the re-birth of theatre that reduced the complex and concrete medieval political idea of re-presenting into the merely mirroring function of words and images, characteristic of the classical age.

Such dualism was bound to explode European thought, and with serious consequences; and this explosion in thinking evidently happened in fin-de-siècle Vienna. How can the very foundations of human existence and the ethical rules necessary for a meaningful life be expressed in words if words do nothing else but represent 'things'? This was the central problem for Wittgenstein, and also for Heidegger, a thinker born just a few months later and only a few hundred kilometres west, in Southern Bavaria, thus in a similar German Catholic environment.

If Freud had a predecessor and Doppelgänger in Schnitzler, Wittgenstein had one in Hugo von Hofmannsthal, another member of the Young Vienna club, Schnitzler's – almost – life-long friend.

Notes

1. From a sociological perspective it is by no means irrelevant that Hegel, Hölderlin and Beethoven were each born in 1770, thus entering the liminal age of 18–19 at the moment of the French Revolution.
2. Kafka's obsession with bureaucracy was implanted onto him by Alfred Weber, not only through his friend Max Brod, who was the student of Alfred Weber in Prague (Radkau 2009: 323), but also directly, as Alfred Weber played a formal role in Kafka's university career (Gray 2005: 292).
3. Borkenau (1900–57) is one of the central figures of 'reflexive historical sociology', together with Eric Voegelin (1901–85), his exact contemporary (see Szakolczai 2000). The two were born a few weeks apart, and both grew up in Vienna (Voegelin only from the age of ten). The depth of their understanding concerning the modern world is thus based on their direct experience of the collapse of 'Austria' at the age of 18.
4. It is this combination that has been captured in an unsurpassable manner in Jaroslav Hašek's *The Good Soldier Švejk* (1921–3).
5. Joachim Riedl similarly entitled his chapter in a volume about Vienna 1900 as 'The City Without Qualities', paraphrasing Musil's title.
6. Borkenau (1938: 141–3) systematically compares Lueger to Stalin.
7. While Voegelin did not link the expression to Vienna, he lived in the city from 1910 to 1938.
8. Significantly, this description is given at the end of a discussion of Grillparzer's version of Calderón's *Life is a Dream*, to be used by Hofmannsthal as model both for his last play and his writings on the 'Austrian idea'.
9. In contemporary folkloristic stories, these origins even became connected with goats, goat-herds and bestiality (Allen 1999: 58–9).
10. The link between coffee-house culture and cabalistic spirit is by no means a trivial detail: a quote from Charles Fourier on the cabalistic spirit and plotting was selected by Bradshaw as frontispiece to his book, while the same quote was placed as the first epitaph to his introduction by W. Scott Haine (2013: 1).
11. Intriguingly, the previous, sixth book ends, just a few pages before, with a distinction between dreams that are true visions and those that tell a lie – a difference certainly ignored by Freud.

2 Hugo von Hofmannsthal
Promises and realities

The name of Hugo von Hofmannsthal (1874–1929) today is hardly known outside a small circle of specialists. Few people even among those otherwise familiar with German literature would be able to mention a work of his. Such failing is not limited to Hofmannsthal, but applies to Vienna literary modernism as a whole:

> the central paradox of the Vienna of these years [is] that whilst the city produced one of the most lively and important movements in modern art, music, and literature, it did not come up with a single major work of art.
> (Kuna 1991: 124)

During his life, Hofmannsthal was a very well known figure in his native city and country, becoming 'the idol of Vienna's culture-ravenous intelligentsia' (Schorske 1981: 16), as '[n]ot since Goethe and Hölderlin had such exquisite lyrics been penned' (Janik and Toulmin 1973: 112); certainly better known than Freud or Wittgenstein. According to Stefan Zweig, in Hofmannsthal his ' "youth saw not only its highest ambitions but also absolute poetic perfection come into being, in the person of one of its own age" ' (as in McClatchy 2008: 4).

Hofmannsthal's times, life and work are tightly interwoven. Yet, quite strikingly, Hofmannsthal did everything in his power to erase traces about his life, and was so successful that – though he died suddenly – until our days no biography has appeared. The first such work, subtitled 'Sketches towards his image' (Weinzierl 2005), made huge efforts to retrieve any available trace concerning his existence, yet could not call itself 'a biography'. One might wonder about the 'big secret' Hofmannsthal wanted to erase at any price, but evidently he had nothing to hide. Though perhaps this was exactly what he had to hide, desperately: nothingness itself, the void; according to Roberto Calasso (1993) 'for all his life Hofmannsthal suffered from the consequences of an original sin that was only his and which only the guilty one perceived: the sin of having understood and seen everything, before having lived it', so 'lacked the force of gravity'.

Even the barest facts about Hofmannsthal's life, seen from the right angle, gain explosive force and meaning. He was born in 1874, thus part of the 'vintage' which produced three of the most characteristic figures of fin-de-siècle Vienna, the others being Karl Kraus, journalist, editor and for over two decades unique contributor of *Der Fackel* ('The Torch'), a satirical magazine that offered a unique, running commentary on the absurdities of his time and place; and Arthur Schönberg. But, perhaps more importantly, and certainly strikingly, he was born on 1 February, which means that by the day nine months after 1 May 1873, or the opening of the Vienna World Fair, which would produce, within nine days, the stock-market crash. One could hardly be born under a worse sign.[1] Just as significant were the signs under which he, and all members of his cohort, matured. Schorske argues that the standard, linear lines of European intellectual history became hopelessly confused with the arrival of Nietzsche. But Nietzsche arrived on the scene when the generation of 1874 reached maturity, starting university, in 1891–2, when he suddenly became the most talked about figure of contemporary culture. Hofmannsthal even here was ahead of everybody, in both absolute and especially relative time, as in 1890, at the age of 16, still well inside high school, he was already reading Nietzsche; while in 1892–3 he attended a university course on him (Ziolkowski 2005: 15).

If Hofmannsthal was born under a bad sign, his death was particularly tragic. In 1929 his older son Franz committed suicide. Two days later, just when leaving home for the funeral, he collapsed on his door. Father and son were then buried together, a few days later.

Hofmannsthal's entry into the literary life of Vienna is a famous story. In 1891 a new essayist started to publish in the most highly regarded Viennese literary journal under the pen name 'Loris'. Hermann Bahr, leader of coffee-house literati, could not believe his eyes when he first read the pieces. The style and content simply soared above everybody else. He absolutely had to meet this genius, and in his mind various ideas ran back and forth how he so far could have ignored such a superb writer – he must have lived abroad, probably in Paris, for decades. He could not believe his eyes when, a couple of days later, he met the Loris, or Hofmannsthal, a seventeen-year-old boy wearing school uniform. His astonishment was raised to an even higher pitch once the youngster started to talk: ' "my soul was inundated by an unforeseen light" ' (as in Calasso 1993).

Bahr was by no means alone with his assessment. After meeting him for the first time Schnitzler claimed that had the feeling ' "of having encountered a born genius for the first time in my life, and never again during my entire lifetime was I so overwhelmed" ' (as in McClatchy 2008: 3–4). His impressions were shared by everyone in the room who witnessed Hofmannsthal's first semi-public reading of his poetry:

> 'After a few minutes we riveted our attention on him, and exchanged astonished, almost frightened glances. We had never heard verses of such perfection, such faultless plasticity, such musical feeling, from any living being, nor had we thought them possible since Goethe.'
>
> (Ibid.: 4)

Similar passages could be quoted from Stefan Zweig, another central figure of the Viennese literary life, or even Stefan George who invited Hofmannsthal to his circle.

The education and upbringing of Hofmannsthal was the best that the German tradition of *Bildung* could offer – thus in a way he received the worst upbringing possible. Being the only son of a wealthy family, Hofmannsthal went to the best schools, was educated by the best teachers in the best possible manner, being 'reared in a virtual hothouse for the development of aesthetic talent' (Schorske 1981: 15), so by the age of sixteen knew all the classical languages and practically anything about European culture worth knowing. The lack of real life experiences under such sheltered conditions were rendered worse by the main preoccupation of his father, transmitted to his son: a boundless love for Viennese high culture, especially theatre (Luft 2011: 3). Hofmannsthal was brought up, like a modern-day Homunculus, in a very special kind of incubator. Bahr captured this in an almost cruel but perfectly fitting manner:

> 'his great art has no feeling; his soul does not have a part containing sentiments. He only lives with the nerves, the senses, the brain: does not feel anything. He does not know passion, outburst, pathos. Looks at life and the world as if he contemplated it from a remote star; just as we look at the plants or the stones.'
>
> (as in Calasso 1993)

Not surprisingly, such a precarious life progressed through crises. The most significant document of his great crisis is the famous Chandos Letter of 1902 – though signs of such crisis can be traced back to 1897 (Bennett 1988: 137), so Hofmannsthal already entered a crisis of writing at an age (23 years) when most others hardly even start to write; a first document of the great crisis of language that was one of the distinguishing feature of Viennese thinking, culminating in the philosophy of Wittgenstein. With this letter, Hofmannsthal not only gave up writing poetry – deciding to lay to waste his main talent – but in a way metamorphosed himself from a poet into a seismograph (Citati 2008: 44–5) – one who simply captures, before everybody else and in a particularly sharp manner, the 'spirit of the times'.

Before going into the content of the letter, some matters of context must be relayed, touching upon the most personal, intimate part of Hofmannsthal's life. The letter, with its utter despair about his loss of language, published 18 October 1902, came at a very particular moment of his life. Hofmannsthal was married on 8 June 1901, his daughter Christine was born on 14 May 1902, while his first son Franz on 20 October 1903. Thus, a time which in the life of most human beings is a moment of unreserved joy, the arrival of a first child less than a year after the wedding, for him turned out to be occasion for utter existential despair – due to the loss of writing; as if such ability depended on the *absence* of strong and meaningful human emotions. Furthermore, his son Franz, born on the third day a year after this letter, was evidently conceived during the worst crisis.

The Chandos Letter

In understanding the letter, the central issue concerns 'interaction' between Hofmannsthal as a concrete person, fin-de-siècle Vienna as a chronotope and the connection between language and reality that is vital for our existence on this planet. The *Chandos Letter* is widely considered as Hofmannsthal's most important writing. It is easily accessible in several translations. From the perspective of a genealogical analysis its significance is even greater as it crystallises the ambivalence of the modern relationship between thought, knowledge, language, theatricality and the self, helping to identify the stamp which the Austrian spirit, through fin-de-siècle Vienna, left on the modern world.

The letter is generally recognised as autobiographical. If so, then it underlines the confessional tendency in modern literature, emphasised by Kierkegaard and Hamvas. Hofmannsthal is outspoken in the letter, not playing games, and is not trying to hide things, honestly confronting the bottom of his crisis. Yet, he is clearly aware of the paradoxical nature of his effort – the impossibility of language to convey the truth of reality, experiences being always different from their representations, advancing the *aporia* of Magritte's pipe. This is why the letter is written in the name of Lord Chandos and transposed to early 1603: not to deny or hide away but *in order to* underline its autobiographical authenticity. Beyond intentions, the letter demonstrates the argument put forward by Calasso and others that at the heart of Hofmannsthal there is a certain void due to the theatrical nature of his education, and which he therefore cannot fully reveal, cannot even grasp – yet, he will generalise on this basis about the heart of the human condition. Through his relentless truthfulness Hofmannsthal arrives at diagnosing the theatrical void at the heart of the modern world, though mistakenly identified as the heart of the human condition.

The letter starts by revealing a personal state of anxiety: Chandos/Hofmannsthal breaks his long silence about a state of 'mental stagnation' in which he has been caught for years. This state is an alienation from his self (he does not know 'whether [he is] still the same person'), a distancing which extends to the future (he is deprived of plans) and which is only further spiralled by any talk or writing about it.

Thus, while recognising the impossibility of penetrating the core of the matter, he offers two central and closely connected hints. First, at the heart of this distancing there is the problem of language. The centre of the phenomenological description of his condition is offered by striking claims about experiencing words flying around him; an alienation that first concerns the use of abstract terms, then any words whatsoever, simply depriving him of speech: 'I have lost completely the ability to think or to speak of anything coherently' (p.3). At the level of interpretation, this condition is revealed as something at the core of his inner self: a certain abyss that can only be identified, from the outside, as its identification from the inside is both a logical and existential impossibility, being a void.

This is a most frightening from inside revelation of nihilism, the most honest since Nietzsche. It must, and does, lead to a search for a way out; but a search which excludes as a starting point two possibilities of renewal, *the* two central modalities of traditional European culture: any concerns with the divine ('To me the mysteries of faith have been condensed into a lofty allegory'; p.2) and with Plato ('Plato I avoided, for I dreaded the perilousness of his imagination'; p.3). Hofmannsthal's education through German *Bildung* not only deprived him of genuine life experiences, but also indoctrinated him with a language that systematically excludes the possibility of finding a way out of the trap. The utmost truth and confessional terminology of the letter reveals the entrapment of an entire culture: one of the greatest geniuses that was ever been gifted to the planet became entrapped through the best education possible, by the end of the nineteenth century, and thus became a mere tool to diagnose the state in which this culture arrived at in fin-de-siècle Vienna.

Thus, instead of turning to the divine and Plato Hofmannsthal returns to the philological reading of Antiquity (he was trained as a philologist, gaining his doctorate in 1899) and the 'great, classical authors', instead of turning to life, to his daughter. In an extremely telling part of the letter he alludes to his daughter, though she is to be made four years old, right after the much quoted sentence about words growing like funghi in his mouth, but through moralisation it only intensifies his condition. Yet, after all, he does receive a revelation, as if a reward for his truthfulness; a most peculiar one, a revelation without words, completely outside the culture and education that distanced him from life and the world; a revelation about the significance of the reality of simple everyday objects, and of the reality of the world and existence as such. The heart of this revelation was that 'Every thing that exists, everything I can remember, everything touched upon by my confused thoughts, has a meaning' (p.3), even his current state. This revelation is characterised by two expressions: first, it revealed to him 'a presence of love'; and second, it taught him that 'we could enter into a new and hopeful relationship with the whole of existence if only we begin to think with the heart'. Yet, this phrase is preceded by the expression 'as if', the perhaps most fateful expression of Austrian culture at that very moment; and followed by the phrase '[a]s soon, however, as this strange enchantment [in the next phrase he conveys it better through the expression "this harmony transcending me and the entire world"] falls from me, I find myself confused'. Thus, in spite of receiving a revelation he somehow cannot fully get it, cannot carry it over into his own life, cannot translate it into a habitus. The terminology of St Thomas concerning grace and habit (*gratia* and *habitus*) is particularly important here (Lonergan 1971). Grace is rare and divine, only few people receive it, and just for short occasions. It is their task to transform this unique gift into something lasting, carry it over into their entire life.

Hofmannsthal received a rare gift, his genius, only comparable in German culture to Goethe, Hölderlin and Nietzsche; and now he received another gift-like revelation. But in between, he was (mis)educated by Enlightenment culture; and this culture made him not only waste his talents, but also to generate such an inner void inside him that he could not even take care of this new gift – all he could do, with utmost honesty, was laying bare his failure, not even understanding what he revealed, at the bottom of the Chandos Letter.

The experience was later re-interpreted with the help of two concepts, 'pre-existence' and the 'allomatic' – terms that try to capture in words the unnameable, so these are expressly and explicitly paradoxical.

Pre-existence

The term 'pre-existence' does not appear in the Chandos Letter, though is its central underlying theme (Bennett 1988: 126–7). It is discussed explicitly in two of the most important plays of Hofmannsthal, *The Serious One* and *The Woman Without a Shadow*.

'Pre-existence' appears around the outbreak of the Great War; a new crisis whose culminating point is not a letter, but a dream where in July 1914 he dreamed that – as if an image from Tiepolo's Pulcinella series would come to life – he was condemned to death by a tribunal of the French Revolution; the last dream he actually dreamed (Calasso 1993), thus a dream to end all dreams. It is an effort to return to the central revelation experience of the Chandos Letter: another attempt at the impossible, putting the unnameable and unsayable into words.

The central theme of *The Woman Without a Shadow* is not simply pre-existence, but the passage from pre-existence to existence, which is highly paradoxical, as pre-existence is itself a passage; a condition of permanent liminality. Pre-existence is something like the state before the fall, a state of pure virginal existence. It is also 'a world of endless metamorphosis which has no aim [*metamorfosi senza fine e senza un fine*]', which does not want anything else but itself (Calasso 1993). In Bennett's reading pre-existence is 'perfect self-transforming freedom' and – in resembling Baudelaire's 'Albatross' – for the poet the real world represents an entrapment. Pre-existence is a 'constant temptation' (Bennett 1988: 251, see also 125–7), a vision of harmony that transforms existence into a permanent state of transitoriness, or liminality: existing now 'means precisely that he is constantly *in transition* from pre-existence, that he must make the transition over and over again' (Bennett 1988: 126; *sic* in original); everything is gliding, nothing solid (Ibid.: 49, 304). This is furthermore identified with the divine, as pre-existence is 'the experience of oneself as god' (Ibid.: 204). Such experience is particularly accessible to artists, through their work, which has no goal, rather is 'a way to the forgetting of goals, a way to the gradual perfection of its own silent, endlessly repeated "transition" into being' (Ibid.: 229). Thus, the story of the original sin or the Fall is interpreted as an occasion for the divinisation of man, directed towards the service of 'others'.

Allomatic

It is here that the other key enigmatic term, the 'allomatic', enters. The source of the term is a 1912 Rosicrucian-alchemical book titled *Twice Dead!* (Bennett 1988: 252, following Ferdinand Maack), reinforcing the link with alchemy already present in the fascination with transformation and metamorphosis. The best way to understand the 'allomatic' is through its twin concept, the automatic. The automatic is what is directed by itself, so the 'allomatic' is direction by others, through the in between, without consciousness (Ibid.: 257–8). Here again Hofmannsthal is entrapped in his present. In the age of technology automatic means being directed by itself in a mechanical sense, thus becomes an occasion to engage in a critique of individualism, helped by the Machian ideas about the absence of the person.[2] Hofmannsthal again ignores Plato, certainly due to the image of Plato circulated by neo-Kantianism, so in spite of his fluency in Greek does not connect 'auto' to Plato's 'care of the self' (*epimeleia heautou*), as Foucault in post-World War II Paris and Patocka in communist Prague, thus the exact opposite of modern automatism. In trying to escape automatism he thus falls into the opposite extreme of 'other'-centredness, anticipating the 'Other' of Levinas, neglecting the person as concrete centre of morality.

From pre-existence and the allomatic to the non-existence of the person

The problematisation of the person was central for Hofmannsthal in his entire career, but became particularly pronounced in *The Serious One*,[3] the play so much connected to pre-existence, but also – through *Andreas*, his unfinished novel – the allomatic. The questioning of the existence of personality, just as the concern with the dissolution of the concept of individuality, are recurrent themes of his notes written around the play (Bennett 1988: 105), just as the play itself. The play is ostensibly about society and the social, the manner in which true humanity is generated through social interaction. Yet, the play demonstrates the opposite. Instead of focusing on dialogues and encounters, it rather contains a series of 'missed meetings' (Ibid.: 156). Instead of caring for others, its heroes are infatuated with themselves; and none more than its main hero, Hans Karl, spokesman of Hofmannsthal. Hans Karl even refuses to acknowledge this self-infatuation, though other characters in the play clearly charge him with this, implying narcissism, and as 'he himself expressed [this] by his fascination with his mirror image in the clown Furlani' (Ibid.: 159). The paradox is resolved by the play's claim that it is such narcissism, if pursued with insistence, that 'becomes the path to a "life" of external engagement' (Ibid.). For Hofmannsthal 'the individual is for all practical purposes identical with what people say and think about him; everybody, so to speak, is everybody else's hallucination' (Ibid.: 227–8).

Theatricality and self-consciousness

One strand of continuity in Hofmannsthal's work is his long-standing, obsessive hostility to Kleist, in particular to the essay on marionette theatre. Kleist was preoccupied with the problem of theatricality and had clear ideas about the problematic aspects of self-consciousness, connected with the Fall. Hofmannsthal, on the other hand, was desperately trying to preserve the value of self-consciousness, perceiving there the hope for redemption, in connection with the theatre.

Hofmannsthal's claim that the theatre is the place where the reality of the real is revealed starts in a relatively innocuous way. The centre of theatre is not the text, rather the actual, physical performance. He argues that it is only in the European tradition that the text gained a primacy over the performance. The reality of theatre is therefore playful mimetic action, the actors who move on the stage and enact something, beyond purely mental understanding (Bennett 1988: 16, 66, 233). The meaning of the play is completed inside the theatre and not outside it, in the material reality of the theatrical building, and with the actual presence of a live audience (Bennett 1988: xi–iii). The intentions behind the text or the poet's original vision are irrelevant, at any rate not communicable (Bennett 2005: 118–20).

Hofmannsthal here makes a further step, and not only claims that a theatrical performance is more real than a mere text, but that it is more real than reality. The aim of his writings on theatre is the 'revelation of the nature of human existence by an unmasking of the theatrical situation as a reality realer than the real' (Bennett 1988: 93). Here we start entering the infinite spiral of Hofmannsthal's related thinking. By real theatre Hofmannsthal means something more than the actuality of a performance, but a concern with truth:

> [t]he artist, of all people, knows most clearly that reality is in truth a mental or poetic act, composed of metaphors [. . . and so] truth is an empty truth, relating to nothing, except insofar as we put it behind us in favor of an absurdly committed activity by which its quality as truth is realised.
> (Ibid.: 91)

By such absurd commitment Hofmannsthal means the spectator going into a theatre, sitting at a place and watching a spectacle; an activity that for him does not mean a vain search for pleasure and immediate gratification, rather a heavy investment in search of the truth of reality. It is furthermore a quite risky investment, as sitting in a theatre reveals our quite precarious situation, involving recognising the truth 'that all life is essentially the living of a lie' (Ibid.: 97). Our situation in the theatre, just as self-consciousness, is absurd, as it is logically unjustifiable (Ibid.: 87). Such 'absurd' commitment is met with a similar attitude by the artist, who 'in spite of his knowledge, must carry out the absurd act of treating the world *as if* it were real' (Ibid.). In contrast to Ortega's analysis of *Don Quixote* Hofmannsthal does not argue that in a theatre we accept the absurdity that what is shown in front of our eyes as a theatrical play is actually real, rather the opposite: in order to generate in the audience the illusion of reality the author rather must temporarily accept the illusion that reality – which he knows as being a mere figment of imagination – is actually real.[4]

In order to make the argument plausible, Hofmannsthal paradoxically takes death as model. We cannot 'live through' our dying, we can only gain an experience of dying, as our *own* death, through a theatrical spectacle (Ibid.: 85). Furthermore, just a theatre creates the experience of death, it also creates life, which is furthermore the same thing (Ibid.). The language of poetry and of everyday life are the same; as language creates both, the logical conclusion is to identify poetry and life (Ibid.: 34–5). Theatre is not only identical to life, but is a source of renewal in life: in theatre '[h]uman life always begins anew, its origin repeated in every instant' (Ibid.: 87).

Theatre, far from being a mere reflection of social reality or individual life, is rather the model of both – the latter through critical awareness and self-consciousness, which offers a key to experiencing the social (Bennett 1988: 163, 211).

The next two sections specify how this was to be achieved for social cohesion and individual self-consciousness.

Society

Given the centrality of in-betweenness for Hofmannsthal's view concerning artistic work through the allomatic and pre-existence, it is not surprising that he primarily conceives theatre as a unique way to bring society together, realising the possibility of building a new community (Bennett 1988: 301), as it is an in-between place.[5] Spectators sitting in a theatre audience are in a par excellence in-between situation, between the dream world of the stage, offering theatrical illusion, and the relative security of their humdrum everyday existence (Ibid.: 95–9).[6] Hofmannsthal turns this in-betweenness into an ethical exercise, a recognition of truth and realisation of a new community.

This starts by claiming that a state of tension between opposites is fundamental for the human condition. The opposition between the infinite character of human intelligence and the finiteness of our animal nature whose limits intelligence continuously violates (Ibid.: 8–9, 274), and which is constituted as a paradox (Ibid.: 13–15), or between social petrification and cultural fragmentation (Ibid.: xiii, 250), is pervasive for Hofmannsthal. It is reflected both in the dichotomy of individual and society (Ibid.: 154, 196), and in the inclination to think in dualistic categories and doubles (Ibid.: 199, 210). The theatre thus acts as a bridge – but in order to do so, it must further separate and liquefy. The atomised, detached spectators sitting in the theatre by no means reflect social pathologies, like disintegration or alienation, rather the necessary conditions for creating a *true* community, for which eventually in 1917 he would explicitly come up with the term 'people' (*Volk*) (Ibid.: 299), considering it as the step towards a new Europe – a central concern of his last period.

Central for this is the mechanism through which individuals as spectators together in an audience constitute a community. Hofmannsthal's idea of the theatre, taking off from the more questionable aspects of Nietzsche's *Birth of Tragedy*, is that the spectator during a spectacle is not simply dissolved into a mass, rather 'his self-detached, self-seeking consciousness as an individual is directly involved in the mechanics of communal participation' (Bennett 1988: 90). The function of the theatre is 'holding together' an audience (Ibid.: 288), establishing 'an area of contact between individual and communal experience', where 'the individual spectator, without compromising his individuality' is engaged in communal participatory experience (Ibid.: 91). Thus, through the sheer presence of others in the theatre, a collective is formed out of isolated individuals (Ibid.: 80–1).

Theatre and self-consciousness

The arguments connecting theatre and self-consciousness take us into the heart of Hofmannsthal's concerns, and also back to his polemics against Kleist. For Kleist, the puppet theatre managed to produce an experience of grace, outside self-consciousness, thus re-evoking our natural condition. Hofmannsthal evidently encountered Kleist's essay only in about August 1895 (Bennett 1988: 3), and his reaction was a violent and immediate refusal, denying every single element in his claims. To begin with, for Hofmannsthal such a 'natural state' does not exist; to be at one with oneself is identical with madness, as it implies a failure to differentiate anything (Ibid.: 12), which accidentally is a strikingly faulty argument; it is an impossible Dionysian longing (Ibid.: 278), which must be restrained (Ibid.: 12–13). Existence without self-consciousness is even identified with magic (in a 1895 poem 'A Dream of Great Magic'), or with nothingness (Ibid.: 15). In contrast to this, human existence is necessarily split and disrupted (Ibid.: 9–10), the clear recognition of such division being a precondition for artistic creation (Ibid.: 15–16). Far from representing the opposite of grace, rational self-consciousness and reflectivity are rather conditions of possibility for grace (Ibid.: 13); the impression of gracefulness being produced by self-conscious posing (Ibid.: 6–7). Kleist is mistaken: '[w]e must learn to experience self-consciousness not as a problem at all, but as a divine gift' (Ibid.: 11); self-consciousness representing our 'essential divinity' (Ibid.: 48). In his last play, *The Tower* Hofmannsthal outright creates a new myth, asserting against Kleist that 'self-consciousness is not a violation of our nature but the very expression and testimony of the divine in us' (Ibid.: 317). The conclusion, drawn by Bennett, commenting on a long direct citation from Hofmannsthal's play, is that 'the basic principle of our self-conscious existence, our situation as spectators to ourselves, even in its terrifying aspects, is God' (Ibid.: 319).

In his early works, poetic language is paralleled to self-consciousness, in that they both transcend the everyday (Ibid.: 19–20); while after the Chandos Letter, he came to emphasise the primacy of language over the individual (Ibid.: 105, 202), arguing – advancing Wittgenstein and Heidegger – that language only capacitates thinking. Before performing the work of connecting, language proceeds by further separating, through the 'paradox of the soul' or self-consciousness, the necessity of self-questioning (Ibid.: 13), a 'quasi-divine capability that liberates us from the bonds of a merely physical or animal existence' (Ibid.: 15–16). This prepares the ground for tying together individual and society (Ibid.: 9), which happens in the theatre, but only through the *consciousness* of an audience (Ibid.: 168); and through the activity of the artist who knows that everything is *poesis*, or a construct, and thus can freely exploit or transcend self-consciousness (Ibid.: 91).

The parallels between theatre and self-consciousness are fully exposed in the 1897 *Small World Theatre*, which at the same time inaugurates his crisis. The play is fully symbolic, with puppets representing the condition of unselfconscious happiness, while the title alludes to the Renaissance idea of microcosm, every human person representing a world in itself, so the theatre can be used to represent 'the internal dynamics of the self', with its climax being 'the happening of self-consciousness' (Ibid.: 12). This comes out most clearly in non-verbal communication, like in pantomime. As Hofmannsthal argues in his 1911 essay on the pantomime, '[a] pure gesture is like a pure thought' (Hofmannsthal 1964: 49), so the theatre can capture the 'intricate dance-figures in consciousness' (Bennett 1988: 92). This takes us back to permanent liminality: the comic pantomime of Vorwitz (whose name means 'pre-joke') in *Great World Theatre* demonstrates, through its manifold plays with time, 'the transition from one moment to the next' (Ibid.: 285).

The use of dance to capture self-consciousness is inherently paradoxical, as dance appeals more to emotions than to the intellect. Hofmannsthal's theatre of consciousness much caters for emotional involvement, and this is where problems with his approach reach their culmination. As for him the truth of experience is reduced to suffering, this rendered possible the reconstitution of the sacrificial mechanism within theatre.

Sacrifice, or beyond the ultimate paradox of self-consciousness

Beyond the somersaults of self-consciousness and its reflections in the acrobatic dance-steps of pantomime, the theatre also educates through experience, but only through experiences of suffering (Bennett 1988: 317–21). While such experiences involves empathy and sympathy, by opening up a contact between the individual and the community the theatre also enables each 'to intrude upon the other at a high level of consciousness' (Bennett 1988: 91; see also p.31). The connection between such intrusive violence and the role of the other is clarified through the surprisingly tight connection between the allomatic and sacrifice, established by Bennett through a meticulous analysis of some notes prepared for the novel *Andreas*. In the search for establishing the relationship between 'self' and 'other', and through expressions like the self being the 'receptacle' of the other, metamorphosis, Doppelgänger and absolute unification with the other, in tracking down the thought-processes of Hofmannsthal Bennett arrives at the claim that 'the allomatic is neither positive nor negative but simply the element or medium of human existence in the world' (Ibid.: 261–2). This existence is tightly connected to sacrifice, whether in the sense that 'it is the allomatic itself that is sacrificed', or whether that 'by way of [a] sacrifice, the allomatic triumphs' (Ibid.: 262).

A similar centrality of the sacrifice for Hofmannsthal is established by Calasso (1993) in his analysis of *The Woman Without a Shadow*, the play dealing with Hofmannsthal's other key term, pre-existence. In Calasso's reading, the clearly symbolical motive of the play, that in order to escape pre-existence the Empress must obtain a shadow from somebody else, has a serious message, revealing the 'magical accountability' that rules our world: to take away something is an act of violence; everything which is taken is literally stripped away from its natural place, which thus sets in motions a series of violent acts that can only be stopped by an act of renunciation, or a sacrificial circulation.[7]

Hofmannsthal's evocation of sacrifice is highly metaphorical, but the theatre, as he emphasises, is a very concrete, material place, and the connections between theatre and sacrificial rituals are tight. Given that both works discussed above were written during World War I, one wonders whether Hofmannsthal had a similar sensitivity to the eerie connections between World War I and rituals of sacrifice as Marcel Mauss. The direction of Hofmannsthal's thinking, however, was different; the extreme events of the war revealed the 'saving power of "suffering as a divine principle"', and furthermore even involved an 'awakening of originary powers [*Urkräfte*]: the *people* [*Volk*], holy and substantial depths, where life was always eternal warfare', evoking a 'Something [*ein Etwas*] that was more real than individuals' (Hofmannsthal 1964: 381). Hofmannsthal even brings in the sacrifice of Christ, through the comic pantomime of Vorwitz. It is done in a particularly tortuous way: our necessary submission to the permanent transitoriness of time, symbolised with the comic pantomime, is 'an image of God's eternal sacrifice as Christ'; thus

> [e]ven our apparently helpless passage from one instant to the next is already a participation in Christ's eternal sacrifice. In our utterest helplessness, in the anguish of the intellectual self-alienation that we experience in time, we thus in truth constantly enact the Creation itself and so realize our union with absolute Being.
>
> (Bennett 1988: 285)

The absurdity of such straight-faced, honest transformation of the theatre, and of all places in fin-de-siècle Vienna, homeland of the make-believe, into an educational institution capable to build a new, truthful society, that furthermore through an evocation of sacrifice culminates in a re-creation of Creation in an evidently recreational (theatrical, *divertissement*) context, could only have been proposed by Hofmannsthal by a complete misreading of his own revelation experience. As the Chandos Letter demonstrates, Hofmannsthal came to problematise the core of his classical German cultural education, recognising that there was something else beyond mere words and language. However, instead of connecting back to real experiences, he rather shifted emphasis to the other central aspect of his upbringing, the obsession with theatre. Still, in this way he not only managed to capture the theatricality at the heart of modern Enlightenment culture, but even the sacrificial mechanism that offers, with another turn of the screw, the hidden truth of theatre.

The Tower

The torturous character of Hofmannsthal's identification of theatre and self-consciousness comes out with particular clarity through his last play, *The Tower*. In this play Hofmannsthal 'out-Lorises Loris' (Bennett 1988: 317), meaning that the playwright, beyond the age of 50 and after the end of World War I and the collapse of the monarchy, manages to surpass the convoluted aestheticism of the precocious titanic teenager. The distance from Goethe could not be greater.

The play is a tribute to self-consciousness, asserting that 'our consciousness [. . .] simply *is* our situation', and that 'the mirror is the reality' (Ibid.: 320). In it Hofmannsthal 'as it were pulls himself together and realizes in unprecedented purity his own earlier thinking, his understanding that self-consciousness is not a weakness but a power, by which even our transience and ultimate destruction become truly our own' (Ibid.: 320–1). The omnipotent constructs of the theatre are asserted without any need for argument: staging '*creates* the committed, finite, helplessly doomed situation that truth requires', and not simply on stage but – through the participation of the spectators who 'understand' – also in the audience. The message is the futility and hopelessness of human existence, but as it is expressed joyfully, it is supposed to generate a cathartic joy among the audience (Ibid.: 322, 337–8). By staging nothingness or the void, the theatre gives shape to it, thus helping to overcome it, generating saving power not through the intellect, but through mere participation in the ceremony. Hofmannsthal not only calls for a sacrifice of the intellect, reducing the message of his last plays to a few formulaic expression, endlessly repeated for easy memorisation, but asserts that such inconsequential social forms 'are needed for the *actual* organization and enactment [. . .] of the ceremony in which precisely intellectual existence finds its highest fulfilment' (Ibid.: 324–5).

The last scene of the second version of the play, thus Hofmannsthal's farewell, reaches unsurpassable levels of absurdity: 'it exists for the sole purpose of giving him room to express his grotesquely sophistical, indiscussible, and therefore perversely irrefutable ideas on politics and fatality' (Ibid.: 340). While written at the moment where Hofmannsthal was supposed to launch a 'conservative revolution', the play is not propaganda in any meaningful sense: it rather 'manifests the decision to write a kind of propaganda where propaganda is impossible' (Ibid.).

Hofmannsthal the playwright could not and did not raise this absurdity at a higher level. Hofmannsthal the essayist, however, manages to surpass even this, when he became spokesperson of the 'Austrian idea' as the salvation of Europe.

The 'Austrian idea'

In a series of essays Hofmannsthal considered the War and the collapse of the Monarchy as an occasion to re-launch the idea of Austria, not simply in order to save and reorient his own country, but to give new directions to Europe, as if to resurrect it out of its crisis. For these purposes Hofmannsthal not simply reconsidered Austrian history, but '[i]n some respects we may say that Hofmannsthal invented the Austrian tradition' (Luft 2011: xi), as a vehicle to promote his own form of Catholic conservatism. The mission of Austria, which he rightly restricted to the 'Crownlands' (Ibid.: 8), thus including Bohemia but excluding Slovakia and Hungary,[8] is to offer some kind of mediation of and defence from the 'East', corresponding to its long-term role, but one which was actually the reason for Austria's historical failure, thus a not simply untimely but counterproductive idea. The weakening of Austria, warns Hofmannsthal, could lead to a victory of Asia, through yielding to the unlimited rule of money, for which he uses the stunning expression 'larval [*verlarvte*] influence' (Hofmannsthal 1964: 377; 2011: 94),[9] possible source of a most dangerous narrowing and degradation, especially when combined with the rule of the machine and the technological exploitation of nature, culminating in an 'intoxicating conquest of the mind' (Hofmannsthal 2011: 93).

The purpose of this chapter was not the critique of a single author, anyway little known in social theory. Following the hints of Broch (1974), Hofmannsthal is rather an exemplary case for a genealogical analysis. It demonstrates what happens with a man who should have become the greatest genius of his age and of European culture due to being educated under enlightened humanism. Even further, Hofmannsthal not simply 'demonstrates' these effects, but reveals them in their functioning, helping to understand how the seemingly self-evident ideals of humanistic *Bildung*, through the intermediary of fin-de-siècle Vienna, could have produced such a devastating effect.

Notes

1. Given that one of the few birthplaces of the modern novel is *Tristram Shandy*, and that this novel starts by evoking not the astrological constellations under which the hero was born, but the emotional conditions under which he was conceived, the symbolic date of Hofmannsthal's conception has its own significance.
2. Concerning the influence of Mach on Hofmannsthal, see Bennett (1988: 105–6).
3. Hofmannsthal discovered Kierkegaard when working on this play (Miles 1972: 90).
4. Such disrespect for reality is not limited to the literati and their fascination with theatre, but can be extended to neo-Kantian thinking, just as fundamental for Vienna as operetta and cabaret. Voegelin paraphrases the neo-Kantians in the following way: ' "We are not interested in reality. We have values, and we have relevant experiences that we relate to these values" ' (Voegelin 1999: 139). And even acting has its relevance for this farce, as Voegelin also relates an anecdote according to which somebody privy to Hitler's private receptions conveyed that Hitler could mimic others so successfully that he could have been the greatest German actor (Ibid.: 119).
5. He started work on his central play dealing with the in-between, *The Serious One*, in 1910, thus a year after van Gennep published his *Rites of Passage*, though – in spite of his extremely wide reading – it is unlikely that Hofmannsthal knew about this book.
6. Pascal calls this in-betweenness of the theatre *divertissement*, the reason why he considers theatre, or *comédie*, as the greatest danger for a Christian way of life (Pascal 1972, No.11).
7. Calasso's analysis can be captured in the various terms connected to the Hungarian word for 'take' (*vesz*), which include *vétel* (buying), linked to *vét* (to err, sin), *elveszik* (gets lost, disappears), *rávesz* (get fooled or conned), but also *vész*, implying threatening events, having a further series of important connotations like *veszett* (raging, rabid), or *veszély* (danger).
8. Hungary, for better or worse, has a different character or essence. The distance of Hungary was recognised in the novels of both Broch and Doderer, presenting Hungarian characters through a somewhat exotic, but certainly benevolent and understanding lens.
9. The term has etymological connection with the Latin word for 'mask' (*larva*).

3 Novel origins
Rilke's *Notebooks of Malte* and Hofmannsthal's *Andreas*

The modern novel has undergone a new birth at the start of the twentieth century in a manner that could not have been at the same time more concrete and more symbolic. The works of the great novelists of the late eighteenth and nineteenth centuries, Goethe, Dickens and Dostoevsky, emblematic figures of their respective countries and easily the greatest novelists of all times culminated, in an ever more pronounced manner, in a striking re-evocation of the Resurrection. In Goethe, this theme is still quite hesitant, timid, appearing at the moment when Faust contemplated suicide and only implicit in the ending of *Faust II* about the Virgin, Queen of Heaven and the eternal feminine. It is explicitly present in Dickens, in *A Tale of Two Cities*, though recognising its centrality requires an interpretive effort. Finally, it is omnipresent in Dostoevsky, culminating in the last scene of his last novel, the *Karamazov Brothers*. In an even more striking and clearly epoch-marking manner, the last great novel of the nineteenth century was *Resurrection* by Leo Tolstoy, who wrote this novel about twenty years after his two milestone works, published it in 1899 and died in 1910. This was the year when a strange book marking the rise of the modern novel, *The Notebooks of Malte Laurids Brigge* by Rainer Maria Rilke was published – a novel (and only novel) by a poet; a work that was not novelistic by any classical standards; a novel much gestated by Rilke's two visits in Russia. In 1899 and 1900, thus the moment the century was closing and he published his first major set of poems, containing the milestone 'I Live My Life in Expanding Rings', Rilke met Tolstoy twice. He planned to close *Malte* by a section on Tolstoy, even drafted two different versions (Rilke 1966: 967–78), but took it out in the last minute, almost at proof stage, closing the novel instead with the parable of the Prodigal Son.

Malte, this quasi-novel, was quickly followed by three further quasi-novels, two written by some of the most highly regarded novelists of all times, while each three being iconic figures of their time and place – however, these coordinates, thus the exact chronotope, require careful introduction and analysis. Thomas Mann was one of the most important twentieth century novelists, Nobel prize winner already at the age of 54, at the same time emblematic figure of German culture, spiritual leader of the German exile community under Hitler. Hofmannsthal was again *the* symbolic figure of fin-de-siècle Vienna, so much so that Hermann Broch, who belonged to a coffee-house group hostile to Hofmannsthal's, ended up calling his milestone book on fin-de-siècle Vienna *Hofmannsthal and His Time*. Finally, Franz Kafka also became symbolic embodiment of the assimilated Central-European Jewish cultural diaspora.

The place is Southern-Germanic Central Europe, the place at the forefront of religious and civilisational conflicts. It incorporates the Western part of the 'Austrian' (or 'Eastern') Empire, prominently Vienna and Prague though not Budapest, and the Southern part of Germany, centring around Munich; thus, the area at the forefront of the struggles around the Reformation, including the Thirty Years' War that was started in Prague; an area much defining the political meaning of Central Europe, in between North and South, East and West, thus a particularly liminal space. The time was also particularly liminal as – beyond the broader issue of the Great War, the emerging Communist revolutions and the collapse of empires on the horizon – it was condensed in the two years following the publication of Rilke's (non-)novel, 1911–12, including both direct and more perplexing connection in between all these works.

Andreas, the unfinished and only novel of Hofmannsthal, was conceived in close interaction with Rilke and *Malte*. The non-novel of Thomas Mann was *Death in Venice*, a short story rather than a novel, written again in 1911–12, ending Mann's decade-long 'crisis' and serving as a springboard for starting *The Magic Mountain*, his main masterpiece. Finally, Kafka's non-novel is a very short story, 'The Verdict', written in one night in between 22 and 23 September 1912, leading to rewriting his first novel, *Amerika*, thus starting a particularly productive period which ended with the sinister 'Metamorphosis'.

It might seem strange to start a book discussing twentieth century novels by the only novel of a poet; yet, a proper presentation of the context makes this inevitable. The novel pioneered an unprecedented inner account of the hero, without any conventional narrative, well preceding Joyce or Proust. Concerning the links between modernity, poetry and novels, it had a close, highly symbolic but also paradoxical (non-)predecessor in Baudelaire, perhaps even in Hölderlin's *Hyperion*. As Baudelaire was a poet of modernity and the novel is the par excellence modern literary genre one could have expected Baudelaire experimenting with writing a novel. However, while he indeed introduced prose poems, evoked by Rilke in *Malte* (Huyssen 2010: 75), he did not write a novel. Thus, one could venture the claim that Rilke wrote the novel that Baudelaire failed to do, stepping into the space as if created by Baudelaire's absence. Thus, if modern poetry starts with Baudelaire, inventor of the term 'modernity', the hypermodern novel starts with his closest heir Rilke. This also gives proper due to their fundamental differences. In spite of his clear perception of the 'horrors' of modernity, Baudelaire could not help looking forward to the 'new'. In Rilke, however, there remained no trace of a romantic apology of modernity.

Rilke was not simply a poet, widely considered as the greatest German poet of the twentieth century, but also had a quite singular background and a series of particular formative experiences, much contributing to his uniquely insightful but occasionally also problematic vision of the world. He was a German, born and raised in Prague, the Czech capital, which at that time belonged to Austria. He travelled widely, both in Germany and Italy, lived long periods in Paris, where he returned so regularly that many documents of his life were lost when his flat was appropriated after 1914; travelled also repeatedly in Russia, while he lived the last years of his life in French Switzerland. Through his travels he learned several languages: he spoke French so well that he even wrote poems in it, and had some Italian and English, even Russian. The latter he absorbed through Lou Salomé, 14 years his senior and still his lover for years, though married; the two stayed in touch, mostly through correspondence, till the end. In terms of religion, Rilke was Catholic, non-practising but with a strong interest in spirituality and even religion, leaning towards both Pietism and hesychasm, a somewhat similar Orthodox ascetic practice. Like Valéry, he had an interest in angels, including the cult of angels in Islam. While of lower middle class origins, he – like Yeats – had a fascination with castles and towers, and spent the last years of his life in a medieval tower in Muzot (Switzerland), renovated specially for his sake; and – like Nerval – he even fabricated an entire mythology concerning his remote aristocratic ancestry. Still like Yeats, and many others of his generation, he had a fascination with the occult, especially alchemy, blissfully oblivious – like everyone else – that alchemy offers no escape from the modern technological-scientific world vision, being one of its sources.

Rilke and *Malte*

Given that Rilke was primarily a poet, and one of the greatest modern poets, the writing of this single novel took up an enormous, truly incommensurable place in his working life. He started to be occupied with it around 1902, shortly after his wedding and during his first long stay in Paris, at the age of 27, without even knowing it consciously (Schoolfield 2001: 154). As – in contrast to Hofmannsthal – Rilke was not precocious, this meant an early stage in his career as poet. Writing the novel was a main preoccupation in the following eight years, so its completion was felt as if he was delivered from an enormous burden (Prater 1986: 173–4). However, his sense of relief turned out to be hasty, as his creativity, instead of receiving a boost, was rather stalled. In 1912 he started *Duino Elegies*, his chief poetic work, but could not properly progress, just as his hopes of 20 June 1914 were similarly not met. Completion would have to wait until February 1922 when, in a few weeks of extraordinary creative surge, he not only finished the *Elegies*, but also the *Sonnets to Orpheus*, claiming that on the night of that first February the words came to him, as if in a boundless storm (Freedman 1996: 480–93). Given that he died in December 1926, his poetic creativity is mostly limited to the few years before and after the two central decades of his life lived under the shadow of his single novel project – which managed to found the hypermodern novel, with all its ambivalence.

Rilke's work hardly corresponds to the formal attributes of a novel. While it does have a hero, it has no narrative structure, nor other protagonists. It consists of an apparently unstructured collection of events that happened to the protagonist in Paris, childhood reminiscences and accounts about his readings, mostly about rather obscure episodes of medieval history, focusing on the early fourteenth century and female mystics. Such lack of organisation is even highlighted by the title, and occasional comments by Rilke, especially in letters, seem to confirm the fragmentary, not to say random character.

Yet, the poet devoted eight years of his life working on the project, of which a fair amount was spent on attempts at organising the material. Rilke was, furthermore and indeed, a poet for whom every letter and movement of thought mattered, thus the order of the 71 sections (Huyssen 2010: 75), published originally in two slim volumes, cannot possibly have been random.

Even further, Rilke was very much aware, like every poet, but much more than most, that poets do not have a full control over what they write. In the terminology of Plato's *Phaedrus*, poets write under the influence of divine madness. Rilke was, with Valéry, the modern poet most preoccupied with such influences, 'waiting for the angel'; and the angel evidently arrived, in full armour, 12 years after completing *Malte*, in February 1922, ending a long creativity crisis. It is thus more than reasonable to assume that the order embedded in the novel goes well beyond the purpose and consciousness of its author.[1]

This is rendered immediately evident today with the first line of the novel, pinning down time and place. It is both extremely concrete and highly significant, containing at once autobiographical and world historical allusions, thus tying together in the first words of the first hypermodern novel the micro-micro (beyond the daily level of social interaction the inner life of the single individual), and the macro-macro (beyond the level of society the fate of world history). The time and place given are '11 September, rue Toullier' (Rilke 1979: 7). 11 rue Toullier was the address in Paris to which Rilke moved in late August 1902, thus the tight autobiographical connections between author and hero are established in the clearest possible terms. This is also the generally accepted reason why Rilke offers 11 September as time. However, for us today, 11 September has a very specific and highly significant meaning, through the 2001 attack on the Twin Towers; an event decisive for the direction where the new century, if not millennium is moving. According to rational considerations, this is pure coincidence. But poets, already for Plato, founder of rational thought, were closest to prophets; in his two dialogues about love, thus closest in theme to this novel, and poetry in general, the inspiration of poets and prophets are connected. Even more, in the *Symposium* Plato's Socrates outrights yields the high place to a prophetess, Diotima (who would be a protagonist of Hölderlin's *Hyperion*, another key novel written by another key poet), making a suggestion about love that evidently only a woman can propose – an idea uniting Goethe, Hölderlin and Rilke, the three most important German poets of the last two centuries who each wrote key novels – which in itself again brings them almost exclusively together. Thus, Rilke's dating of the first hypermodern novel to 11 September, clearly implying 11 September 1902, or by the day 99 years before the Twin Tower attack, at another start of a century, is objectively prophetic. Perhaps we do not stretch this reasoning too far by evoking Rilke's interest in Dante, especially the *Vita Nuova*, and the importance of number 9 for Dante.

The novel moves at three registers. The first relays the fictive personal experiences of the hero, Malte Laurids Brigge, into which the concrete Paris experiences of Rilke, but even his early adult experiences in Prague, as still René, are sublimated. The second is Malte's childhood reminiscences, where again a number of episodes from Rilke's life are incorporated, often with as much accuracy as possible (Huyssen 2010: 74–6). The third is a shift to a completely different register, the dimension of history, especially medieval European history, based on Rilke's extensive though idiosyncratic readings. The first and second dimensions dominate the first part, while in the second part the emphasis shifts from the biographical to the historical dimension, while within the personal, biographical part the emphasis in general shifts from the mere telling of episodes to their interpretation – with the singular difference of the crucial Venice episode, which however is an adulthood and not childhood event.

Given the distinction between the two parts, which remains unexplained yet very real, present in the first edition, the connection of the two is bound to be significant. The first part ends with the first extended medieval flashback, describing the famous fifteenth century 'The Lady and the Unicorn' tapestries.[2] It is inserted into recollections about Abelone, Malte's childhood beloved, and is read through an allegoric-autobiographical angle, with his identifying with the unicorn, seeing himself in the mirror held to him by the lady, an image recalling the most significant and most frightful childhood recollection of Rilke, when he was unable to liberate himself from a suffocating mask.

Part Two continues with the same story, but in a completely different key: through schoolgirls who study, mechanically and without any understanding, the image in a museum. This helps to introduce and identify the contrast at the centre of the novel: between Paris experiences, through the eyes of Malte, where nothing is in order, the city presented as a big hospital where – as the height of absurdity – even young women are denatured of their essence, and Malte's childhood, when things still had their proper, concrete time and place. Rilke offers an uncompromising vision of the devastations of the modern world, anticipating TS Eliot's *Wasteland*; a diagnosis culminating in the visionary Venice experience, taking up more or less the same structural place in the Second Part as 'The Lady and the Unicorn' in the First Part. Here the scenery shifts from Paris, heart of the continental modern world to Venice, heart of the transitory period between the Middle Ages and (early) modernity. Rilke identifies, again with visionary clarity and beyond contemporary decadence, where Venice is only perceived as seat of hedonism and the search for pleasure, the iron will that well over a millennium before made Venice possible.[3] This episode is again framed by evoking Abelone, Malte's Diotima, and concludes by one of the central sentences of the book, a Pascalian call to think by the heart (Rilke 1979: 226), identifying the core message of the book in the heart, in the female capacity to love.

However, the three main levels of the book are also directly connected in another way, captured by a central anthropological concept not accessible to Rilke, though coined in a book published just a year before Rilke's, liminality; and by a scholar just a couple of years older than Rilke, Arnold van Gennep. Paris, for Malte/Rilke, just as for Baudelaire, embodied liminality – the transitory, the fleeting, or passages, being always in movement; but, in contrast to Baudelaire's *flâneur* who in a way finds pleasure in this transitoriness, in *Malte* such liminality is threatening from the start, and soon becomes intolerable. Childhood, being the formative period of human life, is similarly liminal – but there transitoriness is transformed into something stable and meaningful, our own character and inner self, so – far from memories being constructs – they give access to our deepest essence, helping us to find again ourselves, our own force. Finally, even the medieval dimension, for Rilke, is focused on spatial and temporal liminality, on the tormented episode of the Avignon papacy. The great difference is again that, in history just as in childhood, such liminality does not question stability and meaning, rather is an occasion to a search for return; while the specific feature of modernity, implies Rilke, with his description of streets and hospitals, shops and masks, is that there liminality has become permanent. It is this permanent liminality that he tries to diagnose and overcome, through the drive for the extreme, best present in his famous letters to his wife on Cézanne, which even contain a dual evocation of the indestructible. On the first such occasion, in a letter of 8 October 1907, in characterising the presence of objects in Cézanne he uses the word *unvertilgbar* (Rilke 1952: 22). Next day, however, in a particularly important letter, characterising the world outside in contrast to Cézanne's relentless work as where 'something undefinable and terrible is growing' (*ein unbestimmtes Furchtbares im Zunehmen*) (Ibid.: 25), he uses *unzerstörbar* in capturing how reality is pushed through Cézanne's experience of the object up to indestructibility (Ibid.: 23).

These few comments were necessary, and hopefully helpful, to recognise the fundamental unity and coherence of the work. In order to capture its message about hypermodernity, this utterly theatricalised and thus fake endgame, we need to go through the novel, following the sequential order Rilke bequeathed us.

The first, and only, objective, factual line of the novel is followed by a few, still relatively matter of facts claims by which Rilke rapidly takes the reader through the truths of everyday wisdom into his own vision of contemporary reality. Most of his acquaintances must have envied him for living in Paris, just as in our days this is bound to happen for someone living in London or New York. However, for Rilke/Malte, it is rather the city where one comes to die, as the very first sentence states (Rilke 1979: 7),[4] and where silence is even worse than the usual, extreme noise. One can only survive here if one *learns to see* – and, indeed, the city offers such educational opportunities. Learning to see first of all means to realise that here everyone has several faces, wears several faces – the public space of Paris is full of masks. The greatest fright for Malte in Paris is to encounter a man without a face, or the void itself; as, at the limit, a mask hides nothing else but the void.

At this point the novel switches from diagnosing Paris life to presenting Malte's illness, an illness eventually reconsidered as proof of Malte's basic sanity: in this modern public sphere a healthy person, someone still thinking with the heart, becomes so vulnerable that they cannot survive intact. The first allusion to Malte's illness is followed by three crucial diagnoses of modernity. To start with, it is where, anticipating Ariès, one now cannot even die one's own death; then, Rilke adds that today nobody is at home – a diagnosis that would be repeated in a slightly different form at the start of the second part, that today we are only travellers: 'what kind of life is this?' (Rilke 1979: 19). From here, after listing a few masked scenes from the streets, Rilke quickly moves to singling out the theatre, with its inherent unreality and artful void (*künstliche Leere*; Ibid.), and its reversing the logic of everyday life as the culprit for such loss of meaning, and then offers, in two pages, a first summary of the book's rationale. Armed with such trivial discoveries about loss of meaning in the everyday life of a modern city, Malte, identifying himself as a nothing whom nobody knows, offers a series of comments that radically reverses the classical self-understanding of modernity. If what he perceived, based on his teaching himself how to see is right, then a few stunning conclusions follow: that so far nothing important was seen, known and told; that in spite of all the presumed progress of science and civilisation, we remained on the surface of life, and even this surface was covered and suffocated by 'an incredibly boring stuff'; that 'the entire world history so far was misunderstood'; that a series of absurd ideas rule our lives; that people now live who fail to distinguish between reality and unreality, becoming prisoners of generalities, about 'children' and 'women', without recognising that every human being is a concrete singularity [*unzählige Einzahlen*] – culminating in the claim that if this is so, then something must happen (Ibid.: 24–5). The two pages are closed by endless circularity, as they simply return to Malte sitting in the fifth floor in his Paris room, and writing, night and day.

Yet, the book continues, and this is the juncture where the first childhood reminisces of Malte are offered; back at the age of twelve, in the family castle of Urnekloster.

In the ensuing pages there is a continuous back and forth movement between Paris and Denmark, focusing on the contrast between reality and masks, and also the need to escape a masked reality through further masks – especially to escape the outcasts of Paris, most difficult to mislead, as they recognise that he, the nascent poet, is one of them. This rest of Part One contains two crucial episodes. The first is a draft letter, evoking the mood of envy in the starting pages, but – through Baudelaire – gives some voice to his own feelings. It culminates in two diagnostic claims: a truly Baudelairean exclamation about the horrors of modern life, and a revealing of his heart, admitting that Paris is not for him: someone with a limitless heart should have stayed home. These revelations are immediately followed by a series of further, explicit references to masks, and the need to meet the difficult challenge by not giving it up and going to the – masked – men of the city in order to study them.

Here comes the second crucial episode of Part One, where the two threads of Paris masks and childhood experiences, so far kept separate, are joined. Here Malte, alone in the old castle, is unpacking cloths from a wardrobe, first encountering in his life the strange feeling that whenever he took up a clothing, he became as if in its power – it prescribed his gestures, even his ideas. Far from leading to an experience of alienation, it rather gave him inner security. Then, to his doom, he reached the highest shelf, which was full of masks. He first scorned them, due to their 'absolute unreality [*dürftiger Unwirklichkeit*]' (Rilke 1979: 99), but once he found a set of cloths and masks together, covering the Italian sense of *maschera*, his perception changed: it transported him into a feeling close to intoxication, promising an infinite possibility of metamorphosis. This is followed by a cryptic but extremely important claim: though he so far never saw masks, he immediately realised that masks must exist (*es Masken geben müsse*; Rilke 1979: 99): a claim whose structure corresponds to the Biblical definition of the necessity of sin (*Es muss zwar Verführung geben*, 'such temptations must happen', Mt 18: 7, see also Lk 17: 1), thus identifying the two – as if implying that wearing masks were an 'original sin'. He cannot resist the temptation of taking one up – a terminology also recalling the 'temptations' of Paris, in the draft letter – one which had a strangely hollow smell. He goes to the next room (which in this occasion is not called the 'guest's room', but the 'stranger's room'), in order to contemplate himself in the mirror; however, he stumbles and falls down, enmeshed in the clothing, perceives being possessed by a will stronger then him, becoming so much terrorised that he cannot open his mouth. He is eventually relieved by the servants, who at first were laughing at him, taking a long time to realise that he was not playing for fun, rather was terrorised from fear. The First Part ends with the discussion of the 'The Lady and the Unicorn', already mentioned, but not before Rilke offers, just before this concluding episode, a comment about his diffidence of music, since childhood, due to its transformative qualities (Rilke 1979: 117–18).

Part Two takes up and amplifies, literally from its first sentence, the diagnosis of modern unreality. This revolves around the loss of the concrete: in these days, not only men no longer live at home, but even the objects are leaving their place – like in order to be put into museums. This is a major loss and problem, as everything is concrete, belongs to its time and its place, so severing it from its context deprives beings from meaning and living reality. In his search for the concrete Rilke the poet offers a stunning devaluation of imagination:

> No, no, nothing can be imagined in the world, not even the slightest thing. Everything is composed of particular singularities [*einzigen Einzenheiten*] that cannot be foreseen. In imagination we pass over such things and we don't even notice that we miss them, as we are in a hurry. But realities [*Wirklichkeiten*] are slow and indescribably particularising [*unbeschreiblich ausführlich*].
>
> (Ibid.: 146)

Rilke follows Kierkegaard in believing that God is opposed to the universal: the ultimate reality is the individual, something unrepeatable and unique (Sokel 1980: 173).

The most serious undermining of the concrete concerns our own force, the core of our selves. We are having terrible nights, we expose ourselves to become suffocated with fear as we no longer recognise our inner force:

> since a time it seems to me that *our* force [unsere *Kraft*; *sic*], all our force, is what is too much for us. It is true, we don't even know it, as isn't what is most our own [*unser Eigenstes*] that we know least? [. . .] we have distanced from ourselves what was most valuable in us [. . .] Epochs have passed by, and by now we became used to what is smaller. We no longer recognise our own properties and become horrified by its immense greatness [*äußersten Grossheit*].
>
> (Rilke 1979: 153–4)

A crucial role in such loss of harmony and proportionality is due to the scientific vision of the world by Newton and its universalisation by Kant. Soon after his diagnosis Rilke offers a delightful satire, taking up Dostoevsky's motive of the 'double' and presenting a Russian clerk, Nikolai Kusmitch, Malte's neighbour in St Petersburg, who became paralysed once he started to experience time 'as such', and even perceived the earth move under his feet (Ibid.: 159–61). The episode ends on a self-ironic note, as the only thing Nikolai Kusmitch manages to do, lying on his bed, is reciting poems. A similar later diagnosis also ends on an ironic tone: in the loss of our proper reality, we have become in between or liminal beings, in front of both God and the modern god, the spectator; we are mere 'laughing stock and half-lings, neither real beings, nor play-actors' (Ibid.: 210). The ensuing section ironically extends this diagnosis to the theatre, already identified as main source of the loss of reality: our theatres are nothing, compared to the theatres of Antiquity, as a theatre is only possible if there is a community. The next section, as if to close this argument, alludes to the great actress of his times, Eleanor Duse, with whom he spent a summer in Venice, and who – again paradoxically – treated acting *as if* it were reality, offering a full identification with her every role.

Such loss of authenticity and reality even extends to contemporary women – this is the central message of the first sections of Part Two, commenting the episode of schoolgirls studying 'The Lady and the Unicorn' in the museum. For Rilke, by imitating modern men women destroy themselves, giving up what is most precious in them, considering the search for pleasure as measure of progress, and already 'starting to look around themselves, in search: those, whose force always consisted in becoming found [*gefunden zu werden*]' (Ibid.: 125). Beyond such diagnosis, he immediately offers an understanding and a way out: for centuries innumerable women kept alive the flame of love, accepting their fate under most adverse conditions; thus, it is understandable that they became tired. This suggests, as a way out, that now men should take their place in keeping up the 'work of loving [*die Arbeit der Liebe*], that has always been done for us' (Ibid.: 127).

The leads to the concluding message of the book, offered by Rilke as the way out of a world of masks, or the world of dead and death: a return to the way of life, the way of lasting, or the way of loving, that goes beyond the purely passive role, historically assigned to men, or being merely loved: to love is to 'illuminate with an inexhaustible oil [*unerschöpfliche Öl*]', while being loved is only to burn and be consumed (Ibid.: 226). This way goes through the *heart*, a central term in the novel: it means to think with the heart [*mit dem Herzen zu denken*], thus to follow the way of Abelone (Ibid.), where Malte evidently fails, as his heart is not strong enough (Ibid.: 153), perhaps because it is infinite (*unabgegrenztes Herz*; Ibid.: 72), the possible reason for his failure in Paris.

The novel closes with discussing the contrast between loving and being loved, first through the poetess Sappho, and then through a singular, perhaps Kierkegaardian reading of the parable of the Prodigal Son (Lk 15: 11–32), pushing the story to its extreme limit. For Rilke, this parable is not about somebody wasting away his inheritance, rather a leaving home by somebody too tired of being loved, but not yet capable of loving. In a few pages (Rilke 1979: 227–31), he offers an extended interpretation about the existential condition, and reasons, of the prodigal son, leading repeatedly to a series of question marks.

This way of proceeding abruptly changes in the last pages of the book (Ibid.: 231–4). Rilke as Rilke, taking off the mask of Malte, offers a trademark Rilkean shift and poetic gestures. The first sentence, a single word in German, *Gleichviel* ('It doesn't matter') marks the difference not just from the Prodigal Son, but from Malte; the second starts by claiming that he sees beyond the Prodigal Son, the start of a real existence, defined as a long road without an aim (*ziellose*), though directed towards God, thus a long-distance walking trip, where the road is more important than the destination (Doi 2011), except that this road in a typical Rilkean poetic condensation is termed 'a long loving [*die lange Liebe*]': loving as a silent work, thus combining the task assigned to men, once women became tired, the *work* of love, with the basic life atmosphere of Paris, silence – but a silence now filled with love, thus no longer threatening. As a result of this loving walking work, the Prodigal Son, now called as 'the-one-who-became-stranger', returned home[5] – a striking allusion to the *Odyssey*, as Rilke adds that we only know that the prodigal son returned, not that he also stayed. In the following passages his status, just as that of Ulysses, changed to the 'recognised one', who was even forgiven – of love (Rilke 1979: 234). Still, though recognised, nobody fully knew who he really was.

The last sentences contain an open ending, still around the fundamental *work* of loving: that it was terribly difficult to do; that he felt that only one would be capable – but that person did not yet want it (Ibid.: 234).

Hofmannsthal and *Andreas*

> In my innermost core I am indestructible
> Hofmannsthal, *Moments [Augenblicke] in Greece*, 1914

> What he had dreamed, it was already fading away. What he had thought, in the very evening it was no longer that clear.
>
> Thomas Mann, *Magic Mountain*, 1924

Of all the great unfinished novels of hypermodernity, *Andreas* is both the least finished and most enigmatic; the most concrete, but also the most symbolic – and due to its unfinished character such symbolism can be interpreted almost infinitely. Its unfinished, incomplete, fragmentary thus – evidently – failing character is first and foremost a symbol of the incomplete nature of Hofmannsthal's work; of the collapse of the Austrian monarchy; and of the permanent liminality of the entire hypermodern world.[6]

The novel, just as Rilke's, is clearly autobiographical; even the most autobiographical work in an entire oeuvre that was fundamentally autobiographically driven (Bemporad 1976: 161). This is revealed by the name of its hero, as the name of the protagonist of Hofmannsthal's first theatrical play, *Yesterday,* is also Andreas, just as of a clearly autobiographical character in the prologue to his 1893 play *The Door and Death* (Hofmannsthal 1992: 43, fn.1). *Yesterday* has further, crucial, both formal and substantive connections with *Andreas*. It is a very Hamletian, novelistic play, whose only action takes place before the curtains are drawn, written at a period when Hofmannsthal was extensively reflecting on *Hamlet*. Furthermore, it has tight connections with the *Rosenkavalier*, the opera Hofmannsthal finished in between the first draft and the finished sections of *Andreas*, his most famous and popular work. Its protagonist, Octavian, is another autobiographical character, embodying the ambivalent situation of a youth moving towards maturity, playing – even excessively – with sexual ambivalence (a male role, but played by a female mezzosoprano, who during action repeatedly crossdresses as a girl); a character whose age is given as 17 years and two months, corresponding to Hofmannsthal's when composing *Yesterday* (the play was published, in two segments and under a pseudonym in November–December 1891; see Ascarelli 1992: lxiii); and a character who on stage would gain the pseudonym 'Maria', the name of another – and also split – hero of *Andreas*.

Yet, all these, and especially the connection with the *Rosenkavalier,* also indicate that such autobiographical motivation cannot be separated from the inspiration directly exerted by Rilke. The personal and literary connections between Hofmannsthal and Rilke are tight. While there is only about a year and a half between them, Hofmannsthal was phenomenally precocious, while Rilke not at all so, thus during the latter's Munich stay in 1896–97 the poems of Hofmannsthal became a major formative experience, so much so that Rilke was explicitly trying *not* to become too much swayed by Hofmannsthal (Hendry 1983: 26). Still, in 1899 he went to Vienna mostly to attend a reading of his poems by Hofmannsthal. It exerted such a huge impact on him that he wrote a letter to Hofmannsthal, stating that while already thus far Hofmannsthal had been a guide to him, now he became his master (as in Prater 1986: 51). While such letters of course contain exaggeration, but – given Rilke's personality – they could not have been merely rhetorical.

The central issue, however, is different. In 1899 Rilke would publish the first volume of the *Book of Hours*, and in 1901 further two. Already the first contained such milestone of modern poetry as 'I Live My Life in Expanding Rings', establishing the reputation of Rilke, eventually way surpassing Hofmannsthal's. Hofmannsthal was both an extremely perceptive reader and a warm and generous person. He must have noticed immediately Rilke's greatness, which might have contributed to his 'crisis', a central part of which was his abandoning writing poems. This might have something to do with the split personality syndrome of *Andreas*.

The connections between Hofmannsthal and Rilke, or between *Andreas*, *Malte* and the *Rosenkavalier*, certainly go beyond the shared name 'Maria'. Hofmannsthal attended Rilke's reading from *Malte* in Vienna in November 1907, and while it is impossible to trace direct influences, the mutual interpenetration is evident. Perhaps this gave rise to one of the central concepts of Hofmannsthal, the allomatic, that first appears among notes written to *Andreas* (Bennett 1988: 252), and which is usually related to interpersonal relations, like sociability and love, but can certainly extend to intellectual collaboration.[7] Whether due to direct or indirect connections, or mere coincidence, the composition of the *Rosenkavalier* and the finalisation of *Malte* took place at the same time, in 1909–10.

A crucial aspect of such links concerns the attitudes of Rilke and Hofmannsthal to Venice. While Venice was widely admired, it is worthwhile mentioning that for Hofmannsthal Venice was a second home after Vienna, while for Rilke – who hardly had a 'home' – it was the most important destination of visits after Paris. For Hofmannsthal, summer 1907 was an important sojourn in Venice, central for the gestation of *Andreas*, as the first sketch for the novel (Hofmannsthal 1998: 111–14), still in first person singular, was written soon after. Temporal coincidences were again particularly striking. Hofmannsthal's 33rd birthday – a date particularly important for Germanic Christians – was 1 May 1907, so very shortly before this trip, while the trip took place at Midsummer, a particularly 'magical' period, as on 27 June 1907 he was already sitting on the Lido, reading a book about Venice, masks and theatre, which offered the most direct inspiration for *Andreas* (Miles 1972: 174). The other major source for the novel was a book he also recently bought, by the American psychologists Morton Price, on a case of split personality, about which he only heard in February 1907 (Ibid.: 186).

In an essay published about his Venice experiences Hofmannsthal reveals the erotic fascination the place exerted on him. On a walk he met a young couple, the woman being particularly beautiful; and on his return to his hotel room, when hearing voices in the next room, he imagined that this same woman remained there alone, fantasising about Zeus's visit to Alkmene, under the guise of his husband, adding that 'to metamorphosis aspires our deepest desire', which is an ecstatic truth (Hofmannsthal 1959: 351).[8]

If the original version of *Andreas* was supposed to remain close to this level of suggestions, of a youth arriving in Venice for educational reasons and finding instead the enchanting seductions of the city, as the first sketch implies, two major reading experiences evidently led Hofmannsthal to radically redesign the story, shifting from first to third person,[9] and inserting a flashback to an earlier part of the trip. These readings were the *Malte*, in particular its very different account on the charms of Venice and its truth; and the original draft of Goethe's *Wilhelm Meister*, found and published just in 1910, of which Hofmannsthal immediately wrote a review (Hofmannsthal 1964: 70–80). The result was a radical reorientation of the design, leading to his combining Goethe and Rilke into a radically anti-Bildungsroman Bildungsroman.

In the following, staying as close as possible to the sequential structure of the completed section of the novel, estimated as about a fourth of the planned full novel,[10] I'll try to reconstruct the inner logic of this paradoxical and unfinished effort.

The narrative fragment, 1912–13

Andreas' trip to Venice is at once the most normal and most absurd kind of trip a young member of the European upper classes could be involved in before World War I. It was normal, as one was supposed to travel to Italy to gain cultural education, Venice being a choice destination; yet, it was also absurd, as Venice was a city of theatres, masks and women, in particular prostitutes. This split only deepened the inherent tensions of modern European education. The central aim of Hofmannsthal's novel of formation, built upon the deepened encounter with Goethe, is thus clear: how somebody torn apart by such inbuilt tensions manages to retrieve one's inner self, assuming that it was somehow still preserved intact.

Still, this task could be formulated in two completely different languages, so the dilemma Hofmannsthal – just as previously Goethe – faced concerned the choice between them. One is the Platonic-Christian (but actually both much older and wider, as much in Plato and the Gospels was about restoration and remembering) language of beauty, grace, virtue, intactness and integrity, while the other is the alchemic-Hermetic-Gnostic language of a radical and necessary break, a renunciation of the past and any tradition, championing a split, a dying to the old in order to live in the new – and *then* a search for a new unity, a reunification. The dilemma, in the context of fin-de-siècle stale official religiosity and neo-Kantianism, and due to the centuries of crisis in European culture, was that the Christian-Platonic vision was considered as the established ideology of a declining culture, while the 'alchemic-hermetic' perspective, combined with the ideologies of Enlightenment and Revolution, seemed to offer an attractive alternative for re-birth. It would have been all but inconceivable what now became evident: that modern 'culture', since a long time, has deviated from the Christian-Platonic road and became indeed re-founded on a Gnostic and alchemic pseudo-scientific world vision.

Thus Hofmannsthal, just as Goethe in the past, or Rilke and Thomas Mann among his contemporaries, was caught in this fundamental dilemma: to capture the inner struggle of the hero as a search for one's own deepest self, one's soul and heart, instead of just a 'choice' for a new unity; and what possibility could there be in the new century to bring such a search to a fruitful conclusion.

The ambivalences of this struggle are present already in the title of the book. Hofmannsthal seems to have settled on a single name, *Andreas*, with the subtitle '*oder die Vereignten*'. The last German word remains ambivalent, as its meaning of 'become united' can cover a finding or restoring unity.

The fragment (Hofmannsthal 1998: 11–109) containing the first part of the novel starts by a fantasy presented as reality: upon his arrival in Venice Andreas is met by a half-naked man, wearing masks, who turns out to be acquainted with the aristocracy in both Venice and Vienna, suggesting him an affordable accommodation near a theatre.[11] As Andreas would soon state explicitly, it was as if his dearest wishes became true (Ibid.: 20). In order to understand this strange starting scene, however, we need to discuss the motto. Hofmannsthal selected a quote from Ariosto about the enchanter, or trickster. The choice of Ariosto itself is of importance, as he was an important model for *Don Quixote*. The central term of the motto, 'enchanter', is a key word in Cervantes' novel, alluding to the main, invisible but omnipresent enemies of Don Quixote, but also capturing the heart of that novel, the paradoxical relationship between illusion, reality and printed writing. The term also became central for both sociology and modern literature, and right when Hofmannsthal was writing *Andreas*: in between 1912 and about 1920 Max Weber was struggling with the problem of the 'disenchantment [*Entzauberung*] of the world', while Thomas Mann was writing the *Magic Mountain* (*Die Zauberberg*).[12]

Moving to the substance of the quote, it singles out for attention not simply tricksters but *unidentified* tricksters; the figures that Weber failed to incorporate in his political sociology, limiting attention to 'charismatic' leaders, thus helping to misidentify, systematically, the political tricksters of the twentieth century as charismatics.[13] Finally, concerning broad significance, the quote indicates that *Andreas* will move in the same register as *Don Quixote*: the paradoxical connection between reality and fantasy, *as* conveyed by a novel; which also implies that it will move in a Platonic register, in the sense in which Plato in *Phaedrus* made it evident that every writing is a writing and not reality – even if this writing has as its scope to explore reality, and especially the extent to which writing had interfered with reality.

Andreas thus arrives at Venice, the city of his dreams, and everything seems to happen as if in a dream – as if his dreams came true. As it seems proper, he tries to convey this to his parents – except that he can't, as he would need to talk about theatre, which would lay bare the schismatic complicity between the proclaimed educational aims and his own dreams. Even further, this only evokes the shocking experience that occurred him on the road to Venice.

Here Hofmannsthal inserts as flashback the Carinthia episode.

Andreas was supposed to be educated and tested in Venice; but he was actually and literally tested before. On his way to Venice a particularly repulsive figure, one of the tricksters alluded to in the motto, manages to get assumed by him as servant. Both the details and the implications are crucial. Andreas does not need and does not want a servant, yet is weak at crucial moments – weak due to the kind of *mis*-education he systematically received. Thus, he has a trickster servant, who would soon guide him where he did not want to go – to Carinthia. The parallels with *Death in Venice* by Thomas Mann are stunningly close, and again we cannot know whether this is a coincidence or an intentional play. Whatever the case, the outcome is radically different: in the story of Mann Aschenbach is guided by Hermes-like tricksters to Venice and his death; in Hofmannsthal's fragment Andreas is guided away from his target, Venice, towards real life and his true self, offering something stable against the theatricalisation towards which his first Venice guide lured him.

This 'real life' has two aspects. One is Romana, a farmer girl with whom he falls in love, and one of the unresolved dilemmas of the novel is whether Andreas would return in order to marry her. The other concerns Carinthia, its mountains, animals and rivers, or nature; thus, reality is love and nature, in contrast to the theatricality of Venice. Hofmannsthal presents this reality in a particularly delicate manner. The flashback is introduced by the term 'the three disastrous [*unheilvollen*] days in Carinthia' (Hofmannsthal 1998: 22), so the reader doesn't expect anything positive; and indeed, the story starts by genuine disasters unleashed on Andreas by the servant. Yet, once he reassumes his original journey and leaves the region, he suddenly encounters its beauty. This page and half are among the most important of the fragments, and in several ways. It starts by Andreas sitting in his cart, with an empty [*leere*] gaze, thinking only about Romana, left behind. Then he perceives an eagle circling, and opening his eyes to his surroundings he experiences nature as he never did before: he recognises a unity, and power, between his own being, the bird and everything around – as if all this emerged out of himself. It was an epiphany experience about the beauty of the world, quite close to the *thaumazein* of Plato's *Timaeus* – a Greek word that can be translated as marvel or enchantment; a marvel based on an experience of strength and virtue, both in the animal and in himself, thus producing an unprecedented experience of unity: the idea that Romana lives in him; that she was a living essence (*ein lebendes Wesen*), a centre (*ein Mittelpunkt*) and that around her there was a Paradise (Hofmannsthal 1953: 162; 1998: 73).

At this moment, two movements became one: the movements of the bird, the circles they were forming, using a terminology closely recalling the circles of Rilke, Yeats and even *The Woman Without a Shadow*; the other the kneeling and prayers that united him and Romana. This led to a feeling of inner strength, when an 'unutterable certainty' (Hofmannsthal 1998: 73) pervaded him; and then, this entire experience was adjudicated as the happiest moment of his life.

Thus, in full contrast to Thomas Mann's story, Andreas was hijacked by a trickster from his road to Venice, which led him to encounter not death, rather life. His journey to Venice thus literally became bracketed by his experience in Carinthia, almost just an intermezzo until he returns to Romana. Except that now he is in Venice; Carinthia is only a flashback, representing another level of reality (Miles 1972: 177); and thus the very reality of life means that he must take his presence in Venice seriously.

So he proceeds – except that the reality of Venice, even outside masks and theatre, turns out to be less and less comprehensible at every step. And here something quite striking happens: from inspiration by Rilke and parallels with Thomas Mann the novel moves to a register that could not possibly have been known to Hofmannsthal, the dream-like narrative of Kafka (Miles 1972: 180). More than surface affinity, this extends to the entire Venice episode: the discussion between Andreas and the younger girl of his house, Zustina, evokes the conversation between K. and the women in *The Castle*; the visit to Nina the visit of Joseph K. to the court painter Titorelli in *The Process* – not forgetting that Zorzi, who guided Andreas to Nina, was a Venetian painter; while the wondering of Andreas in Venice, before and after meeting Nina, with the small square, the church and the garden, are again straight out of Kafka's *Castle*. Any direct influence is excluded, as the novels were written roughly around the same time, remaining unpublished in the life of their authors. Hofmannsthal and Kafka evidently managed to discover something deep and identical, below and beyond the theatricality of Venice and the bureaucracy of the Monarchy: the thorough Byzantinism of both.

Thus, in *Andreas* Venice becomes bracketed for a second time; and even twice. First, the novel introduces a new protagonist: Sacramozo, a Maltese knight. Sacramozo represents something in between the double and a guide of Andreas: a double, in so far as he is evidently liberated from carnal needs; but also a spiritual guide, close to the similar figures of the *Magic Mountain* – a novel that again would only be completed well after the fragments of *Andreas* were written. While the features of Sacramozo are elaborated in the notes, the other central development, with all its ambivalence, is introduced in the narrative fragment: in a church, when waiting to meet Nina, Andreas encounters a woman, but then all of a sudden she disappears and another woman, almost her copy, appears. This event simply brackets his encounter with Nina, as Andreas can hardly wait to get over with his meeting so that he could return to the church, to see again this – Spanish – woman, *feeling* that he would meet her again – however, nobody is there. At this point, repeating the word 'nobody [*niemand*]' three times in the short last paragraph (Hofmannsthal 1953: 162), as if a magical formula, the narrative fragment ends.

The various notes help to shed some light on the events. Andreas was evidently present the very moment the personality of this woman suffered a split – perhaps as a consequence of his presence. The notes demonstrate Hofmannsthal's preoccupation with this theme and intense efforts to present the duality of Maria and Mariquita through the means of a novel, but evidently did not succeed.

The notes, c.1913–14

Both sets of notes (Hofmannsthal 1998: 115–47, 149–83) are fundamentally concerned with the reasons for undertaking the trip and its connections to the personality of the hero. Andreas is not simply going for a journey of learning cum pleasure. Already before starting it, he encountered problems, as his character was not yet formed, remaining uncertain about his own situation, even – and this is the first statement – having two separate halves (Hofmannsthal 1998: 115); the second set further specifies that he even went through a spiritual crisis, offering the precise diagnosis of *Anhedonia* (the inability to experience pleasure; Hofmannsthal 1953: 221). Thus, the journey is a spiritual pilgrimage (Miles 1972: 152–3). Yet, this crisis was a standard problem due to growing up. Andreas had solid bases, as it is true of every normal, healthy human being; in particular, he had courage, the courage to face storms: moral courage (*moral Mut*; Hofmannsthal 1953: 195). The problem lay at the level of his educators; he was betrayed where he should have been helped. The central blame is placed on his parents, in particular his father and his 'calculating *snobisme*' (Hofmannsthal 1953: 195, 1998: 115);[14] but, strikingly, Andreas could not recall a single relative who could warm his heart (Hofmannsthal 1998: 60). The second set of notes deepens this diagnosis, using a striking language: the negative influence of his father was exacerbated by another 'father', Pater Aderkast, a cleric who annihilated his sense of life (*das Leben aufgehoben*), rendering it illusory, evoking the plays of Calderón (Hofmannsthal 1953: 221). This explains why the personality of Andreas became split (*auseinanderklaffen*, Hofmannsthal 1953: 195, 1998: 115).

However, beyond problems of misdirected family and religious education, the loss of the unity of the person reaches into the heart of contemporary thinking, through the philosophy of Mach. Since his first play *Yesterday*, written when he was 17, Hofmannsthal berated the theories of Mach. He immediately understood that reducing the person to an accumulation of sensations undermines the unity of the self, rendering any kind of ethics or morality meaningless.

Having been systematically mis-educated, Andrea lost belief in his own experiences, so he needs to be guided back to reality, including his *own* reality; to recognise both the reality of a higher realm (*das Dasein des Höheren erkennen*) and the very substance of life (*der Gehalt des Lebens*; Hofmannsthal 1953: 222; 1998: 150). This is what Venice, the city of theatre and daydreaming manifestly cannot do. The novel conveys this by anything having to do with Venice possessing a dreamy, unreal, masked and theatrical countenance; while all those experiences that help Andreas, this twentieth century Wilhelm Meister, find himself are not rooted in Venice, rather Carinthia, in particular Romana; Sacramozo, the Maltese knight (the teacher but also the other half of Andreas, whose autobiographical aspect is undermined by his approaching 40, just as Hofmannsthal, who was much preoccupied with this milestone, calling as a result 1914 his *annus mirabilis*; a year which indeed turned out to be memorable for everybody) and the Spanish lady Maria/Mariquita.

A teacher figure is not present in *Malte* or the novels of Kafka, and the heroes of these novels were indeed lost. Such figures, however, dominate the *Magic Mountain*. Sacramozo is radically different from the Jesuit-Bolshevik arch-Sophist Naphta, modelled on Georg Lukács, or the Enlightenment-free mason arch-clown Settembrini, though having some similarities to Pieperkorn. He is not using rhetoric to convince and indoctrinate into his own position, rather he tries to return Andreas to his inner self – in Hadot-Foucaldian terminology, to convert him to his self. Sacramozo is a proper guide, must possess his own solidity: he has 'inexhaustible inward powers' (*unerschöpfliche innere Kräfte*), in which he can take confidence (Hofmannsthal 1953: 241; 1998: 175); and even knows about it, possessing a conception of inner force that Andreas still has to acquire (Hofmannsthal 1953: 239; 1998: 172).

Such an idea is thoroughly Platonic, indeed Franciscan-Platonic, close to the ideas of St Bonaventure, best visible in the manner Hofmannsthal presents the self or soul of Sacramozo *in work*. Sacramozo misplaced a letter in a state of somnambulism, and then became particularly agitated. However, once the letter was found, he took a step back, through the means of his reasoning power (*durch Vernunft*, Hofmannsthal 1953: 241), offering the Platonic vision of reason, not an a priori fixing of our conduct, which only disempowers our inner essence, rendering us puppets of our own objectified 'purposes', and which can easily be substituted, by tricksters, with other purposes; manages to order his unfettered associations; and discovers inside himself the values of nobility, grace and modesty. These are the same values that Andreas also possesses, except that he needs to recover them, bringing them into his presence: becoming the master of our own self implies that we must have everything present in us (Hofmannsthal 1953: 245), even our past. Thus the road to the recovery of the self is through memory; only a recollected self is real (Miles 1972: 57–8), as the past is just as present as the present moment; indeed, the distinction between past and present is arbitrary, 'yesterday' is an empty word, as everything that happened, that was the past, is also present (Hofmannsthal 1992: 40; 1979: 242). The road Andreas must cross is to reconcile with himself, with his own childhood (Hofmannsthal 1998: 150), to find his own inner force – the most difficult of destinations, to reach his own self, and thus to fulfil his inner nature (Hofmannsthal 1998: 226).

The greatest good is an awareness of our inner forces, or a certain emotional experience of one's unity with oneself (*Gefühl des Selbst*; Hofmannsthal 1953: 247). This expression is in the very last sentence of the second set of comments, thus in a way is the last direct word we have from Hofmannsthal about his novel project; and is connected to Romana, evoking the epiphany experience of Andreas in the mountains, when he left them, on way towards Venice.

The real stake of Andreas' journey is simple and trivial, as most hypermodern, a central concern of innumerable works of art since at least a century, being nothing else but finding or realising oneself. However, it is also extremely delicate and complicated, as the standard modern(ist) search has been radically misconceived, purportedly implying a radical and complete break, and then a free search for 'constructing' a new identity, taking up an alchemical and constructivist direction. It is closer to the 'conversion to self' explored by Foucault, though even Foucault's search was highly tentative and by no means completed, not only because of his untimely passing away, but because of his own inner uncertainties concerning the nature of this quest, attempting to detach himself from modernist presumptions of 'scientifically' true self and returning to classical perspectives like Plato, yet stopping short of recognising the unity of true inner force as heart or soul, just as it happened with Nietzsche's 'will to power'.

The highest mode of human existence is to live in unity with one's own self, free from any internal split. Yet, far from being particularly difficult, this is the natural mode of human Being – this is the way people in the mountains of Carinthia were evidently living, people with an intact heart (Bemporad 1976: 159). Still, Hofmannsthal was attempting to raise even this to a further level, through the allomatic, a term coined against the 'automatic', seemingly implying that we can only find happiness and unity in the 'Other'. Most of the central definitions of inner force are contained in notes written around the location where the allomatic appears (Hofmannsthal 1998: 177). Even further, these notes contain the statement, attributed to Sacramozo, that the greatest pleasure is to leave ourselves (*sortir de soi-même* [*sic*]; Hofmannsthal 1998: 170), as a kind of ecstasy. Yet, there is no contradiction, as the heart of the allomatic is love. Finding oneself, the aim of the road, is to be capable of loving (*liebesfähig*; Hofmannsthal 1953: 226; 1998: 156), which can only be done if one is secure of oneself – and, as Sacramozo intuited, this is what Andreas lacked, as he had a certain self-contempt (*Selbstverachtung*), even faced inner disintegration (*er mit sich zerfallen* [*ist*]; Hofmannsthal 1953: 228). Possessing one's own forces does not mean a monadic prison or iron cage of the self; on the contrary, it implies the capacity to love, thus – paradoxically – of ecstatically leaving oneself, together with the loved one, forming a just as indissoluble union with the other as with one's own force. This is the reason why the highest divine ecstasy of mystics is indeed so close to the highest joint ecstasy of human lovers – and why the two are incompatible, being the two highest states possible for human beings. Both are ways to realise our own deepest selves, at the same time when this achieves a full union with somebody else – either the Divine (the real infinite), or a loved one (somebody concrete).

In lieu of an ending

Andreas remained unfinished. However, given the (non-)ending of the earlier *Malte*, the unfinished character of all the (later) novels of Kafka and Mann's odyssey in completing *The Magic Mountain*, the surprising thing would have been had it been finished. Thomas Mann, after all, was a novelist, so for him finishing was imperative; and by recasting the novel, following – quite closely – the example of Goethe and the rewriting of *Wilhelm Meister* after the French Revolution he indeed managed to produce a work whose importance for its times parallels that of Goethe's novel.

Yet, there are two key instances in Hofmannsthal's work that can be considered as proper culminations of the argument, each with its own striking turn. One is the opera *The Woman Without a Shadow*, while the other is a small segment in a 1914 essay.

The Woman Without a Shadow is one of the most important and also most popular works of Hofmannsthal, conceived at the time when he was working on *Andreas*. It is a striking illustration of the allomatic, while also revisiting metamorphosis, a central preoccupation for Hofmannsthal just as for Goethe. While seemingly a fairy-tale, it is much more, just as the *Rosenkavalier* cannot be reduced to a simple farce.

The protagonist is the Empress, a divine being who, during her frequent metamorphic visits to humans, fell in love with an emperor. As a result, she became mortal, losing her powers of metamorphosis, even becoming inflicted with the curse that unless she acquires a shadow, his beloved husband would be turned to stone. Following the advice of his old nurse, he proceeds to acquire such a shadow by tricking humans, but eventually realising the error of his ways. As taking can only be done through tricking, she renounces the undertaking, admitting that she had lost her way by entering the life of other people uninvited (Hofmannsthal 1993: 84–6). Her act of renouncing breaks the spell, her husband becomes alive again, in a scene recalling the ending of *Faust II*, and the final scene contains the stunning image of a circling falcon (Hofmannsthal 1953: 374; 1993: 91), evoking the poems of Yeats and Rilke as much as the ending of the flashback to Carinthia in *Andreas*.

The second instance is even more striking. It is a passage in the third part of an essay written about Hofmannsthal's 1908 travels in Greece, one of the three epiphanies of Hofmannsthal, according to David Miles (1972: 55–9), only finalised in 1914. It states the following: 'in my innermost core I am indestructible [*unzerstörbar bin ich im Kern*]' (Hofmannsthal 1964: 41, with the next sentence repeating the word; see also Miles 1972: 57).

At one level, this is the strongest version of the inner force whose specification was so central for *Andreas*. Even more strikingly, the same term is central for the November 1917 Zürau aphorisms of Kafka. However, the most striking thing, going well beyond the problem posed by the unfinished nature of their novels, is that the insight became ignored and overlooked by both. Kafka would never publish the passage with the word, while Hofmannsthal would erase the passage from the version of the essay abbreviated for the 1924 edition of his collected works.

This was the year when Kafka died, and when Thomas Mann published the passage selected for the epigraph, to remind us about human fallibility, including forgetting, almost the moment we gained, our most important insights.

Conclusion: the novelties of hypermodern novel

The four (non-)novels of 1910–12 generate the novelistic space for the rest of the book, and indeed for much of the modern novel. A comprehensive analysis of their common points could easily be extended into a book-length essay. Here only a few of their most important common features will be listed, in order to set the stage for the rest of the book, including a detailed analysis of the pieces by Kafka and Mann.

The impossibility to finish

The single most evident common characteristic of the founding classics of hypermodern novel is that they were mostly unfinished, as evidently interminable.

A novel is fundamentally a story, a story is supposed to have an end and most of the major, classic figures of the modern novel had no problems in finishing their work – the only major exception, significant in itself, seems to be Goethe, with the more than half a century spent on finishing – if it was ever finished – *Wilhelm Meister*. But the major novels of Defoe, Fielding, Richardson, Dickens, the Brontës, Thackeray, Balzac, Stendhal, Flaubert, Zola, Dostoevsky, Turgenev or Tolstoy – the list could be continued – were finished without much problem.

With hypermodern novels, the situation radically changes. Kafka wrote three novels, widely considered as *the* most important novels of the twentieth century, yet they all remained abandoned and unfinished. Hofmannsthal – for long promising to become an heir to Goethe – only wrote one, not only left unfinished, but in fragments. Rilke finished his novel, in the sense of completing it for publication, but it does not have an ending in any classical sense of the term. Thus, of the four main inaugural figures of the hypermodern novel, only Thomas Mann finished his, both *Death in Venice* and *The Magic Mountain* – the only 'conventional' novelist of the four.

Such endemic problem with finishing a story, a simplest thing in the world, cannot be accidental. It is clear sign of a move towards the paradoxical condition of permanent liminality, or the taking shape of hypermodernity.

Lost heroes, lost narrative

Still, and furthermore, not only the novels seem to be to 'lost', in the sense of not being finished, but the same applies to their heroes. In the case of *Malte*, the two things even coincide – Malte was 'lost' in the novel, in the sense that the novel, started with his experiences in Paris, increasingly moved to his childhood experiences and then to his readings, so the novel became as if transmogrified into readings and parables. The first novel of Kafka reaches, by different means, the same situation, as the hero of *Der Verschollene* ('The Dispersed One'), as the title clearly indicates, is similarly lost in America, once forced to leave his home, recalling how Malte ended up in Paris. Even the hero of Thomas Mann's story shares this fate, as Aschenbach got also lured away from home into Venice, where he lost himself and eventually died. Finally, Andreas also repeatedly got lost, first in Carinthia and then in Venice, even split and fragmented, and while Hofmannsthal's plan was to demonstrate how he could become one again, he never managed to perform this.

Even further, and entering another circle of absurdity, not just as the heroes but the narrative itself also disappeared, generating an impossible novel without a narrative. Thus, once the novel successfully invaded and carnivalised all other genres, it successfully cancelled itself out of existence. This was again inaugurated by *Malte*, the first novel without any narrative,[15] a paradoxical innovation followed by *Andreas*, also more preoccupied with the inner state of the hero than with whatever happens to him, but is arguably brought to perfection by Kafka, as in *Amerika*, while taking inspiration from Dickens, a great storyteller, and especially from *Martin Chuzzlewit*, manages to get almost completely rid of the narrative, an innovation carried to its ultimate corollary in *The Castle*, where the inhabitants of the village in the novel know better about the arrival of the hero than the hero himself – or us readers.

Generalised sleepwalking, trickster hijacking

The heroes, however, often lose their way not accidentally but are explicitly and purposefully misdirected by strange figures that recall the trickster of comparative anthropology, once their will-power was undermined, thus effectively rendered sleepwalkers and further reinforcing such a state. Rilke's novel, interestingly, has no such characters, though the hero clearly enters a somnolent state. Such figures, however, play a vital role in *Andreas*, the first by hijacking the hero to Carinthia, and the second, in a particularly strange (non-)clothing though wearing a mask by taking Andreas to a room near a theatre. *Death in Venice* simply swarms with tricksters, playing a fundamental role in the narrative, as Aschenbach is literally passed from hand to hand by such trickster characters, from Munich to Venice. The eventual somnambulism of the hero is repeatedly underlined: while Aschenbach is presented as a person renowned of his will-power, he ends up unable to commit himself to do the only act he knew could save him. Kafka's novels again reach an ultimate state, where practically all characters are or end up becoming tricksters. Thus, the world of the *Castle* is 'divine', only in the sense of being literally demonic.

The urge at autobiography

Such a loss of direction and will-power by the heroes of these (non-)novels is particularly striking, as they were explicitly autobiographical. While the novel as genre has evident connection with personal experiences, the classical novels were not dominantly autobiographical, with the exception of Goethe. Quite on the contrary, Bakhtin built his theory about the polyphony of classical novels, on their capturing through the author as medium a number of different voices, where the hand of the author after a time becomes as if guided by the characters themselves, who develop and lead the narrative into unforeseen directions. Here, however, with the pioneering novels of hypermodernity, a completely different dynamics sets in, with the autobiographical figure inside the novel becoming reduced to a somnolent state and 'guided' by demonic trickster characters to his perishing – or the contrary. In this way, instead of presenting the complexity of the modern experience through a plurality of perspectives and voices, the hypermodern novel as if captures the identical fate of each and all in being lulled to sleepwalk in a state of permanent liminality – where, to raise paradoxes at a further level, reasoning in the form of calculating, stimulated rationality is not a way out, rather a central mode for proliferating permanent liminality. This will become particularly visible in the novels of Kafka, especially in *The Castle*, where human life is increasingly reduced to the permanent and ruthless play of strategic games, with rational calculation perpetuating overall madness.

Lost authors

Given that the heroes are lost in these novels, or wondering in a sleepwalking state, it is not surprising that the authors themselves became lost, in their real lives and for long years, before or after writing these milestone pieces; something twice amazing, given the significance and often even evident success of these works. The life of Rilke during the conception and writing of *Malte* was in a permanent state of crisis, which did not end after the publication of the novel, persisting until February 1922. Thomas Mann similarly entered a long crisis after completing the *Buddenbrooks*, only overcome by writing *Death in Venice*, though for various reasons the writing of the *Magic Mountain* also dragged on for quite long. The same can be said about Hofmannsthal, who first entered a crisis already around 1897, only ending with World War I; while the difficulties Kafka encountered in his work were particularly acute and well-known, perhaps again only comparable to Nietzsche's.

The link to Ireland

Finally, it is worth mentioning that the strongest and quite striking parallel with the role played by Germanic Central Europe in launching hypermodern culture through novels is offered at the other end of Europe, by Ireland. The most evident figure is James Joyce, who for a long time lived in Trieste, thus the margins of the same area, and whose writing of *Ulysses* step by step parallels that of the *Magic Mountain*. Rilke as a poet has a close equivalent in WB Yeats, who did not write any novels, but whose work strongly parallels Rilke's, culminating in the spiral metaphor of the falcons gyring in their most emblematic poems, 'I Live My Life in Expanding Rings' and 'The Second Coming'. Finally, Kafka also has his Irish equivalent in Beckett. While Beckett was a generation younger, died well over half a century later and is better known through his theatrical works, he also wrote novels, and the parallels between the atmosphere of their works is undeniable.

Notes

1. The analysis offered in this chapter draws particularly closely on a series of recent articles finished by Agnes Horvath about inner force and personal identity.
2. Note that Raphael's 'Lady with a Unicorn' could not be known to Rilke, as the unicorn became painted over already in the sixteenth century, only rendered visible due to a 1935 restoration (Szakolczai 2007a: 272).
3. In between 1897 and 1910 Rilke made at least six visits to Venice. Each visit was substantial, lasting from several days to four weeks, so Venice was second only to Paris for Rilke in terms of its importance (see Dürr 2006: 51).
4. Interestingly, at the time of Rilke, Venice was rather the city where people went to die. Famous such cases include Wagner, Diaghilev and Browning.
5. Note the contrast with Diderot and Lessing, who rather *became* outsiders.
6. About the link between modernism and a permanent 'liminoid' state, see also Griffin (2007).

7. Simmel was connected both to Hofmannsthal (see Frisby 2011: xli) and Rilke (see Prater 1986: 50), and gave his lecture on sociability in May 1910, or very shortly after the premier of the *Rosenkavalier*, an opera supposedly being all about sociability.
8. Note that shortly before, on 25 November 1906 Hofmannsthal wrote an Introduction to the first integral German edition of *1001 Nights*, focusing on its incomparable, absolute, sublime and unlimited sensuality, which exactly due to such limitlessness inundates existence, transforming the world into a revelation, the presence of God being felt everywhere (Hofmannsthal 1964).
9. Intriguingly, the original 1907 sketch started with a passage about memory, alluding to the famous/providential memory of Hofmannsthal (he had an unique, almost eidetic memory, see Miles 1972: 15): 'I remember things very precisely [*ganz genau*]' (Hofmannsthal 1953: 192; 1998: 111).
10. According to an editorial note (as in Hofmannsthal 1953: 376) the narrative segment (*Anfangskapitel*) was written between 17 September–8 October 1912, and 18 July–20 August 1913.
11. Hofmannsthal dates this arrival 17 September 1778. Such focus on September is somewhat intriguing, especially given the name 'Settembrini' in *The Magic Mountain*. September clearly means that start of Autumn, or the end of the year; paraphrasing Huizinga's original Dutch title, the 'Autumn of modernity'. It is also the ninth month of the year, though in the original Latin calendar, as its name indicates, was the seventh, thus embodying both 'magical numbers'.
12. About this, see the May 2015 special issue of *IPA*, organised around the lead article of Ivan Szelényi; see also the pioneering studies of Goldman (1988, 1992) about the connections between Max Weber and Thomas Mann.
13. See the studies of Agnes Horvath (2000, 2008, 2013a).
14. Note the similarity to *Rosenkavalier*, especially the figure of Mr Faninal, who is not interested in the happiness of his daughter, only in avoiding scandal.
15. An important predecessor is *Tristram Shandy* by Laurence Sterne.

Part II
Suspended in the In-Between
Franz Kafka

4 Kafka's sources and insights
Theatre and other modes of distorted communication

The position of Kafka in the modern novel, even in modern culture in general, parallels that of Goethe. Both are central figures of transition at the two ends of the long nineteenth century: Goethe lived through the *Sattelzeit* around 1800 (Koselleck 1988), marked by the American and French revolutions and the Napoleonic Wars, while Kafka experienced the similarly liminal events of World War I and the Bolshevik 'revolution'. Yet, in spite of such structural analogies, there is a major difference between them, no doubt due to the fact that one was living at the start, while the other at the end of this long transition period: while Goethe is one of the greatest artist of all times, whose impact on German culture is comparable to that of Shakespeare on English culture, Kafka's work not only remained radically incomplete, but also fails to offer cathartic and redeeming features, remaining tied to the nihilism of modernity which it not only documents and analyses, but paradoxically reflects, comparable to the way the work of Callot or Newton 'reflects' the liminality of their times (Horvath 2013a) – with the exception of the Zürau Notebooks.

Goethe and Kafka can also be compared in terms of their impact and appreciation. Already in his life Goethe acquired such a cultic status in German culture that writing about him from the distance necessary to form a judgement is practically impossible. Kafka only acquired a major following after his death, but – after World War II – he became the most widely read contemporary German language author, even gaining the paradoxical status of being a 'permanent avatar of the avantgarde' (Corngold and Gross 2011: vii). The secondary literature on Kafka is unmanageable even by experts, so one needs to be particularly careful to find reliable guides in the jungle, all the more so as Kafka is also unique in escaping any fashion and any effort at a comprehensive and exhaustive interpretation (Ibid.: vii). The specific focus in this book will be to bring out the manner in which through valorising and problematising his own extremely liminal condition Kafka managed to gain unparalleled insights about the permanent liminality of modernity.

Kafka's multiple liminality

Concerning Kafka's background, it is in not sufficient to say that it was liminal. In terms of time and space, including family background and life experiences, it was liminal in such a heightened manner that it could be used as if to illustrate the distinction between a causal explanation and elucidation through liminality.

While Kafka was born in Prague, his father had been born in a small village into a traditional Jewish family, moving to Prague around 1880, so not long before Kafka was born (Robertson 1985: 1–4); a life-path shared by many similar families. His father spent his life trying to acquire stable middle class status, source of a permanent conflict with his son, resulting in a mutual failure to understand and recognise the other. The broader context of such family skirmishes was Central Europe, a liminal space in between East and West; and the First World War, a highly liminal moment. As a combined result, assimilated Jews gained at that particular time and space a kind of perceptivity that would not be repeated again (Calasso 2005: 105), as their lives were not only lived at an impossible place, belonging to neither here (the surrounding Germanic culture), nor there (Judaism), but lived literally through the collapse of these three cultures – the European 'old world', the Habsburg Empire and assimilated Jewishness (Masini 2010: 108, 200–1). Kafka's unique personality managed to transform such liminal sensibility into works of art that captured central features of the modern world just coming into full being with incomparable visionary clarity and philosophical, even theological precision.

Among the various figures of literature and culture who had a major impact on Kafka four figures stand out: Dickens and Goethe in particular, but also Kleist and Dostoevsky. The novels of Charles Dickens were the most important direct sources of inspiration for Kafka, especially evident in his first novel, *Amerika*, also known as *The Missing Person*, closely recalling *Martin Chuzzlewit*. Among the many similarities, perhaps the most important is the visionary character of both: Kafka and Dickens not simply 'wrote' novels, rather they put down on paper the flow of images that literally saturated their minds, so that their pen could hardly follow what took place in front of their inner eyes (concerning Kafka, see Starobinski 2001: 454; Zilcosky 2004: 12). Yet, there are radical differences. In contrast to the ease by which Dickens finished and published his novels, Kafka never actually managed to finish them. Furthermore, the characters in Kafka's novels lack the human depth and understanding mastered by Dickens. Karl Rossmann, hero of *Amerika*, is certainly Kafka's most Dickensian character. Having almost no negative features and possessing unlimited good will, he evokes our sympathy, yet remains strangely colourless. The protagonists of the other novels are rather anti-heroes, only diagnosing the emerging modern condition, which is all the stranger as Joseph K. and K. are both clearly autobiographical. Evidently Kafka's time and place no longer allowed space for the optimism and humanity of Dickens, tying Kafka to the diagnosis of modern permanent liminality. Among German writers, Kafka held a special regard for Kleist, especially for his essay on the marionette (Faber 1979: 63–4). His most important source of inspiration, however, without any doubt was Goethe.

Kafka had an exceptionally intimate relation to Goethe (Robertson 1985: 25, referring to Brod). This can be traced back to his school days, when – alone in his class – he wrote his final year essay on Goethe, titled 'How should we understand the conclusion of Goethe's *Tasso*?' (Wagenbach 2011: 32). He also had special affection for *Hermann and Dorothea*, particularly intriguing given that his father's name was Hermann, and that he did not feel for Goethe the kind of adulation demonstrated by his teachers, rather regarded him as an ancestral figure (Robertson 1985: 8). Still, like any German literary person, he felt the oppressive weight of Goethe's stylistic purity and the practically unattainable standards set up by his work (Ibid.: 8, 25–6).

Goethe's impact on Kafka's novels was shown in detail by Pietro Citati. There are close parallels between *The Process* and *Lehrjahre*, in particular concerning the falsity and deceit attributed to the activity of the divinity (Citati 2007: 155); or between the Tribunal in the former and the secret Masonic society in the latter (Ibid.: 160–1). The parallels are particularly strong with the ending of *The Process*, where the two executioners, behaving like automatons, recall the theatrical scenes of *Lehrjahre*. Parallels extend to *The Castle*, where the mechanical effects repeatedly happening in the village are evoked not in order to illustrate the idea that the divine is deceit, mere fantasy, rather that it is mere appearance (Ibid.: 291). For Kafka, Goethe was not simply a figure of literature, but a philosopher – and much more than 'mere' philosophers (see for e.g. Masini 2010: 100–1).

Still, Kafka made strikingly selective use of his main literary sources. From Kleist, Kafka most read and appreciated his letters; from Goethe, his diaries (Koelb 2010: 29); and he especially intended to emulate Dickens' life, due to the personal intensity with which Dickens lived it – and which returns in his admiration for Goethe as well, especially concerning Goethe's balancing act between life, including public activities, and literary production (Koelb 2010: 29–30). Yet again, the failure of Kafka is striking; a failure of which he was acutely aware, opening up a spiral between the wish to emulate and his failure to do so, certainly contributing to his intention to destroy his oeuvre – an attempt which also failed, no doubt because it was not decisive enough; and where another serpent is biting its own tail.

Kafka was intensely interested in two philosophers, Plato and Nietzsche. Kafka read attentively many of Plato's dialogues, his writings containing ample traces of such readings (Corngold and Gross 2011: 5). His debt to Nietzsche poses a more complex problem. While never mentioning Nietzsche by name, and Brod denying any connection, arguing that Kafka's ideas are the exact antithesis of Nietzsche's (Corngold and Gross 2011: 9–10), there are clear biographical indications about Kafka's great interest in Nietzsche. Kafka was seen reading Nietzsche's works as early as 1900 (Faber 1979: 44), while around 1920 he gifted a copy of *The Birth of Tragedy* to Gustav Janouch (Bridgwater 1974: 11). The impact exerted by Nietzsche on Kafka is now widely acknowledged, Erich Heller considering Kafka as Nietzsche's legitimate heir, while Walter Sokel going as far as arguing that in Kafka there is an almost line by line engagement with Nietzsche (Corngold and Gross 2011: 10).

Kafka's theological leanings are more controversial. Walter Benjamin considered the very idea as revealing a misunderstanding of Kafka, though this was rather a reaction against the excesses of Max Brod. Yet, the theological undercurrents in Kafka's work are essential – and they can be rendered visible, most paradoxically, through another much ignored aspect of the work, its close connection with theatre. This can be shown most directly through the peculiar dynamics of Kafka's life-work.

'The Verdict' as the great leap forward

In terms of quality, Kafka's work can be divided into two parts: the early works, up to 'The Verdict'; and the later, mature writings. In between the two there stands this short piece as a genuine guardian of the threshold; a singular role that is all the more strange as it was written during one night, 22–3 September 1912. The story of how Kafka was glued down to his writing desk on that night, emerging in the morning, with the story in his hand, and reading it to his sister by now has been told so repeatedly that its astonishing features became taken for granted.

The date carries a number of special features. Yom Kippur, the Day of Atonement, in 1912 fell on 20/21 September, a coincidence of particular significance, given the title and theme of the story. Furthermore, Kafka's correspondence with Felice Bauer was started on 20 September; and even more intriguingly, he first met Felice on 13 August, thus exactly forty days before, 'forty' being one of the most cherished Biblical numbers. Such speculation on numbers and coincidences is recurrent in the Kafka literature, reflecting Kafka's own interests.

It is here that another aspect in Kafka's life enters the picture that over the past decades received a fair amount of attention, but whose significance so far perhaps has not yet been fully explored and understood: his involvement with Yiddish theatre. The peculiar theatricality of Kafka's work, its reliance on glaring and gestures, has been identified by early commentators like Walter Benjamin (1977: 418, 31, 5–6), who even asserted that 'Kafka's world is a world-theatre', meaning that human life is lived as if on stage (Ibid.: 422). However, nothing is further from Kafka's style than theatricality in the ordinary sense of the term. It was therefore difficult to make sense of this connection – especially given the scarce importance attributed to theatre in social theory.

Kafka's theatre experience

The involvement with Yiddish theatre covered a short but intense period in Kafka's life. His first encounter took place in May 1910, when Kafka attended a few performances by the 'Spiewakow Trupe' (Massino 2002: 16). It did not leave an impact on him, so much so that the first relevant entry in his diary is from 5 October 1911 (Beck 1971: 13; Massino 2002: 16), connected to a second series of performances, this time by Yitzchak Lowy's group. This interest culminated in a 25 December 1911 diary entry on minority languages and a 18 February 1912 lecture on Yiddish language (Koelb 2010: 33–4; Robertson 1985: 19–23). This, however, also signalled the end, as the actors left Prague and the coming war closed possibilities: the group simply vanished into thin air (*nel nulla*) (Massino 2002: 51).

The encounter with Yiddish theatre took place at a highly liminal juncture in manifold socio-political and biographical senses. In terms of biography, Kafka suddenly encountered his own Jewish background and identity, and in a particularly resounding manner. Kafka gave up on religion already in his high-school years, becoming an assimilated, Western Jew. He was also on a threshold in his writings: he realised that what he had so far written was not good enough and waited for a decisive turning point, a leap in quality (Ibid.: 15–16).

Two pieces of evidence make it evident how much Kafka was dissatisfied with his previous efforts. First, he termed such works as mere 'buffooneries', weightless jokes and tricks on which so far he wasted his time and talent (Calasso 2005: 180; Citati 2007: 26, 73); an activity that strikingly recalls Leonardo da Vinci's pastimes in his youth. The second touches an even deeper level, but was only noticed recently by Roberto Calasso (2005: 165–70), as this particular piece of evidence was omitted from the previous edition of Kafka's diaries. These concern a series of June 1910 entries, among the earliest ones, in which Kafka repetitively, even obsessively, ponders how much his education, in family as in the schooling system, damaged and even ruined him, the guilty including not only parents, relatives and teachers, but even the cook who accompanied him every day to school. According to Calasso, Kafka 'poses no limits to his fury' here, extending his malediction even 'to those he could not remember' (Calasso 2005: 169–70). It is in this context that the striking feature of these entries, forcing previous editors to omit them, gain their significance, as here Kafka, line after line, 'like a broken disc' (Ibid.: 165), wrote down identical sentences, revealing both an astonishing degree of alienation from his own family and surroundings, just as a deeply nurtured desire for revenge.

Yiddish theatre is usually traced to mid-nineteenth century, but the broad genre must be much older. Given that such performances were limited to the Eastern part of the Jewish diaspora, it must have been an inheritance of the Byzantine world, possibly rooted in ancient mime plays. Such a conjecture is all the more likely as the comic roles played in the group reveal a strong affinity with the figures *of commedia dell'arte*. In both improvisation played a central role, making the performances of actors look particularly truthful (Massino 2002: 19–20, 28–9).

The decisive encounter happened on 5 October 1911 when Kafka attended a performance by a group from Lemberg, led by Yitzchak Lowy, at the Cafe Savoy in Prague (Beck 1971: 13–15). At this moment Kafka suddenly and decisively fell under the spell of Yiddish theatre, Lowy becoming an indispensable friend for long months, while for Maria Tschissik, a leading actress, he felt an unconfessed love (Beck 1971: 15–20; Massino 2002: 16–17). The performances struck a chord in him, evoking compassion and pity and producing an intense involvement, mobilising his own failures and aspirations (Koelb 2010: 32). From that moment, his diary entries become saturated with references to theatrical presentations, with long descriptions giving detailed accounts of the smallest acts performed.

68 *Suspended in the In-Between*

The effect mechanism of performances much relied on gestures, in particular exaggerated movements, and 'significant glaring' (Beck 1971: 27–8; see also Stach 2013: 56). The most important such detail, however, concerned music.

The music accompanying performances was no mere addition to the show, rather it was the very 'soul' of Yiddish theatre (Massino 2002: 17). As soon as musical notes were sounded, actors immediately came under their spell, were touched by them, 'irresistibly transported' by them, and the same happened with the audience, pervaded, almost possessed by this music (Ibid.). The music was so full of melody that its effect was not simply the joint fixation and transfiguration of actors and audience but an irresistible and contagious suspension of any structure: suddenly the children of the troupe who so far were only hanging around entered the scene humming the songs, thus the boundary between actors and audience was dissolved in blissful liminal *communitas* (Ibid.). According to a diary entry of 22 October 1911, the central emotion establishing contact through and with the actors is compassion or pity (*Mitleid*).

The impact of this experience of bliss was tremendous on Kafka. It resulted in an alchemic transformation of his very being, reshaping his existence as a writer, even his personal identity (Ibid.: 25): a sudden suspension of his Western assimilated identity and recognition of his fateful but inevitable fragmentariness, yet gaining magically a new confidence (Ibid.: 24). Kafka felt the theatrical performance irresistible: though trying to preserve his distance, he was swept away by audience reactions, (mis)taking theatre as source of real authenticity.

The most important direct expression of his theatre experience was writing: through the encounter with Lowy 'overwhelming forces liberated themselves' on the night between 22–3 September in Kafka (Ibid.: 25) whose full flowering can be traced in Kafka's eventual, overnight transformation into the greatest writer of his times.

As the theatre experience touched Kafka below and beyond the level of consciousness, it is not surprising that the decisive effects on his writing also took place at this level. At the level of conscious plans Kafka re-started work on *Amerika*, discarding previous drafts. However, the effort did not succeed; the idea for this novel was too deeply rooted in his earlier self, and the frame could not properly accommodate the changes. The most successful sections of the novel were the scenes where the new style suddenly fully broke through, like the 'hotel reception' and 'electoral canvass' scenes, and most clearly the concluding chapter, the stunning vision of the Great Theatre of Oklahoma.

The single most important, indeed decisive evidence, at once sign of the change and its operator, in the sense of Foucault's 1984 Introduction to the *Use of Pleasures*, was 'The Verdict'.

'The Verdict'

The most striking feature of 'The Verdict' concerns the perfect coincidence between what it is and what it was supposed to be, given matters of context – conscious and unconscious, internal and external. It was written just after Yom

Kippur, the day of atonement, and it is indeed about a judgement; and its main protagonists closely correspond to the protagonists of Kafka's real life – the father figure, Lowy masked as the Russian friend and even Felice Bauer as fiancé. Yet, none of this was premeditated and consciously produced, just outcome of a night of feverish writing – surprising, even frightening Kafka more than his commentators.[1]

The storyline of 'The Verdict' moves, almost imperceptibly, from matters of family triviality into the complete absurd; according to Calasso the frame of the story is 'of an insolent absurdity' (Calasso 2005: 155). It is the story of Georg Bendemann,[2] a young merchant revealing to his father his plans to get married. The father encounters this with increasingly stronger and more absurd accusations, during which the scenery in the story assumes a dream-like character, with the father expanding into a giant who can touch the ceiling by his hands. He eventually condemns his son to death by drowning; a verdict strikingly recalling the penultimate words of Nietzsche (Nietzsche 1988, XIII: 647). The son promptly obeys by leaping acrobatically into the river, 'dear parents, I still have always loved you' being his final words.

The case of Kafka's 'The Verdict', a short story written during one night which singlehandedly made out of Kafka the most important literary figure of the twentieth century, is so much outside the horizon of the modern episteme that its understanding requires unique guides, like Pietro Citati and Roberto Calasso, each devoting a book to understanding Kafka and mobilising, through Kafka's own words, the most extreme metaphors about the creative process. Citati (2007: 68) emphasises demonic or *daimonic* inspiration, recalling Plato and Goethe. Calasso makes use of Kafka's diaries, containing Kafka's puzzled reflections on his own 'child', comparing the process of writing this story to ejaculation and giving birth (Calasso 2005: 155; Corngold and Wagner 2011: 133–4), singling out the semen and the mucus, thus two liquids – particularly noteworthy given the ending of the story, the death of Georg by water. The analysis can be taken further by comparing this event to the genesis of the quantum leap within Shakespeare's work, after 1592, making use of the striking insights contained in Ted Hughes's (1992) magisterial work.

In trying to render the absurd creative process of Kafka intelligible, Calasso pursues the questions Kafka posed to himself and his tentative answers. While much of contemporary literary criticism, history of ideas and sociology of knowledge, on the footsteps of Roland Barthes and Michel Foucault, John Pocock and Quentin Skinner, focuses on authorial intentions, Kafka was well aware that his writing challenged the authority of the author at another plane. Calasso's effort to read Kafka's diaries as closely as possible is not caught in the paradox of authorial intentions, as he simply follows Kafka's own efforts in trying to make sense, for himself, of the sentences his hand put down to the paper, but which were not directed by his mind.

Turning to Hughes, Shakespeare's mature work is based on a series of shamanistic initiatory dreams that he received after the closing of the London theatres due to plague on 20 June 1592, so just before Midsummer Night. The two epic poems, *Venus and Adonis* and *The Rape of Lucrece,* contain the substance of these dreams, together defining the 'mythic equation' that resulted in Shakespeare's extraordinary creativity.

Given his background, it is not surprising that the 'equation' discovered by Kafka concerns the other basic thread of European culture, Judaism. In contrast to the 'tragic' equation of Shakespeare, this equation could be considered as 'tragi-comic' or even outright 'absurd'. The expression 'development of an equation' is even used by Calasso, at the end of the concluding sentence of his analysis of Kafka's relevant diary entries, having an affinity with the modality of Kafka's own quest which focuses on the effort to 'describe all the relationships' that have 'become clear in the story', thus his effort to understand a story written down by him but not authored by him; a story which he did not conceive, in the traditional sense, only 'gave birth to' (Calasso 2005: 159–60).

Kafka's tragic-comic equation captures the shifting relationship between five figures; figures that have a close, strict correspondence both to the 'mythic equation' of Shakespeare, as analysed by Hughes, thus the Mediterranean, Greco-Roman side of Christianity, and to the Judaic tradition, or the other aspect of Christianity – the aspect that, with Protestantism and especially modernity, started to gain the upper hand within European culture. Such shift can be identified by the difference between the five figures, through two classificatory schemes: presence and absence, and central or marginal significance. Two of the five figures are female, but both of these are absent and marginal. The mother figure is dead and only plays a token role in the story, in the sense of her memory being supposedly dirtied. The fiancé figure, modelled on Felice Bauer, is alive, but is only a distant object of whom Georg hardly reveals more than the bare facts, while his father unjustly accuses her of lewd conduct. In the context of the story such accusations remain unfounded and thus inexplicable, but gain their significance by the stunning fact that in 1919, when Kafka would announce his engagement to Julie Wohryzek, his father would react in a strikingly similar way.

The two protagonists present are the son and his father, but it is the third, absent protagonist, the 'Russian friend' who plays the decisive role. The organisation and dynamics of the story are thus completely different from the Shakespearean equations, where women play a fundamental role. We now must understand the internal logics of the kind of social life in which women are reduced to mere objects of discussion and desire, but have no voice or presence on their own.

These relations, and the equation they map, belong to three different fields: to social relationships; to theatre, through the strong, both explicit and implicit theatrical metaphors and acts used; and to theology. In each the manifold intersection of Jewish, Christian and modern aspects must be kept in mind and explored.

The story, first of all, and most evidently, is about a family affair, thus interweaving depth psychology and micro-sociology, beyond reductivism. But the characteristics of the family immediately bring in the other two elements. First, the kind of family affair presented, with its evident realism of gruesome details and focus on deep-rooted intimate conflicts, evokes an important streak of modern theatre, going back to the 'bourgeois drama' pioneered by Diderot and Lessing, which gained intensification in contemporary German 'expressionist' or 'surrealist' drama (Sokel 1984), of which the most important representatives were Ibsen and Strindberg – of relevance for Kafka, as Strindberg was his favourite playwright. But the obsessive father–son relationship characteristic of 'The Verdict' also has a theological angle, going back to Abraham's sacrifice and the Mosaic law, involving a singular omnipotence of father over son, and excluding any 'female' aspect like grace, beauty and love. The evidently simple, but increasingly more absurd family story is thus intricately interwoven with theatrical and theological components, which now must be analysed on their own.

To begin with, in the theatrical component the 'bourgeois drama' aspect is mixed with East European Yiddish theatre. The hardly imperceptible move to the absurd strongly recalls family relations as depicted in the Yiddish theatre, especially the strong emphasis accorded there to conflicts between fathers and sons. This is further underlined by the 'Russian friend' being modelled on Yitzchak Lowy, leader and main actor of the group and Kafka's real-life friend.

But the importance of the 'Russian friend' motive extends way beyond the theatre as reference point. Here we need to take into account one of the most striking aspects of Kafka's 'self'-analysis, emphasised but left unexplained by Calasso, that ' "the friend is the link between father and son; is their greatest communality" ' (as in Calasso 2005: 159). Something is seriously out of place here, as a mere friend cannot belong to the heart of a family drama, especially given that he plays none of the standard roles (seducer of daughter or wife, or adviser to son or father), is not even physically present and such claim about his importance contradicts the significance of the blood-ties between father and son, so central for Judaism, discussed emphatically by Kafka and Calasso and reasserted by the death verdict and its prompt execution.

The only possible solution is that here the story, of which Kafka was not the author rather the medium, in the sense of Goethe or Yeats, became more modern than Judaic by incorporating a central piece of Christian theology, the Trinity, and that therefore the absurd component concerns the Judaic and Christian elements becoming hopelessly confused and entangled at the heart of modernity – especially the kind of modernity as sparked by the Enlightenment, rendered possible by the acute sight produced by the sudden encounter of a secularised and enlightened Western Jew with the seemingly archaic and oriental Eastern Jewish tradition, through the unique person of Kafka, the 'incomparable' (Max Brod), at the particular chronotope of Prague just before World War I. Thus the 'Russian friend' in the story, or Yitzchak Lowy, somehow came to assume the role of the 'Holy Spirit', though decidedly in an unholy kind of way, recalling Dostoevsky's *Demons* (Girard 1961: 286–7).

Whatever this could probably mean, it can easily hold the key to Kafka's oeuvre.

The theological confusion thus opened up concerns a conflation of the Judaic father–son relationship with the Christian problem of the Trinity. In strict monotheistic context all power is possessed by the father to whom the son owes unconditional obedience and who can put his son to death at his will, a relationship manifest in the attempted sacrifice of Isaac. In Christian Trinity, however, the son *as* Son of God becomes similarly endowed with omnipotence, as all power was granted to him by the Father. Such relationship of equipotence is as if sealed by the Holy Spirit, not simply 'communicating' between but being consubstantial with both Father and Son. Just as importantly, it is through the Holy Spirit that the female component, all but absent from the Old Testament, returns to the centre of the New Testament, through the Annunciation and without the intervention of bodily liquids, renewing the old Palaeolithic tradition that survived in segments in the Mediterranean, and even elsewhere, focusing on Divine Love.

Given that this aspect of Trinitarian thinking has become, over long centuries, even millennia, a central component of Christian Europe, it was inevitable that Kafka, member of European culture, became absorbed into this culture of Divine Love, where the relationship between father and son was not reducible to obedience and the Law. This unbroken unity is the real meaning of the one-ness of father and son, evoked by the Russian friend in the story; a oneness brought forcibly home to Kafka on the day of atonement, the greatest Hebrew festivity, the Sabbath of Sabbaths, devoted to reconciliation, expiation and unification; and it was exactly such a unification with his own Jewish identity that Lowy, through his Yiddish theatre, generated for Kafka.

However, it is also here that troubles start, and at many levels. To begin with, while the original interpretation of such a bringing together happened through the Holy Spirit and Divine Love, it had to imply a move back to strict monotheism with its rigorous blood-lineage. Second, this was rendered even more complicated by the problematic character of Lowy as theological operator. Lowy was far from being a figure of orthodoxy; he rather escaped his family in order to become an actor, due to his love of theatre. Such overwhelming love for the theatre, a distinguishing feature of modern secularism, recalls Enlightenment figures like Lessing and Diderot, the literal opposite of Judaic traditionalism. The rebellious character of the actor was immediately perceived by Kafka's father, who did not hide his scorn for his son's new friend (Koelb 2010: 33). Lowy as Russian friend thus embodied two characteristics radically opposed to the Holy Spirit: archaic blood rule and the modern spirit of revolt.

Lowy enacting the Holy Spirit thus almost necessarily leads to self-destruction, and thus the outcome of the story can be considered as a consequence of this self-elimination. Here we can resume the storyline as reconstructed by Calasso.

As a start, it is not only the storyline that can be illuminated through the theological metaphor of Lowy as (un)holy spirit, but the efforts of Kafka to gain an understanding of his own story as well. At the simple level of the storyline the role played by the 'Russian friend' remains inexplicable, impenetrable. He is the addressee of a letter, by Georg; in fact, the story starts the moment in which he finished a long letter written to his friend, and its first pages are devoted to his thoughts and reminiscences about the difficult situation of his friend, who escaped to Russia but is not doing well there at all. A major problem of Georg, for years, was how to stay in contact with him without hurting his pride concerning his own failings. He then informs his father about the letter – and this is the moment in which the story suddenly shifts gear and becomes absurd, as the father makes ever more peculiar accusations concerning this 'Russian friend'. It is this series of accusations that Kafka's diary comments present in a new light – a path that can be further illuminated through the metaphor of the Holy Spirit.

This is because, first of all, it is only through Kafka's comments that the Russian friend gains the position of a link between father and son – an interpretation that could have been difficult to offer solely on the basis on the story told. Furthermore, after finishing the letter, Georg feels particularly close to the father: *this is why* he enters his room the first time in months (Calasso 2005: 159). Even further, and concerning the otherwise inexplicable, irrational behaviour of the father, Calasso uses a particularly telling language in analysing Kafka's diary, comparing the behaviour of the father to a spirit liberated from the bottle. The overall effect of this 'liberated spirit' is anything but spiritual: it is the restoring of a 'blood-link' (*Blutkreis*, literally 'blood-circle'; Kafka 1990: 492) between father and son, expelling the extraneous element, the Russian friend prorogating the subject position of the Holy Spirit, but having no blood-relationship to the family. Still, given the previous role of the Russian friend, the return to blood alone, thus the archaic Judaic order, cannot function, cannot entail a restoration of order; rather, and inexorably, the father–son relationship cannot stop at the level of family ties, moving inevitably beyond it, into the merciless realm of the Law: the father pronounces a death verdict, and the son promptly executes it, in the double sense of the word.

The role of the Russian friend clarified, we can return to the unfolding of the story. Two modalities gain importance from this perspective, according to Calasso, rendering somewhat intelligible the otherwise perplexing precipitation of the initially banal story through absurd developments to the brutal end: the repeated eruption of disproportionality and an excessively casual attitude with respect to temporal and spatial boundaries and transitions. Everything in the story, since the moment the father 'opened wide his toothless mouth' (Kafka 2005a: 4) and started his series of wild accusations, out of any meaningful proportion, is literally irrational, being without 'ratio' or proportion; a disproportionality corroborated by a series of disproportional aspects that are seemingly innocuously, but have great significance. This starts with the gigantic size of the father, which the son noticed the moment he entered the room, the first time for months, and which gains genuinely frightening aspects when the father touches the ceiling.

All this is reinforced by the peculiar modality of transitions in the story, which can be valorised through the term 'liminality'. The point can be illustrated by the manner in which Georg goes into the room of his father. Nothing could be more simple and banal; yet, Kafka's storytelling contains three points that together produce a unique, hallucinatory effect. Concerning space, the two rooms are separated by a short corridor; concerning time, he adds that Georg has not been there for months; thus it is striking that Georg now enters this room in a particularly casual way (Calasso 2005: 161). The lack of respect for spatial limits, especially doors, is particularly marked in the story, as Georg repeatedly crosses such borderlines nonchalantly.

Such consistent ignorance of limits evokes the visionary imagery of a world without limits, or permanent liminality – a central way to capture the dynamics of our days. Given the role of the 'Petersburg friend' in the story, one cannot avoid mentioning the visionary association with the Petersburg Revolution of 1917. The image of permanent liminality is reinforced by the last two words of the piece: *unendlicher Verkehr* ('endless traffic'). Concretely it alludes to the vehicles moving on the bridge, the last image seen by Georg before he let himself fall into the river. Endlessness or limitlessness is the very definition of permanent liminality, capturing the unleashed dynamics of the story; while the term 'traffic' not only connects it to one of the most mundane aspects of modern 'reality', but is also a word associated by Kafka with sexual intercourse (Corngold and Wagner 2011: 134). Thus the last two words of the novel, through a most banal image, tie together the two extremes of the story: extreme spiritual power, permanent liminality; and extreme materialism, reducing the creative process to a sexual act – while all this takes place on a bridge, which again is something most material, a solid stone structure, while being a metaphor of liminality (Simmel 1994), connecting the adjacent pieces of land above the flux of the water, instrument of death penalty in the story, and would return in the first paragraph of *The Castle*.

With this account on the ending of the story, we can complete the analysis inspired by Hughes's interpretation of the Shakespearean oeuvre. In Shakespeare, the emphasis is still on harmony and proportionality, its loss being the problem, while in Kafka disproportionality dominates at every level. Thus, instead of an equation, the heart of the story concerns a particular kind of *dis*-equation. But what could this be?

The answer is helped by two cues. First, Kafka was well aware that he was *not* the sovereign author of this text. The second hint concerns the theological character of the 'equation' in 'The Verdict'; a relationship between the Old and the New Testament that is radically different from the 'mythic equation' identified by Shakespeare, for the simple reason that while it makes sense to recognise affinities between Catholic and Protestant, Greek and Roman, ancient Mediterranean and medieval European ideas, this cannot be done for the Old and the New Testament, given that the New Testament *incorporates* the Old Testament. At one level, this is a simple historical fact. At a second level, it implies a religious imperative of conversion: between Judaism and Christianity, and also Islam, there are genealogical relations, thus their harmonious integration is impossible; the only non-violent alternatives are conversion or peaceful coexistence. At a third level, moving to modernity, with the Enlightenment and secularisation the theological paradox becomes particularly thorny, concerning the potential affinity in the thinking of figures whose education was rooted in rival theological views. Still, at this juncture Kafka's interpretation of his own text again offers a vital cue: according to him, at the start of the story, after finishing his letter, Georg believes that he has his father 'inside him' (Calasso 2005: 159). The claim is strange enough, and goes beyond the text of the story, as it reflects the relationship between the two religions *from the perspective of Christianity*. This is the starting point of Kafka *as* assimilated Jew, whose behaviour, towards his friend just as his father, is motivated not by obedience but by love. But Georg, and Kafka, is not somebody who converted, rather he became assimilated into European culture through secularisation, and for whom the Judaism represented by the father figure became quite vexingly problematic.

The problem identified through Kafka's writings is thus not a mythic equation, but a theological 'dis'-equation or, perhaps even better, a theological 'absurd equation', sharing many affinities with the world of theatre and the upside down turned world proliferated from there. Central for this 'absurd equation' is the absurd relationship between a theatricalised Jewish family and the similarly theatricalised bourgeois family, where the similarity of the effect mechanism of the two, the focus on the evocation of emotions of pity and sympathy, generating *communitas* through theatrical means, yields similar results in both cases, assimilation (as a problem) for one and secularisation (as an outcome) for the other. The final equation is between secular ex-Judaic and ex-Christian bourgeois families, which should be identical, simply modern and secular, but which still can be conflicting and incompatible due to the radically different nature of the underlying theology that became secularised, a tension felt with particular clarity in the generation of Kafka, but which later became invisible – without resolving the underlying incompatibility.

The difference between the mythical equation, motivating Shakespeare's work, and the theological dis-equation behind Kafka's oeuvre is also visible in the respective character of the major works. For Shakespeare, the mythical equation was transformed into the tragic equation, which produced, almost automatically, his four completed tragedies, greatest masterpieces of world literature. For Kafka, theological dis-equation gave birth to an absurd or tragi-comic dis-equation, which could only produce unfinished novels, and which thus could capture, in all its fragmentariness, the heart of the modern condition, without transcending it. Kafka again had striking insights into his own failure, as in a much-quoted aside made to Brod he claimed that 'there is indeed hope, but not for us' (Citati 2007: 189).

Kafka and the demons

The idea that Kafka wrote his works under the influence of external forces which cannot be reduced to stimulants like alcohol or drugs but were 'phantasms' or 'demons' is so much outside the horizon of possibility of the modern episteme that it was ignored by most commentators. Yet, given the testimony of close friends, and Kafka himself, this is a solid piece of evidence, a data not a fact that cannot be ignored without doing injustice, even violence to the work and especially the creative process that generated it. Kafka made it clearly and repeatedly evident that he had no sovereign control over his night-time writing. Thus, he did not 'decide' to 'start' writing *The Process* in 1914, rather he 'found himself writing' a new book (Calasso 2005: 221). Masini also makes the point about Kafka being not necessarily the author of the work, rather 'lost' in the work (Masini 2010: 211). A particularly explicit account is given in one of his last short stories, 'The Burrow', selected as a motto by Calasso:

> 'In a certain way I have the privilege of seeing the phantasms of the night not only in a state of inertia and oblivious abandon, in dream, but at the same time encountering them in reality, when I possess all the force of wakefulness and a quiet capacity to judge.'
>
> (as in Calasso 2005: 125)

In this account Kafka presents such a direct account of his own creative process that it had to be hidden in a story.

The conviction that Kafka lived in – or rather in between – two worlds, being in daily contact with forces imperceptible to others and outside his control was also conveyed by those closest to him, having access to the most intimate aspects of his being.[3] A particularly significant account is offered by Dora Diamant, his last and in some ways most intimate love. In the rendering of her biographer 'it seemed to Dora that Kafka was in constant connection with something outside himself' (Diamant 2003: 12).[4] Dora conveyed this in particularly striking terms: '[i]t was as if he were saying, "On my own I am nothing. I am only something when connected with the outer world"' (Ibid.).

Beyond their presence, the nature of such external forces also preoccupied Kafka, and his search produced a series of striking results. At a first level, these are 'phantasms'; a relatively harmless term, except that Kafka claimed to have encountered them in a waking state. But he also repeatedly stated that such phantasms had demonic qualities, or were simply demons – clearly implying the medieval-Christian sense of malign spirits. The clearest support for such a claim is provided by those absolutely striking claims in which Kafka associates such demons, and his writing completed under their influence, with serving the devil, 'the diabolical aspect of this service residing in the narcissism that it presupposes, or the fact that the writer lives in his unreality' (Masini 2010: 206). Inspiration for writing for Kafka is a flux, a demonic possession and invasion, transforming life into literature (Citati 2007: 65–9), implying an '"attack on the last earthly frontier"', so his works can be considered as a 'shamanistic confession' (Calasso 2005: 134–8).

Here, beyond Shakespeare and Goethe, Kafka is particularly close to main figures of the Russian novel, especially interesting due to the role played by the 'Russian friend' at the source of his creativity. They include Dostoevsky whose *The Demons*, also translated as *The Possessed*, has evident affinities with Kafka's own 'demonic possessions', but also Mikhail Bulgakov; affinities that become particularly clear through the works of Calasso and Citati. Thus, Calasso ends Chapter 5 of *K.*, devoted to the obscures forces guiding Kafka's work and titled simply '*Potenze*' (Powers), first by a citation from the *Diary* (October 1921), in which Kafka describes his unique internal condition (*innere Lage*) by the metaphor that around his head 'continually flies a lurking [*heimlich*] raven' (Kafka 1990: 865–6), adding the following observation: '[a]pproaching Kafka, the air is hardly perceptibly stirred (*smossa*) by those black wings' (Calasso 2005: 144). Citati concludes the parallel between the room of Kafka and the room described in 'The Metamorphosis' with the following claim: '[t]hus, for a month, his room became the theatre of a tragedy that lasted for a winter' (Citati 2007: 78). As will be discussed in Chapter 10, the circling of black crows will be one of the most striking images of the apocalyptic ending of Bulgakov's *Master and Margarita*, while in the *Theatrical Novel* Bulgakov would describe the creative process of the hero, evidently modelled on his own as his room, in the evening, when returning from work and starting to write, being transformed into a theatre where small figures start to recite a presentation, and he would only need to write down what was taking place in from of his eyes.

Living a life under the sign of a shamanistic initiatory ritual, what's even more, undergoing a shamanistic trip practically every night of one's existence, for years and years on, is a hardly tolerable mode of existence. Kafka's mode of living while writing his masterpieces was extremely schismatic, producing tensions and sufferings compared to which the pains caused by his medical condition were trifles, recalling Nietzsche. Such schismatic mode of being is visible in his dualist relationship to the 'spirits' who visited him nightly: an utter, paranoid fear on the one hand – a fear from the demons, but also a fear of death, a fear to change anything around him, especially in his office, where every single object had to stay at exactly the same place, any displacement provoking a hysterical reaction, but also a fear to avoid *not* being in his room, thus a refusal to move, especially to travel, outside strict medical reasons. This was matched with an obsessive desire for encountering again the spirits, animated by a fear that they would not come back – a dualistic love-hate relationships characterising schizophrenics, *except* that Kafka was not schizophrenic, rather actually, evidently visited nightly by such spirits.[5]

Being aware of his own schismatic being, Kafka was desperately looking for models in the past, finding them in two founding figures of European literature, Ulysses and Sancho Panza. Concerning both, he produced a particularly strange, arguably forced reading, emphasising an ultimate kind of schismatic existence, one being torn between a fight for mere survival, pushed to the extreme, and a wish to be possessed by external voices, or a 'will to be a mask'; two features that again capture the heart of the modern condition, the schismatic tension between a Darwinian 'struggle for existence' as the central feature of animal life, and the Romantic theatricalisation of modern life, captured by Jean Paul in an ideal-typical manner.

Kafka's conclusive assessment of his status is contained at the end of a much cited 5 July 1922 letter to Brod, where he defines the type of writer he felt himself to be as the scape-goat of mankind (*der Sündenbock der Menschheit*; Kafka 1958: 386; see Calasso 2005: 134; Citati 2007: 266–7). Through Girard (1972, 1978), the significance of such a statement is evident, through the implied identification with Jesus the Son – an identification to be traced to 'The Verdict'.

The vanity of writing letters

A radically different yet complementary activity to writing stories was Kafka's similarly obsessive predilection for letter-writing. As it is well known by Kafka scholars, who often expressed their perplexity about such facts, Kafka was engaged in a exhaustive and interminable exchange of letters with all his main female companions, leading to claims that evidently the most erotic act conceivable for Kafka was the writing of a letter (Citati 2007: 255–6).

The interlacing of night-time writing and letter-writing is strikingly demonstrated by the joint and symbolic genesis of both. Kafka wrote his first letter to Felice Bauer, generally considered as the starting point of his obsessive practice of letter-writing, on 20 September 1912, or Yom Kippur Day.

For Kafka writing letters was a surrogate for human relationships, just as writing during the night was a substitute for real life. As he would admit, writing letters was a very peculiar activity: '"how could the idea have emerged that human beings can get in touch with each other by writing letters?"' (as in Citati 2007: 255). Letter-writing was a way to multiply misunderstandings; even worse, it was a way to establish contact with phantasms:

> one's own phantasm, who is apparently sitting at the desk, the phantasm of the addressee who is waiting for who knows what words from us – and all the other ghosts who populate the world, before whom we render ourselves naked, and who wait for the letters brought by the postman at the threshold.
> (Citati 2007: 255; see also Robertson 2011: 136)

Kafka's case was particularly grave, as all his love life was conducted through letters, where he even invited his partners to get involved with this game with ghosts, only as a joke, though with weighty consequences: 'All the misfortune of my life – I don't wish to complain, but to make a generally instructive remark – derives, one could say, from letters or from the possibility of writing letters. People have hardly ever deceived me, but letters always' (Kafka 1953: 229). Yet, he persisted.

Kafka's dogged and desperate struggle against his own habit of letter-writing was captured with particular incisiveness by another major Italian Kafka connoisseur, Ferruccio Masini, in an Introduction written to a 1988 Italian edition of Kafka's letters that position this activity in the context of the problematic relationship between Kafka's life and writings, situated on the horizon of Kafka's encounter with the theatre of Lowy, and paralleled to the practice of night-writing.

In a section entitled 'The avidity of phantasms' Masini argues that Kafka was well aware that both his dominant practices of writing, night-writing and letter-writing as if transferred him into a 'lunar realm', building for himself a labyrinthine world in which he can only lose himself (Masini 2010: 211–12).[6] Similarly to Calasso, but also to Foucault's interest in self-writing and letter-writing, connected to the 'techniques of self', Masini argues that such an activity was a kind of confessional, which however 'often acquires the form of self-denouncing (*autodenuncia*)', building up the 'Archimedean point' in which the *negativity* (*sic* in original) of Kafka's existence could be constructed (Ibid.: 213). Thus, 'Kafka actuated in his letters a kind of premeditated self-sabotage' (Ibid.). His attempt to involve his interlocutors in this letter-writing game attempts to transcend the ultimate possible limit, at once sincerely revealing that he is not pretending to be sincere – a paradox worthy of Epimenes the Cretan – and disclosing the heart of his schismatic existential condition as being at the same time the hunter and the hunted, being aware of the extremely dangerous road which he took, and that the decision to devote himself to writing under the impact of demons destroys the possibility of any happiness in love: '"I cannot hear the terrible voices inside and contemporaneously You"' (as in Masini 2010: 213).

But why did Kafka persist with the practice of letter-writing? What was he hoping to gain from it? How was it related to the heart of his work – both concerning its substance and modality? It is here that Ferruccio Masini offers vital ideas, running parallel to the analyses of Calasso and Citati about phantasms and demons as sources of Kafka's creativity. In some respects Masini echoes Calasso and Citati; in others, his argument is the opposite; yet, they complement each other, forming a whole.

For Kafka writing letters, especially to the women of his life, was the perfect – absurd – spatial complement to his – absurd – temporal mode of living through night-time fiction writing. It represents a parallel fictionalisation of his love life – and not only (Citati 2007: 341). If his 'trading' day-time living into night-time writing, a genuinely demonic pact represented the reversal of the normal priorities of human life, forcing him to live in an upside down turned world, the practice of writing letters became a replacement of genuine, personal and physical relationships of love.

Perhaps the most important reason for his insistence in writing letters, tying further the links with night-time writings, was his desperate need to understand himself – to understand the practice of writing down stories at night of which he was not the author. With the benefit of hindsight, one could compare this to the similarly self-wasting self-analyses of Leonardo da Vinci.

Given the complementariness of Kafka's two obsessive habits, changing one without the other became impossible. Thus, in spite of his misgivings, he persisted with both. The only serious attempt to break this habit indeed happened together with the attempt to give up writing, even to burn everything that he has been written, during his relationship with Dora – and even this was not brought to conclusion. Thus he persisted with his love-hate relationship with the letter-writing practice, this chasing of oneself by oneself, and even attempted to turn it to an advantage, using it to understand the nature of distant communication – an activity quite close to fiction writing, and which in his case was brought even closer by the perception of the intrusive and invasive presence of the phantasms. The result is a unique understanding of the nature of communication, in particular the absurdity of communicating from a distance, of vital significance for the contemporary world dominated by distant mass communication, or rather its *illusion*.

The impossibility of non-personal communication

Communication, understood as the interaction between two human beings through the medium of language, is one of the most fundamental aspects of the human condition. However, communication assumes *presence*. We can only talk to somebody who is nearby; who hears the words we utter. But due to this fact communication is never a mere issue of using language. Words are accompanied by gestures of the hand, movements of the eye, and at any rate every human being has a particular tone and voice; thus, whatever is said cannot be separated from the personality of the human being who uttered such words. Communication is necessarily a total human fact.

Of all forms of verbal communication, this is most evidently true in the case of an exchange of words between persons who are in love. In such case the words uttered dwarf in a particularly significant manner – all that matters is the tone, the eyes, the 'meta' aspects of communication. At the limit, saying 'I love you' becomes the least pronounceable of all possible expressions, as a love that needs to be put in words is almost a contradiction in terms. This is the message of Cordelia's silence in *King Lear*; and there the point is 'just' a daughter–father relationship, not the strongest of all human passions and bonds, sexual passion.

The strongly personal, concrete, existential aspect of communication is visible in the term 'intercourse', being synonym for sexual relationship in most languages, as they refer to an act of intimate commonality. This is why talking to somebody whom we do not know is not simple, as 'communicating' is intensely personal. In order to communicate, to say something, even to ask a question, we need to know the other person; asking something from an unknown person is therefore a kind of intrusion that creates a degree of embarrassment on the part of both sides, even if one is only asking directions in a foreign city. Thus, communication can only take place in the concrete, physical 'in between' of two human beings, where two concrete persons 'open up' to each other and reach a degree of understanding about certain matters; an understanding which thus they come to share.

Writing letters poses the opposite problem. It involves a physical distance, or the impossibility of communicating, of saying something or even making a gesture, for the simple reason that the other person is not present to experience it. In the terms used by Kafka, the difference is thus infinite, with the limit of finiteness being the distance from which the other can still be seen or at least heard, thus he or she could be invited to come closer, so that he or she could be present for concrete communication. And yet, writing a letter, *especially* to a loved one, also implies an emotionally particularly intense relationship, where the words of the letter are addressed to somebody close to us; in fact, the practice allows us to express emotions with such intensity and frankness that is often not possible in real life. Thus, it would seem, letters are unique means to achieve truthfulness.

But this is only an illusion, as – according to Kafka – it is right here that the deceit of letter-writing lies. This idea enables Kafka to give a penetrating analysis of the nature of distant communication and the kind of society produced through the ignorance of this limitation and deceit, moving way beyond most sociologists and philosophers of communication, but having striking affinities with the thought of Plato – a thinker Kafka knew intimately.

The dilemma of distance and closeness, presence and absence, reality and un-reality can be expressed through the mathematical language of zero and infinity (Masini 2010: 186–7, 199). The practice of letter-writing, by prompting the writer to disclose the full truth about intimate feelings, pretends to replace infinite distance, the impossibility to address the other personally by the illusion of zero distance – an intimate union of their souls. Such intimacy is an illusion, as the other is not there, cannot respond, cannot reciprocate a gesture of love, which thus becomes vacuous and stale. The problem is not just a matter of time elapsing, which through e-mails – a particularly tricky mode of communication – can indeed be reduced to zero, but a matter of spatial distance, we cannot be overcome by humans. The intimacy in letter-writing is fake – but an illusion that produces a series of effects, and quite costly ones. Here Kafka offers an understanding about non-direct non-personal communication that constitutes a most devastating critique of contemporary theories of communication, in particular the 'ideal speech situation' and the 'public sphere'.

The first trick is to lure somebody into this peculiar space – a place so close to Plato's *khóra* – to write fully truthful letters, where one starts by completely denuding oneself, rendering oneself vulnerable. This is indeed a precondition of any intimate relationship; however, in this case the 'other' is not present, so the writer who rendered itself spiritually naked cannot find satisfaction. Once tricked, lured or seduced into such state of nakedness, one becomes subject, defenceless, to the 'avidity of phantasms' – an expression uses by Masini (2010: 210) as a section title. Through writing letters one becomes subject to the same situation as through writing fictions during night.

But are these the same phantasms? Or, put differently, what is the 'reality' of these phantasms? At a first level, it seems that Masini's understanding of these phantasms is the opposite of Calasso's or Citati's: they are not external to the writer, rather evoked by the act of writing out of the fantasy of the writer. Such phantasms are related to the 'metaphysical' desire that was incited by the intimacy into which the writer was lured; a desire that cannot be satisfied. The writer is thus not just defenceless but also frustrated; waiting desperately for a response, 'contaminated by this nulla' which is the illusion that the distance might be eliminated (Masini 2010: 217), though his desires cannot be satisfied even through such a response, which anyway take days to arrive.

Kafka uses a series of striking expressions to characterise this trick-ful and illusory game, confusing zero and infinity. Such an idea of communicating through messages is first of all *absurd*. The distance cannot be overcome; the fact of distance is the only reality beyond the fiction of the message, and any tentative to communicate through distance only conjures up an unreality, creating misunderstandings and hopeless confusion, where every act to clarify matters only increases the hopeless confusion, unless a personal encounter can happen – an experience available everyday to anyone who had the foolish idea to resolve a personal matter through the internet. The absurdity of the very idea of 'message' is captured by Kafka in the Zürau parable of the king and the courier which according to Masini demonstrates the 'senselessness of the message itself', its entrusting to the phantasms, as '[t]he nullifying power of the letter is the same as that of a question which already carries in itself the nothingness (*nulla*) of all possible response' (Masini 2010: 217). Masini resumes this line of thought in an emphatic sentence: '*The infinite illusion* (inganno) *of letters evokes erring in the desert, the condition of exile*' (*sic*; Ibid.).

This sentence has a striking force, as it not only connects the desert of exile and Mosaic wandering with the desert of ascetic practices by Christian monks and hermits, but also due to the symbolic significance of 40 days for the start of Kafka's night-writing practice after his encounter with Felice – a love affair that was mostly consumed through letters, thus closing another circle between minute aspects of biography and the heart of Kafka's writing. But here the desert has a very specific meaning; it is not just a metaphor for Kafka. The emphasis in the sentence is on the striking term 'infinite illusion' (*inganno*); an illusion that is outright 'diabolical' (Ibid.), as it plays with the inciting of desire, the presumption that it can be satisfied, while this is false, only an illusion, as the traversing of the distance, bringing the distant close is impossible and only results in becoming lost in the desert: 'How on earth did anyone get the idea that people can communicate with one another by letter! Of a distant person one can think, and of a person who is near one can catch hold – all else goes beyond human strength' (Kafka 1953: 229). The solicitation of desire, the filling of the soul with the impatience of waiting only generates anxiety: the writing of letters is a 'torture machine' which only 'fills with vain words the abyss which separates forever the question from the answer' (Masini 2010: 218).

The writing of letters transforms the distance that separates, rendering any meaningful communication impossible, into a liminal space where misunderstanding and illusion become possible, through the 'phantasms' that immediately populate this sphere. Kafka, however, even after making this discovery, continues the game, thus engages in a most dangerous game of *forcing liminality*,[7] transforming self-confession into self-denouncing, thus self-destruction, closing still another circle.

Escaping the phantasms

In Kafka's life there were evidently three moments in which he came close to breaking the obsessive habit of intercourse with demons on which his writings were based and which they proliferated. Each are of extreme importance, including their consequences, or lack of. The most significant is the time spent in Zürau, resulting in Kafka's most precious pearls, the Zürau aphorisms, theme of Chapter 6. The other two will be shortly discussed now.

The first was a singular but hardly perceptible experience in Kafka's life of which a trace was left in an unfinished short story contained in the Diaries. The couple of pages seem only to contain a draft story. Pietro Citati, however, had the eyes to perceive behind such appearance the trace of a – potentially – most significant experience in Kafka's life.

The draft, dated 25 June 1914 (Kafka 1990: 538–41), so Midsummer Night before the outbreak of World War I, this terrible sacrificial carnival, describes a bachelor, one of Kafka's favourite terms for defining himself (Citati 2007: 28), who spends most of his time in his room, again just like him, but who was preoccupied with watching the ceiling, and who in one evening, the first time he was suddenly overcome by serenity in his room, suddenly had a vision: the ceiling started to move, its centre started to emanate a radiant white light and he became aware 'that a nameless reality was descending into the room and would soon liberate him from the chains of everyday life' (Citati 2007: 149). Not ready to encounter an apparition (*Erscheinung*), the bachelor tore down the light-bulb, but all this was in vain: the ceiling suddenly opened and from great height an angel, dressed in violet-blue shawls with golden laces and great white wings, was slowly descending. Yet, the apparition was delusive, being only 'a wooden figure from a prow that usually hangs on the ceiling of sailors' pubs' (Kafka 1990: 540–1).

The second concerns the encounter with Dora, the only really serious 'love affair' of his life, combined with the attempt to escape the phantasms, at the price of giving up writing, even possibly burning what he had written. Yet, the spectres again had the upper hand: the last extent diary entries, from summer 1923, seem to indicate that 'by now "the spirits" have *taken the hand* of Kafka' (*sic*; Calasso 2005: 144). He felt again defeated, 'in spite of his resolution and all his hopes', resulting in a 'sinister self-portrait' written to Brod in mid-January 1924 in a letter mentioning both Dostoevsky and Goethe, where he describes himself as somebody without a solid ground under his feet, facing an abyss, with vultures circling around his head and a storm breaking out above him (Citati 2007: 356–7). According to Calasso, the most revealing statement of Kafka's condition is a late diary entry describing his own, unique internal condition as having always a raven lurking around his head (Calasso 2005: 144).

Notes

1. His diary entries about the writing process are full of alchemic metaphors, using the language of everything being 'consumed' and 'resurrected' (Koelb 2010: 94).
2. Kafka derived the name from his own, according to a speculation involving names and numbers (see diary entry of 11 February 1913).

3. The parallels with Goethe are again strikingly clear; for details, see Szakolczai (2016a).
4. The name is mere coincidence, the author not being a relative of Dora Diamant.
5. However, Kafka had Gnostic tendencies (see Sokel 2002: 297–302).
6. Intriguingly, Foucault used almost exactly the same language to characterise his own writing practice, without referring explicitly to Kafka – as he almost never did, in spite of his known appreciation of Blanchot, a well-known French Kafka scholar.
7. This point is central for the work of Agnes Horvath.

5 Kafka's novels

In between theatre, theology and prophecy

Before Abraham was, I am

John 8: 58

Given that Kafka was not a religious person, by normal standards, it may seem strange to focus on his 'theology'. In his classic account Walter Benjamin (1977) warned that one of the most fundamental misreading of Kafka is to reduce his ideas to the 'supernatural'. However, he also added that a similar misunderstanding would result by completely ignoring such an aspect of his work. The ambivalence of Benjamin largely reflects his own position between Marxist materialism and critical theory on the one hand, and explicit Messianism on the other, particularly evident in his famous 'Theses on the Philosophy of History'; a Messianism that is quite close to Kafka's, visible in the closeness of Hebrew terms for 'Messiah' (*moshoakh*) and 'land-surveyor' (*moshiakh*), the presumed occupation of K., hero of *The Castle* (Sebald 1976: 47; Robertson 1985: 228).[1]

The clearest example for Kafka's theology is the Zürau aphorisms, strikingly close, even in style, to Benjamin's philosophy of history, in particular concerning their similarly impenetrable, gnomic character. However, according to Pietro Citati, and following a series of precedents, even the two great novels of Kafka, conceived and written after September 1912, not only have a theological aspect, but can be analysed as theological statements as well.

One could object that the abundant Kafka literature is already so full of interpretive efforts that for decades practically every new interpreter starts by lamenting on this fact, trying to justify the – evidently unjustifiable – proliferation of empty chatter. However, the perspective pursued so far, in particular the attempt to give a precise meaning to the 'demonic inspiration' underlying Kafka's creative efforts, not only explains the necessary infinity of such interpretive efforts, but also their turn into a theological direction. As Kafka was not the author of his writing in the conventional sense, rather he was a 'medium' in the service of the 'demons' who suggested for him the content of his work, there was no clear authorial intention that could be pinned down. This, however, does not mean that the effort at interpretation by definition must be boundless; rather, on the contrary, that it must aim at identifying the underlying reason *beyond* any possible intention by Kafka as author.

Kafka's theology, or his relationship to God, was not only implicit, hidden, not revealed, but also desperate (Citati 2007: 153). This was, first of all, because the problem for Kafka seemed the opposite: it was God who was not visible, who was hiding itself, turning his back to us; who cannot be depicted, named or even searched – the search for God itself being blasphemous. Even further, the divine is not only light, but – due to the very nature of light – includes shadow, as the very fact of casting light on some things implies that others will stay in the shadow; and so it should not be surprising that the divine cannot be reduced to truth, but also encompasses *deceit* (inganno) (Citati 2007: 153–4, 276–7).[2] The heart of this deceit concerns multiple games with nothingness (zero, *nulla*) and infinity.

Such game includes the name of the divine, as God cannot be named, and is hardly ever named in Kafka's works, yet has an infinity of names (Ibid.: 152–3). God is also both present and absent: it is omnipresent, invading reality, everything that exists, yet it is also absent, insinuating emptiness; it is omnipotent, its power knowing no limits, yet is invisible and unnameable. Such utter emptiness is evoked in the startlingly powerful opening paragraph of *The Castle*, with the wooden bridge, recalling the ending image of 'The Verdict', which opened to the 'apparent void' (*scheinbare Leere*) (Kafka 2011: 3). From its first sentence, *The Castle* makes it evident that it stands on the borderline, tackling directly liminality: an absolute novelty, as nobody so far 'risked writing a novel on the limit (*linea di confine*)' (Calasso 2005: 65). Such features render Kafka's God fully transcendent: according to Citati, 'perhaps none, not even the great Dionysian theologians or Islamic mystics affirmed the absolute transcendence of God with such a desperate and penetrating (*tagliante*) faith as Kafka in the ultimate decade of his life' (Citati 2007: 153). The distance between such transcendent divinity and us human beings cannot be breeched: God is totally outside us, distant from us, and thus its main feature from our perspective is that it is a '*total gaze*' (sguardo totale; emphasis in original) (Ibid.: 154); while our fate is to be part of an all-encompassing reality which we cannot understand, as we are fully inside, just as we cannot comprehend the divinity, only perceive its distant but penetrating, even overwhelming gaze upon us. Strikingly, even formal details of the writing process have an eerie, transcendent aspect: having started writing on 27 January 1922, Kafka indicated to have abandoned writing, mid-sentence, in a 11 September 1922 letter to Max Brod; thus, by the day twenty years after Rilke dated the start of his novel, and also on the by now infamous day of 9/11.

The two novels offer complementary insights into the nature of the divine-human relationship, but also indicate a decisive displacement. The titles of both novels are metaphors for the divine: the Process is nothing but the effective functioning of the Law, while the Castle is where the Gods reside (Citati 2007: 270). The difference is that while in *The Process* the gods mingle with humans in their everyday life, in *The Castle* they are withdrawn, hardly seen at all. As a result the character of the two novels and the type of action depicted in them become completely different. In *The Process* action is performed by real-life figures, the novel consisting of a series of theatrical scenes with symbolic significance:

a sequence of 'symbolic fragments' (Citati 2007: 270). In *The Castle*, however, while action is less theatrical and events have a more regular, sequential, novel-like character, the protagonists are not real figures, rather it is as if they mime a role, several directly corresponding to standard *commedia dell'arte* figures, with a secretary outright called 'Momus'. High functionaries hardly ever appear; yet, when they do so, they have an 'aquiline' character, an adjective that was central to the characterisation of Pantalone (see Szakolczai 2013a: 204), the same term figuring prominently in their description by the innkeeper – another stock *commedia* character – which at first even seemed ridiculous to K. (Citati 2007: 278). The other main metaphor used for them, the comparison to Proteus due to their permanent metamorphosis, also has strict parallels with the theatre of the sixteenth to eighteenth centuries (Agnew 1986).

Such parallels are further underlined by the central mode of interaction between high functionaries and the inhabitants of the village, sex; just as the central effect mechanism of the type of theatre inaugurated by *commedia dell'arte* was the transformation of love into sex, and human life into a permanent, obsessive search for sexual gratification. The sexual relations taking place between Castle and village are strictly matter of fact. No emotions are exchanged, the word love is not even uttered: functionaries simply use the women of the village in order to satisfy a bodily need. Such acts are comparable to prostitution, except that no money is exchanged and becoming the lover of a functionary is considered a main way for social ascent. Indeed, when K. apparently – as everything is only apparent in the novel – seduces Frieda, Klamm's lover, the hostess considers this the gravest of all acts, destroying the fortune of her stepdaughter. The sexual relations between members of the Castle and the village are reduced to an 'immediate and brutal physical possession', accompanied by obscenity and vulgarity (Citati 2007: 281). The women of the village thus behave like as many Columbines or Franceschinas of *commedia dell'arte*. Such behaviour is, of course, contagious. Thus,

> when the servants of the Castle descend to their villages, they abandon themselves to frenetic dances and orgies, like a pack of savage animals. Nothing distinguishes them from their masters. Sexual passion for them is identical with a profound desire for dirt.
>
> (Ibid.)

This also applies for the first encounter between K. and Frieda, one of the few occasions where Kafka explicitly depicts a sexual act: they make 'love' minutes after they met, and in a particularly brutal manner. The world depicted by Kafka does not correspond to the actual theatrical performances of the classical age; rather it is a nightmarish vision of a society produced by commedification. Its closest equivalent is not Hollywood films, rather the strikingly nihilistic scenes of love-making contained in some late Communist East European films.[3]

A similarly commedic figure is Barnabas, messenger between Castle and village, whose behaviour continually 'reflects' the Castle and whose character evokes the archetypal messenger, Hermes, a major trickster figure, but who is also an outcast. The most evidently clown-like figures are the two aids of K., Arthur and Jeremiah. They represent the lowest hierarchy of the divine for Citati, originally simple inhabitants of the village. However, 'through its extraordinary magic, with its gift of metamorphosis and enchantment, the Castle transforms them at the start of the book into marionettes, into kobolds, who recall Shakespeare, commedia dell'arte, Yiddish drama, romantic *féerie*, and Laforgue' (Ibid.: 282). In this manner, they not simply manifest the lowest level of the divine hierarchy, but also 'the ultimate divine emanation, the ultimate revelation coming from above' (Ibid.: 283). Through them the divine escapes its weight, gains light and 'the metaphysical grace of clowns, a kind of innocence around the enigma' (Ibid.). Yet, while this is a novelty compared to *The Process*, this is not the last word of Kafka about them: 'the aids not always play with childish grace. They are lemurs, spectral inventions: their used bodies are not joyful; and we often gain the impression that in the games they play the disturbing and the sinister accompany the comic' (Ibid.). Thus, Citati's reconstruction of Kafka's theology yielded another archetypical figure, less well known than Hermes but just as important for the modern world: the demonic clown. The process is also similar to the one identified by Richard Pearce, according to which the main heroes of the modern novel reconstruct stages of a 'clownification': '[i]n *The Idiot* and "The Metamorphosis" Dostoyevsky and Kafka create worlds where men are gratuitously transformed into clownish puppets' (Pearce 1970: 2).

This explains K.'s hostility, but also his impotence. He treats them as marionettes, in the most direct sense, hitting them as if they were mere puppets. Yet, his actions only make them realise their demonic potential, playing a central role in his downfall and degradation, usurping particularly well the role of indignant victims.

The equivalent role to these commedic figures in *The Process* is played by compact and highly theatrical scenes. The most important of these are the reception of Josef K. by the lawyer Huld, including the scene with Block; the subsequent meeting with the painter Titorelli; and the penultimate scene of the novel with the sacristan of the cathedral.

Huld and Titorelli offer themselves to Josef K. as figures of salvation. Instead, they only further precipitate the hero's fall, and are surrounded by images of degradation. This is underlined by their living conditions: Huld receives his clients only at night, while Titorelli's flat is insupportably hot, both features recalling Hell. The term 'degradation' plays a central role in Citati's analysis: the way Huld treats his clients is utterly degrading, as shown by the way he makes Block kneel in front of him and crawl on all fours; while the images depicted by Titorelli 'demonstrate us what point of degradation did, in the modern world, the sacred tradition reach' (Citati 2007: 174). Instead of being saviours, they reveal quite different characteristics; and in order to identify them Citati uses, twice on the same page, the English word *trickster*. Titorelli is outright an Ulyssean trickster, best comparable to Goethe's Mephistopheles, having the same 'lucid, corrosive intelligence'. Citati completes this line of analysis by a particularly striking summary characterisation of Kafka's book, according to which 'Heaven loves to select these ironic and indecent mediators between itself and the world' (Ibid.).

The third scene in many ways is even more astonishing, presenting a harrowing combination surrealistic, supernatural and absurd elements. Josef K. is 'lured' into a cathedral by an Italian with a strong Southern accent, who fails to show up. At that moment a sudden, apocalyptic change takes place in the weather, with pouring rain accompanied by full darkness in a late summer morning; Josef K. is again 'lured' into staying in the Cathedral and listening to a sermon by the sacristan (absurdity itself), a paradoxical 'Parable before the Law'. A cathedral is Catholic, the story rabbinic, yet the atmosphere of both scenery and story is thoroughly Byzantine, recalling standard Byzantine jokes about countrymen lost in the great city.

Kafka's theology can be characterised both by what it contains and what is absent from it. Kafka's life-work and world-vision are torn between zero and infinity, failing to contain the *one* of Plato or Heraclitus. Kafka's vision of the world is not a realm of intactness and beauty; it does not contain grace – this is why it cannot be easily recognised as a theology. However, and again – as always – paradoxically, it has much to do with the theologies of grace, even saying something absolutely fundamental about them, or the way they are usually interpreted – and for a very long time.

Kafka was keenly, even desperately aware that his work, and his world, cannot incorporate innocent beauty and saving grace; the angel almost descended into his room, but only almost. He desperately tried to save his hero at the end of *The Process*, experimenting with various solutions, comparable to the way Tolstoy tried to save his heroine in *Anna Karenina*. Yet, none of them found a way – with consequences more tragic in Kafka's case. Still, towards the end of both novels a sudden and surprising ray of light and hope appears. In *The Process*, just where Josef K., condemned, is taken to the scene of execution by two figures who look like lifeless automatons with plastic members, thus recalling the way in which in *Wilhelm Meister's Apprenticeship* the Society of the Tower expresses itself through theatrical appearances (Citati 2007: 187), the beauty of nature erupts into the novel: '"Everywhere there was clear moonlight, with its naturalness and quiet, which is not given to any other light"'. Thus, and '[f]or the first time in the whole book, Nature reawakens from its own absence and gifts to Josef K. the tranquillity and sweetness that he cannot ever possess' (Citati 2007: 188). It also evokes the penultimate scene, the splendour that erupts in the story 'Before the Law'. The grace of all this splendour is pointless, wasted, as it only illuminates the scene of execution; at any rate, the light only came from the Moon – the light of Pierrot-like fools.

The irruption of grace at the end of *The Castle* is similarly wasted, just where meaning finally appears, so is similarly heart-breaking. K. is finally granted, through a series of accidents, a night-time scene with a high functionary, Bürgel, who even discloses to him not only secrets about the functioning of the Castle, but an entire theology of 'the providential harmony of *this* world' (Citati 2007: 314). However, K. fails to get it, as he cannot stay awake, listening to the words of Bürgel in an extremely liminal, half-dreaming, half-wakeful state, not recalling anything.

Thus, just after a ray of hope appears in the novels, it is immediately taken away, closing the opportunity, as if it only appeared to deceive the hero. The ending, or its sign, is K. being treated again as an unwelcome intruder, and eventually degraded into being housed with the servants underground (Ibid.: 318–19). This is elaborated fully with cruel mercilessness at the end of *The Process*, where Josef K. is executed on a large block of stone that recalls a sacrificial altar, with a knife driven through his heart which is even turned around twice. The act is most atrocious, Josef K.'s last words being that he was killed like a dog, while technically recalling sacrificial rituals.

In the world depicted by Kafka's visionary novels, these anti-theological theologies, divine grace and world harmony appear only for instances, immediately lost or transformed into their opposite, like infantile jokes or acts of genuine cruelty. Instead, the world of the two novels is dominated by mechanical processes, suggesting that God itself is a machine, close to the mechanical world-view (and indeed theology) propagated by Descartes and Newton. The Castle itself is a machine, 'that does not know what is charity or love', the same as the Law in *The Process* or even in *Amerika*, identifying God with formalism (Citati 2007: 284). Instead of a serene tranquillity to be reached at the end of a journey, the working of this mechanistic world has two main features, one more frightening and deadly than the other: it *cannot err*; and it *cannot end* (Ibid.: 167–8, 284). The world as machine cannot err, as machines don't err; but error, as Canguilhem and Foucault knew it so well (Foucault 1978), is a condition of possibility of living, thus machine-like perfection only brings about death. In so far as the working of machines assumes human beings, errors happen; however, the Kafkaesque machine does not acknowledge any possibility of error, sticking to the image of its own perfection even when evidently a piece of sand got into its smooth working. The machine, this non-being, attempts to deal with this impossible fact – as in the world of non-reality real events are classified as impossible – by the typical means of non-communication, the writing of letters. The case is demonstrated in one of the funniest and at the same time most anguishing, intolerably frustrating and hair-raising episode of *The Castle*, where the machinery tries to solve the problem of how K. could have been invited as a land-surveyor, when the Castle does not need any more land surveyors. But the same point is elaborated in *The Process*, where Josef K. is told, in impossible paragraphs running to dozens of pages, that a process could never end by absolution, as that would imply the recognition by the tribunal that it made an error by starting the process, which is simply impossible – or where, in the hallucinatory world of Kafka, the impossibility of committing an error and the impossibility of recognising that an error was committed become identical, as if in a Möbius strip or a design by Escher.

Thus we arrive at the other main characteristic of the world as machine, direct consequence of the first: that no process can ever end. Josef K. is condemned to live forever as imputed, becoming an imputed being identical with becoming condemned. Such condemnation, however, never arrives, leading the imputed *wanting* to be condemned, as that at least would end the process – corresponding to one of Kafka's most obsessive dreams, an end that in the novels never comes, as never can come, unless as an execution.[4] Kafka can help us understand why permanent liminality is the paradoxical but necessary flip side of full-scale mechanisation: the rigid order of the machine does not stop movement; quite on the contrary, it rather spins a never-ending but meaningless, circular, nihilistic movement, an unsatisfiable desire for 'change' for its own sake, where the destruction of stability, condition of possibility for a meaningful existence is permanently re-proposed as the solution for the problem itself created, along an infinite spiral: the more 'change' is searched for in order to overcome the boredom of a mechanised life, the more daily life will be replaced by the infinite boredom produced by the ceaseless, repetitive titillation of the senses.

But does Kafka himself escape the kind of world he is depicting? Is his work merely mirroring the permanent liminality of modernity? Even if his anti-theology theology cannot offer any hope, does it at least offer a conclusive analysis of this perpetualised treadwheel? The fact that Kafka's work so far was subject to a more infinite and unending kind of interpretation than any other literary work of the past centuries, perhaps only comparable to Nietzsche, would seem to indicate that there is no end to this process; that in the case of Kafka, more than anywhere else, we are indeed infinitely condemned to an infinity of interpretation.

This would imply that any effort to understand meaninglessness is doomed to meaninglessness – which simply cannot be true. Thus, without pretending to offer a final interpretation of Kafka, one should at least *attempt* to suggest ways to move beyond the infinite circle of interpretation. This starts by returning to the problem of an 'author' who is not fully in control of the messages he transmits.

Various cultures use diverse expressions for figures who utter or transcribe statements that are not of their own making. The Greeks talk about sibyls, the Etruscans augurs, while for poets the word 'medium' is used. Contemporary anthropologists and archaeologists prefer the term 'shaman', following the influential work of Mircea Eliade. However, the term most widely used in European culture is *prophet*.

Archetypical figures of prophecy, like the prophets of Ancient Judaism, and of shamanism, like the shamans of Central Asia, are quite distinct; yet, they share a basic feature. This concerns their attitude to their vocation, which has the specific feature of a *calling* coming from outside. In most traditions not only priests but prophet-like figures like magicians, diviners or medicine men belong to certain families, inherit their position and *want* to become seers, a feature captured in the expression 'vision quest'. However, Old Testament prophets and Central Asian shamans belong to a select subgroup of the category who are very much aware that being selected by the powers above is a very ambivalent blessing.

Becoming a prophet or a shaman is not a social privilege, rather an individual burden. It implies to be set apart, even to sever one's family ties, preventing the possibility of living a normal life.

Kafka's anti-theology, the product of quasi-prophetic inspiration, thus must be considered a kind of anti-prophetic prophecy; a term developed for his contemporary Max Weber. Still, Kafka's work was even more theological than Weber's, thus a more specific formulation is needed.

This can be done by paying close attention to the most important and singular instances of anti-theological theology in Kafka's writings.

Some of these are very evident and present in the whole work. These centrally include the father–son relationship, its exclusivity and its connection to the Law. Kafka's interest is not only obsessive but concerns in particular the presumed right of the father to kill his son, which must be connected to Abraham's sacrifice. This is all the more evident as the motive is emphatically evoked at the end of *The Process*, thus establishing a particularly strong connection between two of the most important writings of Kafka, 'The Verdict' and *The Process*: two works that even through their titles form a coherent whole, as a (legal) process usually ends with a verdict – except that in the chronology of Kafka's work 'The Verdict' comes before *The Process*, and that *The Process* remained unfinished – just as no process ever ends in it. Significantly, Kafka always looks at the father–son relationship from the perspective of the son, identifying himself with the son figure.

Other aspects, which nevertheless belong to the heart of Kafka's anti-theology, are more difficult to perceive. One of the most important concerns the idea of 'searching out God', a feature characteristic of both Josef K. and K., alter egos of Kafka. Thus, according to Citati, the 'Process' is not only a metaphor of the Law, but also of the mode of acting by the gods. Josef K.'s insistence to be involved with his own defence, of investigating details of his process is thus an outmost blasphemy. Similarly, K. in *The Castle* is not satisfied to be merely called by the Castle whenever he is needed, but outright tries to get access there, wanting to talk with luminaries of the Castle, chasing the high functionaries, who are most upset by his insistence. Such a behaviour is radically opposed to the classical model of Hebrew prophets or Asian shamans, yet has been identified as a central feature of Abraham by Thomas Mann at the beginning of *Joseph and his Brothers*, started the year after Kafka died. Kafka's anti-prophetical prophecy thus has a concrete target: not Old Testament prophets, not even Moses, main repository of the Law, but the founder of the tradition, Abraham.

The most important relevant point, confirming the previous line of analysis, concerns the very heart of Kafka's anti-theological theology, identified both by Calasso (2005: 16–17) and Citati (2007: 185). This is the identity of being elected and condemned. The striking character of this point can be realised if we omit the – more or less irrelevant – prefix of 'con'-damnation, in the model of Elias's omission of the same prefix from 'con'-figuration, which leaves us with the identity of being elected and damned, which from the perspective of Augustinian medieval Christianity, Reformation Protestantism or Ancient Judaism is equally nonsensical. One could even argue that it is even nonsensical in Kafka's novels, as this is why their outcome is absurd, simply does not make any sense – and yet, it evidently means something quite different than it sounds. What could this be?

Let's try to make sense of this absurdity from the perspective of the two main prophetic/shamanic traditions, from which Abraham looks an outsider. Far from trying to escape his mission, Abraham outright *searched out* God, and eventually found him – or perhaps he only *thought* to have found him. Thus, the moment he received the greatest gift from this Power, his first son – a strange gift indeed, as becoming a father is a most natural 'given' of human life, while becoming a father only at an old age is a rather strange sign of electedness – he came to think that he now has to *sacrifice* this first and only son – a strange manner to establish a new religion, given that human sacrifice was a standard form of the previous, *corrupted* kind of human existence of the planet; or perhaps he only deluded himself to have received such a demand from the deity. At any rate, even this very sketchy analysis is sufficient to identify Abraham as a very strange kind of religious founder, who seems to innovate where it is not necessary – searching out the deity instead of just accepting a call; and who continues the practice that should be discontinued – human sacrifice.

Through such preparatory distancing of Abraham we can understand the weight and gravity of the charge Kafka formulates against him. It is that at the very moment when the deity evidently intervened, stopping his atrocious act – as Kierkegaard analysed it so well in *Fear and Trembling*, not an act of piety, rather outrageous universalising, thus blind faith – that be becomes convinced of receiving a promise: his offspring would rule the world. The nature of this promise is just as absurd as the conditions under which it was made, the two being no doubt tightly connected. So it is this kind of *perceived* election that becomes identical with a (con)damnation, defining a self-proclaimed 'people of god' who believe themselves to be not simply decisively different from all other human beings, but to rule them by 'right'.

Kafka was thus not simply any anti-prophetic prophet, rather anti-Abraham; a figure so different from, yet so similar to Nietzsche's self-identification as Antichrist.

The nature of this subject position can be further illuminated through the meaning of K. being a Messiah figure.

K. arrives at the village lying at the foot of the Castle being called by the Castle as a land-surveyor. This call at first is recognised by authorities, but then it transpires that the Castle does not need a land-surveyor. The entire thing is evidently absurd, but – in case this needs repeating – everything is absurd in Kafka, though only apparently, so its underlying sense must be established.

For this, we must understand the meaning of K's occupation and the reason why there is no need for it. The question is not what Kafka could have meant by it. Kafka was evidently only a medium; while the message is concerned with the nature of the manner in which he came to be a medium – an anti-prophetic prophet, an 'anti-Abraham'.

94 *Suspended in the In-Between*

The term must be symbolic, as being a land-surveyor is a trivial occupation. A symbol, however, in the etymological sense of a *symbolon*, has two parts. One aspect of the dilemma has recently been identified by Kafka scholars, though the point is still by no means a common knowledge. The other half, it seems, has never been mentioned in the literature of Kafka.

The first concerns 'land-surveyor' in Hebrew being all but identical with 'Messiah'. This is a striking result, as it means that the refusal of K. by the Castle, and by the village, is identical to the refusal of Christ. Kafka here, more than ever, approaches Dostoevsky, as in this way the refusal of the land-surveyor they themselves 'called' is identical to the way the Second Coming of Christ was refused by the Grand Inquisitor.[5] The meaning of this fact, however, remains obscure until complemented with the other half of the *symbolon*. This is contained in Edmund Burke's *Reflections on the French Revolution*, where the 'land-surveyor' is presented as symbolic figure of the Revolution.

The figure being symbolic, the meaning of the symbol *conveyed* by Kafka, the 'anti-prophet' can be understood by putting together the two symbols. According to Burke, the 'land-surveyor' is symbolic of the new order inaugurated by the French Revolution, which implies the – alchemic – dismantling of the historically and culturally bound territorial entities and their replacement by a series of artificial, geometrically conceived, more or less 'identical' segments, in terms of shape and size. The 'land-surveyor' is therefore the *par excellence* instrument of the new order, who literally transforms the earth, or the globe, making – as a Gnostic demiurge – a tabula rasa of the complex set-up of interconnecting social networks that was pre-revolutionary France, replacing it with a series of artificial constructs. Thus, if the Revolution, as it fancied itself, brought about a new type of society, driven by its secular Messianistic belief, then the 'land-surveyor' is its main instrument, the 'effective force' of Messianism.[6]

Visions of modernity: spatial and temporal

Distorting space: the fake promised land

Amerika, also called as *The Missing Person*, is Kafka's first novel. Various drafts, all destroyed, existed before writing the 'The Verdict', but the version that we have was started in late September 1912, thus fully the outcome of Kafka's new writing method; in fact, the result of his effort to make use of it and bring to completion the old idea (Citati 2007: 93–6). Kafka wrote the draft particularly quickly, as if in ecstasy, in one of the happiest moments of his life, only comparable to the autumn 1917 months in Zürau, and the first months spent with Dora Diamant in the last summer of his life.

This mood and the eventual completion of the novel was literally undermined and destroyed by writing 'The Metamorphosis', another poison-gift from the 'other' world, widely considered as Kafka's first real masterpiece, which 'arrived' upon him in one night of November 1912, forcing him to abandon the world of *Amerika* and descend into the abyss (Citati 2007: 95). While Kafka returned to the novel, he abandoned it again around January–February 1913, after which he only took it up to compose, in two feverish weeks in autumn 1914, its crucial visionary scene and – according to Brod – planned last chapter about the 'great theatre of Oklahoma'.

Amerika is the most novel-like of Kafka's novels, taking inspiration from the novels of Dickens. Its depiction of America, however, is particularly close to how Dostoevsky experienced London – except that Kafka was never there. Just as for Dostoevsky London first seemed an astonishing place, the centre of the world, for Kafka as well the new continent was a genuine 'new world', not a land of mere appearances, as Europe has become, but where 'the "signs and miracles" of the Old Testament remained alive' (Citati 2007: 105). Karl, hero of the novel, tries to absorb and learn as much as possible, following also the counsels of his uncle, according to which 'the first days of a European in America can be compared to a new birth [*einer Geburt vergleichbar*]' (Kafka 2013: 20). However, due to the same thirst for knowledge, again just as Dostoevsky, Karl/Kafka also came to change his view, arriving at a new vision of America, comparable to Tiepolo's vision of 'Mondo Novo'.[7] This new and truer vision focused on mechanisation; the realisation that all the presupposed miracles of the new world were mere by-products of its utter fascination and obsession with the machine, with mechanism and technology. Karl came to understand, or thus the spirits led Kafka, that 'the essence of American life is automatism' (Citati 2007: 105–6). The great and stunning discoveries of American technology are nothing but products of mechanical engineering to satisfy trivial, even infantile needs; mechanical games which however transform in depth and minute detail human life, best visible in the genuine sanctuaries of American life, the offices where 'automatisms stage a grandiose and absurd comedy of marionettes' (Ibid.: 106). The central aspect of technology, an insight whose consequences will be drawn in the two other novels, is that it eliminates the possibility of error: 'every error is excluded from the great American machinery, which operates above and outside humanness' (Ibid.) It is thus hostile to life, or – according to the definition of Nietzsche – is nihilistic. Through Kafka nihilism is recognised as the essence of the American way of life.

But why did Karl manage to see all this so clearly? Kafka offers in Karl a kind of self-image; the portrait of the artist as a young man. The affinity between Karl and America lies at the level of childish innocence; a basic prerequisite of a healthy and good life, and yet one which, when taken to extreme, preventing maturity, becomes utterly (self-)destructive, even nihilistic. Karl, alter-ego of Kafka *and* perfect subject for the American dream, is the personage Kafka most loved of all his creatures, who possesses a '"natural grace", the highest possible gift a human being could receive'; he is lively, playful and ingenuous; and, most important of all, he simply cannot lose his 'childish faith in existence' (Citati 2007: 96–7). Yet, at the same time, as if to preserve forever his gift, he refuses to grow up. In this way his gift gradually turns into a poison: preserving the childish eye about the activity of adults, the reduction of human life to eating and copulation, Karl decides to do such activities as little as possible, which would not only prevent him from living life to the full, but also renders him victim of occasions. Thus, a servant manages to seduce him, even becomes pregnant, as a result of which his father throws him out of the family at the mere age of 16 – following the typical Kafka motive of a father's extremely severe, even cruel verdict.

It is thus through the absurdly infantile eye of Karl that Kafka introduces us into the absurdly infantile mechanical world of America as the land of perfect utopia. This is done through three particularly enticing image-scenes, capturing the heart of the modern (American-globalised) world: traffic, communication and the mass-democratic circus.

The first such scene is the vision of continuous traffic as seen from the fifth floor balcony of his uncle's house. Looking down from such quasi-divine height, everything below seemed to move in perfect order, not needing human guidance, except that it was indeed inhuman, as if only spectres were moving around (Citati 106–7; Kafka 2013: 76–8), recalling a film by Jacques Tati, *Traffic*. This spectacle would be repeated with particular emphasis towards the end of the novel with Karl witnessing an electoral campaign from similar height (Citati 2007: 108–10; Kafka 2013: 282–7). From above everything is visible, but also totally unintelligible and utterly comic, combining the mechanical clapping of hands with rhythmic, incantatory shouting, trying to defeat, orally, the opposition by alternatively using silence and loud crying, transforming American electoral politics in the footsteps of Dickens into pantomime.

Just as revoltingly funny and absurd is the scene with the porter's lodge of Hotel Occidental, and just as revealing about the absurdity of perfect communication, another of Kafka's major themes. The reception at the hotel was organised in a most rational way, trying to provide the maximum amount of information with the minimum amount of resources being spent. Two porters were present in the booth, changed at every hour, who responded to any question addressed to them by the cosmopolitan clientele on the language in which they were addressed. They shouted this response directly at the questioner, looking straight at them, but immediately after turning their head into a different direction, so that another inquiry could be dealt with efficiently. The result was a total lack of understanding and thus communication as the answers were unintelligible, while porters became fully exhausted after a mere one-hour work; so the end result of such perfectly rational, mechanically organised communication was complete stasis: zero understanding and infinite exhaustion.

The novel containing such genuinely Kafkaesque visions of the future, our present, culminates in a vision that is not Kafkaesque at all, but even more striking.

The 'great theatre of Oklahoma'

The chapter on the 'great theatre of Oklahoma', an 'uncompleted miracle' (Citati 2007: 105),[8] was the unfinished last chapter of the unfinished novel. It was written during a paid leave of absence, in between 5 and 18 October 1914, together with an effort to finish *The Process* and 'Penal Colony' (Ibid.: 123). The start of the chapter in form recalls the last – finished – chapter of *The Process*: it starts as if anew, separated by an abyss of space and time from the previous chapter – as if Kafka knew perfectly *where* he wanted to arrive, but did not know *how*. Karl notices a placard with a text combining marketing tricks and secular apocalypse – a characteristic rendered intelligible by realising that eschatology was the source of commercials (Calasso 2005: 219). The text is particularly exaggerated: the offer is for one day only, today; for those who miss it, the opportunity will be lost forever; and the ad even ends by a threat, unusual for ads, but standard for apocalyptic messages: 'Damned are those who do not believe in us!' (Kafka 2013: 134). The call is to work for the 'Theatre of Oklahoma', the place of recruitment being the Hippodrome of Clayton. Such a name is again most perplexing, though the connection between the Hippodrome of Constantinople and modern theatre offers a clue.

The reception of the message, by the general public, was quite lukewarm: 'there were too many such billboards, and nobody believed in them anymore' (Ibid.). In contrast, it strongly appealed to Karl, due to its all-inclusive and apocalyptic character, features that, as the novel makes it evident, appeal in particular to outcasts and outsiders, as Karl has become: it invited everyone, *thus* also him, again connecting zero and infinity, Kafka's central tools.

Upon his arrival at Clayton, Karl is first struck by the loud and cacophonic sound of trumpets – another clear apocalyptic allusion, here to trumpets marking the opening of seals in the *Book of Revelation*. In the Hippodrome he witnesses an even stranger scenery, as the trumpets are blown by hundreds of girls, dressed as angels with white robes and wings, dancing on enormous horseshoes, evoking the horses of the apocalypse. The scene, typical of dream-visions, mixes distinct components like angels, horses and trumpets into a single entity; and, even further, the scene manages to combine and confuse the apocalyptic and the carnevalesque, offering a stunning image of apocalyptic carnival. Finally, placing emphasis on vision and not dream, such a scene advances the Hollywood musical, decades before the genre would appear in real life – if 'Hollywood musical' could have any relationship with reality.

Kafka's vision-image of America as the fake promised land is now complete: the American dream is identical to a complete, absurd mechanisation of human life, combined with the similarly absurd transformation of entertainment into an apocalyptic carnival, sealed by the Hollywood industry, with the machinery kept in motion, with full popular legitimacy, by the panto of American democratic electoral politics.

This vision of America as the fake 'Promised Land' is complemented by a similarly stunning inside into the future of totalitarian politics, by foreseeing and presenting two of the most harrowing techniques of the Stalinist secret police, in terms of the upsetting the regular alternation of day and night, with a proper period of transition in between.

Distorting time 1: the day turned upside down

This prophetic insight is offered in two major vision-scenes of Kafka's two main novels, both at prominent places: the opening scene of the first, *The Process*; and one of the last chapters of *The Castle*, arguably its last great scene. These two aspects are singled out for attention in Calasso's masterpiece, selecting as the titles of respective chapters on *The Process* and *The Castle* 'The most risky moment' and 'Night-time interrogations'.

The Process starts with the hero, Josef K., being woken up suddenly by two strangers who came to arrest him to his great perplexity, and who also behave in a most arrogant manner, like eating his breakfast (Kafka 2005b: 4). Both the fact and the modality of such behaviour advance perfectly the way the Stalinist secret police would operate decades later, a form of behaviour not known before. Kafka also offers a reason, arguing that such interruption of sleeping and dragging out of bed renders those arrested so confused that it offers a perfect way to handle them, a strikingly valid observation in its own nihilistic madness.

Even further, towards its end, *The Castle* evokes another favourite device of Stalinist secret police: the night-time interrogation.

Distorting time 2: night-time interrogations

The scene between K. and Bürgel, high functionary of the Castle, contained in Chapter 18, is the culmination of the unfinished novel: unfinished – in contrast to the *Process* – in the sense of simply not having an end. After this, the story would soon arrive at its dead end, evidently not able to progress anywhere.

The 'night-time interrogation' is not really an interrogation, rather its opposite, as K., far from being interrogated, is rather offered revelations concerning the secret of this practice, of the mechanism of the castle, even the order of the world (Calasso 2005: 300, 8).[9] In the 'monotheistic' context usually angels offer revelations. Bürgel is rather a 'guide of souls' (*psychopompos*; see Ibid.: 311), but this recalls Hermes,[10] the Greek divine messenger (*aggelos*), so is quite close. It is fitted, following a standard structuring device of Plato, into a multiple set of onion-like contexts, and is ended by a burlesque coda, with the chaotic distribution of files in the early morning hours.

The context has three aspects. The first is K.'s partial success in getting admitted to an interview with Erlangen; a very partial success, as he is first repeatedly bypassed by his new arch-enemy, Jeremiah – a very telling name, given that Jeremiah is perhaps the most famous Old Testament prophet, renown about his complaints; and then the eventual interview would lead nowhere. Second, before and after the (non-)interrogatory K. has repeated meetings with Frieda and the innkeeper, both being particularly desperate, focusing on the same dual accusations, steadily increasing in force and hostility; accusations touching the moral and intellectual insufficiencies of K. who doesn't understand anything and thus destroys every chance, including the possibility of happiness – a particularly sensitive matter for Kafka (Calasso 2005: 337; see also Citati 2007: 257–8).

Finally, the most important aspect of context, also hinting about the reasons for the novel's incompleteness, is K.'s reflection on his increasing tiredness, a state he indeed fails to understand; and which we, with the benefit of hindsight, and spurned by the narrator, can easily attribute to being faced, on the one hand, with a world that is indeed impenetrable, as turned upside down; while on the other also being worn down with temporariness becoming permanent, a situation where nothing is ever final, nothing can ever be decided and resolved, and which even alludes to the impossibility of ending the novel. Calasso also remarks on the permanent condition of tiredness in the novel: not only K., but all characters are continually tired and enervated, in lethargy (*spossatezza*), as being pushed to the extreme limits of their forces, without ever achieving anything, waiting for an epiphany that never comes – living in the void and looking into the void (Calasso 2005: 301–3, 316–17).[11] This tiredness gives rise, at the start of Chapter 19, to a stunning reflection by Kafka through K. on permanent liminality, with K. comparing his own tiredness to the fatigue characteristic of the functionaries of the castle, being similar only on surface, but in actual fact completely different. It was something overtaking at noon those happily working all morning, and which 'in fact was an indestructible quiet and peace [*eigentlich unzerstörbare Ruhe, unzerstörbarer Frieden war*]' (Kafka 2011: 157). This perplexing use of the term – perplexing both because it actually occurs and because the meaning is so different from the Zürau aphorisms, applied to permanent liminality – is confirmed in the concluding sentence of the passage, with K. murmuring to himself that 'for the masters here there is always midday' (Ibid.).[12]

The night-time (non-)interrogation between K. and Bürgel is a complex comedy of errors played at several levels. Most evidently, it is sparked by the error of K. in knocking on the wrong door. It continues with Bürgel being frightened, pulling the blanket over his head and bitterly complaining about the fate of functionaries who are never left alone, as they cannot even close their doors by key – a section deleted by Kafka, certainly an instance of decontextualisation, again trying to achieve ballade-like terseness. At the next level the comedy moves to problems with sleeping: having been woken up, Bürgel cannot go back to sleep, so gives a gratuitous introduction to K. about the functioning of the castle, except that K., who thought himself strong enough to face Erlangen, is rather desperately tired and – though keenly aware of the importance of Bürgel's revelations – cannot follow him, falling repeatedly into deep sleep. Still further, we reach the heart of the comedy, as whatever Bürgel tells in general about the functioning of the 'system' and its justification or – in Citati's reading – the world of the 'gods' actually applies to the concrete situation, describing what is actually happening through a stunning 'exercise of transcendental acrobatics', resulting in a momentary coincidence of 'maximal generality and the most irreducible singularity' (Calasso 2005: 315). However, this concrete reality is presented as an error that should not have happened, even could not have happened, and which yet exists – thus defining the concrete, existing world of K. from the perspective of the supposedly universally valid logic of the castle as not simply an error but an impossibility. Still, at a further turn of the screw, even this is justified, and considered in its very

100 *Suspended in the In-Between*

absurdity as part of the world, thus animating an ever spiralling, unfinished as interminable circle of absurdity. The level of paradoxical paradoxes reached here is only comparable to *Don Quixote*, a favourite reading of Kafka, central for the Zürau notebooks, helping to understand the reaction of Einstein who returned Kafka's book sent to him by Thomas Mann with the comment that ' "[t]his is too much for the human mind to grasp" ' (as in Hatfield 1969: 49). In this chapter Kafka evidently reached such heights in paradoxical thinking, trying to take up the paradoxes of modernity to their ultimate limits, that it simply could not be either continued or concluded.

The failure of redemption

Merely reflecting chaos is the biggest reproach that can be formulated against the art of a decadent period – a charge indeed formulated by Hofmannsthal against the literature of his times. This is by no means what Kafka did – and yet, he certainly found no way out of permanent liminality. K. the land-surveyor-Messiah who was called, though evidently only due to error, and so found himself superfluous when he arrived is the most emblematic figure of such failure, a failure also 'reflected' in the unfinished character of the novel. Furthermore, Kafka's failure in coming up with any idea about redemption involves a direct contrast with Goethe, concerning their visions of women. For Goethe, salvation was fundamentally connected to women; his last words were about the eternal feminine, closely connected to the Virgin. Kafka, however, as it was already recognised by Benjamin, had a low opinion of women, bordering on misogyny; quite striking for someone who wrote his high-school thesis on Goethe's *Tasso*. For Kafka, according to Benjamin, women were swamp beings (*Sumpfgeschöpfe*), animated of lasciviousness (*Üppigkeit*) (Benjamin 1977: 429), as if embodying seasickness on solid earth (Ibid.: 428). This is a particularly striking expression of permanent liminality – but also an amazingly limited vision of the feminine that is not only light years away from anything Goethe ever wrote, but is also a clear expression of the worst aspects of patriarchal monotheism; a clear failure of Kafka's own calling as an anti-Abraham.

Notes

1. It should be noted that in German *landvermesser* also might gain the negative sense of mis-measuring, see Corngold and Gross (2011: 8).
2. According to Citati (2007: 155), this vision of the deceiving character of the deity brings Kafka close to the Greek gods, Goethe, especially the *Lehrjahre*, and Dostoevsky. However, at the same time, this understanding is radically different from the focus on light, characteristic of the Platonic aspect of Eastern Orthodoxy, where even the representation of shadow was not permitted.
3. For a particularly interesting example, see *Pure America* (1987) by Péter Gothár, who in 1982 with *Time Stands Still* won the New York Film Critics Award.
4. The endless process as the worst nightmare in Kafka's anti-theology has striking parallels with the endless search for the 'better' argument in contemporary philosophy, similarly meaning that nothing ever reaches a stable conclusion, humans

being permanently suspending in the endless arguments of the 'open public sphere' – except that this nightmarish state of things is considered as a desired utopia, raising processuality into the normative cornerstone of social order,
5. Benjamin also emphasises the similarity to the Grand Inquisitor (1977: 422).
6. The symbol has further significance through Plato, including the inscription above the entrance of the Academy ('Let no one ignorant of geometry enter'), the origins of geometry and the theories of Hobbes, and especially by *geo-metron* implying Earth-centred proportionality, beyond the Copernican vision of the world and Newtonian science, among others, making geometry both the cornerstone of the modern scientific vision of the world and its overcoming, which cannot be further followed here.
7. See also Calasso's (2005: 211) repeated evocation of the zero (*nulla*), as connected to New York as 'new world' (*mondo nuovo*), the association with Tiepolo being particularly justified, given that Calasso's next, 2006 book was devoted to Tiepolo.
8. The title word *Naturtheater*, or 'nature-theatre' was given by Brod, and does not seem warranted.
9. Given Calasso's interest in the Sanskrit term for world order, *rta* (see Calasso 1983, 2010), it opens up a series of important parallels.
10. On Hermes as psychopompos, see Kerényi (1986).
11. The parallels with Beckett, especially *Waiting for Godot* and *Endgame* are tight.
12. There is another and just as striking use of the term in Chapter 10 where K. now accepts the characterisation of Klamm as an eagle, being inaccessible high up there, moving around in his 'indestructible circles [*unzerstörbare Kreise*]' which follow 'incomprehensible laws [*unverständliche Gesetzen*]' (Kafka 2011: 68), recalling the poems of Yeats and Rilke about the gyres of the falcon, but even more Hofmannsthal's *Andreas*, where outright an eagle is circling above. Furthermore, the secret of Klamm, a true 'Dappertutto', according to Calasso (2005: 36), is his secretary, with the extraordinary name Momus.

6 The Zürau Notebooks
The indestructible and the way

> To believe is: to liberate the indestructible in us; or better: to liberate ourselves; or better: to be indestructible; or better: to be.
>
> Kafka, *Zürau Notebooks*

Apart from his anti-theological theology, contained in his novels, Kafka wrote a work that combines theology and philosophy, while being both anti-theological and anti-philosophical. These are the Zürau aphorisms, written during the autumn of 1917, 'the best time of his life' (Citati 2007: 207).

Both in terms of form and content, this writing is radically different from anything that Kafka ever wrote. It is not fiction, rather a collection of reflections having evident philosophical depth. The ideas are extremely concentrated; they are reduced to the barest essences, and are extremely enigmatic; compared to them, the ideas of Heraclitus 'the obscure' are transparent as a mountain creek. Their closest parallel for Citati (2007: 212) is John Scotus or Byzantine mystics, while Calasso (2004: 12) compares them to Hebbel and especially Kierkegaard, a philosopher Kafka was systematically reading in November 1917, with a particular focus on Abraham's sacrifice (Stach 2015: 235). For Stach, they are closest to Valéry, and also Pascal's *Pensées*, which Kafka was indeed reading shortly before moving to Zürau, thus instead of (Nietzschean) aphorisms, they should rather be called (Pascalian) meditations (Ibid.: 229). But they are also different by their outlook: while the manuscripts of the major novels are contained in densely written, overcrowded pages, here only one, and usually very short, saying is contained on a single, clean sheet. Their character of standing apart from everything else is also marked by the fact that Kafka never referred to them. The aphorisms were carefully copied from two other notebooks, on 103 pages,[1] numbered and corrected. It was evidently carefully prepared for publication – yet, there is no trace of any attempt at publishing it (Calasso 2004: 11–12; 2005: 335).

The period in which they were written was highly specific and particularly liminal, both in terms of Kafka's life and world history. Kafka first coughed blood on the night between 12 and 13 August.[2] He was diagnosed with tuberculosis, and the doctors advised mountain air. As a result, on 12 September he left for Zürau, where his favourite sister Ottla lived, and stayed there for over half a year. There were several reasons why this was the best time of his life, some evident, some utterly strange. He was away from work duties, in the countryside after a life spent in a big city – in 1916–17 Kafka moved in Prague to 'Alchemists' Street', a most symbolic name, feeling that everything is out of joint (Stach 2013: 141–4); now enjoying the company of wild animals. He was also particularly happy to abandon fiction writing, and for long months he thought he managed to escape his phantasms. But the strangest of all was the fact that being diagnosed with a serious, easily mortal illness did not make Kafka anxious; quite on the contrary, he considered such a verdict as liberating.

In terms of broader historical context, autumn 1917 was not only the fourth year of World War I, but on 7 November the Bolshevik Revolution broke out. The time in which Kafka started to pin down the aphorisms, 18 October, is particularly close to this date – especially if we consider that in the traditional Russian calendar 7 November fell on 25 October. Even more intriguingly, Max Weber delivered his 'Science As A Vocation' lecture on the same day, particularly relevant in light of the fact that in his lecture Weber, in a much-quoted passage, centrally alluded to his 'demons'. Furthermore, the Fatima apparitions also took place between 13 May and 13 October 1917. Finally, to close this line of argument, there are few important pieces of work by great artists which include exactly 103 sheets; but this is true for Giandomenico Tiepolo's 'Pulcinella' series (*Divertimenti per li ragazzi*, or 'Fun for the boys'), whose theme in several ways parallels Kafka's philosophy, and which was sold, after a century-long oblivion, in 1920, after having been dismembered.

The order into which the aphorisms – not quite the right term (Calasso 2004: 12–13) – are arranged is difficult to establish (Calasso 2005: 329–30), just as it is impossible to understand the choices for selection (Citati 2007: 212). Some of them are impossible to make sense of; others make points that seem trivial; still others seem obscure due to Kafka's tricky technique of 'decontextualisation', a technique going back to 'The Verdict' (Koelb 2010: 95). Still, this book is 'the purest of diamonds' (Calasso 2005: 330); or, 'if Kafka wrote these phrases, then we humans belong to a marvellous race, superior to the race of angels' (Citati 2007: 213).

Any interpretation of these enigmatic fragments is highly risky. Yet, in the footsteps of Calasso and Citati, a few points can be ventured – all the more so as the anthropological concepts explored in this book, like liminality, trickster and imitation, are particularly helpful here.

What are the Zürau aphorisms? As their spatial and temporal coordinates make it evident – in the full ambivalence of appearance as revelation and as a mask hiding the essence – they were destined to be a last word: of 'Kafka's'. Concerning time, they were written after Kafka received his 'verdict', confirmation of his illness. Concerning space, Zürau was a mountain village, remote physically and culturally. They were reflections about ultimate matters, on the 'ends' of the world, at the end of the 'world'. Their ultimate nature is undermined by a formal characteristic of the name: 'Zürau' is bound to be the last entry in any index, all the more so as German 'ü' is identical with Greek 'y', and no word starts with Zz.

The Zürau aphorisms thus emphatically contain Kafka's *last* reflections. They are based on memories and reflections, on his intimate understanding of the two cultures to which he belonged and on his writings, hopefully the phantasms left behind, in his room.

In terms of their theme, they evidently centre on art and life; the life of an artist, and the paradoxical relations that exist, for an artist, between art and life. But, as it is imperative for any significant artist, they are also about the 'world': the world in the Biblical sense as the human condition on Earth after the Fall; the Paradise, meaning the Golden Age before the Fall, and also as the promise at the end of times; and the current state of the world, modernity as we call it, in so far as it is a special modality of the 'world' – perhaps as a bridge towards the return to the Golden Age, perhaps an accentuation of the Fall. These two central concerns, the artist and his task and the current state of the world and its relationship to the Golden Age, are evidently related; and, given the nature of this work as ultimate reflections, thus some kind of 'anamnetic exercises' (Voegelin 1978), one could expect that Kafka must have pulled out, at this moment of his life, a memory of his last high school year, around the year 1900, another symbolic moment, the time when he was familiarising himself with Nietzsche, the year in which Nietzsche died, the theme of his 'last' lyceum essay, on Goethe's *Tasso*, and its central claim about the poet as being the 'bridge' towards the Golden Age – thus, the *only* human being comparable to Zarathustra's 'overman'.

At any rate, this piece of Kafka's life history immediately gives us access to the central themes of the aphorisms: the question of the Paradise, its presence and accessibility; the 'indestructible' in us, the single most striking expression of these aphorisms (Calasso 2005); and the qualities and character of a poetic work that can help to give us access, again, to the Golden Age.

The very first and last aphorisms of the collection, No.1 and No.109/2,[3] introduce Kafka's vision of the task of an artist that can be understood through Nietzsche and Goethe, in particular Nietzsche's *Zarathustra* and Goethe's reflections on his demons, and some attention to Greek etymologies. The last aphorism captures, in a particular striking though coded manner, Kafka's standard writing habit – is almost its apotheosis. The first, however, is about the 'way' – so the way must be understood as the way *of the artist*. It is from this perspective that we can understand its thrice stunning character: first, that it presents 'the way' as walking on a rope, evoking the figure of the 'tightrope walker'; second, that such a walk takes place only a few inches above ground, so by no means implies a stunning feat; and third, that the central problem is not falling down, rather stumbling, a word having close affinity with 'scandal'.

The image of the 'tightrope walker' immediately evokes Nietzsche's *Zarathustra*; but the closeness to the ground adds a comic touch to the scene, alluding to Tiepolo's Villa Zianigo 'Pulcinella' fresco, now in the Ca' Rezzonico museum, though Pulcinella there only sits on the rope. In the famous prologue, Zarathustra starts to teach the overman in this scene, at the marketplace (which is also the scene of a carnival, so is rather a *fairground*), where the 'tightrope walker' is followed by a jester, imitating him and bringing about his suicide-like fall and death.[4] The 'tightrope walker' is a joint metaphor for the human condition and the condition of the artist, and – as Marion Faber (1979) argues in her excellent book, comparing this and similar self-referential circus-metaphors in the works of Nietzsche and Kafka, and also von Kleist and Rilke – such metaphors are central for Kafka's self-understanding as artist.

This establishes clear ties with the last aphorism, which evidently and emphatically contains Kafka's *ars poetica*, capturing the habit of night-time writing in a particularly striking manner. It argues that the best way to gain knowledge of the world is to remain at home, glued to one's desk, without listening or even waiting for anything, and then the 'world' would come to 'you', offering itself in a particularly striking way: it would first throw off his masks (*Entlarvung*) – it simply could not do otherwise; then would enter an ecstatic state (*verzückt*); and finally it would be laying there in a twisted or broken state (*winden*).

The term phantasm or spirit is not mentioned there, but a series of other aphorisms give a sense of the world that is fully spiritual. Thus, the type of unique, non-sociological understanding of 'the world' Kafka offers here clearly refers to the spiritual world: the world as spirit, or the world of spirits.

The question now is to find a way to connect the first and last aphorisms, as the two metaphors through which Kafka offers his *ars poetica*, the circus and the writing desk, are connected. Focus is not only on circular movement, but the trapeze as a particularly important metaphor. It is through this image that we can bring in the other object central for Kafka's self-understanding as an artist, the writing desk. And the two can be simply brought together by the fact that the Greek word for 'table', both in classical and modern Greek, is *trapeza*. Thus Kafka, who knew his Greek well, so much so that he was reading Plato's dialogues, one of his favourite writings in the original, could identify himself sitting at his writing desk as a 'trapeze artist'. According to Citati (2007: 33–4), such self-identification reaches far, into an entire theology of sin and Fall. It is even identical to permanent liminality, given that for such an artist time is reduced to the fleeting instant.

The connotations of the Greek word extend far. Classically denoting an eating table, *trapeza* came to be used for moneychangers: in Greek banks are still called *trapeza*, paralleling the conceptual development in Italian (see *banco* 'bank', source of the modern term for financial institutions in most European languages). However, and further confirming the links between eating, money and religion, *trapeza* in Greek had another meaning, the place on which the offerings to the gods were laid; a meaning that might have been the original one, also explaining the unequal sides. Eventually the term acquired the abstract meaning of any 'flat surface on which a thing rests' (Liddell and Scott 1996: 1810), quite close to *khóra* (the empty space of the 'public sphere'; Plato's receptacle of Being in *Timaeus*). The word *trapeza* is not simply 'connected' to money or religion, rather it goes into the heart of both: the exchange of money on the one hand, and offerings (not necessarily sacrificial killings) on the other.

Finally, among derivatives of the term, there is *trapezétai* ('parasite'), developed through dogs being fed by leftovers thrown off the table; a term significant due to

Kafka's (self-)identification of the artist in 'First Sorrow' as a parasite (see also Faber 1979: 77). This idea is taken up into a particularly dangerous direction by Maurice Blanchot (1981: 83), obsessed with Kafka's negation, arguing that for Kafka 'art carries a name: destruction of oneself, infinite disaggregation'.

After the frame

If the very first and last aphorisms provide the frame for the undertaking through an *ars poetica*, the immediately following and preceding ones define the basic mode in which a philosophic-poetic attempt at reaching the Golden Age can be conducted. The central elements of this attitude are 'patience' (No.2 and No.3) and 'humility' (No.106). Both are the par excellence anti-Titanic virtues, most opposed to the arrogant self-assertive egoism of Enlightenment modernity, visible in the modern cult of Prometheus or in Blumenberg's attempt to legitimate modernity through such self-assertion.

While not values usually associated with modern artists, patience and humility are indeed central to the particular artistic attitude characteristic of Kafka: withdrawing from public noise into the eerie silence of a room, at night, patiently waiting for the 'phantasms' to arrive, and subordinating oneself humbly to their inspiration. For Kafka both values require constant attention and steady application. In this manner they give strength, even to those who – like, evidently, Kafka – 'despair in solitude' (No.106), offering the necessary methodicity to work. Their absence not only interrupts the regularity of work habits, but also interferes with receiving the inspiration that is the source of any poetic work. Here the word *scheinbar* ('appearance'), that appears twice in the three lines of aphorism 2, can be understood to mean the second time apparition.

But there is something else there, far from 'pure' art and close to theology. Impatience is not only an error, upsetting proper work habits, but outright a capital sin; one of the two capital sins, the other being inertia; moreover, as inertia can be traced to impatience, there is only one capital sin – so, raising things in the crescendo of four short sentences so quickly so high that is probably unique even to Kafka, impatience is outright the reason why men were expulsed from Paradise, and also why they cannot return there. Thus, in Kafka's anti-theological theology, from an error that most philosophies and religions consider a minor character fault impatience becomes the greatest of human sins: a genuine monstrosity.

In attempting to understand this claim, let's return to context: it is aphorism 3, in a collection of aphorisms representing according to Calasso and Citati the distilled 'pure diamond' of his mind, and where the tone of the collection is set up by a search for the 'true way'. We must thus turn to the heart of Kafka's other arguments about the Paradise, or the Golden Age, keeping in mind this stunning starting point about the incomparable monstrosity of impatience.

The Paradise in the Zürau aphorisms

Kafka devoted six of the aphorisms to the theme of the Paradise: Nos 3, 64, 74, 82, 84 and 86 (Calasso 2005: 335). Thus, after introducing impatience as capital sin, cause of all our troubles with Paradise, we have to wait, patiently, until aphorism 64 for him to return to this theme. The reference then is repeated, with Nos 74 and 84 – indicating that a game with numbers is going on, especially if we take cognisance of the manner in which the 103 or 105 sheets are numbered until 109. To begin with, two numbers are missing, 65 and 89, as inconspicuous numbers as possible – except that 65 comes after 64, which is 8x8, while 89 comes after 88. This means an evident, emphatic play on the number eight, but also on four, as eight is twice four, or two added together four times; a play that is valorised in all kind of ways by the numbering of the aphorisms connected to Paradise: the first one is exactly No.64, after which there is the first of the two breaks, No.65; among the following five on Paradise, two others end with 4, forming the series 64, 74, 84; and while 64 and 74 stand alone, the third one – as if evoking the number of the first aphorism on Paradise, No.3 – is the centre of a trio, surrounded by 82 and 86, each number in the series starting with 8, while after 88 – not about Paradise, but alone devoted to death – 'comes' the second missing number, 89. Whatever the meaning of these plays with numbers, they certainly emphasise the centrality of Paradise in the aphorisms.

Aphorism 64, which according to such logical order comes right after No.3, not only follows its theme, the expulsion from the Garden of Eden, but also its internal rhythm: it takes up a seemingly trivial statement, but – just as a hound-dog bites into the game – captures a piece of it, torturing and investigating it until it wields its deepest inner truth in the form of an utterly astonishing claim. The starting claim, the eternity of the expulsion (*Vertreibung*) from Paradise, is not only simple, but particularly depressing; but Kafka, true student of Nietzsche's genealogy, recognises that no historical event can represent a complete break. Thus, expulsion from a single and once for all event becomes a *process*; it is *this* process that is eternal; but if this is so, then it also means that something in us is still preserved from Paradise; and thus, in so far as this is still with us, by implication we are still in Paradise, whether we take cognisance of this or not. Thus, through another series of machinegun-like claims, Kafka's inexorable iron 'logic' leads us from utter hopelessness into an almost blissful state.

But the nature of whatever is preserved in us is still to be ascertained. This is named in the next aphorism about the Paradise as the *indestructible* (*unzerstörbar*), perhaps the central term of the aphorisms,[5] and of Kafka's philosophico-theology; a word that appears four times here. Most importantly, however, this is not the first but the *last* appearance of the word; it is therefore not introduced here, only given a definite meaning. We thus have to retrace here the way it was introduced previously.

The term appears in aphorism 50, again a momentous number. Given its significance, it almost comes out of the blue; at least, the previous three aphorisms map a quite peculiar context: No.47 is the important statement about the king and his courier; No.48 also has its significance, as the interpretation of history as progress discussed there has ties to interpreting history through the Fall; while No.49 is one of the clearest cases of decontextualisation where the meaning is completely lost. It is in this context that the term *indestructible* appears, carrying a very emphatic meaning: it is simply impossible to live without a confidence (*Vertrauen*) that within us there is something that is indestructible, even if both (the indestructible and belief in its existence) can be hidden from us. One modality of such belief is the belief in a personal god. This claim prepares both No.64 and No.74.

The other two appearances of *indestructible* are in two subsequent aphorisms in between 64 and 74, Nos 69 and 70/71; leading up to 74. Both are of extreme importance. No.69 defines not simply happiness, but the *perfect possibility* of happiness, or the way to happiness as believing (*glauben*) in this indestructible in us, but not trying to reach it (*streben*), clearly alluding to the possibility of an unconscious presence in us.

A potentially important step towards understanding Kafka's meaning is offered in a 6 August 1920 letter to Brod, in which the aphorism is quoted almost in full, as the theoretical possibility of a perfect happiness on earth, except that the word 'indestructible' is replaced by the expression 'decisively divine' (Calasso 2005: 334; Kafka 1958: 279–80). The meaning, however, according to Calasso, even in this way remains inaccessible. It is evidently connected to a sense of immortality associated with certain types of conduct, close to the sense of being alive, but we can't go beyond; and 'perhaps it is better that it is so' (Calasso 2005: 335).

The next aphorism completes the path towards bringing together the two key terms of the aphorisms, the Paradise and the Indestructible, disclosing the heart of Kafka's philosophico-theology by defining, in terms clearly recalling Plato's *Philebus*, thus the heart of Plato's philosophy, the indestructible as being what makes us human *and* social, thus the heart of the anthropology and sociology of the Golden Age, or what is remained is us from it. In this case it is impossible to do away with a full citation: 'The indestructible is one; every single human being it is and it is at the same time common to all, thus the connection (*Verbindung*) between human beings is indissoluble like nothing else' (No.70/71).

With this, we can return to aphorism 74, or the joint appearance of 'Paradise' and 'indestructible'. To start with, here – and here alone – the term appears as an adjective, not a gerund. The aphorism directly, though only hypothetically, connects the Fall and the indestructible: if whatever was destroyed was destructible (thus by definition was not 'indestructible'), it does not matter. If, however, the 'indestructible' was destroyed, than there is a big problem, as all our convictions are wrong. This, however, again by definition cannot be true – as the 'indestructible', if truly so, could not have been destroyed. The Golden Age, as a possibility *and* as a reality inside us, it still given – in other words is our gift: our most precious gift. A late March 1918 letter to Brod illuminates this, through Kafka's reading of Kierkegaard: one should stay with one's original nature, and *this* results in a transformation of one's entire existence (Stach 2015: 243).

The connection between these two terms thus could not be tighter, and indeed within the aphorisms there is no further mention of the term 'indestructible'. Yet, in the original notebook from which the aphorisms were taken, there is a further mention of the word, and both context and substance are absolutely important

– starting with the fact that it precedes all others, and is thus the very first occurrence in Kafka (1992, I: 55). This is in between Nos 42 and 43 in the published aphorisms, where there is a quite long time gap. No.42 was written on 26 November; the next series of remarks, containing these two citations, are dated 31 November, but according to the editor were probably only written down on 1 December. No.43 is preceded by four not published aphorisms, each of exceptional importance, the second containing the first mention of 'indestructible', and followed by three others which were published, then followed on the next day, 2 December, by No.47, the famous aphorism about the king and his courier. This context is related to one of the most striking and thorough omissions, the erasing of all direct references to the name of Christ and the figure of the Messiah.

The entire set starts and ends with two unpublished aphorisms about the coming of the Messiah. The first sentence of 1 December, written down after a gap of four days, states that the Messiah will come once the most unfettered individualism of faith becomes possible, and no one will be able to destroy (*vernichten*) this possibility; so the graves will open themselves (Kafka 1992, I: 55). This claim is then possibly identified with 'Christian teaching', focusing both on the actual individuality of the example and 'the symbolic presentation of the resurrection [*der Auferstehung*] of the mediator in a concrete man' (Ibid.). The first aphorism of 4 December, written down after a stormy night, states that 'The Messiah will first come when he will not even be noticed, he will first come after his arrival, he will not come on the last day, only on the very last day' (Ibid.: 56–7). This omitted aphorism is between two particularly important published aphorisms, no.47 (2 Dec) on the courier of the king, and No.48 (4 Dec) on progress, stating that believing (*glauben*) in a progress that already happened is not a faith (*kein Glauben*) (Ibid.: 57). This is followed, on 7 December, by No.50, the first kept aphorism on the indestructible (Ibid.: 58).

This context only underlines the significance of the first (in fact double, both noun and adjective) omitted mention of 'indestructible', and its omission. The aphorism states that 'to believe (*glauben*) is: to liberate the indestructible (*das Unzerstörbare*) in us; or better: to liberate ourselves; or better: to be indestructible (*unzerstörbar*); or better: to be (*sein*)' (Ibid.: 55). The tight connection between Christ, Messiah, faith, resurrection and the indestructible are evident, though not only failed to make way to Kafka's publications, but were edited out even from the polished notebook.

The centrality of this first occurrence and its more than paradoxical omission receives further support by the two other cases where the name of Christ appears (see Becker 2003). It is present twice in the original version of No.102, devoted to the theme of the suffering common to mankind. This appears in Octave H, written down on 21 February 1918, and is identical except that the second sentence is omitted: 'Christ suffered for mankind, but mankind must also suffer for Christ' (Kafka 1992, I: 93). The third occurrence concerns two words jotted down as part of a series on 7–9 February 1918, of which almost everything was discarded. It only contains two words: 'Christ, *Augenblick* ['blink of an eye']', the last annotation of 7 February (Ibid.: 87). It probably alludes to a sudden vision-image.

110   *Suspended in the In-Between*

We can now return to the remaining three instances of Kafka's discussion of the Paradise, Nos 82, 84, and 86. According to the logic of numbering, analysis must start with No.84, with its meaning to be attenuated through the ones before and after.

Given the centrality of No.84, it is particularly reassuring that it is one of the most affirmative, indeed radiating texts that Kafka ever wrote. Beyond the paradoxical puzzle raised by No.74, it not simply asserts the indestructible inside us, but that the Paradise is our destiny: we were created to live in the Paradise, and even the destruction of the Paradise was only done in order to help us. The previous aphorism, No.82, which is closely combined with No.83, discusses the trees that caused our Fall, placing the emphasis on the Tree of Life: we were chased out not because we ate from the Tree of Knowledge, but because we failed to do so with the Tree of Life – indicating that much of the rest will be concerned with the Nietzsche-Foucaldian dilemma of knowledge and life.

Aphorism No.86, on the other hand, closes the theme of Paradise in a truly concluding manner. To begin with, it is by far the longest of all. Second, it shifts the emphasis from Paradise to the situation after the Fall, or – as it is explicitly defined in No.85 – the 'world'. The central feature of our 'world' is defined by our fate, through the Tree of Knowledge, or the knowledge of knowing the difference of good and evil – which means that as all of us know this difference, in *this* we are not different. The real difference of us human beings living in the world (*though* also having the indestructible in us) concerns something else: whether one is able to act accordingly. It implies a preoccupation with motivations, concerning finding the right kind of conduct: this is what the *entire world* (*die ganze Welt*) is about – how to move back to right way.

Thus, with aphorism 86, the emphasis is displaced to the proper way of conduct in our environment after the Fall, which is 'the world'. The key to this situation is offered in the absolutely crucial aphorism that is *in between* the last series of aphorisms about the Paradise, connecting it and them to the world, and establishing this connection by placing emphasis on connection, the in-between, transition, passage, or liminality.

Aphorism 85 starts with a striking definition of evil (*Böse*): startling again both because of its modality and substance. The modality is striking, as – with Kafka's impenetrable density reaching its height – a crucial statement about evil is offered in the form of a pure definition, as if out of a neo-classical textbook of law. But the content is also striking, as evil is defined as the 'irradiation of human consciousness in certain positions of passage'. Passage means liminality, so evil is defined through the human energy liberated in liminal moments *by consciousness*. The second part of the aphorism simply clarifies that this evil is not rooted in the sensible world, but only in its interpretation. This, however, is only a first approach into the next major theme: the link between the world – the world of knowledge, thus also the world of deceit, as No.106/2 identifies knowledge and deceit (*der Betrug*) – and evil.

The world and its evil as outcomes of liminality, and the way in it (inside us)

Having been thrown out of Paradise, the central fact of our existence according Kafka's Zürau 'theology', so similar to and yet so distant from Heidegger's existential thrownness, a concept on which Heidegger was reflecting at the same time, though only published in 1926, we now live in the 'world'. The character of this 'world' in which we live and the task a poet has there is numerically the central preoccupation of the aphorisms.

Three questions appear here, before a more detailed analysis of the meaning of the 'world' for Kafka: the cosmos-chaos pair, central for Greek thought; the link to evil, as thematised by the serpent or devil, central to Judeo-Christian thought; and the question of modernity. This world, as the analysis of the nature of our expulsion already established, is not identical with a reversion to chaos, as a piece of the Paradise is still with us; yet, the threat of such regress is ever-present. Furthermore, this world is evidently penetrated by evil, a term almost as much discussed as 'world', and most often in close connection. Finally, the question of modernity, this unique development of Judeo-Christian culture raises all the previous questions in a particularly cornered way: does modernity offer us the possibility of a return to the Golden Age, as precursors to sociology like Saint-Simon or Comte argued; or, on the contrary, represent the threat of a full reversal to chaos?

The central question, thus, is the 'way' to follow in the world; the question of the 'right way', as the very first aphorism defines it; finding the way that might steer us back towards to Paradise, an undertaking in which the poet has no small role to play. But before we can discuss Kafka's ideas about 'the way', we must reconstruct his insights concerning the world and its evil; and, first of all, this is the very starting point of the analytical undertaking about in-betweenness or liminality, the state of transition that emerges between the Paradise and the world; a condition so central for understanding modernity.

Liminality (transition, passage) is discussed in three aphorisms: 13, 85, and 105. No.85 was the point of entry, singling out this condition to be discussed immediately after the expulsion from Paradise; so we must continue with the other two. First of all, their situation and numerical value are both extremely privileged and important. They are at the beginning and end, though not the beginning or the end, thus connecting both to the central line of argument. No.105 is just before No.106, which introduces the theme of humility, while No.13, though not coming after the aphorisms about patience, still numbers 1 and 3, thus connects the 'way' and 'patience'.

Both aphorisms define this world, thus our existence as a passage or a liminal situation, close to Plato's *metaxy*, as introduced in the *Symposium* and the *Philebus*. Both furthermore connect this to desire, which again closely follows Plato's argument in both dialogues, but especially the *Symposium* concerning Eros (Horvath 2013b; Szakolczai 2013b); but, and here taking the road of Freud, in one aphorism it is connected to death (No.13), while in the other to sexual desire (No.105) – a connection all the more relevant as in German the word expulsion (*Vertrieben*) and the word used by Freud for the sexual drive and the death 'instinct' (*Trieb*) are closely related. Even further, in both cases liminality and its link to desire are also connected to a sign (*Zeichen*); a sign that further connects the liminality/desire complex to a Foucaldian understanding of knowledge as power, but of a particular kind: power not as leadership, but as mis-leading, or seduction (*Verführung*). Finally, in both cases this liminal situation is connected to a particular figure that is the main agent of this liminal situation. In order to identify and understand the similarities and differences of these central figures of liminality, or 'liminal authorities' (Horvath 2013a), however, we now need to first analyse the two aphorisms separately.

No.105 is about female seduction, clearly present in the original form, but the first sentence that made it evident became erased, as another clear instance of decontextualisation. This female seduction is conceptualised as the 'good' being attracted to 'evil', even identifying the female gaze as being central for seducing one to her bed. No.13 captures a quite different in-betweenness; there, in one of the most desolate aphorisms of the collection (see Citati 2007: 226–8), human existence is defined as completely insupportable, being caught in-between two worlds, also defined as 'cells' (*Zelle*), the intolerable situation of the 'present', and the unattainable 'other' world, the Paradise. The only residuum of hope is the faith that, when we are moved from one 'cell' to another, the Lord (*der Herr*) happens to pass by and call us.

Here we encounter a number of extraordinary aspects that, with relevant information from other aphorisms and their sources can illuminate the passage, offering a central and astonishing message. To begin with, this is the only place in Kafka's *Nachlass* where the expression 'the Lord', evidently meaning Christ, is used.[6] Christ as the agent in liminality is thus comparable to the female. Their role is quite different – one offers a rare chance for salvation, the other seduces to evil. What units them, seemingly a merely editorial change, is that they are among the few instances where a full sentence was deleted from a selected aphorism. All this establishes commonality between the two figures of liminality, evoking Goethe and the closing sentences of *Faust Two*.

Having clarified the meaning of 'passage' and identified the main agents with potential of redemption, we need to enter into the details concerning Kafka's understanding of the world and the agent that was luring *into* the world (*Welt*), through 'mis-guiding' the feminine, evil (*Böse*).

The world and its evil

The writing of Notebook G was started on 18 October. In a diary entry of 15 September, thus after spending only three days in Zürau, Kafka claimed that he was given the chance (*Möglichkeit*) of a new start (Calasso 2005: 328; Kafka 1990: 831). He only started to write down his ideas in writing a month later, no doubt based on month-long intense reflections. The idea about the right way that became the start of the collected aphorisms was only put down on 19 October, the second day of writing, as if he were resurrected from his own gap and absence. This helps understand the vital importance of the fact that the explicit discussion of both 'world' and 'evil' starts when Kafka returns to the study of the 'right way', in some of the most crucial aphorisms, No.26–7. The first major mention of the 'world' takes place in No.25, while of evil in No.28–9; thus immediately after. Matters of context are again fundamental, and in various ways.

To start with, each these themes were alluded to before, but without emphasis. The 'right way' is casually discussed in No.14–15, then a slightly more important mention is in No.21, followed by No.22, which is about 'following', indirectly advancing a central idea of No.26–7 – but which only becomes intelligible through the latter. Similarly, 'evil' is mentioned in No.7, and connected even to the fight with the female and its ending in bed, close to the meaning of No.105, but remaining cryptic; while 'cage' is identified with the world in No.13 (incidentally, the word 'world' is not present in No.13; the term used there, close to sense 'world' elsewhere, is *Leben* 'life').

The broader context of these passages is quite significant. The aphorisms dated to the first weeks of November 1917 – a period of exceptional significance for 'world history'– did not contain observations of particular interest; for e.g. the only lines jotted down on 7 November were No.17, decontextualised and not terribly relevant. This lasted up to 12 November. The five aphorisms of that day, No. 21–5 are of moderate significance, preparing a return and joint discussion of evil as the way of world and the true way, that would come in aphorisms 26–9. Between No.25 and No.26 there is a considerable gap in the original notebook, as No.26 was jotted down on 18 November (the second such gap, the first being after No.13 on 25 October, as the next entry was dated 3 November). Furthermore, while practically all the sentences written down between 3 and 12 November were kept in, the key aphorisms No.26–7 were followed by a number of omitted ones, just as it happened with No.28–9, again followed by omitted aphorisms, about evil, some of considerable importance, discussed by Calasso and Citati.

This helps us to formulate some hypotheses about the manner how the original sentences were written and selections made. To start with, the most important ones were not conceived and written down continuously, as after and before particularly important statements there is often a long gap. This indicates that these were outcomes of Kafka's own reflections, not products of 'phantasms'. Thus, once a particularly important idea was conceived, he needed time to go beyond; and that some of the least important ones simply signalled his own 'way' during the reflection process. Second, selections were made in a way that, while maintaining linearity, an attention was paid to internal numbering; both concerning the total number of sheets and the numbers that aphorisms inside were to take up. Here one should note that while the number 109 is not only a prime, thus indivisible, but seemingly innocuous, it gains a certain importance in the sense of containing the three most important single numbers, in terms of first and last matters, or matters concerning the beginning and end of 'the world' (meaning after the expulsion, theme of these aphorisms): it contains the number 1, the first number; number 9, the last single number; and in-between the zero, the (non-)number of in-between and deceit. Thus, 109 is indeed the 'perfect number' for Kafka's concerns; a number that marked the limit.

After this contextualisaton we need to analyse, first separately, the interconnected discussions of world and evil, to understand the exact nature of their connectedness.

The world

The three first instances in which the concern with the 'world' is introduced, through No.13 and especially 16 and 25, are only allusive, not going into the heart of the matter, yet reveal themselves strikingly important and illuminating. In particular, they bring together the metaphors of 'cage' and 'refuge'. At one level, this identifies a paradox, as cage represents enclosure, while refuge openness – except that an enclosed area can also serve as a refuge. Two suggestions can be made to connect them. The first concerns the condition of modernity, the paradoxical combination of freedom *and* constraint, or 'autonomy and discipline' (Wagner 1994), captured with particular force in the life-works of Weber and Foucault, as reflected in titles of books by important interpreters (Bernauer 1990; Scaff 1989). The second – a parallel in itself perplexing – evokes animals, as human beings are rarely put into cages or refuges, while both are often used for animals. Such a link might even have been intended by Kafka, as a central aspect of his stay in Zürau was his unprecedented and intense contact with animals, especially those in a 'semi-liberated' (or 'liminal') state. The opposite of cage-like existence in cities is the garden, which evokes the Garden of Eden, and also establishes links between Kafka's vision about the Garden of Eden and the close connection in which humans lived in the Palaeolithic with animals. The link between the mistreatment of animals and the loss of Eden is even alluded in the identical words used for hunting and expulsion, both in German (*jagen*) and Italian (*cacciare*), somewhat similar to English (*chase*) or Hungarian (*űz*).

The problem of the 'world' is discussed in four clusters of aphorisms, connected to the 40s, 50s, 60s and 100s. They are introduced through an aphorism with important content and a most peculiar, indeed unique position, 39a. This particular 'traffic jam' around No.39 (No.39a being one of the eight added aphorisms and the unique with double numbering) indicates that the position of No.40 was rock solid while its content most important: this is the only apocalyptic aphorism, having a particularly Kafkaesque message: we mistakenly understand the term 'Last Judgement' in a temporal sense, but its real meaning is 'summary verdict'. This is the context in which we need to interpret the liminal No.39a, which defines a feature of the 'way' – it is unending; but which also offers a peculiar understanding of childhood, which would be central for understanding No.47, one of the most important aphorisms and the only one where the term 'infantile' reappears: while the road is given, fixed to everyone, childhood peculiarities might deviate one from pursuing it. This offers a singular interpretation of childhood: providence defines the path to follow for everyone; all that childhood can do is to mess up one's life through infantilism. One must preserve and develop through the temptations of childhood, as only the self can destroy itself.

The aphorisms in the 40s do not give a clear image about Kafka's vision of the world. They contain interesting insights, which however remain cryptic and disconnected – like No.41 about disproportionality, central both in the context of 'The Verdict' and the etymological interpretation of rationality as proportionality; or 47, discussed above. In between these dispersed allusions to the world we have another most important and stunning aphorism, No.43, with its reference to hound dogs, evoking the most creeping sentence of *The Process* and also mirroring the apocalyptic start with No.40. In order to understand what is going on here we need to return to the omitted passages, as it is here that the most striking omissions were made, justifying the apocalyptic tone and establishing connection with the 4s and 8s, or the heart of the aphorisms about the paradise; as it is here that the two discarded passages about the Messiah can be found, analysed before.

The second cluster of references to the world is contained in the 50s (Nos 52, 53, 54 and 57), evidently sparked by the crucial appearance of the indestructible (no.50), and a reference to seduction and a serpent that will be analysed in depth in the next section. They contain two main points. One relies on points already discussed: a fight with the world is meaningless, the suggestion itself being a main instrument of evil, or the serpent, tricking one into a fight with the feminine. The second is new, highly Platonic, and would be repeated in the 60s: *being* is only a feature of the spiritual; the material world of senses is only a word of appearances, dominated by the misleading tricks of language, knowledge and possession. The 60s only reinforce these points, emphasising the inner and the spiritual, and even propose as ideal the renouncing of the (sensible) world, connecting it with love, leading up to the crucial No.64. The directness, linearity and centrality of the line of argument pursued here is underlined by the fact that there are no gaps or main omissions in the Notebook; from 7 to 12 December there is a steady advancing of the argument until the conclusive No.64, even having, with No.63, a preparatory claim, defining his own art as concerned with light: the setting of reflectors on truth – though adding a slightly preoccupying and Walter Benjamin-like modality: the true light is on the face of whoever is receeding/retreating.

After such centrality in the middle aphorisms, from 41 to 64, the world all but disappears as a concern until the very end – appearing only in some passages about the Paradise, but merely as a reference point. The return, however, is emphatic, and brings up important new points. It erupts in No.97, a peculiar aphorism on suffering, returning on the same note as it was last discussed, an orthodox understanding of Christianity, here justifying suffering, just as No.60 justified the renouncing of the world, and for the same reason: only the spiritual has real reality, or being; so suffering in this world is indeed identical to beautitude in the other world – a term which incidentally also brings in the concern with beauty, identified by the Greeks, and in particular Plato, with the cosmos. Such link to the Greek idea of cosmos is by no means a forced interpretation as it recurs, again alone in the *Nachlass*, in the next aphorism, No.98. The same theme of suffering as our common fate is the common concern of the last aphorisms about the world (Nos 102 and 103), which lead the discussion up to the male-female contrast, about will and seduction, already discussed, close to the end. In between, there are a series of important statements. First, right after the only mention of cosmos, in No.98, there is the only reference to modernity, in No.99, in terms of the oppressive nature of 'our contemporary state of sin' (*von unserem gegenwärtigen sündhaften Stand*), thus defining modernity as a continuation of the Fall, and in a particularly oppressive way; all of which is reinforced by the added comment, which contains, as a particular feature of the *modern* world, a theatrical reference – again a single case in the aphorisms. It evokes a kind of aside, a false smile as if a wink, that is lanced at the spectator in sentimental comedies, which in its seductive intent and falsity even goes beyond the original deceit – quite a strikingly claim. The series is closed with No.100, stating that while there is diabolic knowledge, there is no diabolic faith.

In order to further illuminate Kafka's understanding of the 'world', the interconnected passages on evil need to be reviewed now.

Evil

Concerning Kafka's understanding of evil, we must start by recognising that it is primarily a 'something', and not a feature of an entity: there are nearly 20 occurrences of the noun, and only one as an adjective, in an aphorism (No.54) where the substantial is also present. They are grouped in three clusters: 19, 28, 29, 39; 51, 54, 55; and 85, 86, 95, 105. This demonstrates that, just as the concern with the Paradise was concentrated in aphorisms dominated by two numbers, 4 and 8, the aphorisms about evil are similarly associated with two numbers, 9 and 5; here the last and middle numbers. This also indicates that the middle numbers of the 109 sheets would have special importance – which is indeed the case with 54 and 55, which together add up to 109; and also that middle aphorisms of the other two series, 28–9 and 95 should have special importance – which in the latter case is further undermined by this number containing both 9 and 5.

Moving to matters of content, the first series is concerned with the manner in which evil can enter the inside, the heart and mind of human beings, and the various deceits evil can mobilise for this purpose. Nos 19 and 39 are an introduction and coda to the argument, the heart which is contained not simply in Nos 28 and 29, but also in a series of important aphorisms left out, perhaps because of a sheer *embarras de richesse*, and which were collected and analysed together with the included aphorisms in a particularly insightful manner by Citati, bringing out the theatrical metaphor that is always central, though often implicit in Kafka (Citati 2007: 222–7). According to Citati, the metaphysics of evil offered here by Kafka is unique, dwarfing even the insights of Baudelaire, concluding the great analysis of 'absolute evil' by nineteenth century novelists to which Citati devoted a magisterial book (Citati 2000). Evil, first of all, is not a substance; it does not exist, has no being, only the divine exists (Citati 2007: 222); it is only appearance, imitation, mimicking, seductions, deceit; not real feature of a thing, but a 'something' that is literally 'no-thing'. It is the greatest of actors; a genuine transformationist illusionist, while the Good is incapable of acting (in this sense); and does so furthermore by being capable of self-knowledge, through self-observation, to which the Good is again incapable – thus demolishing with a slant of hand Hegel's philosophy of history. It is especially skilful in faking to be good – and here Kafka offers us a series of 'terrifying spectacles' (Citati 2007: 224). What we see in front of our eyes as good is most often not manifestation of the divine, rather evil faking to be good, taking up the mask of the good – a seduction even more attractive than the mere teasing of evil; so effective that as its result by now the Good has practically disappeared from the visible world: thus, '[t]he world is occupied by this enormous, most intelligent, agile and mobile', purely negative quasi-being (Ibid.: 225). It is at this moment that we can witness 'the masterpiece of the scenic art of the Demonic', as 'the old actor transforms itself to you yourself' (Ibid.), pulling out a series of most seductive tricks, the most simple but efficient, as Baudelaire already revealed, is that it makes you believe that it does not exist, making use of the ultimate paradox, first tackled by Plato in the *Sophist*: evil has no being, yet it exists in the form of not-real-existence, as a mime, a copy, a fake. Getting rid of this demon inside is particularly difficult, as even our hidden thoughts about this evil inside us are not ours, but its (Kafka, No.29). It is to this aphorism that later Kafka added another one, 29/2, stating that a slave-animal can never become a master – this is only a new illusion. The content of this aphorism is most significant, being another affront to Hegel's philosophy; but its language is also important, being the only other one using the term Lord (*Herr*), thus implicitly identifying Hegel's master-self dialectic with the Antichrist.

The aphorisms about evil in the 50s are mostly connected to the link between evil and the world, and their meaning was mostly already covered. The novelty is contained in No.55, one of the longest in the collection, which connects evil to deceit (*Betrug*) – a word introduced here, and only contained in two added comments, No.99/2 and No.106/2. This has its own importance in defining the modality of evil and its relationship to the world, especially through the added part of No.99, on modernity, which retrospectively identifies the expulsion of the Paradise, through the activity of the serpent, as the 'original deceit' (*Urbetrug*). Taken together, Nos 54 and 55 define, at the mid-point of the collection, evil as non-existing, mere illusion, though – for the same reason – having affinities with knowledge.

The last trio, Nos 85, 95 and 105, offer a proper conclusion to the previous discussion at the middle of the aphorisms by focusing on evil as being located in the in-between. Of these, Nos 85 and 105, offering vital insights, even a definition of evil, were already analysed in the context of liminality. It is from this perspective that we can capture the significance of No.95, which otherwise does not look particularly interesting, but which – in light of the evident significance of numbers – *had* to be central. In its context it indeed becomes so – almost an ethics about overcoming evil; also strikingly close to the philosophy of Heidegger. It states that evil, in so far as sometimes it is a means that is at hand, can simply be disposed of (*zur Seite legen*). Here we first need to take notice that a 'mean', as an instrument, is another word identical to liminality, or in-between-ness, as it is etymologically connected to 'mean' as the middle of something. This immediately gives an insight concerning instrumental rationality, heart of the sociological 'critique' of modernity since Weber, but goes beyond Weber in recognising (also in light of No.41), that such 'instrumental rationality' in a substantive sense is simply and by definition irrationality. Here Kafka adds that it is also evil; and so, making now the similar kind of inversion that was the case with the Paradise inside us meaning that we are therefore still inside Paradise, it means that the instrumentalisation of Being is evil itself. It is in this way, and through the emphasis placed at the 'hand', that it advances Heidegger's famous diagnosis of technology (Heidegger 1977). Thus this short and seemingly plain aphorism becomes an ethical manifesto: if evil has no substance, no being, it is merely an actor and mime in one sense and mere instrument in another, then the solution is simple: we need only to stop following or using it, putting it down and throwing it away. Offering one concrete interpretation, the noise proliferated by the media (a name again identical with the in-between, the heart of evil according to Kafka, though also the possibility to escape it) can be ended by turning it off; or, even better, not turning it on.

Thus, given that we identified in No.95 one of the cornerstones of the collection – a paradoxical cornerstone, as it identified the heart of evil; even twice paradoxical, as such heart is non-being, mere liminality – the immediately following aphorisms gain a potential significance as being at the heart of Kafka's redemptive message. They indeed deliver. Nos 96 and 97 offer a pair of paradoxes that illuminate each other. No.96 states that the joys of our life become torments, if we fail to follow the advice offered in No.95, and rise above the in-between; while No.97 asserts the opposite, that suffering in the here and now is beatitude in the other world – this other world being defined in the following No.98 as *cosmos*, followed by the decisive – and sole – critique of modernity in No.99. Thus we join, from a new angle, the analysis already completed.

It is also here that this chapter can be concluded, as following the internal logic of arguments we returned back to the starting question of the right way.

We only need to collect all relevant instances.

The right way

The explicit discussion of the way (*Weg*), after the introductory aphorism, is contained in three sets: Nos 15, 21 and 26/2; 38, 39a; and 76 and 104. The surprising element is that such references are not too many, and concentrate on the early part of the collection; as if somehow the concern with the 'way' became lost – or reformulated, as the introduction of the 'indestructible' and the analysis of No.95 above intimated.

Nos 15 and 21 are only minor characterisations of the modality of the way, and by implication, through this meaning, No.14 can also be included among them.

Such an inclusion is all the more relevant as No.26/2 only receives its meaning through references to the world and evil, contained in the immediately preceding and following ones (Nos 25, 28–9, and the series of deleted ones, analysed above), and also through No.22, in which the word 'way' does not appear. In this short – but, as we'll see, crucial – aphorism, however, none of the key words of the aphorisms appear; in fact, of the two nouns it contains only one appears in another aphorism, 94, which thus needs to be brought into the analysis as well.

The most important context, however, is elsewhere; and to identify this we need to return to evidence about Kafka's life. While the escape from his night-time demons worked for a long time, in a night in the middle of November, thus about two months after his arrival and a month after he started to write they returned, in the form of a mice-invasion which gave him tremendous trouble. As a November 1917 letter to Felix Weltsch makes it evident (Calasso 2005: 326), Kafka perceived this invasion as not simply bestial, but demonic; a perception made most evident in the word used for the sounds emitted by the mice, *pfeifen* 'piping', evoking the 'pied piper', one of the most famous German folktales. It is after this most significant interruption that, on 18 November, No.26 was penned down, where the term 'way' again does not appear, neither in the unselected notes immediately following No.27, though implied in both, and in close connection with No.22 – where the word *Weg* is spelt out most explicitly (twice in a single line) and significantly, giving an interpretation and bringing together all the others, in the added part.

Let's start the interpretation with No.22. This is most clearly a Nietzsche-inspired statement: the task is you yourself, says Kafka to himself; and there is no student, disciple or follower in sight. The two aphorisms jotted down after the mice-invasion further elaborate it: all the hideaways from this task are false; only one is true that does not hide away from the task, rather it offers a refuge which enables salvation – meaning not cosy personal escape, the one offered by the 'salvation religions', but completing the task, a *positive* task which is simply *given*; a givenness which does *not* implies an imposition, nor a mere command which Kafka in the first part of No.27 reserves for merely *negative* obligations, and which therefore can only be interpreted in the original and etymological sense as a *gift*.

All this becomes confirmed and rendered clearer through the added passage which, however, is problematic, confirming the lingering doubt that over time Kafka became more and more *distant* from the spirit in which the aphorisms were written; perhaps even more cynical. In some ways the meaning is the same, as it asserts that there *is* an aim, which could be assumed to be identical with the task; but here he denies the existence of a way, as what one believed was a way is redefined as hesitation (*zögern*). What could this mean?

The reaching of any aim, any goal means that one must find and *follow* some kind of way to reach it. Following, however, also implies some kind of imitation; and here it is important that a German word used by 'student' or 'disciple' is *Zögling*, having the same etymological origin in *ziehen* 'draw' as *zögern* 'follow'. The dilemma into which Kafka bumped here is the standard modern dilemma of *refusing* to follow anything or anybody, insisting about one's own absolute originality and singularity. But the aphorism can also be interpreted as Kafka actually realising the paradoxical absurdity of such a position: as, if one refuses to follow *any* way, then the goal cannot be reached. Thus such refusal poses again the starting point of the entire undertaking, the point that *thus* could not be included in the collection: should one follow the demons of the night? As formulated in the dilemma of the very first entry of the Notebook, 18 October 1917: '[f]ear from the night, or the no-night' (Kafka 1992, I: 29)

It also explains that, after this, the question of the way could not be discussed much further. The next, short series, Nos 38 and 39a, do not add anything substantial – No.38 is only a reformulation about the paradox of easiness, while No.39a, at that crucial juncture, as analysed before, only restates the given and unending nature of the task.

The question concerns whether the third group manages to take the argument further. Here the situation turns out to be particularly tricky. First, No.76 is a false path – not surprising in a search for the meaning of the 'way': the term *Weg* 'way' has no emphasis, and the aphorism is just about a hide-and-seek played between the question and the answer – as if telling the (re)searcher that he or she has nothing to find here. No.104, however, the second longest of all, is most important, and in some ways conclusive; the only, singular and central return to the problem of the 'way' after the aphorisms jotted down around the return of the mice-demons. The central question concerns not simply the way, but our freedom concerning this way – or *our* way – posed in terms of the 'free will' debate, centre of German theology and philosophy since Luther; the loss of the way for Germans, according to a famous poem by Auden, '1 September 1939'. At one level, the aphorism is an aporia. It starts by asserting three senses of free will, then claims first that they are the same and finally that not only free will does not exist, but even the 'will' has nothing to do with it.

Turning to the character of the – evidently non-free – road defined in No.104, it has a number of conclusive features. First, it indeed leads to somewhere definite, the only possible aim, which is finding ourselves, or being itself, *evidently* the condition of the Paradise, *evidently* through the indestructible in us; through a road which is extremely difficult and labyrinthine, and which touches upon every aspect of our lives. This aim is given; and our freedom only consists in accepting or refusing it, our task – which is not really a free choice, but a question of succeeding or failing.

Now we can, and indeed must, return to No.94, the only other containing any of the nouns of No.22, furthermore a most significant word for the 'road', as *task*. We must start by noticing that, according to the logic of our hypotheses concerning Kafka's concerns with numbers, such combination of 4 and 9 should be particularly significant; a way to combine the two central numbers of the different sets, 4 and 8 on one side, and 5 and 9 on the other; of which the largest, thus in a way possibly conclusive number is 98 – which indeed identifies, uniquely, the cosmos.

The finality of this aphorism can be seen in the fact that it (re)incorporates the arguments taken up in No.1 and No.109/2. It is about the self; the finding of the self, which for an artist coincides with an *ars poetica*, or the way to follow; and also formulates it through the metaphor of the circle, central for Kafka's self-defining short stories about the artist. But it is not just about the artist, as – in the context of the aphorisms through which we got there – the central issue at the heart of one's being is the inner core that was kept from the Golden Age and that can guide us back to Paradise. It also implies a return to *patience*, etymologically connected to the Greek term for 'experience' (*pathos*), implying a primordial *passivity* (a word also etymologically connected to *pathos*) in contrast to the frenetic and meaningless movement of permanent liminality, the modern Newtonian flux. This does not mean not doing anything, which is just another face of nihilism, through the identity of infinity and zero (here in movement), rather recognition of the primordial primacy of Being as given, thus a *gift*. So finding ourselves as something already given, as gifted in our inner essence, requires – of all virtues – nothing more than patience.

Here we might capture the ultimate paradox Kafka faced, and evidently could not resolve: given that any artist, in the sense of Plato's *Ion*, is not just an imitator, but an imitator of the imitators – can it give us insight into the nature of Being?

Notes

1. The critical edition, Calasso – who studied the MS – and Citati all claim that the collection (the *Gesamtkonvolut*) has 103 sheets (Calasso 2004: 11; Calasso 2005: 329; Citati 2007: 212; Kafka 1992, II: 48). However, the book as edited by Calasso, which aimed at faithfully reproducing the structure of Kafka's arrangement, in contrast to the previous editions that simply listed the aphorisms after each other, as they were in the original notebook has 105 pages, corresponding to the fact that they are numbered up to 109, with one extra (39a), two missing (64 and 89), and three dual-numbered (8/9, 11/12 and 70/71) all of which again results in 105 sheets. From the perspective of the 'hypermodern' novel offered in this book it is particularly striking that Rilke used the word 'notebook' in the title for *Malte*; thus, while the Zürau aphorisms are clearly not novelistic, there is yet a tight affinity between these two crucial works by these two Prague artist-thinkers.
2. Kafka first met Felice Bauer by the day five years before; 13 August 1917 was also the date of the planned Fatima appearance when the children could not be present as detained by the mayor of Ourém.
3. The sign /2 indicates that the aphorism is a late addition, at the time of collating.
4. This point leads to the theme of 'fairground capitalism' (see Szakolczai 2014a), which cannot be further pursued here. I'm also making use here of Brian Finucane's 2011 PhD thesis 'Unmasking Nietzsche: Exploring the Symbolism of the Death of God'.
5. This centrality also transpires through Dora Diamant: '[h]is search for what he called "the indestructible" was at the core of his being' (Diamant 2003: 12).
6. The word *Herr* is also used in No.29/2, but there it refers to the owner of dogs. While seemingly trivial, through the interpretation of Thomas Mann's 1918 story 'A Man and His Dog [*Herr und Hund*]' offered by Crescenzi (2011: 85–96), it might not be so.

Part III
After World War I
Hypermodernity as sacrificial carnival

7 Thomas Mann

Death in Venice and
Magic Mountain

Introduction: the *Magic Mountain* in context

The *Magic Mountain*, together with *Ulysses* and *Castle*, its exact contemporaries, is one of the greatest masterpieces of the twentieth century novel, having a status comparable to *Faust* or *Demons*. The three novels with their contrasts and similarities map the space on which the contemporary novel can be situated. Ulysses is never at home, always on the road, wandering (though in Joyce's novel only in Dublin), while the protagonists of the *Magic Mountain* are all fixed to one place, into a great alchemic incubator, which however is also not their home. The *Castle* combines both situations, as its hero K. is away from home, in a village having a closed, incubator-like atmosphere, where everybody else is formally 'at home', though nobody really is. The title locations of Mann's and Kafka's novels are the same, a 'mountain'; yet, while the action of *Magic Mountain* takes place in and near the sanatorium, in the *Castle* the 'castle' is never shown from the inside. The hypermodern novel is thus mapped in between the agoraphobic experience of an infinite space of eternal wondering and the claustrophobic experience of being enclosed in a single, tight spot, the two being united by the experience of never being at home, or unlimited homelessness, an experience stamped through hypermodernity on the entire planet.

In terms of its substance, the *Magic Mountain* is a masterpiece, read and appreciated by generations, an evergreen contemporary classic. Yet, it not only had detractors, including even Citati (2010), but generated controversies that radically questioned its merits. While Thomas Mann won the Nobel prize in 1929, it was for the *Buddenbrooks*, as a member of the Swedish Academy awarding the price loathed the *Magic Mountain*, founding it ' "a nihilistic, decadent, and demoralizing book" ' (as in Goldman 1992: 309). It is also situated at a unique juncture, being the 'eye of the needle' through which the novel passed, from Goethe, Dickens and Dostoevsky, the novels analysed in *Novels and the Sociology of the Contemporary* to the five novels discussed in this Part Three.

Thomas Mann started writing immediately after finishing *Death in Venice*, in late 1912, thus just when Hofmannsthal and Kafka took up *Andreas* and *Amerika*. Yet, while both these, just as the other two novels Kafka started while Mann was struggling with his one before, during and after World War I, were left incomplete,

Magic Mountain was brought to completion, as Mann managed to re-tune the book after the war experiences, incorporating them in a vision of the 'new world' (Crescenzi 2010). Such differences of course are due to all kinds of inexplicable singularities; yet, there were three basic and general reasons behind Mann's success. To begin with, Mann managed to exteriorise, as the theme of the novel, the pervasive condition of internal split and inertia that prevented the completion of the novels by Hofmannsthal and Kafka as an existential pathology dominating modern Western civilisation. Second, he gave this collective illness a name, melancholy. Finally, he found a particularly good guide in Dürer, through the works of Giehlow and Bertram, the latter being a close friend, both of whom for various reasons became forgotten, thus rendering all but impossible a proper appreciation of the novel.[1]

Dürer

'Melencolia I' is one of the three famous large engravings made by Dürer in 1513–14, the other two being 'The Knight, Death and Devil' and 'St Jerome in His Cell'. While the significance of these three images, just as their importance for Nietzsche, Wagner, Weber and Mann, among others, is widely recognised, their understanding requires some attention to context. This involves a genealogy of modernity, in particular the relative roles played by the Renaissance and the Reformation, more concretely, the extremely liminal nature of the years just before 1517, or Luther's act. The central event is the War of the League of Cambrai (1508–16), background condition to a series of developments defining modern thought and culture. These include writings, like Machiavelli's *Prince* and More's *Utopia*, which together span the space in which modern political philosophy was born, or the *Christian Prince* by Erasmus, model for the modern concern with education and civility;[2] and a series of visionary paintings, including the apocalyptic 'Deluge' drawings of Leonardo, the Marian visions of Raphael ('Sistine Madonna' and 'Madonna di Foligno') or the *Isenheim Altarpiece* by Grünewald. The three engravings of Dürer can best be understood as striking visions of the incipient modern world.

They also fit into a context mapped by Dürer's life. It includes his two trips to Italy (1494–5 and 1505–7), and three sets of visionary images, depicted before, in between and after these trips. The first are the 1494 illustrations of Sebastian Brand's *Ship of Fools*, which would be considered by Michel Foucault (1961) as a uniquely powerful symbol of the late Renaissance; the second a 1498 series about the Apocalypse, the most famous image being the 'The Four Horsemen'; the third being the three 1513–14 engravings, digesting all previous experiences and condensing them into three archetypal images.

The unique specificity of 'Melencolia I' can be brought out by analysing the three engravings together. The lonely, relentless knight and the monk-scholar embody the two central figures, and values, of the closing Middle Ages (Huizinga 1990: 63). The novelty, thus premonition of modernity *as a difference,* is contained in the enigmatic third figure, which threatens the first two by dissolving from inside their seemingly unshakeable inner strength and resolution; destroying the indestructible.

The difference is visible through the contrast within what is shared by all three images. There are four such basic similarities. The first concerns the presence of a dog-like animal in each image, identifying the prophetic nature of the image, given the association of dogs with prophecy (Crescenzi 2011: 85–96). The second is the intense, fixed glance of each figure, underlining the visionary character of the images, but also alluding to something problematic in such a rigid way of seeing; particularly so in 'Melencholia I', where inner force is about to be dissolved in aimlessness. This is marked by the instruments of knowledge being dispersed in the foreground of the image (Ibid.: 136), strikingly similar to Raphael's contemporary 'St Cecilia', but lacking its transcendent serenity. The third and most obvious presence is an hour-glass. Beyond measuring time and alluding to death, it captures in a more general sense the connection between consciousness and care.

The fourth common feature is the most innocuous, almost imperceptible by its triviality, yet most fundamental: all three figures are *sitting*, though differently. The knight is still moving, as sitting on a horse; Jerome is in his cell, but surrounded by light and exuding serenity; the figure of melancholy, however, is utterly lost, inflected with inertia (Crescenzi 2011: 27). Through it the previous figures of the series, representing central values of European culture, become redefined as pathological, steps in a sequence of increasing existential loneliness; though, as a reverse move, the third figure thus gains value as lonely genius, gathering all strength to transcend this condition.

The novel, according to Crescenzi, diagnoses melancholy at the heart of the modern condition. While Mann follows a series of important figures in modern culture, from Shakespeare and Cervantes through Goethe and Dostoevsky, the proposition of centrality requires further arguments. This will be done in three steps. First, and most evidently, melancholy is not simply an individual condition, but sign of deeper social, even civilisational pathologies. Second, while it is clearly a troublesome condition, it is also a paradoxical *anti*-illness, a melancholic person being not simply 'sick', but literally and technically a 'non-sick sick', thus extremely difficult to cure. Finally, melancholy will be identified as the par excellence existential feeling corresponding to permanent liminality, thus central for a world moving towards such a state.

Melancholy as anti-illness

Melancholy tests the limits between illness and health, body and spirit, individual and social order. In our days it is called 'depression' or 'bipolarism' – a particularly revealing word. While various drugs are available to treat its symptoms, it is by no means certain that modern medicine offers a better understanding of this condition than classical efforts to cure the human spirit or the soul.

The characterisation of melancholy at a first level is simple: it is to feel sad or gloomy without a reason; it is to consider life itself as a burden; it is a loss of being. Melancholy is often described as mourning when nobody died. As it is a condition without an evident reason, it involves a paradox, and a complicated one. Melancholy at face value is a psychological condition; yet, at the same time it has evident social correlates, as the illness is contagious, though without a virus as its source. For centuries it hardly appears, and then suddenly spreads as an epidemic. A particularly strong outbreak hit England in the seventeenth century, captured in Robert Burton's famous *The Anatomy of Melancholy* (1621); but the most important efforts to analyse and overcome melancholy, by Pascal and Kierkegaard, were also connected to their time and place, the same applying to Thomas Mann. Melancholy proliferates in moments of transition; it is a disease of transitions, including transitions to modernity, especially the transitionality of modernity.

The connections between melancholy and modernity were studied by two important contemporary social theorists, Wolf Lepenies (1992) and Harvie Ferguson (1995). Both being sociologists, concerned with renewing sociology by restoring the centrality of understanding for the discipline, liberating it from positivism and critique and profoundly interested in novels (Lepenies 1988; Ferguson 2010), they place emphasis on the social as opposed to individual character of the disease.

For Ferguson, melancholy is the 'most pervasive and significant experience' of modernity, which became 'almost indistinguishable from being itself' (1995: i, xiii). Even further, 'for modern society [. . .] melancholy alone has "depth", [gaining a] "presence" which lends expression to the profound unease within, if not disease of, existence' (Ibid.: xiv). It is, however, a most paradoxical 'depth' of 'being', as it had already been defined as loss of being, and as it has no depth whatsoever, being identical to continuous change, metamorphosis or flux. Using a particularly important metaphor, Ferguson characterises melancholy as being 'a modern Proteus, transforming itself with every twist and turn of existence' (Ibid.: xiii), identical to flux, or continuous instability (Lepenies 1992: 20; see also Crescenzi 2011: 138). Yet, for anything we assert about melancholy, the opposite is true, almost by definition, given its bipolarity. Beyond permanent flux and instability, modern melancholy is also symptom of an excess or 'surplus of order' (Lepenies 1992: 47). Ferguson lists a whole series of such bipolarities, including the switch from 'lethargic immobility to perpetual useless movement, from darkness to transparent heaviness, or from cosmic dislocation to inner loneliness' (Ferreira 1995: 537). Such bipolarities have a common root in a unique experience of the void – which again is a non-experience, as only what is real, concrete and existing can be experienced: one cannot experience the void, just as one cannot have an experience of one's own death. Such a sense of void has repeatedly been identified both as a central manifestation of modern melancholy, defining its novelty, and as one of its origins. This void is a central consequence of modern science, as for classical thinking, but even up to Leibniz, existence and the world were conceived of in terms of plenitude (Ferguson 1995: 12; see Horvath 2013a, 2015); a change that can be traced to Hobbes abandoning the Augustinian separation between the two cities (Lepenies 1992: 20), but that is already prefigured in the ideas of Cusanus (Ferguson 1995: 11–12).[3] This void is present, with the pervasive absence it spreads, in the experiences of solitude and boredom, two central aspects of modern melancholy (Ferguson 1995; Lepenies 1992: 62–6, 86–130), at one level direct consequences of the spreading of such void, but at another level purposefully spread by the technique of reducing individual lives to the pursuit of objective private interests, or 'passionate interests' (Latour and Lépinay 2009; see also Horvath 2010, 2013a), – another paradox, as interests, being by definition manifestations of in-betweenness,[4] cannot be objective. Isolating individuals through inducing them to follow their private inklings is an old trick, stemming ' "from the clown's repertoire" ' (from Benjamin's analysis of Poe, as in Lepenies 1992: 220), thus bringing together not simply theatre and knowledge, but technologised science and the clown act. The central consequence of this unholy alliance is the spread of secularism, at once symptom and agent of modern melancholy and its void, melancholy being both a key feature of modern, secular individualism and symptom of 'the secular world of endless and fruitless diversions', which reveals a 'boundless spiritual longing' and yet can be diverted because it is vain (Ferguson 1995: xiv).[5]

Not surprisingly, apologues of secular modernity find this diagnosis particularly inconvenient, while its best analysts are the outspoken opponents of modern secularism, Pascal and Kierkegaard. Melancholy is 'an embarrassment to modern thought', where 'every effort is made to overcome [it] by "rationalization" ' (Ferguson 1995: xiv). Yet, such efforts are pointless, as melancholy is incommunicable (Ibid.: 3), even unnamable (Ibid.: xii); so '[t]he Enlightenment project foundered upon melancholy' (Ferguson 1995: xiv).

Pascal and Kierkegaard stated as much way before, so listening to them could have saved a lot of ink, and even more blood. For Pascal, melancholy is a sign of lost innocence, thus rooted in the Fall (Ferguson 1995: 12), a main consequence of the modern predilection for *divertissement*. The outcome is the spectacle of modern life as melancholy: a ' "vast, infinite ocean of incredible madness and folly" ' (as in Ferguson 1995: 22). Not surprisingly, together with Dürer's 'Ship of Fools' Foucault chose Pascal as another symbolic source of modern madness, starting his Preface to *Folie et déraison* by a quote from Pascal; a passage also selected by Hofmannsthal in his *Book of Friends*.

For Ferguson, Kierkegaard's work centrally revolves around the diagnosis and study of melancholy, making him 'the most important, and most typical, psychologist of the modern era' (Ferguson 1995: i); a view shared by Béla Hamvas and Karl Mannheim. Through Kierkegaard we can understand how something that was merely a 'transient "colour" ' has become the defining tone of [modern society's] every experience' (Ibid.: xiii), thus making him a first diagnost of modern permanent liminality. It is due to such extension and permanentisation that melancholy from sadness without reason becomes despair, another central term for Kierkegaard, a condition that – even etymologically – is identical to being without hope.

The ultimate, and deepest, paradox of melancholy, however, also carries the seeds of its own (self-)overcoming. Identifying melancholy, just as nihilism according to Nietzsche, can only be done through one's own awareness of one's condition; yet, immediate self-knowledge is a central source of melancholy and unhappy consciousness (Ferguson 1995: 26). The solution is simple and crucial: far from signalling hopelessness, recognising melancholy is also a major sign for hope; while it is not a proof for the existence of god (something impossible, but also unnecessary), it is rather an infallible sign that God *cares*. Melancholy is a warning for us to recognise that something is not going right, but also that we are not abandoned by God (Ibid.: 28–30); that we have to think and care about our worries, a complex task encompassed by the manifold meanings of Hungarian *gond* (meaning 'care' and 'worry', but also 'think'; thus, in Hungarian 'to think' *gondolkodik* and 'to care' *gondoskodik* are practically identical verbs).

Melancholy for Mann

In Crescenzi's reading, melancholy is *the* central concern of the *Magic Mountain*. Hans Castorp, the hero, is clearly melancholic, but so is everybody else in the sanatorium, where melancholy is a universal condition, so the 'magic mountain' is identical to a 'mountain of melancholy' (Crescenzi 2011: 67). Through this, Mann offers a diagnosis of modernity, following Bertram's joint reading of Dürer and Nietzsche (Ibid.: 48–51), as a loss of virtue and vigour, resulting in a condition of 'total inactivity' (Ibid.: 41–2), or an incapacity to live (Ibid.: 81–4; 2010: lxix); a 'genuine stigma [*vero e proprio stigma*] of Western civilisation' (Crescenzi 2010: lxiv). For this, through the work of Carl du Prel, another major source of Mann, Crescenzi introduces the term 'somnambulism' (Ibid.: 157), while Michael Neumann uses an even more striking terminology: according to him, in the section 'Hippe' in Chapter 4 a particularly striking childhood reminiscence of Hans Castorp is presented as a 'quasi shamanic experience', where Mann 'refashioned himself to descriptions of religious possession and somnambulism' (Neumann 2010: xxxiii). Through the sanatorium Mann searches out a cure for this civilisational pathology (Crescenzi 2011: 80), using the 'seismographic sensibility' of the hero (Ibid.: xxxvi).

It is here that the figure of Karl Giehlow (1863–1913) as a guide to Dürer becomes important. In 1903–4, thus just the moment when Max Weber wrote his *Protestant Ethic* essays, as an effort overcome his personal depression, Giehlow wrote and published a series of essays on Dürer's 'Melencolia I' and its sources. Giehlow had an anomalous career and died young, before completing his work, enabling Panofsky and Saxl to appropriate his unpublished manuscript and publish his ideas under their own name (Crescenzi 2011: 22–7). Apart from the not negligible moral dilemma, in the process the central ideas of Giehlow became disregarded. Giehlow's central idea concerned the link between words and images, based on his study of Egyptian hieroglyphs (Ibid.: 55–7). His work pioneered the joint study of image and knowledge, art and science, anticipating Francis Yates (1966) and Michel Foucault (1966). As Giehlow developed his work after he moved to Vienna in 1898, he could be considered as the anti-Mach.

Dürer's image was already central for *Death in Venice* (Crescenzi 2011: 27–9), while the 1912–15 draft of the *Magic Mountain* shows the importance of the Dürer-Giehlowian theme of melancholy for the novel, melancholy being one of the central connections between these two works (Ibid.: 121–1). The influence of Giehlow can be shown in those central concerns of *Magic Mountain*, where Mann goes beyond art historians, whether Wölfflin (who read Giehlow) or Panofsky. For Mann, according to Crescenzi, the primary aim of education should not be to think 'rationally', rather to learn how to see (*imparare a vedere*, title of a key chapter in Crescenzi, 2011: 129–38), as if following Rilke and anticipating Hamvas. Furthermore, this is no mere academic matter, but a central cause of the pathology of Western civilisation, as the kind of technologico-rational thinking dominating modernity is the way of death. Central for this diagnosis is the chapter on the cinema (the 'Bioscope-Theatre'), this technological projection of moving images, which 'pretends to show life, yet transforms the entertainment (*divertimento*) of the masses into a spectacle of death' (Ibid.: 136). Together with the macabre vision of radiographic images in Behrens's study (and closely recalling Goethe's joint problematisation of microscope and telescope), it helps to understand the 'hermetic and magical nature of Western civilisation', which pretends 'to look outside the realm of physical reality' in order to find its 'spiritual essence, unlimited and eternal' (Ibid.: 137). This reveals the 'melancholy essence of Western culture' in the intimate connections between art and technology (Ibid.). Technology demolishes everything that is concrete and real in order to render the ever smaller fragments available for re-aggregation in the 'public' interest, into new forms conjured up by art. Everything must permanently be 'in transition', serving the 'permanent revolution' conjured up by Joseph Schumpeter (1883–1950) and Leon Trotsky (1879–1940), exact contemporaries, connected through the medium of technology and the 'public'.

Educating Hans Castorp thus means to overcome the disease of melancholy by recognising this link, going jointly beyond the fixity of death and the flux of becoming – only another form of death – and realise, *by learning how to see*, that 'it is life, and not death, which is the true mystery of existence', thus restoring life 'from death to its more authentic condition, its true metaphysical form' (Ibid.: 138), evoking the Resurrection. This is also where the erotic story in the novel would play its role, confirmed in the message of its last word, love.

Death in Venice

'Death in Venice' is not simply one of the best-known short stories of Thomas Mann. It is his 'greatest story' (Luke 1998: vii); even further, it is 'possibly the most artistically perfect of all Mann's works' (Ibid: viii). It was also one of his most popular works, becoming a great success immediately after its first 1912 journal publication, so a book version appeared already in 1913. It also accompanied the writer throughout his life: the theme returned, in the form of a parody, a quarter of a century later, with 'The Beloved Returns'; then at the age of 75, with an essay on Michelangelo's erotic poetry; finally, there are clear allusions to this work in Mann's very last writing, a tribute to *Billy Budd* (Heilbut 1996: 262–6, 557, 592).

The story is also a clear illustration of Mann's strong reliance on autobiographical elements in his works, fitting into the series of his works most clearly inspired by his life, starting with the 1897 'The Joker' (*Der Bajazzo*, or the clown), and continuing with 'Tonio Kröger' (1903, a self-portrait of the artist as young man). Autobiographical reflections, however, can have odd side-effects: in between 'Tonio Kröger', which followed his highly acclaimed novel, *Buddenbrooks*, winning him the Nobel prize, and 'Death in Venice', Mann failed to produce any significant work, while soon after 'Death in Venice' he would start *The Magic Mountain*.

'Death in Venice', however, was much more than autobiographically inspired; nothing was invented in it, with '[v]irtually every detail [. . .] based on fact' (Heilbut 1996: 247). In his autobiographical sketches and notebooks Mann tells us that every single striking detail in the story, including the most bizarre figures – the shipmen, the foppish old man or the sinister singer – happened as it was described in the story (Luke 1998: xxxv), as ' "a series of curious circumstances and impressions combined with [his] subconscious search for something new [came to] give birth to a productive idea" ' (as in Heilbut 1996: 246; see also Goldman 1988: 187; 254, fn.38).

In his excellent Introduction Luke takes the point a step further, by making explicit the striking manner how 'the strange complex of real-life experiences on his Venetian journey, this uncanny coming-together of seemingly significant and interconnected events' gave an extremely direct inspiration for Mann to the story, as if the events themselves were guided 'by some unwitting and magical authorial command' (Luke 1998: xxxvi–vii). For a proper understanding, we need to recur to Plato: to *Ion* and the metaphor of the rings that transmit the divine inspiration, and to the *Laws* and the metaphor of the puppets and the strings. When writing the novel Mann clearly perceived his own 'in-between', middle or mediating – if not outright 'medium' – situation: he acted upon Aschenbach, the hero of the novel, just as he himself was hardly more than a puppet of those peculiar, uncanny 'forces' that evidently guided his strange real-life travel-experience to Venice.

The broader context of the novel was also significant, both concerning the world at large and Mann's own situation. The spring and summer of 1911 were pregnant with threats of the immediate outbreak of a major war, so represented a political crisis; while Mann was in an ever deepening writer's crisis since completing 'Tonio Kröger'. This was the context in which he travelled to Venice; and the experiences he encountered there, in his real life, helped him to overcome this crisis, as if exorcising his evil spirits by writing 'Death in Venice'. In fact, the situation was even more uncanny, recalling Goethe's experience of writing the 'Aegean feast' in *Faust Two*. In order to get out of his writer's crisis Mann was planning a story about Goethe who in his old age, in 1821, fell so much in love in Marienbad with a 17-year-old girl, Ulrike von Levetzow, that two years later, he even proposed marriage (Heilbut 1996: 246; Goldman 1988: 187). It was this project that he set aside, due to his Venice experience (Goldman 1988: 187).

Writing took place from July 1911 to July 1912 (Heilbut 1996: 259), so almost perfectly coincided with the 37th year of his life.

While Mann was candid about the close correspondence between events told in the story and the actual details of his Venice trip, he did not reveal the same about the eventual basis of the striking visions contained in the story. The reasons for his shying away are evident: even as it was written, and in spite of its great public success, the work was submitted to consistent attack on the part of critics and younger writers,[6] so much so that already by 1915 Mann backtracked and claimed that the work was solely a parody, even outright a caricature (Heilbut 1996: 250, 262); a move all the less intelligible as humour was clearly absent from the work (Ibid.: 262). It seems most likely that while writing the piece Mann experienced genuine visions, the ones described in the work, which remained with him so strongly that this would contribute to some of the most striking scenes of *The Magic Mountain* as well. Such visionary elements of the writing process would also explain the strong cinematic qualities of the work (Ibid.: 250–1).

The manner in which the context of events is presented in the story both reproduces and elaborates on the real-life context of Mann's experiences. The background at world scale is the looming war, the unhealthy state of things at large, which would protrude in crucial moments into the storyline; and there are also allusions to the unhappiness of Aschenbach, protagonist of the story, about his own writings. The most important background to the story, however, is provided by Aschenbach's character, described in the second section.

Being a writer, Aschenbach is presented through his writings, especially three main novels. These include a prose epic on Frederick the Great; a novel called *Maya*, a name recalling several *femme fatale* figures, most notably Goya's famous painting, just as the Hindu term for illusion; and a tale entitled 'The miserable' (*Ein Elender*), with evident allusion to Victor Hugo (the German translation of *Les misérables* is *Die Elenden*). The list also contains works that Mann actually failed to write. The single most important characteristic of Aschenbach is his resistance, determination and moral commitment, or will-power, a kind of intellectual heroism, making St Sebastian his favourite saint and him ignore the playful aspects of existence. Emotional ties, especially women, are absent from his life: his wife died young, and he cultivated a distance if not alienation from his daughter.

This is the context in which in an afternoon, after a hard morning's work and unable to get some rest our hero goes for a strolling and something happens to him that he would not have ever imagined, best captured as an epiphany of Hermes. The manner in which this happened is of utmost interest, as even minor details possess significance. Aschenbach decided to end his stroll and take a tram back home. At that moment, suddenly time stood still; the city that so far was buzzing with noise and movement suddenly became deserted and silent; and the tram did not arrive. Time became liminal, and at the same time the place revealed multiple liminal characteristics. The rails of the tram were pointing towards Schwabing, famous centre of bohemian life in Bavaria (underlined by Achenbach's mother being the daughter of a music director from Bohemia); while the tram-stop was at a cemetery, near the walls of the stonemasons's yards, full of crosses and tomb-parts ready for sale, and with the mortuary chapel across. This chapel was made in Byzantine style, continuing the associations between music and the bohemian life, incorporating the origins of *commedia dell'arte*, with a number of mystical inscriptions and two 'apocalyptic beasts' guarding its steps (Mann 1998: 198). It was above them, a context uncanny yet grotesque, that a man appeared. Aschenbach immediately identified something unusual (*nicht ganz gewöhnliche*) in his appearance (*Erscheiung*; Mann 1996: 8), and not just because he was visibly a foreigner, though his outfit incorporated traditional Bavarian elements. He was red-haired, with pimples and small lips rendering his teeth visible, turning his expression into a grimace, 'as if he had some permanent facial deformity' (Mann 1998: 199). Standing in the portico, just above the apocalyptic beasts, his posture seemed bold, even wild and threatening; and he returned the writer's gaze which such an intensity that Aschenbach had to turn away and start strolling along the fence, still waiting for the tram. Note Mann's claim that everything actually happened as described in the novel, including '"the wanderer at the Northern cemetery in Munich"' (Luke 1998: xxxv).

It was during this stroll, in the direction of Schwabing, and once he – quite strangely – immediately forgot about the appearance, that a strange kind of feeling literally overtook him (the term used is *Anfall*, which can be translated as fit, attack, or seizure; Mann 1996: 9–10; 1998: 199). It was a restless 'desire to travel [*Reiselust*]', which 'presented itself [. . .] with intensely passionate and indeed hallucinatory force, turning his craving into vision' (Mann 1998: 199). Here the English translator, as if frightened by so much 'mysticism', adds the clause that it was only a product of imagination due to the hard morning's work, not present in the original.

Aschenbach's vision had a strange combination of attractiveness and repulsiveness, showing at the same time 'the wonders and terrors of the manifold earth' (Ibid.). Once the vision faded away he resumed his stroll and for long pondered on the pros and cons of travelling, at first resisting the impulse, but at the end making up his mind to go for the trip. At this moment time, so far suspended, as if for an eternity, resumed its course, the tram arrived and the stop was suddenly filled with passengers; only the stranger disappeared, as if vanishing into thin air (Ibid.: 201–2).

Aschenbach took a train to Trieste and then a ship to a small island near Pola. Not at ease there, it occurred to him that he should go to Venice, so travelled back to Pola and took the first boat to Venice. Two instances are of particular importance here. The first is a conscious play with not spelling out the name of Venice, only alluding to Aschenbach finding the proper destination, as if Mann wanted to force the reader to guess the only city in the world attuned to his vision experience. The second is a striking coincidence, as Trieste was the city where James Joyce was living and would start writing *Ulysses*, a novel paralleling *The Magic Mountain*; and before moving to Trieste in March 1905 Joyce spent half a year in Pola.

When buying his ticket to Venice the first in a series of extremely peculiar encounters happened to Aschenbach, rendering even more vexing Mann's claim that this happened just as described in the novel. The moment he arrived on the ship he was grabbed by a 'grubby hunchback seaman' who was 'grinning obsequiously' and led him to 'an artificially lit cave-like cabin' inside the ship where, with his cap askew and smoking a cigarette, 'sat a goat-bearded man with the air of an old-fashioned circus director and a slick caricatured business manner' (Mann 1998: 210). So after the Hermes-like figure in Munich, we have first a Victor Hugo-like grotesque gnome and then a devil-looking-alike character, closely recalling Diaghilev. This latter made particularly strange, hypnotic and distracting movements, acting in a great hurry when nobody was around, as if he were trying to make it sure that the traveller does not reconsider his destination.

Soon after the ship departed another strange character grabbed Aschenbach/Mann's attention. In the company of particularly high-spirited young men there was a fake youth: while mimicking others, the wrinkles in his face and a false teeth revealed a 'dandified' old man, leaving a particularly distasteful impression. This bizarre figure turned out to be the fourth strange guide – as many tricksters – for Aschenbach, as watching the man gave him the idea that something not right is bound to happen; that 'the world was undergoing a dreamlike alienation [*träumerische Entfremdung*], becoming increasingly deranged and bizarre' (Mann 1996: 23; 1998: 211). At this moment two things happened in quick succession. First, the thought occurred to him that in order to arrest this process he should cover his face, and thus take a new look at things. The gesture is particularly revealing for a trip to Venice, as it mimed the taking up of a mask – and was indeed the right advice that might have saved Aschenbach from his fate.[7] Second, however, he was prevented in thinking through the idea as at this very second the ship started to move, diverting his attention.

The trip turned out to be a strange experience, unusual for his trips to Venice, and particularly liminal: the sky was damp and grey, everything was enveloped in thick mist and fog, creating an unbroken horizon, surrounding him with a complete circle and producing an eerie impression, as 'in empty, unarticulated space our mind also loses its sense of time and we enter the twilight of the incommensurable [*wir dämmern im Ungemessenen*]' (1996: 24) The gestures of the strange figures around him became dreamlike, and he fell asleep.

While hoping that by his arrival the city would show its usual, sunny face, it did not happen, and the same scenery would receive him as during his departure and travel: sky and sea were dull, even leaden, while the foppish old man got into a particularly undignified state, as he drank too much and could no longer control himself. All this reinforced his earlier impressions about the state of affairs, the world 'slightly but uncontrollably sliding into some kind of bizarre and grotesque derangement' (1998: 213). His arrival to Venice, this most unreal of cities (*die unwahrscheinlichste der Städte*), to which one should only come by the sea (1996: 26, 1998: 213), turned out to be a genuine *adynaton* experience.

All this got Aschenbach again distracted, and before he could realise what was going on he was handed over to another trickster guide, a gondolier taking him from the port. He was soon enwrapped in reflections, in another liminal trip in the fog, on the strange character of the gondola, comparable in its blackness to a coffin, evoking death, an impression reinforced by the eerie silence and mist and fog, yet its armchair providing the 'most voluptuous' and at the same time 'most enervating', thus again death-like seating in the world (1998: 214). Thus, before Aschenbach could come to his senses, the gondolier was taking him not where he wanted, the *vaporetto* to the hotel, but directly to the hotel, producing the uncomfortable experience of not managing to have his will even in this simple case being only heightened by the character of the gondolier – a displeasing man with a brutal, evidently non-Italian face, talking insolently (Ibid.: 215). Thus, the different guides not so much help Aschenbach, but come out of the blue in order to take possession of him at a moment when his will became weak – while his central character trait was will-power.

Upon his arrival, soon another liminal experience takes hold of Aschenbach: solitude. This is just as fundamental for the story as it was different this time from his actual experiences, as Mann was accompanied to Venice by his wife and children. This is the context in which another guide appears on the scene, most different from the previous, bizarre trickster-like characters: Tadzio, a 14-year-old boy of singular grace, belonging to a Polish aristocratic family. The first characterisation of his attraction both to the boy and his family is particularly telling. The family consisted of three adolescent girls and the slightly younger boy, led by a governess, whose attitude was 'cool and poised', her hairstyle and dress manifesting that 'simplicity which is the governing principle of taste in circles where piety is regarded as one of the aristocratic values' (Ibid.: 220). Even their movements, the way they entered the dining room, had a certain air around which was not remarkable in any particular way, yet 'had been carried out with such explicitness, with such a strongly accented air of discipline, obligation and self-respect, that Aschenbach felt strangely moved' (Ibid.: 221). The only moment when they almost lost their composure was when coming close to a Russian family, whom they handled with hostility, disdain, even open contempt.

Aschenbach's attention is soon focused on the young boy who captivated him, since the first moment with his perfect, god-like beauty and grace, comparable only to the best of classical Greek statues, recalling the graceful movement of the *Boy Extracting a Thorn* (Ibid.: 220). Aschenbach could not help but contemplate this beauty, which soon developed into an obsession. That this had much to do with the heightened liminal conditions of his trip is underlined by a striking image which followed his reflections on his Venice experiences, culminating in recognising the reason for his profound longing for the sea: the need to escape daily drudgery and tedious complexity, and just 'lie hidden on the bosom of the complex and the tremendous', following his 'longing for the inarticulate and the immeasurable, for eternity, for nothingness' (Ibid.: 224). At that very moment 'the horizontal line of the sea-shore was suddenly intersected by a human figure, and when he had retrieved his gaze from limitless immensity and concentrated it again, he beheld the beautiful boy, coming from the left and walking past him across the sand' (Ibid.). From then his infatuation would only grow, as when contemplating his figure, rising out of the sea as a young god, he recalled mythical and poetic images of a primeval age; but it would soon conflict with another feeling increasingly getting hold of him: the stuffy, humid, foul air of Venice was no good for him; he needed to leave.

After days of hesitation Aschenbach finally made up his mind and was set to depart. Everything was arranged, with the taxi waiting to take him to the station; yet, he was delaying his departure, and when in the last minute he left the hotel, his baggage somehow got sent to the wrong address, so he had to return. This again produced a highly liminal experience: a combination of departure and return, a sense of new adventure, with a strange, wild joy about the failure to leave, to flee, to cling to his last piece of will-power and reason: an 'unbelievably strange an experience it was [. . .] like a dream in its bizarre comedy [*komisch traumartiges Abenteuer*]'; especially as he had to conceal 'under a mask of resigned annoyance the anxiously exuberant excitement of a truant schoolboy' (1996: 47; 1998: 232; alluding to the infantilising aspect of the mask).

His dizzying return to Venice was followed by a reflection and a vision. The reflection finally made him understand why he had such a strong attachment to Venice. While anywhere he went, his work and duties had the better of him, it was only in Venice that he could genuinely relax and leave his routine with good conscience: 'Only this place enchanted [*verzauberte*] him, relaxing his will, making him happy' (1996: 50). Another vision came to him next day, a charming (*reizend*) vision this time, on the seashore, after again contemplating the beauty of the boy; including an old plane tree, near Athens, at a sacred place, the tickling of a stream and the music of crickets; and Socrates walking with Phaedrus, instructing him in desire and virtue, and arguing about the centrality of Beauty over Reason, Virtue or Truth, as Beauty alone of these can be directly perceived (1998: 238–9).

While the vision instigated Aschenbach to write, the work did not go well and he would soon be disturbed by signs around him indicating a trouble more important than his personal problems with unhealthy air: Venice was evidently infected by an epidemics. From this moment, the central dilemma of the story was displaced from Aschenbach's struggle with himself to the parallel progress of two infections: the infection of the city with plague, and Aschenbach's infection with an obsessive and absurd love for the boy. The terminology of infection is explicit in Mann, and the parallel infections show a strange dynamics: while Aschenbach tries to confirm his doubts, this is difficult due to the irresponsible game of the authorities who – in order to secure the income from tourism – hide the facts, in complicity with his hotel manager who is identified as 'trickster' (*Schleicher*; also meaning 'hypocrite') (1996: 68; 1998: 250). The more his suspicions are confirmed, the more he abandons himself, ignoring any sense of shame, to the open courting of the boy, leaving himself prey to the infection, which would eventually kill him on the seaside.

A crucial moment in this process, the most striking scene in the novel is another bizarre figure leading a Neapolitan band of street singers ('beggar virtuosi') performing under the hotel terrace. He was lean and red-haired, with a brutal face, striking a 'posture of insolent bravado'; a mountebank, half pimp and half actor, having neither voice nor musical talent, yet stealing the show 'with a mimic gift and remarkable comic verve [*komischer Energie*]' (1996: 68; 1998: 251). His act was hilariously entertaining, yet also upsetting and even dangerous: '[t]he actual words of his song were merely foolish, but in his presentation, with his grimaces and bodily movements, his way of winking suggestively and lasciviously licking the corner of his mouth, it had something indecent and vaguely offensive about it' (1998: 252). This applied particularly for the way he sang the refrain, every time performing 'a grotesque march round the scene', with Aschenbach noticing 'that this suspect figure seemed to be carrying his own suspect atmosphere about with him as well' (1998: 253). The reception of his antics was revealing. The public, in particular the Russians, responded with wild laughter and applause, failing to realise how much all of them were made fun of by the singer. In his increasingly liminal state Aschenbach was almost carried away, his facial features being distorted into a painful 'rictus-like smile' (1998: 251), while Tadzio looked at this scene of debauchery with distraught attention and remote curiosity, in a posture of 'innate and inevitable grace' (1998: 251–2).

After the show he led the collection of money, and in doing so changed his character: '[s]aucy as his performance had been, up here he was humility itself' (1998: 253). Aschenbach became increasingly uneasy about the events: '[r]emoval of the physical distance between the entertainer and decent folk always causes, however great one's pleasure has been, a certain embarrassment' (Ibid.). Eventually, the band gave a bonus number, in which the performance became even more exaggerated, 'with such authenticity that it was infectious and communicated itself to the audience', where the singer 'nearly burst with what was no longer laughing but shrieking', which turned out to be ever more hilarious, until the entire public – except for Aschenbach and Tadzio – became infected (Ibid.: 254). When the troupe was leaving, he continued his act, even mocking a collusion with the gateway – but the moment he got out, 'he suddenly discarded the mask of comic underdog, uncoiled like a spring to his full height, insolently stuck out his tongue at the hotel guests on the terrace and slipped away into the darkness' (Ibid.: 255).

From this premonitory scene onwards events took a dark turn and quickly precipitated towards the end. Aschenbach finally confirmed his suspicions: Venice is hit by a plague. Yet, he fails to leave, fails even to inform the Polish family, becoming an accomplice, joining the great process of undifferentiation, so characteristic of plagues (Girard 1972), which by now has been completed, with a series of identities established between the complicity of public authorities and private entrepreneurs, the general public and comic entertainers, and finally between all of them and Aschenbach, who should have maintained his stand as cultural authority, and yet cascaded head over heals into moral and intellectual debauchery – as made clear by Mann. Not surprisingly, this is followed by another vision: a terrible, apocalyptic nightmare, returning in a crucial scene of *The Magic Mountain*, born out of a sense of guilt and complicity, the exhilarating freedom of chaos (Mann 1998: 259–60). It was not a dream, rather a 'bodily and mental experience', that indeed overtook Aschenbach during sleep, with his will being disarmed and his soul being scene of events that 'irrupted into it from outside, violently defeating his resistance – a profound, intellectual resistance – as they passed through him, and leaving his whole being, the culture of a lifetime, devastated and destroyed' (Ibid.: 259). The dream-vision was started and dominated by fear, yet it was mixed with pleasure and joy, 'a terrible sweet sound of flute music' (Ibid.); with only a single and obscure word being heard in the noise: '*the alien god!* [Der fremde Gott]' (1996: 78). The scenery was full-scale ecstatic late Dionysian rite, with 'a human and animal swarm' running down from the mountain, in frenzied dancing, naked women carrying serpents, crying, shouting and shrieking, culminating in bloody sacrifices, lewd gestures, the tearing up of human and animal limbs, and the licking of blood. The most terrible part of the dream was him no longer being separate from this mob:

> the dreamer now was with them and in them, he belonged to the stranger-god. Yes, they were himself as they flung themselves, tearing and slaying, on the animals and devoured steaming gobbets of flesh, they were himself as an orgy of limitless coupling, in homage to the god [*dem Gotte zum Opfer*], began on the trampled, mossy ground. And his very soul savoured the lascivious delirium of annihilation [*Unterganges*].
>
> (1996: 79–80, 1998: 261)

Mann would learn from his experience (though arguably not enough); but Aschenbach couldn't. He woke up not as somebody determined to reverse direction and set things right, rather as one 'powerlessly enslaved to the daemon-god' (1998: 261). He abandoned himself to his passion for the boy, giving up decency and self-control, starting to dress like a young man, and even let a hairdresser transform his facial complexion. He only found solace in his – systematically distorted – reading of Plato's *Phaedrus*: artists must 'necessarily remain dissolute intellectual adventurers', possessing an 'incorrigible and natural tendency towards the abyss', not capable of decency and rigour, only of self-debauchery (1998: 265).

Aschenbach would soon succumb to the plague.

The Magic Mountain

According to several formal characteristics *The Magic Mountain*, a work that directly followed 'Death in Venice', could not be more distant from its predecessor. It was a long novel, not a short story; it took place in the high mountains, not the seaside, in most orderly and bourgeois Switzerland, not in chaotic Italy; it was about individual illness and recovery, not about social epidemics and death. Furthermore, while the Carnival was absent in the Venice story, a central event in *The Magic Mountain* would be a masked carnival ball. Yet, such differences only reinforce their fundamental unity, and read together they deliver a coherent and still most valid, even untapped message.

This starts with *The Magic Mountain* not intended to be a massive novel, rather another short story. This is visible in its structure: the first two of the seven chapters are quite short, 16 and 19 pages in the English version, while the third is more extended, running to 35 pages. It is with the fourth chapter, counting 90 pages, that the novel starts to explode; the last three chapters are well over 150 pages each, novel-length themselves. Even further, at the start of Chapter Five Mann reflects on this unexpected explosion of length, meditating on the nature of time, continued at the start of Chapters Six and Seven.

Perhaps nothing is more trivial than a writer starting a short story and ending up with a long novel. However, the actual context suggests otherwise. This includes the warning of World War I that at first was looming large at the horizon and then broke out when Mann was working on the novel, and the previous work also pursuing an unexpected direction. So one can argue that Mann was similarly 'driven' when writing this novel.

While the figure of Hermes is not directly present in this novel – though would again feature, and quite prominently, in Mann's next, even longer epic novel, *Joseph and his Brothers* – the novel clearly shows affinities, both in its structure and content, through alchemy. Hermes was 'patron saint' of alchemy (Horvath 2015), visible through classic works about alchemy and magic, attributed to Hermes Trismegistos, becoming enormously popular in Europe in the fifteenth and sixteenth centuries; texts which in their final form are dated to the Hellenistic times, but which certainly incorporate much earlier tradition. The book has seven chapters, corresponding to the seven stages of alchemic initiation; it takes place in an isolated place, a sanatorium at Davos, about 5000 feet above sea level, perfectly corresponding to an alchemic 'incubator' (Szakolczai 2013a: 147–8). Its hero, Hans Castorp, would define his experiences as 'alchemistic-hermetic pedagogy' (Mann 1999: 596), given that he was not simply taught by his main interlocutors, Settembrini and Naphta, but these two figures, representing two different streams of thought within the Enlightenment, were literally fighting for his soul, with a crucial chapter titled *Operationes spirituales*.

The parallels between the two works, and Mann's 'drivenness', are best brought out in his reflections on time, which are also reflections on space, rooted in the experiential bases of both works. This starts with Mann being present in Davos, in between 12 May and 15 June 1912, thus the moment when finishing 'Death in Venice', during his 37th birthday. Recognising the fundamental parallels between contemplating the infinite sea at the beach and the infinite snow in the mountains defined the horizon of the novel since its beginnings, literally launching it and expanding it, physically and spiritually, in time as well as in space, into infinity.

The manner in which Mann begins his reflections on infinity at the start of Chapter V clearly indicate his awareness about being guided, and its link to 'Hermes'. This is visible in a series of formal features, starting with the last section of Chapter IV, innocuously entitled as 'The Thermometer'. However, the material inside the thermometer is nothing else but mercury, Latin name of Hermes; and the section indeed explicitly reflects on the main characteristics of Hermes/ Mercury, repeated in the fourth section of Chapter V, 'Whims of Mercurius'. Furthermore, the first section of Chapter V is titled 'Everlasting Soup and Sudden Clarity [*Ewigkeitssuppe und plötzliche Klarheit*]', a title with manifold allusions. The eternal soup evokes the Last Supper, especially given the infinite number of meals consumed in the Sanatorium, while the sudden illumination, combined with allusions to Hermes/Mercury, might refer to Mann's reflections on his own work.

Reflections on time

At any rate, this is the context in which Mann's reflections on time appear at the start of Chapter V, to be repeated in the first sections of the last two chapters, each carrying meaning with their titles. This is rather straightforward for Chapter VI, with the starting section titled 'Changes'; but more substantial, and poetic, for the last chapter, starting with a *Strandspaziergang* (beach-walk), with the felicitous English translation 'By the Ocean of Time'.

These three reflections on time form a tight series, progressively increasing in depth. In spite of its complex title, the first is relatively straightforward, little more than an afterthought, the surprised realisation of the author that his work, just as the stay of his hero in Davos, has gone way beyond originally plans. The consequence is a peculiar experience, living an extended, 'continuous present' (*eine stehende Jetzt*); in an everlastingness (1995: 254; 1999: 183). The central element of this experience is the loss of temporality, resulting in a 'dimensionless present [*ausdehnunglose Gegenwart*]' (1995: 254; 1999: 184). The potentially mysterious aspect of this experience is alluded by Hans Castorp's arrival on Midsummer (1999: 37).

The starting section of Chapter VI gives a much more comprehensive and startling analysis of the complexities of experiencing time. It starts by directly posing the question 'What is time', and gives three remarkable words as an answer, one noun and two adjectives, forming a tight net: it is a mystery, which has no essence (*wesenlos*), yet is all-powerful (*all-mächtig*) (1995: 472; 1999: 344). In order to unravel this mystery, time is compared to space, both at a general level, where the identity of time and space is pondered upon, and concretely, through the image of a circle, which is a spatial concept, capturing motion, and yet an accepted way to measure the passing of time. Apart from motion, time is also linked to action, alluding no doubt to the 'unmoved mover', which – at least according to the English etymology – is the original source of acting; and finally, both time and space are connected to the problem of limit. Here we re-join, at a deeper level, the central theme of the previous discussion, the experience of a loss of limits; and Mann connects here this experience to the destruction of the very idea of limits, the impossibility of conceiving a limit for either time or space.

In this way the discussion reaches philosophical heights, as the concepts of action, limit, time and space are central terms of Kant's philosophy, time and space in particular being his basic transcendental categories. An even more clearly philosophical polemics is voiced in the next sentences, where Mann claims that such an affirmation of the infinite is a consequence of the mathematical-logical destruction (*Vernichtung*) of all boundaries and limits in time and space, and their corresponding (*verhältnismässige*) reduction to zero (*Null*) (1995: 472). Mann formulates here a subtle critique of neo-Kantianism, all-powerful at that time. The application of a mathematical type of reasoning to human experience results in promoting nihilism: meaningful human life cannot exist without limits, yet the abstract type of reasoning, as promoted by neo-Kantianism, systematically eliminates them (Szakolczai 2011).

In the novel the problem is only discussed at the level of questions. Mann contrasts the philosophical questions of his hero with the attitude of his cousin, Joachim, who could not even consider such questions. Yet, such questions are characterised with the term 'sinister [*schlimme*]' (Mann 1995: 472–3), moving beyond mere philosophy and speculation; and in the coming pages the reason for such an adjective becomes evident. The argument reaches a further depth and higher pitch in a paragraph whose opening words radically move outside the reach of Kantian philosophy, as they picture mountains and valleys lying 'for six or seven months under snow, thus evoking infinity and undifferentiation (Mann 1999: 346). Such levelling of mountains and valleys unmistakably alludes to one of the most famous apocalyptic passages in the Old Testament, the starting image in Deutero Isaiah, the voice spoken in the wilderness: 'Every valley shall be exalted, and every mountain and hill shall be made low' (Isaiah 40:4). The next sentence in the English translation contains the word 'prophecy', alluding to a prediction that Hans Castorp made, in a rush manner, provoking the chastening of Settembrini, during the carnival (Mann 1999: 347). The apocalyptic imagery is clearly intended, though Mann transmits the vision of a peculiar, carnevalesque apocalypse. The circle is closed by identifying the 'prophecy' Hans Castorp made at the start of the carnival: it was related to the identity of the seasons, the loss of count about the passing of the days and months due to the dead monotony of the time up there (Ibid.: 322–3). The evocation of Settembrini's name is also not without a reason, as it opens another circle, through his apocalyptic Biblical allusions, when a few pages later, at the start of the Carnival, he identifies Madame Chauchat with Lilith (Ibid.: 327).

While the word 'prophecy' is not spelt out in the German version, the idea is clearly present, the term appearing a few pages later (1995: 480; 1999: 350). The number seven would also be re-evoked in the following paragraph: six weeks have passed since the Carnival, so we are in the seventh week (1999: 347).

Reflections about time reach a third and final level at the start of the last, seventh chapter. Closing another circle, we move back to personal experience, after philosophical heights and prophetic depths, but an experience of a very different kind: from recognising the puzzling quality of infinity we are faced with a genuine *adynaton* kind of experience: the impossibility of capturing or even narrating time (Ibid.: 541). From Hans Castorp the novel moves back to the autobiographical level, the experience of the story-teller who makes this shift evident by stating that time has moved from being the medium of the story to becoming its subject (Ibid.: 542). This, however, happened not before two further examples were brought into the analysis: the contrast between the time element in narration and in music and the sinister experience of opium dreams (Ibid.: 541–2).

From here, the book moves to explore further the nature of this 'impossible' or 'incapacitating' experience, using Joachim as a contrast to Hans Castorp. While it was possible to induce the latter to philosophical speculation, Joachim in his 'simple good nature' was originally incapable of such ideas (Ibid.: 542). After spending some time up there, he even became incapacitated to answer a simple question about his age (Ibid.: 543). Yet, after some further stay, he was capable of sophisticated reflections about music and time – which induced the narrator to state that such remarks indicated a certain alchemistical elevation of his nature (*alchimistische Steigerung seines Wesens*) (1995: 740). This implies a three-fold sequential structure: an original level of capacity, which at a second level becomes disturbed and disempowered, while at a third level is replaced by some kind of empowering, a process which Mann calls an 'alchemic' type of transformation, explaining the prominence of number seven in the book.

At this point Mann closes in on the conditions under which such 'alchemistical elevation' takes place, both in the debilitating and empowering senses (1999: 543). After the previous evoking of altered states of consciousness through the use of drugs as opium and hashish, Mann here brings in the example of miners buried underground for ten days, but thinking they were there only for three days – a type of experience that evokes the conditions of a cave, so central for archaic initiation rites, which arguably go back not to thousands but ten of thousands of years. Mann is clearly circling around the idea of liminality and characterises liminal conditions with two crucial terms: they are bewilderingly confused (*verwirrend*), and also generate a sense of helplessness (*Hilflosigkeit*) (1995: 741; 1999: 543); so we are back to the *adynaton* experience.

The problem is now identified; and without being aware of the work of van Gennep – which was contemporaneous and had the same 'driven' character (Thomassen 2014) – he could not go analytically further. Still, as the danger of an impending liminal confusion, crisis and chaos has been recognised, Mann makes two gestures at this time, trying to return his characters to the right road, appealing for objectivity and a healthy sense of judgement. Yet, these suggestions no longer work, as it is rendered clear, both directly and allusively, in the next few paragraphs. Directly, as the liminal conditions of confusion and alchemic elevation are actually 'objective', just as being sealed physically under the ground is a fact which produces, in a 'laboratory-scientific' manner, the confusion we are grappling with. Here another example, the 'hermetic' sealing of cans (*hermetische Konserve*) (1995: 743; 1999: 544) is evoked; an example pregnant with meaning as it returns, through generating vacuum, to the problem of emptiness and zero. Concerning allusions, Mann keeps playing with the number seven at any possible mode: whether, as another case of freezing time, by evoking the dormouse (*Siebenschläfer*) (1995: 743, 971), which recalls the seven dwarves, also miners, thus connected to caves; or by his invitation to the reader to count the exact time our hero spent in the Sanatorium, which turns out to be seven years – a number Mann would reveal in the first word of the last section of the last chapter (1999: 706).

As this indicates, the call for a return to reason could not work, and for two reasons: first, as the game with number seven indicates, because the problem goes way beyond the rather limited powers which human reason could master; and second, because reason, in the form of Kantian individualistic rationality, has become deeply implicated, corrupted and rendered accomplice to the confusion. The ensuing sentences are devoted to the phenomenology and diagnosis of this confusion, which extends to both nature and culture, involving the seasons and the senses. It also identifies the source of the latter confusion – though one must be extremely careful here. This is none else than Mme Chauchat (1995: 742; 1999: 544); not incriminated or identified, only as if shown up from a distance; but a careful reading had already revealed her presence, recalling her association with Lilith. However, such an association became visible through the – highly distortive – prism of Settembrini, the liberal Enlightenment rationalist. This perspective, however, has been identified as the real source of nihilism, which confirmed at the end of this introductory section that the restoring of powers to perception and the senses can only come by setting bounds to reason (*der Vernunft Grenzen anzuweisen*) (1995: 747); a passage followed by a half-ironic salute to Settembrini.

This is Mann's last word in these series of introductory sections concerning the problem he conjured around time, space and infinity, concerned with 'the measure of dizzying identities [*Es wuchs der Maßstab der schwindligen Identitäten*]' (Ibid.: 744), followed by one of the most poetic and intellectually captivating passages about strolling along the beach, characterised as a most magical experience (Ibid.: 745). The same experience is evoked at one of the most important moments of the book, just before Castorp had his vision in the snowstorm, where a parallel is made between walking in the infinite snow in the mountains and on the beach at the sea's edge (1999: 473), rounding up the parallels between 'Death in Venice' and *The Magic Mountain*.

What directly follows, however, is just as important, giving the direction in which the book draws to its end, and which will be pursued in the remaining part of this analysis as well. Mme Chauchat represents the principle of confusion from the perspective of cold Puritan rationality, but also the basic human values of feeling and love from the perspective of life. These values must be properly evoked and channelled, which requires not reason, rather something much more important for human life: *personality*. So the next three chapters introduce a new figure, Mynheer Peeperkorn, a Dutch coffee-planter from Java, who managed to bring back Mme Chauchat into Davos through the elementary force of his personality, immediately revealing the insignificance of the rationalistic debaters, Settembrini and Naphta. Still, the passage introducing Peeperkorn also hinted at a principle of confusion much greater than Mme Chauchat, a direct consequence of her mishandling by Puritan rationalistic excess: this resides in an Egyptian princess, a 'sensational person' who not only combined the most exquisite Parisian toilette with dressing up as a man but, 'scorn[ing] the world of men', laid a 'fitful siege to an insignificant little Roumanian Jewess called Frau Landauer' (1995: 748; 1999: 548).

In order to follow this conflict to its conclusion in the book the internal unfolding of the novel must be reconstructed. This will be all the easier as this is contained in three sequences that structure the last three chapters.

Chapter V

This chapter has a clearly accelerating structure, culminating in the first great concluding moment of the novel, a masked ball organised for the German carnival (*Fasching*) at the end of February. The seminal character of the event is emphasised by the section title, '*Walpurgisnacht*', and the play with number seven: the event takes plays almost by the day seven months after Hans Castorp's arrival at Davos (1995: 442, 1999: 322). The build-up of the events is concentrated in the penultimate section. The title, 'The Dance of Death', startling in itself, has clear affinities both with the 'Witches' Sabbath' and the medieval carnival, just as with plague epidemics which often culminated in such macabre scenes. It also contains, in a short but extremely important and revealing part of the section, the main instrument for the *opus* or 'incubation' (Horvath 2015), the cinema, named 'Bioscope-Theatre' (1999: 316). The account is no doubt based on Mann's first experiences with the new art, and so it is a truly extraordinary document, helping to face up to the radical novelty and problematicity of something by now taken for granted.

The experience can be resumed in four main points. To begin with, it makes us aware of the singular condition which becoming part of a movie audience represents: one enters a small and dark room to become subjected to being bombarded with quickly changing images. Second, the direct effect is utter absorption: anybody present in a darkened room is bound to be glued to the glowing screen where these images are unrolled. Early films were saturated with such illusion-mongering, showing in quick sequence images from quite different times or spaces, or that were specifically geared to incite the senses, like the Moroccan dancer, shaking her half bared breasts, who was 'suddenly brought so close to the camera as to be life-sized; one could see the dilated nostrils, the eyes full of animal life' (Ibid.: 318). Third, Mann managed to weave into his description the reaction of the audience during the showing, which had three crucial elements: a shocked silence in face of the appearance and vanishing of illusion, in which he found something 'nerveless and repellent' (Ibid.: 317); the experience of powerlessness with respect to the force of this illusion, or an *adynaton* experience; and finally, the recognition that ultimately behind the magic images there lay nothing else but nothingness itself, confronting the viewers: that this new form of entertainment had a central role in eliminating the boundaries and distinctions in space and time. The concluding point concerns the way in which the audience left the theatre, in stunned silence, as if dazed and confused; though, just as importantly, the new audience was already there, looking towards the spectacle with 'eager eyes' (Ibid.: 318).

The conclusion, especially in a novel saturated with alchemical allusions and numbers, is clear: the cinema is not a neutral medium, rather a genuine instrument of alchemic transformation. It is not accidental that this episode is inserted at the end of a section entitled 'The Dance of Death', providing the introduction, striking the tone, for the carnival that is the main subject matter of the last section entitled 'Witches' Sabbath'.

Given the title, the events of the carnival are rather mild. No exceptional events take place, and even the call for dance (Ibid.: 333), preoccupying after the title of the previous section, fails to produce spectacular incidents. The only emphatic element concerns the repeated identification as central for the 'carnival spirit' the call for licence and abandon and the resulting loosening of the principles of self-control, stimulated through the wearing of masks and cross-dressing. The calm flow of the carnival indicates that in so far as such a lapse is circumscribed and controlled, no harm is done; problems only emerge when this is combined with a more general and systematic loosening of the sense of judgement, as characteristic of the movie theatre. The problematisation of such a schismogenic[8] pairing of purposeful incitement with a call for abandoning self-control is characteristic of the chapter throughout, marking the complicity between liberty and illness: liberty as the systematic trespassing of borderlines is paired with illness, in particular fever, the type of illness measured by thermometer, thus involving Mercury. The final stage of this pairing, and the concluding moment of the entire chapter, takes place in the encounter at the end of the carnival in a private room between Hans Castorp and Mme Chauchat. Castorp is head over heels in love with the elusive and cat-like Russian lady, whose name in French – the language they use in their conversation – means 'hot cat', with the second syllable all but repeating the first; but due to his lack of personality he can't act, can only watch her. It is only under the general conditions of abandon, during the carnival, that he gathers enough courage to talk. Their conversation, predictably, gyrates around the question of love, and even has apocalyptic aspects – though these only become visible through the next chapter. Now as in their later encounters, Mme Chauchat tries to establish a strong boundary line between ordinary time and carnival time, warning Castorp to respect his own limits by calling him 'prince Carnival' (Ibid.: 343); and – half-jokingly, but only half so – identifies first Castorp's falling in love with illness, even death: '*Le corps, l'amour, la mort, ces trois ne font qu'un*' (Ibid.: 342, 'The body, love and death, these three are all the same'). This is the moment in which the carnival experience turns apocalyptic.

Chapter VI

Chapter V is a first, relatively harmless culminating point of the novel; Chapter VI constitutes a second, increasingly dark build-up for the true explosion to take place at the end of the last chapter. The central role in this chapter, as in most others, is played by a new character, this time Naphta, the radical Communist Jewish Jesuit, modelled on Georg Lukács, at once mirror image and polar opposite of Settembrini. The two are the same, as both represent versions of the same modern Enlightenment rationalism, unable to realise that the narrow vision they have of the world does not correspond to the astonishing manifoldness of life and spirit. But they are also radically different, as Settembrini stays at the relatively harmless level of a benevolent secular liberal freemason armchair intellectual revolutionary, while Naphta moves a further step, taking everything to its logical conclusion, not shying away from extremist thinking and violent action. Though raised and maintained by the Jesuit order, he supports the position of the Sophist Protagoras about man being the measure of things (Mann 1999: 398), and repeatedly and emphatically endorses terror (Ibid.: 400, 645–6, 697), even making the hair-raising argument that slaying a human being is 'the heart's deepest desire' (Ibid.: 462). His conversations with Settembrini, including the 'Great Colloquium' that constitutes the core of the section *Operationes spirituales*, turn around the problem of health and sickness, having the question of evil as its background, and attempt to bring the discussion to a rational conclusion, though only manage to proliferate, hopelessly, confusion (Ibid.: 406, 415, 469, 525–6, 544, 594), which is eventually explicitly sought by Naphta (Ibid.: 691).

It is after this great disputation that the crucial event of Chapter VI happens, as if the 'spiritual operations' had produced a real effect, invoking the spirits to conjure up a vision for Hans Castorp. After the great discussion Castorp needed some time to be alone with his thoughts – and found more than he was bargaining for. Going on a skiing excursion he entered a snowstorm, got lost, and the moment when fighting for his life, half-asleep and covered in snow, he had a vision. The content closely corresponds to Aschenbach's vision had on the Lido, tying further together infinite sea and endless snow.

The vision had three stages. At first, Mann/Castorp was overwhelmed with idyllic images of an archaic seaside culture. Then, in the middle of his vision-dream, his heart became heavy, increasingly darkened, overcome with dread and anguish. At the end, when approaching a sanctuary, the original joy turned into screaming terror, as within the sanctuary two grey-haired witches were dismembering a child. At that moment, while still half-asleep, he started to reflect on his vision, related to the problem that preoccupied him: health and illness, love and death, spirit and desire. This was resolved in a series of fundamental identities and differences established, beyond the facile identification thrown up, elusively, at the end of the carnival by Mme Chauchat: death is a great power, and it is 'release, immensity, abandon, desire' – but it is purely lust, not love; as love is the opposite of death, and it is love, not reason, which alone is stronger than death (Ibid.: 496). Once he came to this conclusion and formulated it as a maxim, he started to gather the will-power to separate himself both from his vision and snowed-in surroundings, managing – now solely by his own force – to return to his senses and stand up. The threatening experience was over, and within an hour he was back home.

Yet, the adventure had a surprising corollary: though through his vision Castorp found a conclusive response to his queries, once back in the safety of civilisation he immediately forgot it (Ibid.: 498). Even more amazingly, the same can be said about the writer: Mann would also forget his conclusion, just as several other central elements of these two crucial writings by World War II.

Chapter VI finishes with the death of good and simple Joachim; but there will be much graver and more complex catastrophes to be dealt with in Chapter VII.

Chapter VII

The protagonist of this last chapter, and in a way of the entire novel, is Mynheer Peeperkorn. This is quite striking, given that he only enters in the last chapter of an 800–page-long novel, and that he doesn't share the usual characteristics of the heroes of major European novels: a colonial coffee-planter, he is an old-fashioned aristocrat, quite old as well, and his discourse is hardly intelligible, repetitive and often annoying. Yet, as it eventually becomes evident, he has the one characteristic that the other figures lack: he has not so much unique charisma, in the Weberian-heroic sense, rather real personality. As a result, we have a truly Weberian dilemma, in the sense emphasised by Wilhelm Hennis (1988), at the heart of the novel: how far can the human person stand up against the diluting, levelling, destructive, nihilistic forces of the modern world, as embodied in the alchemical operations jointly performed by individualistic rationalism and the image-magic of movie theatre (see also Goldman 1988, 1992)?

In so far as he is alive, by the sheer force of his personality Pieperkorn maintains balance: as if an Atlas, keeping the world upon his shoulders. A flick in his eyes is worth more than hours of sophisticated talk by Naphta or Settembrini; in his presence everything is suddenly restored to its proper place and gains weight. He still has, and not just knows, intact, the principles on which alone decent human life can be based, like the maxim that one should under no conditions complain:

> 'You don't complain?' asked Pieperkorn, and turned his face. It seemed ashen in the twilight, the pale, weary eyes stared out beneath the great folds of brow, the large chapped lips stood half open, like the mouth of a tragic mask.
>
> (Mann 1999: 609)

Needless to say, Castorp hardly had the force to open his mouth. Most importantly, Pieperkorn knew that the core of human existence is feeling and passion; this is what is truly god-like in humans, not rationality or even reason; and that feeling is by no means 'feminine', rather the exact opposite – it is only through passionate feeling that a man can become worthy of gaining the full confidence of a woman:

> Man is nothing but the organ through which God consummates his marriage with roused and intoxicated life. If man fails in feeling, it is blasphemy; it is the surrender of His masculinity, a cosmic catastrophe, an irreconcilable horror –
>
> (Ibid.: 603)

Until Pieperkorn was alive, Chauchat-'Lilith' was happy and tame. But once he died, things soon got out of control: the preoccupying signs visible before multiplied, until the full storm would break out – meaning, obviously, the Great War. These signs all belong to the schismogenic horizon of increasing self-abandon on the one hand, and incitement and excitement on the other. Such signs are brought together in a section entitled 'The Great Dumbness', describing entrapment in various monomania, including collecting, betting, fashion, amateur photography, at the limit even the squaring of the circle. The section starts and ends with two significant, conclusive assessments of the state of the world, recalling similar diagnoses in 'Death in Venice', but going beyond them. At the start, shortly after

Pieperkorn's passing away, it seemed that 'the entire world, "the Whole" [*dem Ganzen*]' arrived at a dead end, with everything going wrong, as if a demonic power, called 'Dumbness', had taken control (1995: 860). The diagnosis is repeated towards the end, in explicitly apocalyptic terminology: Great Dumbness is an apocalyptic, evil name, announcing an impending catastrophe, a rising storm and whirlwind; a terrible Judgement Day (*jüngste Tag*) (Ibid.: 869). Other signs include predilection with rights and whatever one deserves, characterised as a spirit of egotism, the repeated transformation of *Hofrat* ('court consultant') Behrens, director of the institute, into a mime; or the conducting of spiritistic sessions through a medium.

From here, things move inexorably to the final, apocalyptic explosion. The penultimate chapter documents in the Sanatorium the impact of a demon, spirit or 'evil genius' (1999: 682). While always present, not the least in the increasing promiscuity marking life in the Sanatorium both before and especially after the carnival, now it began to spread through increasingly escalating negative feelings of anger and irritability. The crucial terms for this social disease are the same as used for the epidemic in 'Death in Venice', and also in Shakespeare's diagnoses of his own times, propagated then by the image-magic of living theatre and not yet by alchemical-mechanical moving-theatre: infection and contagion; animating the proliferation of arguments, quarrels and mimetic rivalries (Ibid.: 681–9). The visible features of such negative incitement are rising tempers and acute irritability, the suspicious glances thrown around, the words that blame and indict others, in increasingly hostile and malevolent manner, including the appearance of a particularly disgusting anti-Semite, Wiedemann (Ibid.: 683–4), escalating alongside a spiral: assuming hatred and malevolence on the part of the other, an assumption that is always confirmed as a performative speech act, it soon led to the 'horrid sight' of guests scuffling like small boys, but 'with the grimness of grown men', with foaming mouths (Ibid., 684), and even the at once literal and explicitly apocalyptic gnashing of teeth (Ibid.: 697; see Mt 13: 41–2, 49–50; 24: 50–1).

Castorp sees all this, but he can only see, cannot do something about it; he does not have the personality, he can only recognise his own weakness (Mann: 1999: 689). He has hopes in Naphta and Settembrini, but this is in vain, as they are not only weightless intellectuals, but to his great surprise they cannot even resist the stream, rather become adrift in it. Given the 'critical intellect' of Naphta, this is even intelligible: as he sees the entire word under the sign of illness, it is not surprising that he himself only reflects this illness (Ibid.: 689–90). Instead of showing example, they challenge each other to a pistol duel, where in a fit of rage and hurt pride – as Settembrini fails to aim at him, thus demonstrating the fallacy of Naphta's life philosophy – Naphta shoots himself.

The escalation of negative feelings can only have one result. A storm must break out, and indeed the last section is entitled 'The Thunderbolt'. After seven years our hero leaves the mountain sanatorium and returns to the plains to participate in the war. Mann leaves us with a question mark, which is *still* our question today, as so far we not only failed to answer but even forgot it, so at least since the First Great War, but probably since many centuries before, we – all of us in Europe, and increasingly in the entire, apocalyptically globalised world – are just wondering around, aimlessly, losing sense and purpose, as many Dantes lost in the forest, unable to handle Mann's final question: whether Love can re-emerge once, out of this 'universal feast of death' and 'extremity of fever' (Ibid.: 716). As the central word of Thomas Mann is the same as that of Shakespeare and Molière before, or Karen Blixen, Mikhail Bulgakov or Béla Hamvas after; *love*, not as foolish love-at-first-sight of Romanticism and mimetic rivalry, but Love as playfulness, grace and gift-relations; as eternal existential commitment that sets limits which one no longer even conceives of trespassing; Divine Love that emerges out of the joy of festive spirit into order to penetrate everyday existence, and which is the Way by which humans can become caretakers of this beautiful world that has been entrusted to us.

Notes

1. For details, see the excellent studies of Luca Crescenzi (2010, 2011).
2. See Elias (2000), though Elias focused on a later work of Erasmus.
3. Nicholas of Cusa (1401–64) lived during the final collapse of the Byzantine world.
4. See the etymology of 'interest' in Latin *inter essere*, or 'being in between'.
5. Vanity is a central aspect of the modern 'democratic' condition (Girard 1961), and etymologically connected to the void.
6. Mann was terrorised by such 'young titans', afraid of being considered 'old-fashioned' (Heilbut 1996: 250), forecasting his future weakness.
7. The mask of the plague doctor is to prevent contamination.
8. On schismogenesis, see Bateson (1958, 1972); Horvath and Thomassen (2008).

8 Karen Blixen

'Carnival' and *Angelic Avengers*

Karen Blixen (1885–1962), also using the name Isak Dinesen, is a Danish storywriter. She is best known for *Seven Gothic Tales* (1934), which almost procured her a Nobel prize, and *Out of Africa*, on which the 1984 Oscar winning movie featuring Robert Redford and Meryl Streep was based. For this book, however, most relevant is her short story 'Carnival', about a party with several participants dressed up as *commedia dell'arte* characters. The story, based on her life-long infatuation with the genre, accompanied Blixen throughout her life. A first version written in 1910–11 was titled *La danse mauve* (The wild dance), given a definite form as 'Carnival' in 1925–6, re-elaborated in the 1930s and touched again in the 1950s, but remained unfinished and only appeared posthumously in 1977. Given that the story was turned into a metaphor of its times, thus of modern life in general, its full thrust and relevance can only be understood in the context of Blixen's own life and times.

Born into an aristocratic family, Blixen did not have much formal schooling. Her upbringing, however, had elements highly unusual for a member of the social elite and provided intellectual stimulation in all kinds of ways. Being close to her father, who also wrote books, even a minor classic in Danish literature (Thurman 1984: 10), she became something like his confidante at a young age, which made her precocious, problematic especially given that he contacted syphilis (his daughter's fate in her first years of marriage), and that due to this he committed suicide at her age of ten (Ibid.: 28–9). An even more direct intellectual impact was exerted on her by a friend of his father, Georg Brandeis (Ibid.: 11), the most famous Danish intellectual figure of his times: Kierkegaard expert, author of influential monographs on Shakespeare and on the Romantics, legendary 'first discoverer' of Nietzsche and *enfant terrible* of Danish culture – a charismatic dandy and 'angry Jew', denounced as 'corrupter of youth', being a 'vigorous and indiscreet adulterer', an iconoclast like Heine, promoter of the poetry of 'romantic Satanists' – considered in one expression as 'that great Scandinavian Lucifer' (Ibid.: 63–4), indeed signing his scathing articles, attacking feminists, as 'Lucifer' (Ibid.: 63–6).

A central part of her childhood experiences were regular visits to the Tivoli Gardens, the centre of popular entertainments, a pre-World War I version of Disneyland (Thurman 1984: 43–4), close to Vienna's Prater. Participating in such popular entertainment was unusual for a girl raised in an aristocratic household. Furthermore, this was the place where Denmark, alone in Europe, comparable only to Russia, preserved the *commedia dell'arte* tradition. With her three sisters they frequently re-enacted performances at home. She assumed the role of Pierrot, which sort of became her fate.

At the age of 19 she wrote a play for a family theatre performance with the strange title *The Revenge of Truth*. This also stayed with her, as she re-wrote it in 1912, again in 1925, then recast it as a marionette comedy, which was eventually performed in the 1950s (Thurman 1984: 83, 316). The central idea of the play, explaining the strange title, is that every lie one utters immediately becomes true. Just as peculiar and fateful as her identification with Pierrot, in this play she cast herself as an intruder witch – 'an old gypsy woman who appears in the first act and interrupts a squabble' (Ibid.: 82). Shortly before her death she would instruct the actor playing that part that 'the witch should look like Isak Dinesen' (Ibid.: 83). She also wrote a few short stories in her early 20s that, according to Pietro Citati, were already masterpieces, comparable to the greatest works of an age that was highlighted by Proust, James, Conrad, Kafka, Yeats, Rilke or Joyce (Citati 2008: 131). The central liminal experience that directly led to the first draft version of 'Carnival', however, came with her 1910 trip to Paris.

Both the context and the modality of the trip were particularly liminal, rendering possible a genuinely shattering formative experience. Before leaving, she was assailed by horrendous melancholy and extreme depression, combined with frequent thoughts of suicide, compensated by fantasies of great love and a mad escape into freedom (Thurman 1984: 95–9). The train trip to Paris took place under particularly bad weather, with fog and rain, so much so that 'the journey began to acquire "an eternal character. We fall asleep and wake up and read again and fall asleep and wake up"' (Thurman 1984: 99, quoting her diary), underlining the liminality of such travel, strangely recalling Wagner's trip to Paris (Szakolczai 2013a: 264–5).

Her arrival to Paris on 25 March 1910 coincided with the festivities for the Annunciation. While going to Paris in order to study art, it was rather through a series of personal experiences that her outlook was decisively formed. This included encountering Eduard von Reventlow (1871–1918), a young diplomat from an old Danish aristocratic family, relative of Fanny Reventlow, centre of the German Bohemian community in Schwabing, then Monte Verità in Ascona, and his future brother in law, who also had something '"of the Devil in him"' (Thurman 1984: 38); and visits in the Louvre, where her interest focused on the French eighteenth century, and in particular Watteau, author of an archetypal representation of Pierrot. Most important were a pair of theatrical spectacles, Sarah Bernhardt's *Hamlet* and Diaghilev's Ballets Russes. While Blixen biographers do not agree on the very fact whether she actually saw the latter, the premier was 4 June 1910, so quite close to the two-month period she was supposed to have spent in Paris. Reasoning backwards from her carrier, she simply *had* to be in the audience, as in 1910 the Ballet performed *Scheherazade*, with Nijinsky as Scheherazade's favourite slave, and also *Carnaval*, danced to Schumann's music, with a Pierrot, a Harlequin, and a Columbine' (Green 1986: 70). In the next year Stravinsky's *Petroushka*, the Russian equivalent of Pulcinella, was staged, which remained her favourite music, played endlessly on the gramophone throughout her life. She would have to wait for her last years to see on stage Shakespeare's *The Tempest*, one of her favourites, though this was compensated by the fact that she saw it with John Gielgud, at his personal invitation, and the performance inspired her to write her last great story, 'Tempests' (Thurman 1984: 450–8).

The combination of time and place with childhood experiences, and the Hamlet-Harlequin/Pierrot parallels, evidently proved explosive. The most important impact turned out to be her identification with Scheherazade as a storyteller, and the eventual development of her *ars poetica* that could be termed the 'Scheherazade method', which represents a unique combination of existential reality and sheer provocation and seduction; of utter truthfulness and sheer masked play (Thurman 1984: 79, 210). For Scheherazade, the stakes of her stories were nothing less than life or death; it was literally in the shadow of instant death that she had to renew, night by night, her powers of seduction, closely associating erotic pleasure and story-telling with the risk of death. At the same time, at the level of content, the stories were about capturing the infinity of the world, indicated by the number in the title, where the eventual changes from 1001 to 1000 and back themselves merit a section in a history of infinity and the zero. In all this, she became fascinated with the figure of the *virtuoso*, or even 'aesthetic daredevilry', centring upon the 'impossible feat' – where, as a last and truly astonishing turn, she came to discover, as the ultimate hero of her stories, given the sacrifices and suffering that are necessary to accomplish such feat, the personality of the Catholic priest, eventually embodied in the figure of Cardinal Salviati: the price of potency, for artists as for priests, is impotence (Thurman 1984: 193, 210–11, 241–2, 403–4).

World War I exerted little influence on Blixen's work, not only because she had little interest in politics and social movement, including socialism and the social question, democracy, Freud and feminism – which she considered Puritanical (Thurman 1984: 66–7, 289, 292–3, 458), but because in 1913 she got married and travelled to Kenya, where she lived until 1931. Her marriage gave her little emotional satisfaction, confirming her views about the irreconciliability of marriage and love, while their coffee plantation was always on the brink of bankruptcy. Living in Kenya, however, turned out to be a decisive experience for Blixen as an artist, leading to her autobiographically inspired *Out of Africa*.

Kenya with its landscape and animals was a place so incredibly beautiful that she could not even imagine such a thing in her dreams. It was a present-day re-living of 'the ecstasy that must have felt the first inhabitants of the Earth' (Citati 2008: 132). Living there was sheer happiness, where she was a 'queen-witch of the animals' (Ibid.), comparable to Minoan 'Potnia', and also St Francis at Verna. Her favourite animal was a wild bushbuck (antelope) called Lulu (after the Swahili word for 'pearl'), and source of priceless stories (Blixen 1986a: 70–89; Thurman 1984: 199–200). The animal was captured and being sold, hanging with his ankles tied up, by children near the road. Blixen did not have the time to stop, but woke up at night with a terrible fright and immediately dispatched her attendants to fetch the animal. Bushbucks are the most graceful and beautiful of antelopes, and Lulu was particularly so: it 'was a rare experience to hold such a perfect thing in your hands' (Blixen 1986a: 74). Lulu demonstrated with her being the power of grace: '[o]n the strength of this great beauty and gracefulness, Lulu obtained for herself a commanding position in the house, and was treated with respect by all' (Ibid.: 75).[1] Still, her taming was not completely successful, and eventually she returned to the savannah, as 'she had the so called devil in her', meaning 'the feminine trait of appearing to be exclusively on the defensive, concentrated on guarding the integrity of her being, when she really, with every force in her, bent upon the offensive' (Ibid.: 78). This became particularly prominent when 'her discontent with her surroundings reached a climax', and when 'she would perform, for the satisfaction of her own heart, on the lawn in front of the house, a war-dance, which looked like a brief zigzagged prayer to Satan"' (Ibid.).[2]

Blixen also had the chance of familiarising herself intimately with the local popular version of the *1001 Nights*, as its stories were frequently told in the evenings around the fire. Their spirit was different from the way it was transplanted, through the Enlightenment of the eighteenth century, into Europe, as can be shown in the way Shakespeare looks through their morale. One of her closest domestics, Farah, had a quite peculiar understanding of the culminating event of *The Merchant of Venice*. According to him, Shylock by no means should have given up his claim for the pound of flesh; he should have been smarter than that, maybe cutting out small bits and pieces, until the exact pound was reached (Ibid.: 276–8).

Her experiences in Africa convinced her about 'the divine beauty of the universe' (Citati 2008: 134), best transpiring in correspondence with her mother, capturing the range of her feelings with 'perfect grace' (Ibid.: 133). Such an astonishing experiential background, bringing together in a unique synthesis Minoan Crete with its cult of nature, beauty and grace; the Plato of the *Symposium* and of *Phaedrus*, with its 'fusion of erotic and philosophic ecstasy, of earthly and heavenly love' (Ibid.: 142); and the Franciscan-inspired Tuscan Renaissance, left a definite stamp on her work, which in her mature stories came to formulate an 'apology of *harmonia mundi*' (Ibid.: 134).

At the same time she also realised, almost obsessively, and closely related to her life experiences that everything has a price; that the world of beauty that she had just discovered is collapsing around her, with everything precipitating, as a whirlwind, into 'the total failure of her life. *Failure*, she repeated: *failure* and *failure*' (Citati 2008: 138, *sic* in original); her 'ruin was, in fact, complete' (Thurman 1984: 283). The coffee plantation was not economically feasible, her debts accumulated, and in December 1930 she had to sell everything, escaping the creditors; the airplane of Denys Hutton-Finch, her companion and lover, crashed on 14 May 1931; while the syphilis infection, which she thought had been cured in one of her trips to Europe, returned and systematically destroyed her body, until it became little more than a larva. Yet, with astonishing persistence and genuine '*amor fati*', following Thomas Mann (Thurman 1984: 422), she turned all her tribulations into inspirations for work. In her writings she followed as a principle the way a pearl grows, around a grain of dust, elaborating the stories as a true 'spiritual artisan', without regard to cost (Ibid.: 291–2). She was only concerned with two things, as if constituting the two poles of her writing: the concrete, rooted in reality: 'what am I to do in this next moment?'; and its opposite, the most ultimate and distant question: 'what did God mean by creating the world, the sea, and the desert, the horse, the winds, woman, amber, fishes, wine?' (Blixen 2002: 242). As a true follower of Kierkegaard, Shakespeare and St Francis of Assisi, Blixen considered whatever fell in between as mere chatter, irrelevant triviality, 'full of sound and fury, signifying nothing'.

'Carnival'

A prime example for her way of proceeding was 'Carnival', on which she kept working for decades. While conceived after her first visit to Paris in 1910, she was much taken by her second visit there, in 1919–20, when she saw a version of Dostoevsky's *Idiot* and Pirandello's *Enrico IV*, but was again probably mostly taken by the Stravinsky/Picasso/Diaghilev staging of Pulcinella, premiered on 15 May 1920. The story, however, was only given a definite shape in 1925–6, at another liminal moment in her life, when she again sailed back to Europe, in March 1925, hoping for a definite treatment for her syphilis.

The story was explicitly written to capture the 'spirit of the twenties' (Green 1986: 243), in order to unmask the decadence of the post-war generation (Thurman 1984: 240), which showed no courage (Ibid.: 238). It is one of only two writings by Blixen that take place in the present: in February 1925, near Copenhagen, a party launched at the vigil of the opening of the Copenhagen Opera. Its formal structure could not have been more classical with its unity of time and place, a feast as theme, and characters wearing mask and disguise: four men and women, cross-dressed, most wearing *commedia dell'arte* masks (two Harlequins and one Pierrot). Its actual unrolling, however, is far from being orthodox, rather it follows a reversed logic, as if time would flow backwards. The feast has just started, but its participants are not enjoying themselves: they are bored, melancholic and blasé, desperately in search of excitement that could revitalise their spirit. The theme, instead of marriage, classical subject matter of comedies and their source rituals, is love, understood as mere sensuality, and getting increasingly more frivolous, not to say perverted. As a last resource to stir up sentiments, somebody comes up with the idea of a game of chance: they should all throw their names into a hat, and the winner will enjoy for an entire year the income of all the other participants, and can select any one of them as his companion. Thus, instead of the classical model of a contest (winning the bride), followed by a feast, it is a feast followed by a contest, where neither the feast nor the contest is right: coming before the contest, the feast is without a stake and thus without interest; while the contest is a matter of pure chance, with the missing stake replaced by the excitement of having the possibility of choosing as companion somebody different from one's legitimate spouse – as some participants were married.

Just when they are about to make the draw, opening a bottle for a drink, the lights of a car appear: the bell rings, and at the door there is another masked figure, dressed up as Zamor, the black servant of Madame Dubarry (1743–93, mistress of Louis XV), who became a Jacobin during the Revolution and had his former mistress guillotined. The scenery again could not be more classic: an intruder arrives, in black dress; furthermore, introducing himself as the stepson of Rubinstein, the Antiquarian, he evokes a combination of Othello and the merchant of Venice, thus becoming the third Harlequin in the group.[3] After being asked to participate in the game, he refuses and threatens them with a pistol, claiming that he had already killed somebody that night – his own stepmother; but eventually, given that he is just as unhappy as all the other participants of the feast, he decides to join the contest. It is won by one of the Harlequins; and he (or rather she) selects Zamor as her companion, in order to redeem him for his innocence lost when he became seduced into playing.

The story ends by a cryptic exchange of words. In response to this explanation, one of the participants, Rosenthal,[4] a Jewish painter – the only older person in the group – quotes from a classic Danish comedy: 'everything has got an end, and foolery as well' (Blixen 1987: 119). But Harlequin (the winner) responds that even she is also well versed in the classics, and rather 'everything is infinite, and foolery as well' (Ibid.; last sentence of the story).

While the story remained unpublished, as it remained too close to her (Thurman 1984: 238), it served as material for some of her published work, like 'The Roads Around Pisa', the most highly regarded story in *Seven Gothic Tales*, whose heroes are also desperately unhappy, though they don't know why. Not surprisingly, the central events of the play are story-telling, of which one leads to a duel – though it becomes defused; and a fairground puppet show, which plays 'The Revenge of Truth'.

Blixen's masks

One of Nietzsche's most striking sayings, both for its honesty and yet revealing the deeply problematic character of the work, is the claim that only a nihilist can diagnose nihilism. The same idea holds true for Blixen as well: the precise diagnosis of carnival society, or the modern world as the absurd place in which everybody turns into his or her own mask, could only have been made by a person who, in a way against herself, turned herself into her own mask, and even justified this – a problem that would be repeated with Bulgakov and Hamvas. The necessity of wearing masks had already been suggested by Nietzsche (*Beyond Good and Evil*, No.40), while Kierkegaard not just often published his works under pseudonyms, but hid as the author under a quite complex set of masks. None of them made it, however, into such a tight principle as Blixen, who literally transformed her being into a mask, so much so that even her closest acquaintances often lost the plot, and did not know where the real Karen Blixen ended and the mask began – as she did not know either. Her most favourite mask, since childhood, was the figure of Pierrot, which she kept using even in her adult years, so much so that by his last years, also due to the loss of weight and the transformation of her physical, even facial features due to the effects of syphilis, she was literally transformed into a Pierrot – with elements of tragedy and farce becoming inseparably mixed. In fact, she not just looked like Pierrot but managed to produce the real effect of a Pierrot or a Harlequin: in her presence 'the boundary between "the inner and outer" dissolved' (Thurman 1984: 424, quoting Aage Henriksen). She also published her writings under various pseudonyms, the most persistent being Isak Dinesen: Dinesen was her mother's family name, but Isak – a male name – was chosen because it means 'the one who laughs' (Ibid.: 2). The most disturbing of her masks, however, was the mask of the witch, into which, according to some testimonies, she transformed herself (Ibid.: 211, 438; Green 1986: 244).

Blixen certainly took masks seriously. She knew that tearing off the mask of a person, especially of a woman, was considered a mortal offence in many cultures,[5] and she was fond of quoting the Venetian custom according to which even a token of incognito was respected (Thurman 1984: 340). However, a diagnosis of the carnivalesque spirit of the times could lose seriousness if one is too willing to become a mask oneself; and thus Blixen had to face occasionally violent critiques in this regard which much upset her. She was in particular hurt by the charge that her stories contained not a single normal human being (Ibid.: 298) – a charge voiced by Sainte-Beuve in his famous critique of Baudelaire, and that could also be formulated against Bulgakov or Hamvas. She was particularly fascinated by sexual misconduct, an obsession she evidently shared with her Puritanical aunts (Ibid.: 328). The problem was that she took not only masks, but her own masks, thus inevitably herself, too seriously – though again she was also capable of self-parody as well (Ibid.: 290). A good example for this problem was the story of a pact made with the devil, selling her soul in exchange of her artistic gifts, where it is impossible to know whether she really became convinced about it (Ibid.: 372–4). Such games, and the recurrent confusion between play and reality where even she frequently lost the plot, resulted in a kind of split personality (Ibid.: 423–4). These were reflected, according to Henriksen, in the central myth and symbol of her life: the Biblical myth of the Fall and the symbol of the marionette, especially as elaborated by Heinrich von Kleist (Ibid.: 421–2). In this way she came to represent almost perfectly the typical Romantic: estranged from her family, even from her homeland, living a cosmopolitan life and writing in a foreign language – recalling Nabokov (Green 1986: 241). Thus, 'her inner life was at odds with her reality' (Thurman 1984: 287); yet, again comparably to Nietzsche's nihilism, it was through her profound immersion in the worst excesses of Romanticism that Blixen managed in her work to understand and overcome it so thoroughly.

Even further, Blixen explained and even redeemed her most bizarre obsessions with mask in a way that remained faithful to her theology of *harmonia mundi*. For her God was less concerned about true knowledge – this bored him thoroughly – rather with whatever changes and transforms itself; with playfulness and fantasy, her favourite creatures being Proteus and the actor; thus, 'the history of the world is nothing else but the history of its theatrical transformations' (Citati 2008:

146–7). As a result, 'given that God created it and continues to model it, our world is not just beautiful, but is also happy' (Ibid.: 147); a position culminating in a theological world-vision, close to St Bonaventure: 'everything is sacral' (Ibid.); a manifest, aesthetic justification of existence.

Blixen was aware of the rare, almost unique character of the vision she came to acquire. Though atheist when young (Citati 2008: 134), she assumed her new position with 'Don Quixotesque heroism', as if ignoring the fact that 'she remained the only person on the planet' who still behaved as if God still lived (Ibid.: 148).

These qualities of the world, however, can only be revealed through mask, mystification, even outright lie, as 'only behind the dusty curtains of the theatre opens up the road that leads to mystery, to the symbol, to the sacred' (Ibid.). As the hint about lies already indicates, Blixen does not ignore the dark sides of life; the shadows of decay and decadence are always present in the background; in her stories everything has its double, there is darkness lurking behind the light. Yet, all her stories inexorably lead to their end, which is never forgotten; and at this end she always shows that 'the tragedy is resolved in conciliation, a coincidence unites the dispersed signs, and thus the marvellous harmony of God rules again over the winters of this planet' (Citati 2008: 149, referring to the second collection of her stories, *Winter's Tales* (1942), an evident allusion to Shakespeare's *A Winter Tale*).

A scenery that keeps returning in these tales, where God's epiphany in nature becomes most visible, is the 'enveloping blueness' that one can observe when walking on the seaside, 'in which the horizon dissolves and the sea and the sky seem to be the same element' (Thurman 1984: 327). Staying with the same imagery, Blixen was fond of the symbol of the fish (Ibid.: 423), but was even more fascinated with the snake, which occasionally even appeared on her path in particularly significant moments of in her own life (Ibid.: 409). She was especially taken by the symbol of the 'brass serpent' (Moses IV, 21: 6–9), a metaphor she applied to herself in Europe, as representing the values of the dying aristocratic world, and which her servants applied to her in Africa (Thurman 1984: 367). As a last related example, upon the publication of a popular 1949 novel she identified herself with the figure of the Centaur, a tragic, repulsive redeemer (Ibid.: 369–70).[6]

Blixen wrote her only novel during World War II as – in contrast to World War I – she was now caught in the whirlwind of events.

The Angelic Avengers

The Angelic Avengers is Blixen's only novel. It is not counted among her best works, rather considered a mere adventure story, at best a simplistic allegory for Nazism (Thurman 1984: 339–40). This is usually explained by the conditions under which it was written: having nothing to do under Nazi occupation in Denmark and also short of money, evidently Blixen wanted to escape and have some fun. An oft-quoted, evidently self-referential passage from the book, also used as its motto, seems to say as much: what is wrong with having some fun if one is shut up in a prison and not even allowed to say so? (Blixen 1975: 110).

Yet, Blixen was not only too good a writer to pin down pointless stories, the opportunity was also special. She did not live in any prison, but under occupation by a most brutal totalitarian regime. And at that time it was still possible to penetrate the actual, daily mode of operation of the Nazi regime, as today this is hidden by its greatest evil, the Holocaust, from the perspective of which the Nazi regime metamorphosed into its own, magnified caricature: so thoroughly evil that the possibility of its existence becomes incomprehensible. It was furthermore written during the darkest period of World War II, 1942–43 (published in Danish in 1944), when the war had already been dragging on for years, with a serious possibility of Hitler winning it. This was the moment when Auden wrote his extraordinary *The Sea and the Mirror: A commentary on Shakespeare's* The Tempest (August 1942– February 1944),[7] while Hamvas was composing the first two volumes of *Scientia Sacra* (August 1943–February 1944). Furthermore, her 'prison' was Denmark which, given her lifelong interest in Shakespeare, must have been particularly eerie, rendering the famous quip 'Denmark's a prison' (*Hamlet* II.ii.239) into effective reality. There must have been a reason for writing the particular story as it came out. As always, we can trust the flair of Roberto Calasso, who selected the back cover she wrote for this book among those hundred he republished in a separate volume, recognising that this 'disquieting' entertainment was one of the most risky works of Blixen and, beyond its misleading ease, also one of her most coded (*cifrato*) (Calasso 2003: 164–5). And whether Blixen was playing hide and seek with the Gestapo, was intending to penetrate the heart of the current evil, or her hand was as if driven, stumbling upon archetypal characters, it does not make much of a difference.

To be sure, the book is about prisons, quite a few of them, and escapes, testing the heroine's 'force of flight' (Bernauer 1990). It is also about evil, in manifold enactments. But it is also about masks, both real and imaginary masks, and these provide the central connection between prisons, flights and the depths of evil. Finally, it is full of paradoxes, starting with the title, an utter paradox, as being angelic is hard to reconcile with vengeance – except for the angel expulsing Adam and Eve from Paradise.

Regardless of all such exceptional situations and circumstances, the novel starts in the most classical manner possible – Lucan, one of the angelic heroines, must leave her home in England as her father died bankrupt, so became tutor for the son of a rich businessman. While sounding trivial, it is not so for two reasons. To begin with, Blixen was primarily not a novel-writer, but a storyteller, and – as Propp has shown – the basic motive of every folktale is leaving home; and second, because the motive of failing businessman fathers would recur centrally.

The father of her pupil, a very rich but widowed businessman, falls in love with her but, instead of asking for her hand – which she in advance decided to refute, as she cannot reciprocate his feelings – proposes to support her, and her brother, for life in exchange of her becoming his lover. Thus, still within the 'pure' world of business, a second step is made towards evil: people who live in a world dominated by money come to think that any human being can be moved around solely by monetary concerns.

Lucan escapes again and reaches the home of Zosine, her best childhood friend. There she literally tumbles into the centre of a ball celebrating the eighteenth birthday of Zosine, becoming one of the highlights of the feast. Yet, already before dawn, out of this blissful state she is dislocated by a most painful realisation. Behind the scenery of the ball a real masked game took place: in the midst of the birthday celebration Zosine's father became replaced by a dummy, as his business also went bankrupt, the police already there to arrest him. So Lucan is again forced to fly, though this time she is not alone.

A social life organised around the economy is an upside down turned world where one can easily be forced to give up one's home, resulting in a joint mechanisation and theatricalisation of human conduct and thinking. If Lucan's first employer is an example of the former, Zosine's father embodies the latter. Thus, as Lucan reproached to Zosine: 'You talk as if you and your father were on the stage, where the great thing is to make an impression by words and gestures' (Blixen 1975: 72). Taken together, mechanisation and theatricalisation prepare the conditions in which the eruption of evil, in various guises, becomes possible.

Evil enters the novel at the moment the two girls realise that they must leave, though at first at a great distance. It appears in a story told by Olympia, Zosine's nanny from Santo Domingo, and involves events that seem to belong to a world of nightmare, not real life: many decades ago her daughter was snatched, sacrificially killed and eaten back home by a white man who sold his soul to the devil and became a priest in a local voodoo cult. The story evokes the evils of Blixen's present, racism and profit-driven conquest; the ancient practice of ritual sacrifice, in its most horrific form; and the archetypal modern myth of Faust – all in a single mixture.

After this freaky episode, arising as if out of the 'collective unconscious' of modernity, or perhaps the planet itself, during the liminal period of a World War, the story promptly returns to its present. Their money running out, the heroines are searching for employment together, as they refuse to part from each other. This proves difficult, so – to keep up their spirit – they formulate a strange pact, contained in a chapter entitled 'Against all the world': they do not give up and challenge the whole mankind – though nobody in particular (Ibid.: 75). Finally, an evident stoke of fortune arrives: a reverend and his wife take them to their home in France.

While for long enjoying near-idyllic conditions, after a time they discern that the house keeps some secret behind its façade (Ibid.: 116). Soon after, through a visitor, the story of selling one's soul to the devil is brought alive, though forgotten again. This is followed by a visit from an investigating judge and a detective who are asking some uncomfortable questions to the reverend, but – through the girls' help – he is cleared from all doubts. However, shortly later they accidentally find a letter revealing that the reverend and his wife are involved in the slave trade and even the killing of girls of their age. They were thus only canary-birds in a cage – kept to testify the character of their patrons. Yet, as they are spotted with the letter in hand, they have to release their proof – though they have the presence of mind to act as if they did not know what it contained. With this, a spiralling double guessing game starts, characterised as a masked ball (Ibid.: 200), where nobody can be sure what the other persons know, resulting in the kind of infinitely reflective strategic games so characteristic of court societies: 'they cannot be sure that we know that they know that we know that they are murderers' (Ibid.: 201).

With this the prison turns into a strange mousetrap – they cannot leave, feeling it as their duty to unmask the murderers, but also knowing that finding a proof would sound their death knell. They several times believe that the nightmare is over – only to realise that what they read as a sign of their liberation was only another turn of the screw towards their doom. The decisive moment comes when, out of thin air, Olympia arrives on the scene, though she couldn't even have known about the place where they were staying. Ignorant of her arrival, the reverend enters the room and is identified by Olympia as the same 'Papa le Roi' who killed and ate her daughter – though that was actually his uncle. With pistol in hand Olympia forces the 'reverend' to put his head into the rope he prepared for the girls. However, undisturbed, the monster claims that no human being can harm him: the bargain he made rendered him invulnerable, while – evoking the Erinyes or Furies, alluding to the story of Orestes – he claims that those killing him would be forever tormented by their consciousness. Undeterred, Olympia pulls the trigger, which fails. At this moment Lucan asks grace for him.

Here we come to the genuine culmination of the novel, most likely the reason for its lack of popularity with critics – and also the moment when it goes beyond its title. As, instead of fulfilling the search for revenge, the main 'angel' of the novel, Lucan, rather asks mercy for the villain. This is the only thing the 'reverend' cannot tolerate, that he was not prepared for, as it means that he lost the bargain. So in utter despair he hangs himself, while Lucan repeats: 'Yes. Grace! [. . .] Forgiveness! Mercy!' (Ibid.: 266).[8]

The novel might not be as polished as Blixen's short stories, which reached crystal-like perfection. It was written and published relatively quickly by her standards. But its content is by no means trivial. At one level, it offers a literal combination of *Hamlet* and *Faust*, the two most famous figures of modern European art, standing at the two moments of threshold in the rise of the modern world. At another, however, the hesitations of Hamlet and the Titanism of Faust are dwarfed by the angelic features of the heroine. She is rather a modern-day Iphigenia, a parallel all the more valid as the novel brings in the gory anti-tradition of child sacrifice and ritual cannibalism, the kind of ritual practices which Iphigenia was fighting against. At any rate, their central modes of action are identical, and closer to Pascal than to Hamlet or Faust: it is to only act in a way that is compatible with the dictates of the heart, evoking not justice or revenge, rather grace and mercy. Revenge never yields any result, this much we know; but we should still learn again and again that the call for justice can be very close to the pursuit of revenge: and where all justice fails, mercy – not pity, and especially not self-pity, the escape into the identity of victimhood and the tearing up of wounds – and grace always brings relief, and in the most unexpected ways.

Thus, in one of the darkest periods of European and world history, and certainly in a unique moment in the history of Denmark, Blixen not only gained an insight into the heart of darkness and the depth of absolute evil, but also reasserted the principle that can triumphantly transcend it. Calasso is quite right in asserting that in this book Blixen demonstrated 'one of her most rare merits: to have created a convincing, chemically pure and novelistically vivid image of Good and Evil' (Calasso 2003: 165). In this achievement Blixen comes close to Bulgakov and Hamvas, in whose writings we can revisit the sacrificial carnival at its peak, and also its overcoming.

Last works

Her last collection of tales, published simply titled *Last Tales* (1957), was intended to be a final statement. This was realised through another stunning surprise: a fusion of Scheherazade and the Catholic priest in the figure of Cardinal Salviati, through which Blixen exalts the beauty of the world through 'a defence of the splendour of the form, the impeccability and the rituality of the modes, and the elegance of irony', singing the glory of God through the playfulness he created (Citati 2008: 151). The stories mostly take place in small, provincial places of an almost static Italy, focusing on Catholic rites, the sensual aspects of religiosity, especially the cult of the Madonna, recalling Tarkovsky's *Nostalgia*. They reassert Blixen's quixotic belief in *harmonia mundi*, reflected by everything resembling everything else in this world, given that they all come from the same workshop and bear the same divine stamp of love, revealing to the world God's love for the human race (Blixen 1995: 99–100), a proportionality and harmony only recognised by few: at a moment, only seven people (Ibid.: 372). This harmony is threatened by the demons, the same ones who in the region of the Gadarenes invaded the pigs,[9] but who by now became tired of staying in pigs and looked for others to invade (Ibid.: 129). The other key theme of Dostoevsky, the Resurrection, is introduced through a musical metaphor offered by Pellegrina Leoni, one of her recurrent heroines, as an example of how much the Lord likes teasing, *da capo* being one of his favourites (Ibid.: 180). The last section of these *Last Tales*, called 'New Winter Tales', closes with two tales about Copenhagen. They start by introducing the principles of inheritance and heredity, central for the Danish nobility, as being in harmony with the logic of the world, in contrast to the logic of quantitative accumulation, which only leads to anonymity and thus annihilation (Ibid.: 280–2). They end with nothing less than reasserting the order of the world, through a discussion between Yorick, the poet-jester, and Orosmane, the prince. Both agree that all men were created much more noble, elevated and worthy of love than they would seem (Ibid.: 372), and even name three ways of perfect happiness in this world: to feel inside oneself an excess of force; to know with certainty of completing the will of god; and the ending of pain (Ibid.: 374–5); a condensed essence of Nietzsche, Pascal and Kierkegaard.

Still, even *Last Tales* could not be a last word; Blixen kept working on stories that did not make it in the collection, returning even to 'Carnival', though leaving it unpublished. She managed to complete, however, *Ehrengard*, which appeared as a separate volume posthumously in 1963, her true testament.

The story is about a painter, Wolfgang Cazotte, who considers his art as a form of seduction: he tried with patience to induce the objects 'to reveal him their most intimate essence' (Citati 2008: 152). When he becomes acquainted with the young Ehrengard, he cannot help but try to do the same with her, even though he knows it too well that this would reveal his own fallen being. As simply seducing her in the classical way would not be sufficient, he devised a particularly shrewd strategy of seduction: he wants Ehrengard to pronounce her own fallenness and blush at that very moment (Blixen 1986b: 56). This would make his seduction a true work of art, as 'every work of art, when revealing the reality and appearance of things, seduces and corrupts them, leading them to their twilight, and let them fall into the abyss of a definitive *nulla*' (Citati 2008: 153). Luck comes to his help: he spots when Ehrengard, with her servant, comes to take a bath, nude, in a nearby pond; so prepares a painting of Ehrengard entering the pond, which would not reveal her face, so she alone would recognise the real subject of the painting, and at that moment her whole body, 'from heel to forehead would blush into a deep, exquisite crimson, a mystical *rose persan* [Persian rose]' (Blixen 1986b: 68). Everything runs according to plan, but at the crucial moment not the youth but Cazotte would blush deeply, falling into his own trap. This is, according to Citati, Blixen's last word about the fate of the artist: 'having falling into temptation and sin, having yielded to the irresistible gaze of the world, she now dissolves itself, is lost and fades away, while her hands design a rosy and snow-white sunset of words' (Citati 2008: 153).

This is a true last word from an artist who not just hid but erased herself under her art. About this she was keenly aware. Shortly after her death the following sentence was found on her desk, written by her calligraphic script: ' *"forfeited my claim to a real human life"* ' (*sic*, as in Thurman 1984: 485).

Notes

1. About similar reverence for eland antelopes by the San, see Guether (1999: 166–74).
2. See also her identification with stork (Blixen 1986a: 267–70).
3. The name Rubinstein is intriguing, as Ida Rubinstein played the title role of Scheherazade in the 1910 Russian Ballet version. It also means 'ruby stone', something close to a 'pearl'.
4. Leon Bakst, main choreographer of the Russian Ballet was called Rosenberg. Ida Rubinstein was his protégé.
5. In most cultures women were explicitly forbidden to wear masks.

6. See also the discussion of the Centaur constellation, the one closest to the Southern Star, in Hamvas's *Karnevál* (1997, III: 38–48, 67–8).
7. While Blixen's work is considered a parody of Charlotte Brontë's Gothic novel *Jane Eyre*, the motto of Auden's epic poem is from Emily Brontë.
8. While the acts of the 'reverend' are not explained from the inside, an important conversation does hint at the motivation of his wife, alluding to her utter disgust of female body functioning and a vicious hostility to 'Papism', revealing in her a genuine streak of extreme fundamentalism. The scene also recalls Naphta shooting himself at the end of the *Magic Mountain*.
9. See Lk. 8: 32–7, selected as motto for Dostoevsky's *Demons*.

9 Hermann Broch

Sleepwalkers

The title of Broch's key novel fits into the series constituted by the *Demons*, *Magic Mountain* and *Carnival*, and continued by Bulgakov's *Master and Margarita*, Doderer's *Demons* and Hamvas's *Carnival*, capturing an activity situated in between the wakeful and sleeping states, recalling a permanent carnival night, thus having a particularly liminal, unreal character. Beyond the title alluding to activity, there are concrete human beings who are engaged in it; who are or act as sleepwalkers. Broch has important precedents in identifying contemporaries as sleepwalkers. They include Heraclitus, classical prophets like Isaiah and Jeremiah, calling for watchfulness, or Gabriel Tarde (Szakolczai and Thomassen 2011: 53–4).

The theme of the book and its author can perhaps be best introduced through reflections by Milan Kundera, one of the most acclaimed novelists of the last decades, contained in his book of essays *The Art of the Novel*. According to Kundera, of all great modern novelists Broch is the least known (Kundera 1986: 88), due to a series of historical and artistic reasons. 'Sleepwalking' is a confused condition, based on a mistaken exchange (or *scambio*, using the unique Italian term here) between the sleeping and waking states; an error particularly revealing of the current human condition. The source of the error had already been identified by Baudelaire, even though Baudelaire – just as later Kafka, one could add – contributed as much to analysing the error as to its further dissemination. The world is full of correspondences and echoes, where everything resembles everything else; the world is a 'forest of symbols'. This reveals a basic, hidden order of the world, an underlying *harmonia mundi*. However, when this order is expressed in images, such symbols can be confused with the order that they only re-present, and then hypostased as having a reality on their own.[1] When one thinks of acting upon reality, one only reacts to symbols, with the system of symbols creating an entire irrational system of confusion, which can even gain dominance in politics (Ibid.: 83–4). In contrast to Kant, the real criterion of maturity is not related to the use of reasoning power, rather the ability to resist symbols. In this sense, far from entering maturity, modernity rather represents an increasing state of infantilism. This is the reason why, following Broch and also Bakhtin, Kundera asserts the all-inclusive character of the novel, beyond poetry and philosophy: its task is 'to mobilise all intellectual tools and all poetic forms to illuminate "what only the novel can discover": the essence of man [*l'être de l'homme*]' (Ibid.: 86).

The genre of the novel allows Broch to literally *re*-present sleepwalking as embodied in literary characters. They are captured in the three part titles: the 'romantic' (*Pasenow oder die Romantik*), the 'anarchist' (*Esch oder die Anarchie*) and the 'realist' (*Huguenau oder die Sachlichkeit*). The three terms constitute a strange series as modalities of sleepwalking. A romantic can easily be considered as a 'sleepwalker'; an 'anarchist' might also fit; but a 'realist' seems out of place. Familiarity with the protagonists at first generates further confusion. Joachim von Pasenow,[2] protagonist of Part One (taking place in 1888), is hardly a normal romantic. He is a Junker and military officer whose behaviour is not animated by Romantic passions, rather a vague feeling of unease that neither lets him follow his call of duty, nor to leave it in the name of another ideal. Romanticism is usually associated with the middle classes and their efforts to imitate the aristocracy; but his case is the opposite, an aristocrat imitating, rather half-heartedly, bourgeois Romantics, for example by having an affair with a Czech dancer. The logic of mimesis is even more complicated, as in seducing the girl Joachim follows the lead of his father, while the father himself has become thoroughly 'embourgeoisified', shown in his obsession about receiving and reading his mail. Joachim is a 'sleepwalker' not because he is a true Romantic, rather by being a *fake* Romantic. The depth of his sleepwalking is revealed by the modality of his marriage: neither in love, nor following tradition, going through the motions without passion or conviction, thus failing to perform even on his wedding night – though the novel assures us at the end of the first part that 18 months later an heir was born (Broch 1985: 158).

The protagonist of Part Two (1903), August Esch is not a true anarchist either. The real anarchist is rather his friend (sort of), Martin Geyring, member of the Social Democratic party, who would even get arrested. But Esch[3] is also a kind of anarchist, though a fake and imitative one, paralleling Joachim's 'romanticism'. He does not like his life and situation, tries to escape it, leaving his job and moving to another city, but this hardly makes him happier, so he eventually returns to Hamburg, trying to become an entrepreneur (sort of), with a variety theatre show. He even marries a widow – showing the same degree of resolution as Joachim: he does so neither for sentimental or carnal reasons, nor even for the money, just going through the motions for lack of anything better.

By now one could guess that the protagonist of the third and longest part of the novel, taking place in 1918, during the last months of the Great War, would also be a sleepwalker realist, if such a thing were possible. The designation of Wilhelm Huguenau[4] as a 'realist' is certainly ironic, though with a sour tone – different from the previous. Huguenau is a realist, and in the most modern manner possible – he is a model figure of rational choice theory, *avant la lettre*. Every move he makes follows a strict calculation of interests and maximisation of pleasures. Thus, towards the end of the war, he deserted the army, once the opportunity presented itself; made his way to a small Alsatian town, where he insinuated himself into the elite, with the pretence of buying the press; and managed to mislead everyone so shrewdly about his identity that nobody even doubted it, in spite of the wartime conditions. Even further, when the occasion presented itself, in the confusion of a local riot in the last days of the war he raped the wife of Esch (who also ended up in this town, owning the local press, thus becoming a rival to Huguenau), and then simply killed him. Yet, while all such actions seemed very 'rational' in the sense of promoting his 'interests', Huguenau gained little if any genuine pleasure and happiness; he sleepwalked through his life, just as Joachim or Esch.

This leads to the heart of the book's message: the reality of sleepwalking; life as sleepwalking. Beyond a metaphor or an abstract generalisation, through the carefully constructed texture of the novel, with the help of everyday figures Broch gave substance to the problem he was tackling: how reality itself can be falsified; how we all can live in a fake reality, without taking notice of it. Broch made it evident that this was the central reason why he wrote this novel both in asserting that reality itself has become falsified (Ibid.: 501), and by posing a set of crucial and by no means merely rhetorical or provocative, rather existentially startling questions: 'Can this age, this disintegrating life [*zerfallende Leben*], be said still to have reality?' (1978: 615; 1985: 557); 'Can this age be said still to have reality? Does it possess any real value in which the meaning of its existence is preserved? Is there a reality for the non-meaning of a non-existence? [*gibt es Wirklichkeit für den Nicht-Sinn eines Nichts-Lebens?*]' (1978: 618; 1985: 559). Broch took seriously the metaphor of an entire society walking in sleep (Hatfield 1969: 110), only underlining the need for the novel to present a comprehensive knowledge, as times of decay can't understand themselves (Ibid.: 109, 112). Broch considered the period 1888–1918, marked symbolically by the rule of Emperor Wilhelm II, as a single, catastrophic development, culminating in the utter immorality characterising every act of Huguenau (Ibid.: 112–14). As philosophy, due to positivism and neo-Kantianism, lost the ability to understand contemporary reality, its task must be taken over by the novel (Kaufholz 1986; Steinberg 1984: 2).

Yet, between sleepwalking rendered perceptible through the three main protagonists and extremely broad set of questions about the unreality of the real there was still a gap and tension. Broch used two means to bridge such a gap and ease the tension: a fourth protagonist, bridging parts One and Two, Bertrand; and a running commentary and essay inserted into Part Three, 'The Disintegration of Values'.

Bertrand, the trickster-outsider-businessman

Joachim, Esch and Huguenau are sleepwalkers: they either act without any conviction, or act decisively but without any inner meaning. Eduard von Bertrand, however, is not even a sleepwalker; with him the zero degree of sleepwalking is reached, comparable to Stavrogin, this zero-degree revolutionary.

Bertrand is a (sort of) friend of Joachim, from the military, evidently his only friend there, who left service and became a successful and wealthy businessman. The relationship between the two men is enigmatic, not exposed explicitly, yet belong to the heart of the novel. Sleepwalkers have no friends; they are not capable of close human relationships. Bertrand is by no means a real friend: he even takes revenge against Joachim (Broch 1985: 138), evidently because Joachim could stay, having a minimal degree of attachment to a concrete institution and role. Bertrand was incapable of this, embodying the void itself.

The question of ethics, in particular responsibility, was a central concern for Broch throughout his works. Sleepwalkers are not responsible for their actions, thus guiltless – the title of his last novel, published a year before he died in 1951. Not being a sleepwalker, Bertrand should be responsible for his actions, yet he isn't, in a perhaps even more profound sense. He represents Broch's take on the problem of evil, much influenced by Nietzsche's idea of nihilism beyond good and evil. Bertrand repeatedly interferes with the life of Joachim, his friend, at its most intimate levels. Yet, he is not motivated either by his self-interest or sheer malevolence. What then drives his actions, evidently beyond good and evil, though in a manner even worse than evil?

Bertrand is not only a businessman, but also an actor. He is repeatedly recognised as such, and – a most revealing detail – by people way below his social standing: by Ruzena, the Czech dancer, to whom he offers a toast on the 'imitation of life' (Ibid.: 57), thus she identifies him as 'a sort of actor [*eine Art Schauspieler*]' (1978: 78; 1985: 69), and who would later even shoot at him, being so much upset by his non-realness (1985: 120–3); and by Esch, who would even consider him as a mere symbol (Ibid.: 297). This characterisation is of great importance, as here a fleeting episode in the novel and its deepest philosophical level touch upon each other: Bertrand's nature as a mime reveals the deepest essence of the modern businessman;[5] a point to which Broch would return, clarifying it in one of the culminating, visionary scenes of the novel.

A mime, a human being whose nature is to act up, has no substance, no nature, no depth, is mere emptiness, making people around him profoundly uneasy. This is why, in her confusion and despair Ruzena shoots at him – yet, as one cannot kill the void, the effort is only half-hearted and not successful. The same intention of killing Bertrand drives Esch, who is even identified by his would-be victim as his murderer. Esch even succeeds, though only in an indirect way, adding to his characterisation as a fake: having denounced Bertrand for homosexuality, the latter would commit suicide. But emptiness can be significant through its effects; just as any actor, Bertrand lives for, and through, the effects generated in others. Such effects have only one direction: dissolution, destruction and split. The void, the *nulla* transforms everything it touches into its own shape. It is the eponymous agent of nihilism, transforming by contamination like a virus everything into its own non-shape, central for Broch's diagnosis of formlessness.

This starts with Joachim who after his first meetings with Bertrand *as a* businessman perceives the dinners at home with his parents as a genuine affliction (Ibid.: 75). Joachim at first does not understand what is going on, tries to be more intimate with his parents, which is an absurd impossibility and unconscious imitation of Bertrand – with one's parents one can only *be* genuine, one cannot perform this as a purposeful action. In his naïveté Joachim even invites Bertrand to his parents' house, which deteriorates his relationship with his father, eventually making him mortally sick. So Joachim now desperately wants to escape his parents' house, returns to the military, but the Bertrand effect has already eaten inside his soul. He now perceives military duties as circus; he cannot even take refuge in Ruzena, as her face disappears, he can no longer recall it from the distance. He starts to suspect Bertrand being behind his afflictions, confirmed when he is tempted to perceive the Sunday mass as a circus (Ibid.: 115).

The manner in which Broch presents this recognition and identification of Bertrand by Joachim as source of his troubles is crucial. Joachim identifies Bertrand as a liminal being, who is in between of everything; even associated with the *demonic* (*dämonisch*; Ibid.: 114; see also p.142 on the 'demon' of Bertrand). The demonic, even in Plato's *Symposium* as *daimonic*, is embodiment of in-betweenness, connected in particular to the treacherousness of Eros (Horvath 2013b; Horvath and Szakolczai 2013; Szakolczai 2013b). Broch plays on the treacherous emptiness of Eros, in connection with Bertrand.

Joachim *now* knows – but it is too late, as Bertrand by now not only infected his father, but even his fiancée, Elisabeth. Trying to seduce the prospective wife of one's friend is one of the most abominable immoral acts possible. But Bertrand is not trying to do that. He does not want to seduce Elisabeth; he is not in love with her, following the logic of mimetic desire. He does not *want* to do anything with her, he simply cannot do anything else but to re-enact his essence, which is acting and enacting, the void itself: enacting the void is the same as being void. In *this* particular instance, the essence of the classical episteme, duplicated representation, the identity of the sign and the being it represents (Foucault 1966), works perfectly.

Thus, Bertrand succeeds. Had he tried to seduce Elisabeth, she might have resisted, and thus come out stronger of the encounter; but no one can resist the void, any encounter with it only saps one's strength. The encounter left Elisabeth with two extremely significant and purely negative effects: first, it generated a split inside her consciousness, preventing her from acting, even to say farewell to Bertrand, as she felt that her own actions would only be out of place and theatrical; and at the same time she felt an external split, with respect to her own world, in particular her family, with her parents appearing on the other side of the 'frontier line' of a world cut into two (Broch 1985: 103).

Elisabeth would encounter Bertrand for a last time under most significant circumstances. The meeting takes place in the hospital, where Bertrand was recovering from injuries caused by Ruzena's shot, thus he can play on the role of suffering victim – the ultimate trick of non-entities; a position he gained through Ruzena, due to his being a *nulla*. Before this last meeting, Bertrand was pulling some further tricks on Elisabeth – for example by asking for her hand, only to save her from Joachim – another particularly egregious action (Ibid.: 132–3); but the woman also was increasingly recognising him for the better, just when Joachim also perceived his 'repulsive cynicism' (*widerlicher Zynismus*; Broch 1978: 150), being no true friend at all (Broch 1985: 134). Thus, in the hospital she was not taken in by Bertrand's declaration of loving her, as 'something [did] not ring true' (Ibid.: 138); yet, given the conditions, it had an effect on her soul. In their last meeting Joachim had a similar recognition of Bertrand's faking, as 'his words sounded warm and sincere, yet mocking'; Bertrand lured him with devious cunning (*Winkelzug*; Broch 1978: 163), and the 'shaking off responsibility', talking like a base *agent provocateur*' (Ibid.: 165). Thus, Joachim and Elisabeth would never mention Bertrand's name again (Broch 1985: 150). Yet, by that time the damage was done, and could not have been undone; Bertrand's physical presence was no longer necessary for his effect, as even from a distance he would be unsettling (Ibid.: 140). The shadow would extend to the unconsumed bed of their wedding night.

Further details are offered in conversation between Bernard and Esch. Its context is the first long digression by Broch, on the state of travellers, a typical liminal condition, which offers the first definition of sleepwalking. This context must therefore be reconstructed, before turning to the conversation.

The metaphor of travellers

The reflection on the liminal status of travellers starts once Esch embarked on the train to reach Bernard (Ibid.: 292), but its proper meaning is gained through a statement made by Esch a few pages before: '"For we don't know black from white any longer. Everything's topsy-turvy [*Alles geht durcheinander*]. You don't even know what's past from what's still going on . . . "' (1978: 326; 1985: 290). The experience of travelling both illustrates this claim and gives it meaning – the vision of a world in which everybody becomes a 'traveller'.

The reflection starts with an aside on dreaming; not any kind of dreaming, certainly not Freudian, rather prophetic dreaming which forewarns about the great crises of life, and which comes to someone who so far was sleepwalking; even further, it offers a definition of a sleepwalker as a traveller yearning for home from the distance; a concern that would return at the end of Esch's trip, offering it a kind of a frame (1985: 303).

After this reflection on dreaming and sleepwalking, Broch develops a second set of reflections out of the mundane details of travelling: a travel not only lifts one out of one's everyday life setting, but also forces one to reflect on one's life – starting with recognising the 'socially constructed' nature of the contemporary world, where everything around is a matter of human manufacture – and even one's own thoughts are manufactured that way. This recognition immediately leads to two further basic stances; moods, no longer thoughts: first, anger against the main agents of such 'social construction', engineers and demagogues, who would be repeatedly singled out for attention as main culprits for such state of the world, and even called sophists (Ibid.: 295), and considered responsible for sleepwalking and the ensuing 'state of detached irresponsibility [*Zustand unverbindlicher Verantwortungslosigkeit*;]' (1978: 330; 1985: 293) – a state induced especially by travelling, together with dreaming, again closing a circle; and a word (irresponsibility) repeatedly identified with travelling and by sleepwalking.

The state of irresponsibility induced by travelling is characterised by three further features: a state of mind biased towards the future, insinuating that only the future is real (about this, see Riedl 2010); false community between fellow travellers; and a state in-between slumber and dream. The reflection is closed off with a paragraph (Broch 1985: 296) which defines the traveller as one who has begun his sleepwalking; claims that one thus becomes oblivious even to engineers and demagogues; and compares this state to a tightrope walker[6] and to trance, where one even forgets one's own name. The closing reflection, in italics as the starting one, brings in the 'eternal dream' of mankind for a new innocence, to be gained through sacrificial death.

Esch travels just in such a state of trance, finding Bertrand's house without knowing the road, thus technically sleepwalking; and when arriving before the house, he saw it only as a symbolic representation of itself, as if a 'dream within a dream' (Ibid.: 297).

Such a sense of unreality continued inside the house, dominating his first impressions about Bertrand: the rooms seemed to be extended into infinity, as if guarding a holy of holies, an inner shrine called 'presence chamber [*Thronsaal*]' (1978: 335; 1985: 298). As Esch went there to promote the case of his friend Martin, who was in prison due to his protests against Bertrand, he considered Bertrand as representative of 'power', thus 'evil', but found something quite different: unreality and the void. The unreality of Bertrand, whom he immediately recognised though they had never met before, was striking: 'it seemed to him that this man was only the visible symbol of another, the reflected image of someone more essential and perhaps greater who remained in concealment' (1985: 298), thus as if behind a mask – so Bertrand was his own mask; even further, he was 'like an actor and yet was not an actor' (Ibid.) – so Bertrand looked like a fake mask and a fake actor, which – given that the actors of *commedia dell'arte*, who wore masks, were also called masks – is the same thing again. In such a height of unreality it is not surprising that Esch did not seem real even to himself, as he was not saying something, only hearing his own voice speaking, thus rightly identified by the narrator as a 'dreamer' (Ibid.: 299). The ensuing conversation also had a profoundly dream-like character, underlined by Esch's paradoxical characterisation as 'an overwakeful dreamer', and concluded by Bertrand's Thomas Mann-like sentence, assuring to Esch that he 'will forget what I say to you now, forget it like a dream' (Ibid.: 302).

As Bertrand commits suicide shortly after this conversation, his role as businessman-mask is taken over by Huguenau, a perhaps even more sinister, but just as 'guiltless' figure.[7] The central role of keeping together the threads, including the third protagonist, is taken over by the running commentary entitled 'Disintegration of Values [*Zerfall der Werte*]'.

'Disintegration of Values'

It has been often claimed, and even accepted by Kundera, that this commentary is too much of a philosophical essay, thus alien from the rest of the novel. Yet, it is mistaken; the commentary comes at a particular context, and is well integrated into the storyline. Even further, the ideas were sparked by the story; it was only through the animation of his experiences and ideas in the form of the fictional characters that Broch managed to arrive at such ideas about the truth of reality – which was the unreality of the apparently real. Thus, by no means was the novel a simple 'vehicle' of a pre-existing philosophy, and so this running commentary offers a perfect means to end the chapter.

The first disquisition on the disintegration of values emerges in a very precise context, as the twelfth chapter of the third part. Having introduced Huguenau, the third, 'realist' sleepwalker, Broch makes him meet Esch (Ibid.: 358), and – woven into the texture of the events – introduces a series of substantial points. First, recalling the paradigm of the travellers, Broch repeats the idea that longing and flight only lead to death, and – anticipating contemporary arguments about globalisation – identifies the annihilation of all measurable distance as a central feature of the current world. Then, moving to a more general level, and bringing together book-keepers, Kantian philosophers and Don Quixote, he identifies in bookish knowledge a major source of the unrealism and sleepwalking that rendered the war and the increasing disappearance of the reality of the real possible. Book-keepers, just as Kantian philosophers, like to operate with clear-cut and absolute dividing lines, but

> the frontier between reality and unreality [*die Grenze zwischen Wirklichkeit und Unwirklichkeit*] in life can never be clearly drawn, and a man who lives within a world of precisely adjusted relations will refuse to allow that there can be another world whose relations are incomprehensible and inscrutable to him: so when he steps out of his firmly established world or is torn from it he becomes impatient, he becomes an ascetic and passionate fanatic, even a rebel.
>
> (1978: 413; 1985: 369)

As a result, European society, pervaded by such neo-Kantian mentality, became unable to perceive the dangers to which it was drawn: 'Among the many intolerances and limitations which were so common in pre-war days, and of which we are now rightly ashamed, there must be reckoned our total lack of understanding when faced with phenomena that lay even a little way outside the confines of a seemingly rational world' (1985: 371). The war, with all its horrors, was only a 'secondary thing' (Ibid.: 539); the central matter concerns the historical developments that transformed European culture into a mass of sleepwalkers. This phenomenon was introduced through the four main protagonists of the novel. In the running commentary Broch draws the consequences of his narrative and searches for causes.

The first of the ten sections on disintegration occupies a prominent place in the book, cutting right into the heart of the matter: 'Is this distorted [*verzerrte*] life of ours still real? Is this cancerous [*hypertropisch*] reality still alive?' (1978: 418; 1985: 373; first sentences of first section on disintegration of values). Such questions emerge out of the 'reality' of the war, in its last year, when it has become since long evident that people die in unprecedented numbers without any reason, having no idea what for and why, even though 'without a hold on reality they fall into nothingness [*ins Leere*]' (Ibid.). With the unreal reality of the war, the mixing together of violence, sacrifice and profit-making, everything has been turned upside down, as if in a comedy or a farce: 'Fantasy has become logical reality, but reality evolves the most a-logical phantasmagoria' (1985: 373). As all forms were blurred, all stabilities undermined, the world became ruled by a 'twilight of apathetic uncertainty', where man can do nothing better that wobble 'through a dream landscape that he calls reality and that is nothing but a nightmare to him' (Ibid.).

The age of such total confusion is characterised by some as great, by others as insane, yet both sides fail to realise the obvious: such characterisations can only be applied to individual human beings, and not to an 'age'. This leads to the heart of the problem of the book: an attitude to understanding rationality that takes as its starting point individual reasoning confuses order and harmony, the etymological source of 'ratio', and individual motivation. In such a world turned upside down the distinction between rationality and insanity becomes impossible: action that looks insane and/or immoral from one perspective looks perfectly rational from the other and vice versa. It is this dilemma that is formulated at this juncture of the book, after an encounter between Esch, the 'murderer' of Bertrand, and Huguenau, Bertrand's 'heir' and murderer of Esch, in a striking language that seemingly searches for effects through paradox-mongering, but which merely expresses the actual unreality of the real that has been increasingly unleashed on Europe, and the world, through institutionalised sleepwalking. In this world, the world of Broch's times *and* our world of globalised modernity,

> [o]ur common destiny is the sum of our single lives, and each of these single lives is developing quite normally, in accordance, as it were, with its private logicality. We feel the totality to be insane, but for each single life we can easily discover logical guiding motives. Are we, then, insane because we have not gone mad? [. . .] Are they [the soldiers of the war] insane because they did not go insane?
>
> (1985: 374)

Huguenau embodies this dilemma,

> [t]he rationality of the irrational: an apparently completely rational man like Huguenau cannot distinguish between good and evil. In an absolutely rational world there would be no absolute value-system, and no sinners, or at most, mere detrimentals [*höchtens Schädlinge*].
>
> (1978: 597; 1985: 541)

The point is taken further at the start of the last running commentary. Huguenau is unable to draw the line between real and unreal, rational and irrational, failing to 'recognize the irrationality that had pervaded his actions' (1985: 625).

In this unreal and insane because at once depersonalised and individualised world, deeds of genuine social value and meaning are replaced by their ideological masks, as 'any superpersonal idea, even a destructive one' could be made accepted by large numbers, even become ruling, 'provided that it could masquerade as socially valuable' (Ibid.: 374). The reality of a world war, with its intimate ties to profit-making and, one could add, the eventual camps and genocides, proved that human beings could be made adaptable to practically anything. The price of social 'comfort' was giving up personal integrity, a phenomenon that Broch captures through the metaphor of the split. The combination of heterogeneous and mutually exclusive realities within one individual, the everyday reality of the war with its mass killing, the disinterested slaying and the publicly vindicated slayer, the institutional and moral justification of utmost immorality does not simply generate splits within nations, societies and classes, but 'it is a split in the totality of life and experience, a split that goes much deeper than a mere opposition of individuals, a split that cuts right into the individual himself and into his integral reality [*in seine einheitliche Wirklichkeit*]' (1978: 420; 1985: 375). About this split, every one of us is deeply aware; yet, we cannot help it and thus, inevitably, we are looking for a leader who could explain all this and restore sanity; in Weberian terminology, a 'charismatic leader'; yet, in Broch's times, just as in ours, we know very well that instead of genuine leaders, our 'reality' only produced the same trickster figures who actually created this modern world.

The possibility of redemption is arguably *the* central theme of the novel; however, for a time the running commentary focuses on the formlessness of modern art, the utter lack of style, paralleling the narrative, which lays bare the increasing formlessness and meaningless of life itself. It also presents a twice absurd paradox: modern art, which refuses to 'merely' represent reality and nature, ends up mechanically miming the formlessness of reality; and this new art, with all its avant-garde and 'l'art pour l'art' aspirations, ends up being a *non*-art, as art is nothing else but form.

While a reflection on art is fully within the remit of an artist, the running commentaries soon address much broader and basic themes: the fifth and sixth offer an excursus into logic and rationality (1985: 422–6, 445–8), while the seventh and eighth into history (Ibid.: 480–6 and 523–7). As Broch already indicated that he considers the war an almost logical outcome of previous developments, these latter are searching for causes. They are also closely interwoven with two central events in the novel.

The first is unique on a number of counts: by bringing together all three sleep-walker protagonists; by presenting the dialogue in the form of a theatrical play; and by its theme which – recalling again *The Magic Mountain* – is entitled as 'The Symposium or Dialogue on Redemption' (Ibid.: 497–507). It touches upon the Original Sin, arguing that one error is sufficient to render the entire world false, and a series of other central themes – except that none of this matters, as the protagonists reveal themselves, heightened by theatricality, as mere masks, actors enacting themselves, talking past each other and not getting anywhere in their ideas, except for occasionally stepping out of their roles. Even the truths they utter become distorted and turn banal, like the non-substantiality of evil proclaimed by Pasenow (Ibid.: 500), which does not mean that evil is only an illusion. Quite on the contrary, and rhyming with analyses of the demonic offered elsewhere, the conditions of a falsified, fake and theatricalised reality only multiply the power of evil, leading to the fear that 'in a world of illusion and semblances nothing but evil could take on bodily form' (Ibid.: 534). The colloquium thus could only draw one conclusion, substantiated by itself, that 'we are all still living in a false reality [*falsche Wirklichkeit*]' (1978: 555; 1985: 501); followed up in the final scene, subtitled 'Transformation [*Verwandlung*]' (1978: 560; 1985: 505), evoking the famous 'transformation' scene in English pantomime, inaugurated by Lun in *Harlequin Sorcerer* (see Szakolczai 2016a).

In the ensuing, second major event Broch reaches the height of his visionary power. On the back of Dostoevsky's *The Demons*, and anticipating the *Carnival* of Blixen and Hamvas, the war-ending collapse is preceded locally by a celebration of the 1914 victory in the Battle of Tannenberg (Broch 1985: 507–20). The increasingly wild and absurd scenes scandalise Pasenow, who perceives that these 'turned war itself into a bloody caricature of corruption', helping the world become featureless and faceless, an empty pit; so in his 'icy immobility [*eisiger Bewegungslosigkeit*]' he was overtaken by a 'dreadful desire' to 'destroy this demoniacal rabble [*das dämonische Gezücht zu vernichten*]' (1978: 570; 1985: 515). But of course he does not do anything as, having sleepwalked his life, he has already become transformed into a puppet. For others the scenes evoked the 'annual fair [*Kirchweihfeste*]', though a 'hysterical fair', offering '[e]mpty forms that still live', which 'looks like a fair, but the people in it don't know any longer what's happening to them'; and which, even further, recalls 'Judgement Day', or an apocalyptic carnival (1978: 572; 1985: 517). Broch here reaches into the fairground origins of the modern world, an insight leading right towards his striking analysis about the sources of the present condition in the eighth essay.

Broch roots the disintegration of values, beyond the Renaissance individualism discussed in the seventh essay, to Protestantism, the major sect-formation out of the decay of Christianity (1985: 523). He terms as the most characteristic Protestant idea the categorical imperative of duty, rooting Kant's purported universalism inside sectarian religiosity; and, even further, identified as the 'silence and ruthlessness of the Absolute', links this to 'the structure of the Jewish religion' (Ibid.: 525). This is the prelude to Broch's radical critique of modern rationalism, which requires further introductory comments.

A convert to Roman Catholicism, Broch was born Jewish, and after the Anschluss escaped into the US, where he died in 1951. The novel was written in Vienna during 1928–31, published 1931–2, thus just before Hitler's rise to power. The place, time and person guarantee a unique access to truth that within a year became closed.

The problem of Broch, as we have seen, is the thorough modern confusion between the rational and the irrational, the normal and the insane, the real and the unreal, which render practically each inhabitant of the modern world a sleepwalker, culminating in world wars and ideological totalitarian systems. Trying to reach the heart of this nihilism, understood – following Nietzsche – as an alienation from the real world, he found it in an abstract rationalism rooted in the peculiarities of Jewish religion, a vision of the divine which, due to its 'immolation of all sensory content', can be considered as the 'root cause of the prevailing disintegration of values' (Ibid.: 526). The next paragraph starts by defining 'the Jew' as the 'really modern, the most "advanced" man' (Ibid.). This is due to the 'abstract rigour of his conception of infinity', through which he 'surrenders himself with absolute radicality to whatever system of values, whatever career he has chosen'. Anticipating the ideas of Henri Frankfort (1948: 337–44), Broch traces modern nihilism to Hebrew monotheistic transcendentalism; the paradox that an absolute belief in divine transcendence could easily switch over into radical constructivism, being liberated either from the need to conform to nature as given, or to other human beings as a concrete community. In such a vision of the world pure spiritual enlightenment and absorption into materialism again become identical – just as in Gnosticism, one could add – leading to the 'absolute Abstract', which Protestantism liberated from its ghettoes, rendering it both inner-worldly and omnipresent, by

> inflam[ing] to virulence all the dread ruthlessness of abstraction, [. . .] as if it had released that absolute power of indefinite extension which inheres potentially in the pure Abstract alone, released it explosively to shatter our age and transform the hitherto unregarded warden of abstract thought into the paradigmatic incarnation of our disintegrating epoch.
>
> (Broch 1985: 526)

Abstraction here focuses on thought and religion, yet complements the analysis of travellers, where the modern, non-religious outcomes of abstract religiosity were already identified in technology (the 'engineers'), and in mass politics and its 'public sphere' (the 'demagogues') – each direct descendants of the late Renaissance fairs and their theatricalised public, spellbound by the magic of alchemy; direct sources of the modern fascination with the supposedly universal benefits of technology and the democratic public sphere.

This crucial section has a just as significant coda, in the last segments of another thread woven into the narrative, entitled 'Story of the Salvation Army girl in Berlin' (see especially No. 14, in Broch 1985: 574–8). Here the narrator is an inmate in a Jewish refuge-hospital, characterising the times, and the place, as a heightened state of provisoriness, where '[t]he provisory seems to have become the definitive', offering him the paradoxical 'certitude of living in a sort of second-class reality, giving rise to a kind of unreal reality, of real unreality', hovering between various states and sleepwalking, in an 'unstable flux' (Ibid.: 575–7).

We are getting ever closer to the heart of the book, as not only events in the story and the war are tied together with the running commentary, but also the author as impersonated inside the novel. It culminates in the last two running commentaries. The ninth essay (Ibid.: 559–65), subtitled *Epistemological Excursus*, starts with the most comprehensive problematisation of unreality, thus making it evident that epistemology for Broch does not mean the validity of knowledge, rather the much more troublesome question of assessing the unreality of the apparently real but actually mask-like, inauthentic, fake. The discussion culminates in the last, tenth essay (Ibid.: 625–48), a symbolic number, and subtitled *Epilogue*; the concluding and longest section of the book, combining the form of Mosaic laws with the substance of ethical prophecy. Starting with the figure of Huguenau (Ibid.: 625), twice identified shortly before as a 'clown' (Ibid.: 570, 620), and the phrase 'All was well', first pronounced after Huguenau killed Esch (Ibid.: 614), this culminates in analysing the quintessential outcome of abstract, world-negating thought, the revolution, and presenting a Christian-Platonic framework to go beyond such nihilism.

Any revolution implies a break away from the whole, a questioning of the world as it is in the name of a part: a race, a class, group, a 'chosen people' of a kind, so it must be partial; yet, at the same time, it must also absolutise itself as the genuine representative of the whole, thus 'lead[ing] by a plain, undeviating path to the absolute revolutionary disintegration of values' (Ibid.: 636). This leads to a necessary ambiguity, which 'amounts to dishonesty, epistemologically speaking' (Ibid.), as such revolutions, while asserting their absolute, abstract righteousness and justice, also and inevitably are rooted in and promote the irrational: as

> revolutions are insurrections of evil against evil, insurrections of the irrational against the irrational, insurrections of the irrational masquerading as extreme logical reasoning against rational institutions complacently defending themselves by an appeal to irrational sentiment: revolutions are struggles between unreality and unreality, between tyranny and tyranny, and they are inevitable [. . .] once the disintegration of values has advanced to its last integral unit, the individual

thus, a '[r]evolution is the breaking through of the irrational' (Ibid.: 636–7). This irrationality is best shown by the protagonists of the revolution also becoming its choice victims. Broch was particularly and tragically prophetic here.

Yet, even this is still not the last word, as the ultimate irrationality of all revolutions is still bound to culminate in some ultimate rationalism. Irrationality is a terrible threat, dissolving everything stable, so the task of all formation, and of the Church, is to encircle and transform the irrational (Ibid.: 626). However, and still, every value system is rooted in irrational impulses, and thus pure rationality, without feelings, is the greatest evil (Ibid.). Differences between modes of revolutionising are minor, and bound to become less and less marked; what matters is whatever is common to them: 'a preliminary revolution based on the irrational does not matter in the long run [. . .] for it cannot prevent the definitive rational revolution' (Ibid.: 638). The book ends by characterising the substance of this presumed 'rational' Revolution: it will be a 'churchless "Church in itself"', animated by a spirit of positivism, and having as its (anti-)ontology 'an abstract natural science without substance', and as its (anti-)morality 'an abstract ethic without dogma' (Ibid.: 639). It will be a 'church' that is 'deliberately setting itself up as an anti-church with machines as the apparatus of its cult and engineers and demagogues as its priesthood' (Ibid.), having as its asymptotic end, in infinity, 'the pure deed-in-itself, the idea of a pure organon of abstract duty, the idea of a rational belief without a God' (Ibid.).

Revolutionary nihilism culminates in the atomised individual, with its presumed rationality and irrational impulses, the 'last product of every disintegration of values', the 'point of absolute degeneracy [*Verworfenheit*]' or the null-point of the atomic dissolution of values [*Nullpunkt der Wertatomisierung*]; (1978: 712; 1985: 645). It is, however, not simply an end-point, but also a new beginning; and here Broch, just as later Borkenau (1981), would shift to the classical, Platonic meaning of 'revolution' as a revolving movement (see the *Statesman*, 269C–74A). This is explained with the help of two crucial conceptual pairs, concrete-Absolute and rational-irrational. The concrete is the central source of value for Broch; it is the historical and the personal, whatever lives and exists, and thus requires freedom to fulfil its existence at a given time and place (Broch 1985: 640–4). The Absolute is the divine that exists outside time and place, giving the Law, but which for the same reason doesn't belong to the reality of the concrete, thus cannot be brought down or evoked at the level of reality without serious consequences, ultimately rendering reality unreal. Here comes the second pair, the rational and the irrational, as together they are both 'partakers in the overarching and majestic Being which is at once the highest reality and the profoundest unreality' (Ibid.: 643). This is because life, with its freedom, is fundamentally irrational, governed by impulses contained inside every living being; yet, it is also subjected to and limited by the rationality of the Absolute, its *ratio*, the divine Law. It is the balance between the rational and the irrational, and the concrete and the Absolute, which gives integrity and style to every concrete system of values; every culture and civilisation. Broch's world vision is indeed profoundly Platonic, as these pairs perfectly correspond to the pairs One-Many, and Limit-Unlimited, formulated in one of Plato's most important and conclusive dialogues, the *Philebus* (16C–7A), and characterised a 'divine gift'.

But Broch defines his own position as 'Christian-Platonic', based on the 'Platonic unity of the Church', whose disintegration was brought about by Protestantism, and which necessarily culminates in the Antichrist (Broch 1985: 486, 638–9). So, while the disintegration of this value system is inevitable, Broch contrasts such nihilism with something indestructible: the unity of world and of mankind is inamissible and inalienable (*unverloren und unverlierbar*; Broch 1978: 624), as every man is an image of God and the Word of God, 'measure of all things' radiates in every thought humans create (Broch 1985: 564–5), and so our Hope in the Messiah remains 'indestructible [*unzerstörbar*]' (Broch 1978: 715), even when our concrete hopes fail. Broch ends on such a note of hope, focusing on the 'binding' of our loneliness to the loneliness of others, and a 'voice' offering comfort in love *against* self-harm, in the togetherness of being there; and uses in the last page of his book, though differently, the same central word of Rilke, Hofmannsthal and Kafka, the indestructible.

Both Broch's diagnosis of increasing unreality and his 'Christian-Platonic' vision of the world (Broch 1985: 639) are strikingly valid. Yet, there are certain problems in the conclusive formulations, just as important omissions. While the concluding words are cathartic, they are caught in a double negation. There is an excessive important attributed to voice, in contrast to presence, which parallels the downplaying of the aesthetic in contrast to the ethical (Ibid.: 646–7). While the word 'Messiah' appears on the last page, the book hardly mentions Christ, and not at all the Resurrection, which is problematic for a 'Christian-Platonic' world vision.

Thus, arguably, the ultimate position reached in the novel is contained in its middle, expressed by the Salvation Army girl, who manages to see 'the grace of God on all things gleaming' (Ibid.: 384; last line of the second segment about the 'Story of the Salvation Army girl in Berlin', which would gain such an importance for Broch); a great lesson for the self-declared functionaries of modern European culture, who – in their obsession with formal rationalism – failed the foresee the coming storm, and yet exposed anyone outside their orbit, whom they could not understand, like the Salvation Army girl, to 'endless ridicule' (Ibid.: 371; in the first paragraph of the first segment).

Notes

1. On the links between reality, art and technology, see also Szakolczai (2015).
2. The name evokes Joachim Ziemssen, Hans Castorp's cousin in *Magic Mountain*, also military officer.
3. Broch calls the protagonist of Part Two by his last name – evidently, a sign of depersonalisation.
4. In this case Broch gives the personal in brackets (p.343), as if he were ashamed of attaching a 'personal' name to this figure.
5. This is a point of great significance, given the neoliberal vision of everyone becoming an entrepreneur of oneself.
6. This is also a central metaphor of Nietzsche and Kafka.
7. See the parallels with the 'innocent fraud' of economists (Galbraith 2004), just as Voegelin's 'we did not mean it'.

10 Mikhail Bulgakov
Master and Margarita

Mikhail Bulgakov (1891–1940) was born into a most orthodox Kiev family: his father taught at the Theological Academy and both his grandfathers were priests. Not surprisingly, most of his family left Russia soon after the October Revolution, while he was being looked at with great suspicion throughout his life by Communist authorities. It therefore created quite a surprise and uproar that in 1965–6 two of his novels, *Black Snow: Theatrical Novel* and *Master and Margarita,* were published posthumously. Reading them, especially *Master and Margarita,* at the time of their publication produced an 'electrifying' effect, as if publication itself were due to a stunning oversight (Pevear 1997: vii). The 150,000 copies of the literary journal in which *Master and Margarita* first appeared were sold out within hours, and people talked about nothing else for weeks. This excitement was repeated with the first book-form edition of the novel, which also included *Theatrical Novel* and the earlier *The White Guard*: on the black market the volume fetched 50 times its original price (Curtis 2012: ix). Its very language was different, a breath of fresh air; phrases were passed from ear to mouth, becoming legendary sayings overnight; in particular the sentence, repeated several times in the book, that '"cowardice is the most terrible of vices"' (Pevear 1997: viii). The surprise was all the greater as nobody knew about the existence of an entire unpublished Bulgakov novel – and what a major novel: 'above all, the novel breathed an air of freedom, artistic and spiritual, which had become rare indeed, not only in Soviet Russia' (Ibid.). Being unlike anything preceding it, the novel gave rise to intense efforts at decoding, started with the Afterword by A. Vulis to the first edition (Milne 1990: 228), which emphasised its links to the Menippean satire, through Bakhtin (see also Proffer 1996: 98, 117).

The two later novels are closely related: *Master and Margarita* is the undisputed masterpiece of Bulgakov, a key novel not just of the Russian and East European Communist experience, but the modern world; while the other, highly autobiographical novel was written once *Master and Margarita* was all but complete, giving vital insights about Bulgakov's creative process. Both works were written without any hope of publication within his lifetime.

Bulgakov: life and times

Trained as a doctor, Bulgakov volunteered for frontline service and was badly injured twice. His early writings were based on his front experience and the ensuing civil war. His first major novel was *The White Guard* (1924), partly published in 1925, on which his first play *Days of the Turbins* (1926) was based. The play was extremely successful but also controversial; Stalin liked it, and this gave a degree of protection for the artist throughout his life. Still, by 1930 his situation became so difficult that he applied for permission to emigrate (Ginsburg 1988: viii). This was denied, but he was given work at the Moscow Art Theatre, where he worked until 1936 on a play adaptation of Molière's life, entitled *The Cabal of Hypocrites*, and also wrote in 1932–3 a biography on Molière (Clayton 1993: 202–4).

Bulgakov's interest in Molière is not surprising, given the manifold parallels between the two authors. These include a passion for theatre – which Bulgakov would eventually regret; living under autocratic regimes, which continuously interfered with their work; maintaining a fearless and uncompromising attitude in face of the storms which their work unfailingly evoked; and finally, having an 'infinite capacity for capturing the absurd and the comic, the mean and the grotesque' (Ginsburg 1988: vii). Though a writer and not an academic, Bulgakov conducted extensive research when writing his biography, striving for absolute authenticity, motivated by the belief that a true artist must love his subject. His work was also stimulated by parallels recognised between Louis XIV and Stalin, and the similar helplessness of the artists living under despots (Clayton 1993: 203). Given his understandable interest in the fate of manuscripts, he was particularly taken by the curious fact that all of Molière's manuscripts and letters simply vanished, 'as though conjured away into thin air' (Bulgakov 1988: 246).

The play was performed in February 1936, but after seven performances, provoking the usual combination of success and criticism, was taken off the programme. As a response, in 1936–7 he wrote *Black Snow: Theatrical Novel*, fictionalising his experiences with book publishing and theatre production under Soviet Russia; while in 1937–8 he was working on a scene adaptation of Cervantes's *Don Quixote*, a work never performed in his lifetime (Doyle 1983). *Don Quixote* was one of only three literary works mentioned in *Master and Margarita*, the other two being Gogol's *Dead Souls* and Goethe's *Faust* (Doyle 1983: 869), both serving as direct precedents: Gogol with his description of a tightly knit yet completely absurd system of administration, to be traced back to the Persian Empire – recalling thus, perhaps not so paradoxically, the *1001 Nights*; while Goethe with the Devil as protagonist and the Witches' Sabbath. Don Quixote was important for Bulgakov as a hero with whom he could identify, a 'figure of sanity in an insane world', thus comparable to two heroes of *Master and Margarita*, Yeshua and the Master, just as to Dostoevsky's Prince Myshkin (Doyle 1983: 873, 6; Milne 1990: 221). He learned Spanish in 1937 in order to understand the work better and – following a long line of interpretation – for him the novel was a profoundly philosophical work, though reaching the aims by non-conventional, even absurd means (Doyle 1983: 869–70).

The novel had to be substantially cut, but Bulgakov still managed to add a few innovations, focusing on the myth of the Golden Age, central for his reading. For him Don Quixote as a knight (*rytzar'*, a word derived from German *Ritter*, thus evoking Dürer's 'Knight, Death and Devil') stood for the key virtues of courage and justice, and was fighting for honour, so the central speech was delivered not to the goat-herds, but directly to Sancho Panza, as virtue can only be based on nobility, and not mass consensus. This had a not simply anti-Soviet, but deeply anti-Marxist and anti-populist message, moving beyond the conventional mass-media democratic message that has become taken for granted in Western intellectual circles, a vital message of Eastern or East-Central European novels also emphasised by Kundera (1986). In Bulgakov's reading the aim of Don Quixote was no less than 'to convert [*prevratit'*] our Iron Age into the Golden Age' (Bulgakov 1974: 14); or, in an even more striking formulation, to 'revive [*vozrod'it'*] this sparkling age' (Ibid.: 23); in both cases implying the religious terminology of conversion as a new birth. But in order to be seriously promising such attempt requires a sober and concrete ethos guiding everyday conduct: it is not to impose one's ways, and especially not through violence, rather to do only good deed (*dobro*) to everyone, and don't procure evil (*zla*) to anyone (Ibid.: 74); a speech which thus also reflects the famous 'Funeral Oration' of Pericles, according to Thucydides. The ending of the play, with a sunset and storms about to spring up (Doyle 1983: 873–4), closely recalls the end of *Master and Margarita*, drawing even more closely together the religious-eschatological and not simply secular-eschatological parallels.

Still, during all this period, starting from 1928, Bulgakov was primarily working on *Master and Margarita*, his key novel. Recalling Kafka, the novel was mostly written at night, in order to avoid surveillance (Curtis 2012: ix). Recalling Dostoevsky, the novel was several times completely re-written, and he actually burnt the first draft, giving rise to the famous saying in the novel: 'manuscripts don't burn'. The novel is widely acknowledged, together with Boris Pasternak's *Doctor Zhivago* (1957), its closest parallel (Milne 1990: 220–1), as the most important novels written during the Communist experience in Russia, comparable to the greatest nineteenth century novels. Bulgakov and Pasternak knew and respected each other, Pasternak even visited Bulgakov on his death bed and the two had a long talk (Ibid.: 224). The autobiographical elements of *Black Snow* offer keys to the composition of *Master and Margarita* as well.

Black Snow: theatrical novel

The novel is a thinly veiled autobiographical account about how Bulgakov became a writer. It uses a Kierkegaard-like construction: Bulgakov presumably only edited a manuscript written by one Sergei Nikolaevich Maksudov, an author contemplating suicide. The game of distancing is repeated concerning the motto of the manuscript, 'for their actions follow them', from the *Book of Revelation*

(14:13), just as the second motto of *The White Guard*, 'and the dead were judged out of those things which were written in the books, according to their works', was also from there (Rev. 20:12).[1] While in his mock Preface to *Black Snow* Bulgakov pretends to disown this motto, its centrality is evident. Evgeny Dobrenko's Introduction to a recent English edition of this novel is subtitled 'Writing Judgment Day', and in its conclusion he argues that the 'unexpected aspect to this apocalyptic theme' is its association, by a main character, with operetta, evoking the 'tragic paradox of Russian history' (and, following Girard, not only): 'what the people of this country perceive to be a dreadful judgment, as well as their hopes for purification and a way out of the endless cycle of tyranny and slavery [. . .], all just returns to its normal course, and becomes deceit and "operetta". An Apocalypse in operetta mode' (Dobrenko 2008: xli).

The quite peculiar account about how he started to write both works should be taken quite seriously. The two accounts, reconstructing the experiential bases of the works, are interesting both in what they share and in what they differ. Bulgakov hid the revelation of his visions behind a game of masks even when he knew it could not be published in his lifetime.

Writing *The White Guard* was conceived after the wars. Bulgakov tells us of having lived a lonely and boring life, in a small room with a cat, when one night he woke up, among tears, as he had a vision of his native city, and memories of the wars returned to him, seeing again people, friends and acquaintances, who died in the wars. His vision focused on a snowstorm and on people moving around a black piano. He started writing with the night-time dream-vision (Bulgakov 1986: 18–19).

The scenery was repeated, in a way, in the story about conceiving the play based on the novel. The existential context is different, provided by the often absurd vicissitudes he had with trying to publish his novel, which had as its central character the editor Ridolfi, explicitly identified as Mephisto-like; events having the character of a tempest. The first moment is again waking up from a dream and snowstorm; but this time a real storm wakes him up and then, with tearful eyes, he sees around him the people who previously populated his dreams: relatives, friends and acquaintances from his native city who died during the wars. Now these were no longer fragments of memory: '[b]orn in a dream, these people were now emerging from their dream and coming firmly to life in my cell-like room' (Ibid.: 51). This event led him eventually to transform the novel into a play: when he returned to his writing, '[t]hrough the lines of the paper I would see a light burning and inside the box those same characters in the novel were moving about' (Ibid.), and eventually the box was also filled with sound, especially with music, played by a pianoforte during the day, while at night by an accordion. So while previously he only saw, in a dream, the body falling to the ground after being shot, he now actually saw the shooting. He did not tell anybody about it, as he knew they would advise him to see a doctor; and yet, the voices did not come from outside: 'No, someone was playing on my table: I could distinctly hear the gentle tickling of the keys' (Ibid.). He could only keep asking questions: 'Why did the little room grow dark, why did the pages fill with a winter's night in the Dnieper' (Ibid.)

This gave him the idea of writing down what he saw: the movement of the figures inside the 'magical little room' (Ibid.), after which the images even became colourful, and at the third night he came to realise that he was writing a theatre play. It is only after this event – at least as told in the novel, though Bulgakov had a great interest in theatre since his childhood – that he started to go to the theatre, taking particularly great pleasure in the costumes of a French play and the funny servant in a Spanish play. He kept working, and by April the first scene was finished (Ibid.: 52).

Master and Margarita

Already at a first glance the novel demonstrates a number of astonishing features. It combines easy accessibility with a difficult, complex structure. Since its publication the book has been extremely popular, both in Russia and abroad, and due not simply to the circumstances of its publication, but its artistic merits: it is both easy and entertaining to read, and yet intellectually challenging and rewarding. Still, behind such easy accessibility there lies an extremely complex organisation; conceiving this book was a genuine *tour de force* of imagination and creative intellect, while its writing involved meticulous artisanship. The book incorporates three different storylines: the arrival in Moscow of a strange group of beings, the devil with some assistants who create havoc in the everyday boredom and hypocrisy of Communist Russia; the Master, a writer, alter ego of Bulgakov, and the love of his life, Margarita; and finally the story of the Crucifixion, a novel written by the Master, having Matthew Levi (the Evangelist) and Pilate as protagonists, and told as a 'play-within-the-play'. The novel takes place within four days, from Wednesday afternoon up to Saturday night, with action running parallel in Moscow (real time) and Jerusalem (the Biblical time of the Crucifixion).

The book is structured around a number of further paradoxes. Its basic tone, struck immediately in its first pages, is burlesque-like, recalling a caravan carousel (Bethea 1982: 390); yet, at the same time, it is full of apocalyptic signs and allusions. Furthermore, while the novel-within-the-novel is confirmed by an eyewitness account of the Crucifixion by Satan, the 'plain' novel has Satan as one of its protagonists, shown in a clearly positive light – especially as compared to the inhabitants, in particular the officialdom, of Moscow under Communist rule. Still further, the heroine, Margarita, otherwise model of Christian love and grace (Weeks 1984), ends up being the witch-queen of a midnight party, a kind of Witches' Sabbath, given by the Devil.

Resolving these paradoxes and explaining the lasting force of the novel can be helped by taking into account three elements. The first is Bulgakov's experiential background, both concerning his highly orthodox education in Kiev and far from orthodox war-time experiences. The second point is the visionary character of Bulgakov's work: similarly to main figures in the European tradition like Dante, Shakespeare, Milton, Goethe, Dickens, Dostoevsky or Thomas Mann, Bulgakov did not simply have great powers of imagination, but his works were rooted in undergoing genuine vision experiences. Finally, through this combination of experiences Bulgakov acquired a position from which he gained direct access to the heart of the modern condition.

This can be shown by unravelling the structuring paradoxes of the novel.

While the novel starts as a satire, or even farce, its basic structure is plainly apocalyptic. This is shown by its strange of 'unity' of time and place. At one level the novel jumps between Jerusalem and Moscow; at another, there are strict parallels between a spring week in 1930s Moscow and the week of the Crucifixion in Jerusalem. Evident apocalyptic imagery includes the tempests that break out in both places around Friday and Saturday evenings (Bulgakov 2008: 185–9, 378, 385, 390), underlined in the Jerusalem scene with the carrion-crows (*sterviatnik*) circling around the scene of the Crucifixion, waiting for their prey (Ibid.: 181);[2] the allusion to Rome or Babylon in the Moscow scenes (Ibid.: 374), a reminder that Moscow was always considered as 'Third Rome'; the way in which at the closing or opening parts of crucial chapters Jerusalem or Moscow emerged from or disappeared into mist and fog (Ibid.: 310, 374, 393–4); or the direct evocation of the four horsemen of the apocalypse (Ibid.: 387–8, 391–2), depicted with particular visionary power by Dürer in 1498–9. The carnevalesque nature of the Moscow scenes could be considered as a technique to lighten up the novel, while contrasting the serenity of ancient Jerusalem with the buffoonery of Communist Moscow. Yet, the novel captures the heart of the present exactly through weaving apocalyptic and carnevalesque elements into a tight unity.

This can be best seen through one particular symbol, the horse – perhaps one of the most complex and important symbols of the book; and one scene, the 'black magic' spectacle at Moscow Circus – certainly one of its culminating moments.

As analysed in detail by the excellent article of David Bethea (1982), images and words evoking the horse are omnipresent in the novel.[3] The significance of this imagery can be best seen through three central instances. First, Bulgakov ends two chapters with practically identical words about Pontius Pilate: the novel-within-the-novel, as read by Margarita (Bulgakov 2008: 344); and the last, 32nd chapter of the book (Ibid.: 400). Yet, there is a slight but important difference in the wording; the second version adds two qualifiers to the name of Pilate: he was a *cruel* procurator, and was a *knight* (*vsadnik*).[4] The two bring together cruelty and horsemen, perhaps another allusion to the apocalyptic horsemen. Second, one of these horsemen in the novel is Behemoth, an apocalyptic Biblical monster, a huge (man-sized) black cat in the novel, and funniest of all characters. Furthermore, in Russian, this is the common name for hippopotamus, meaning 'water horse' in Greek, thus another way of bringing together the grotesque and apocalyptic through the horse. Finally, much emphasis is placed both in Jerusalem and in Moscow on the hippodrome or circus (Greek and Latin names for the same building), again connecting horses with entertainment and apocalyptic scenes at the same time.

This also takes us directly to the second point, a central scene in the novel, the 'black magic' performance of Woland (Satan in the novel), in the circus in Moscow.

The scene takes place at a particularly important juncture. It is the moment in which the various threads in the novel come together. It is Chapter 12 – a number of considerable symbolic significance, in a joint cosmological and sacred sense. It is at the end of Chapter 11 that the Master first appears: an appearance literally interrupted with the Circus scene, as the only thing the – as yet unidentified – Master does is putting a finger on his mouth, whispering 'Psst' (Bulgakov 2008: 123); while in Chapter 13 the Master would not just re-appear, but tell his story, immediately re-connecting, through 'Homeless' the poet and Pilate, the Jerusalem and Moscow storylines. Furthermore, the circus performance is on Thursday evening, the Last Supper in the Gospel chronology, an event omitted from the Master's novel, yet – being a feast – with evident parallels with the circus performance, just as – being last – with apocalypse.

We know from previous chapters that Woland (the foreigner-consultant) promised to perform 'black magic', and also 'revelations', so suspense is guaranteed, both in the circus audience and at the level of the reader. The chapter starts by a clown in motley trousers circling around the circus on a bicycle; while in the ensuing interval Rimskij, administrative director of the circus, much preoccupied about whatever was going to happen, can only repeat for himself one short sentence: 'but why' (*no za shto?*) (Bulgakov 2008: 122), identical to the famous gesture of Pulcinella, *ma perchè?*, chosen in the Italian translation of the novel (Bulgakov 1997a: 159). This is when Woland enters the scene, with his assistants Korov'ev and Behemoth, wearing a black mask (*polumaska*, Bulgakov 2008: 124: a Russian term denoting Venetian style half-masks). The performance produces quite different revelations than officials or the public could have imagined: it is the deprived state of 1930s Moscow that was revealed there, literally unmasked and even physically rendered nude, as the cloths that were distributed for free and for which members of the public frenetically traded their own clothes would vanish into thin air, leaving their owners naked in the streets of Moscow.

The crucial scene of the chapter comes after the first few tricks demonstrating that Woland and his assistants are indeed in capable of performing magic. At that moment they suddenly end the hilarity and start to silently scrutinise the public (Bulgakov 2008: 125). The scene closely recalls how Meyerhold's Pierrot scrutinised the public a few decades earlier in *The Fairground Booth* (Szakolczai 2013a: 289); but the purpose and effects are radically different. Bulgakov is not trying to assert his own superiority by confusing the public, rather he tries to have them return to their senses. It is the most serene moment in the book, not comic or parodic in any way, though not apocalyptic either, rather orthodox Christian. The question Woland asks from his assistants is whether the inhabitants of Moscow have genuinely changed, as the Communist propaganda wanted to have it: not just externally, but internally, which is 'the much more important question' (Bulgakov 2008: 126). The answer is so evident that it needs not be spelt out. The actual flow of events reveals an even more depressing answer: yes, they have actually indeed changed, and internally, but in the wrong direction. So in the novel egregious hilarity, apocalyptic doom and calm serenity all belong together, forming an in-depth analysis and comprehensive diagnosis of the modern condition.

This can be seen by presenting the main figures of the novel.

The Muscovites: secular modernity

As the novel takes place in its present, the 1930s in Moscow, the first question to discuss is what it says about the people of this time and place. The answer is simply nothing: these people were measured and found wanting (Daniel 5:25). They are nobodies, weightless beings, carrying on meaningless nullity existence. Bulgakov by no means diabolises these unhappy wretches, in search of immediate bliss, rather shows that their human substance has been so profoundly emptied by the experiences of the past decades that they no longer possess any weight: their lives have become so meaningless that they do not even notice it. Officials simply abuse their power and privileges to the maximum degree possible, while at the same time live under a terrible fear, as anything can happen to them at any time: they can be unmasked. The general public does not fare much better; they have become obedient puppets of the authority-less apparatchiks of the Soviet regime: terrorised to keep the rules and fulfil orders, the horizon of their lives has been reduced to the satisfaction of the most mundane material goods and bodily functions.

Significantly, the fate of some prominent figures of the corrupt and empty officialdom is beheading: whether for good, as in the case of Berlioz, or as a farce that can be reversed, as in the case of Rimskij. This recalls the guillotine, famous 'invention' of the French Revolution. The similarity is certainly intended, underlined by the start of Chapter 29, beginning of a series of apocalyptic chapters, where Woland and Azazello sit on the stone terrace of a beautiful Moscow building, built about a century and half earlier, so just before the French Revolution (Bulgakov 2008: 373).

Only few persons are exempt from this general picture. One is Praskovja Fjodorovna, the nurse in the psychiatric hospital, who is good in her simplicity (Ibid.: 176, 390). Born before the apocalyptic times of the World War and October Revolution, due to her plain, solid goodness she was not formed or transformed by these events. But not everybody born before the twentieth century was 'immune' from these experiences, as shown through Annushka-the-plague (*chuma-Annushka*; Ibid.: 306), who is without redeeming qualities, becoming something like the 'exterminating angel' in the novel, spilling out the oil that would help Berlioz meet his fate – and who almost pocketed the horse-shoe lost by Margarita.

The people of Moscow who resigned themselves to the experiences of the twentieth century must convert. Two paradigmatic cases are presented: the poet 'Homeless' (*Bezdomnij*), who first became witness, together with Berlioz, a particularly repulsive official of the Writers Union, to the 'materialisation' of Woland and his company, but who then meets the Master in a psychiatric ward and comes to his senses there, even becomes a professor;[5] and Varenusha, the theatre administrator, who is transformed into a vampire by Hella, becoming so excessively nice and courteous 'that the masks called him their benefactor-father' (Ibid.: 407).

Woland and company: Old Testament

Woland and his suite create havoc, in Moscow and in the reader, not simply by their materialisation and by their antics, but because the Devil turns out to be a positive character. The paradox is resolved in an excellent article by Laura Weeks (1984), who argues that Bulgakov is using the Old Testament sense of Satan.

Woland is nothing else but Satan. The name helps to overcome the standard image of the Devil; indeed, the question 'but who is he?' is repeatedly posed at the beginning by the two Moscow characters, Berlioz and Homeless, who meet him first. The answer suggested by Laura Weeks is that Woland is the Satan of not the New but the Old Testament. This means that while he is 'the prince of this world' (Jn 12:31, 14:30, 16:11), with respect to higher powers he is a servant executing orders. This becomes clear in Chapter 29, when Matthew Levi gives orders to him, in the name of Yeshua, without showing much respect, labelling Woland as an 'old Sophist' and the 'spirit of evil and sovereign of darkness', and Woland – though protesting that he is 'not a slave [*rab*]' – still has to obey (Bulgakov 2008: 374–5).

This combination of rulership and obedience indicates Woland/Satan as an in-between, liminal being, which indeed corresponds to his image in the Old Testament and in the novel, as well as to the etymological root of the word, *sut* 'rover' (Weeks 1984: 231). Satan is an unsettled spirit, a traveller perpetually moving between the upper and lower worlds, and is therefore first of all a messenger in the Old Testament (Ibid.: 228). Still, his role as communicator between the two realms is not restricted to delivering messages, rather it incorporates a complex set of administrative-legal functions, and Bulgakov shifts emphasis here. This includes the testing of human beings; then the role of the public prosecutor, a task specifically assigned to him in the Old Testament tradition, which also came to be emphasised recently by René Girard (1999); and finally the administration of justice. It is these legal roles that, according to Weeks (1984: 225–33), were at the centre of his 'materialisation' in Moscow. And, for once, this is no joking matter: in one of his last utterances Woland reassures Margarita that 'everything will be right (*pravil'na*), the world is based on this' (Bulgakov 2008: 397).

Furthermore, this etymology opens up a genuine treasure trove for Bulgakov, as in Russian *sut* means 'fool', while *sutka* 'joke', tying further the knots around demonic and parodic, apocalyptic and carnevalesque.

Apart from his materialisation in Moscow, Woland was present at crucial moments of history and loves to perplex his audience by jovially telling about his talk with Pilate on his balcony (Bulgakov 2008: 44), or his breakfast in Königsberg with Kant. This latter enables Bulgakov to express his views on the founder of critical philosophy. Taking up a rush comment by the illiterate poet Homeless, Woland agrees that the asylum is Kant's right place. He told him during their conversation: 'as you wish, Professor, but you got yourself into some awkward speculation! Perhaps it is smart (*umno*), but desperately unintelligible (*boljno neponjatna*). You will be laughed at' (Ibid.: 12).[6] Apart from frightening them out of their wits, Woland exerts another quite specific and most alarming effect on human beings: he numbs their will, preventing them from carrying out actions they want to perform or should be doing (Ibid.: 49, 123). Finally, his apartment in which the Witches' Sabbath reception takes place also contains some interesting objects, related to the room being lit by candles, as Woland could not stand electricity. These include a candelabra with seven legs in the form of claws; while the branches of another formed the shape of a serpent (Ibid.: 261), interpreted as Satanic parodies of the *menorah*. However, given that candelabras are usually made of bronze, this also recalls the bronze serpent of Moses in *Numbers* (21:9).

Woland has four aids in the novel; each with a name and characteristic that closely recall episodes of the Old Testament that are more central to the apocryphal traditions than the Scripture. The first is Korov'ev, also called Fagot. The Russian name recalls the word *korova* 'cow', alluding to the golden calf or cow (Weeks 1984: 237).[7] His other name evokes a musical instrument, the bassoon. The figure is one of the greatest pranksters in the book, though not without tragic undertones: in his real life Korov'ev made some jokes about light and darkness, and for this he had to repent for quite a long time; his punishment only expired with his Moscow activities (Bulgakov 2008: 395).

The most peculiar thing about Korov'ev is his appearance, in both senses of the word: the way he looked and the manner in which he materialised 'out of thin air'. Concerning the latter Bulgakov is most careful and precise, and is literally Shakespeare on the reverse: while in *The Tempest* (IV.i.150) the figures of the masque vanished 'into air, into thin air', here the materialisation of Korov'ev takes place twice, first by the air becoming suddenly thicker (Bulgakov 2008: 6), and then as if stepping out of vapour (Ibid.: 46). Concerning the former, attention usually focuses on his physical features, being extremely high and thin and having a moustache that recalls birds' feathers, or the strange kind of pince-nez he was wearing. The most interesting element for this book, however, is his 'motley' trousers. The Russian word used is *kletchatyj*, which means motley in the sense of 'checkered', while the other Russian word meaning 'motley' is *pjostryj* 'multi-coloured'. Taken together, these are the two terms used in Russian to characterise the clothing of Harlequin, while the classic, 1867 translation of *As You Like It* by Piotr Isaevich Veinberg used the adjective *pjostryj* for the 'motley' coat of Jaques. This clearly identifies Korov'ev as a Harlequin figure. Combined with his Russian name meaning 'cow', this indicates that in Soviet Russia Harlequin became outright an idol; while his not wearing a 'motley coat' but a 'motley pantaloon' jointly evokes the two main characters of Venetian *commedia dell'arte*, Pantalone and Arlecchino, helping to recognise Bolshevik Russia as commedic buffoonery.

The 'inseparable companion' of Korov'ev is Behemoth, a black cat, which – together with the black Venetian half-mask of Woland – tightens further the net around Venice, *commedia dell'arte* and the Shakespeare of Jaques, Iago and Othello, but also the Paris cabaret, metamorphosis of the commedic, the most famous cabaret being *Le Chat Noir*. In the Old Testament Behemoth only appears in *Job* (40: 15), but is also present in the *Book of Enoch* as a male monster, always together with Leviathan, who is female (Hamvas 1989: 82–3; Weeks 1984: 237). While Leviathan is considered a dragon or sea monster, it is not clear what kind of animal Behemoth was, though due to its enormous size it came to be identified with the hippopotamus (Batto 1995: 319).

The other two members of the company are not as frequently present in the novel, but carry just as intriguing and mostly apocryphal references. The identification of Azazello with the Azazel of the Old Testament is evident. Both appearances of this figure carry exceptional significance. In *Leviticus* 16 Azazel is a demon associated with scape-goating: during the ritual priests offered two scape-goats for the sins of the people, one to Azazel, driven away into the desert (Janowski 1995). The role of Azazel in this rite is not clear, a problem not helped by the uncertainty of its etymology: it might stand for a desert demon, or for a precipitous place like a rugged cliff. This ritual is not Biblical in origin, as it can be traced back to the South-Anatolian and Northern Syrian region (Ibid.), birthplace of agriculture and location of the first stone temples, in particular Göbekli Tepe.

Azazel is also prominently present in the *Book of Enoch*. This work is considered as Hebrew Hellenistic apocryphal prophecy, but Hamvas (1989) traces it to a much older tradition. Azazel leads a group of rebel angels who lusted after women, their blasphemous unity generating a monstrous race (Ibid.; see also Weeks 1984: 237). Azazel also taught a number of arts and crafts for humans, including astrology, metallurgy, sword-making for males and the art of make-up for females (Hamvas 1989: 36). The fallen angels were condemned to a punishment recalling Prometheus the Titan, which – as Prometheus was also considered as inventor of sacrifice – can be tied back to the *Leviticus* story. In Rabbinic Judaism, Azazel is simply ignored (Janowski 1995: 245).

In *Master and Margarita* Azazello shares several features with the Old Testament Azazel: he has mastery of firearms, and gives to Margarita 'the cream with the power to beautify women and bewitch men' (Weeks 1984: 238). His most peculiar bodily feature, however, was his fiery-red hair (*ogn'enno-ryzhij*), as if crowning a particularly repugnant face (Bulgakov 2008: 86).

The last member of the entourage, Hella, similarly has red hair as her most distinguishing feature. In both occasions where introduced attention is called immediately on her red hair (Ibid.: 117, 131). The word used for red (*ryzhij*) has its importance, as the usual Russian word for red is *kracnyj*, etymologically linked to 'beautiful' *kracivyj*, while *ryzhij* is chestnut or ginger-red, used for circus-clowns (in colloquial called *ryzhego*), or for horses. Black (as the night) and red (as the fire) are thus the two colours clearly marking the company, and such a combination with its symbolic power leaves no doubt that it represents the dark underworld, hell, with its burning fires.

Hella carries such an association even in her name, but has a series of further identifying features. When she first appears, she is completely nude, a beautiful young woman with one disturbing feature: a scar on her neck. She also has ice-cold hands and phosphorescent sparkling eyes, identifying her as a vampire. Her first act is to kiss Varenusha, the theatre administrator, transforming him into a vampire. According to Weeks, these features also identify Hella with Lilith, present according to some translations in *Isaiah* (34: 14), also identified with the whore of Babylon in *Revelation* (17–18), even considered according to Jewish folklore as the first wife of Adam; a divinity that can traced back to Mesopotamia, with her name as Lilitu first appearing in 2400 BC Akkadic inscriptions (Hutter 1995: 973–4; Weeks 1984: 238–9). Lilith is a beautiful nude woman, vampire and seductress, often represented with the wings and feet of an owl and surrounded by two lions, recalling the Minoan *Potnia*. She preys particularly on the most vulnerable: mothers at childbirth; newborn infants; and men who are spending the night alone. She has no husband and cannot bear children, so tries to ensnare men, in particular by being one 'with whom a man does not sleep in the same way as with his wife' (Hutter 1995: 974). As a demon, she is also linked to stormy winds (Ibid.). In the cabalistic literature, known to Bulgakov working on *The Cabal of Hypocrites*, she appeared as having long red hair (Weeks 1984: 239). The names Azazel and Lilith also share a repetition of the first syllable.

The Master and Margarita: New Testament

If Woland and company did not conform to the classical image of the devil, rather standing for the Old Testament idea of administering justice, recalling the 'cruel horsemen' of the Apocalypse and placing the inhabitants of Moscow on trial, then the title heroes, the Master and Margarita, stand for the New Testament and its central values, love and grace (Weeks 1984: 225, 240). The perspective that sins must be condemned according to justice and can only be redeemed through the graceful gift of love is one of the central messages of the novel, characteristic in particular in the way in which at the end the Master liberates the hero of his novel, Pilate, whose punishment closely recalls the fate of Titans (Bulgakov 2008: 397–8).

The Master is true master of his art and knows it; this is how he introduces himself (Ibid.: 142), without the slightest pretence. He can sound out anything that is not genuine, fake, false (Ibid.: 150). Furthermore, just as Bulgakov, he suffered too much in his life, and – more than the author – became broken by it. This is revealed in a particularly captivating passage of the novel, dictated by Bulgakov in the last months of his life, when already blind (Pevear and Volokhonsky 1997: xix), and considered as pure autobiography by the most authoritative Bulgakov scholar, Marietta Chudakova, about the tiredness of those who carried a too heavy weight in their life (Bulgakov 2008: 394; see Bethea 1982: 392). This passage offers an apotheosis of noble suffering, recalling Baudelaire and Nietzsche. However, in his life, the Master could not always stand up to this value; he proved to be too weak; in particular, he yielded to the most common and most infectious illness of life under Communist Russia, fear; and due to this fear, he has lost the most important thing in his life, Margarita. Being afraid, too weak to commit himself fully, he rather escaped into a mental hospital, leaving their common hide-away and Margarita could not find him.

Bulgakov even names this illness, the reason why the Master could not fully stand up to his task: he was too romantic; in the words of Woland, even 'thrice Romantic' (Bulgakov 2008: 399). Thus, according to the final judgement, delivered by Matthew Levi to Woland, he 'did not merit the light, only merited peace' (Ibid.: 376). This peace he indeed receives at the very end of the novel, when he is re-united with Margarita, and the two are taken by Woland to their final resting place where they could live in peace until the end of times, an idyllic home surrounded by quiet and silence, which can be accessed through a stone bridge over a trickling creek; a stone house with a Venetian style window (*venetsianskoe okno*) (Ibid.: 399), with vines running up the roof.

The true hero of the novel, however, in the classical, ritual sense of contest and victory, is not the Master, but Margarita. She is the one who has the force to pass all the tests, meriting the reunion with the Master and gaining for him the place of rest. Margarita is a figure of practically unlimited love and grace, marked only with one romantic blemish, which is not shared by her real-life model, Bulgakov's third wife: she is told of having an enviable life, including not having children (Ibid.: 223).

In the novel, Margarita embodies *the* female, both close relative and radical opposite of Lilith. She does not have the writing talent of the Master, and willingly subordinates herself to his genius; but, in contrast to the Master, she has courage and strength. She not only cannot be discouraged by critics belonging to the Communist officialdom – against whom, again characteristically, she entertains an unlimited passion for retaliation, and only his good luck saves her worst enemy from the terrible end that would have been his fate, had he been at home at the moment when Margarita was finally empowered to act out her revenge. More importantly, she stood up fully to the task of confronting the messenger Woland sent to him, the particularly repulsive and fearful Azazello, who in her hands became powerless, even invoking Behemoth for help; then accepted and fulfilled the task, serving as Queen to the Satan's ball, that taxes to the limit any mortal. In doing so she was helped by the fact that – as intimated by Woland just before the feast – she had 'royal blood [*korolevskoj krovi*]' (Bulgakov 2008: 260). She even passed the most difficult test of all: once having fulfilled her task, she was ready to leave, without asking anything in recompense, thus standing up to the maxim, explicated by Woland later: 'Don't ever ask for anything! Never anything, and especially not from those who are stronger than you' (Ibid.: 292). She therefore fully merited her reward, the only reward that interested her: she got back the Master, and the two could depart towards their eternal repose.

Notes

1. The first motto is also of exceptional interest, as it reproduces an experience central for both Thomas Mann and Karen Blixen, the manner in which water and the snow can melt into air: 'A light snow was falling, which suddenly changed to thick, heavy flakes. The wind began to howl; it was a snowstorm. Within a moment the dark sky had merged with the ocean of snow. Everything disappeared' (from Pushkin, *The Captain's Daughter*).

2. The word *sterviatnik* is derived from *sterva* 'dead animal', an obsolete meaning as the word became a term of abuse in the sense of 'bastard', 'shit', bitch'. See also the related expression *stervenetj* 'get mad, furious'.
3. Russian has two terms for the horse, *konj* (most used by Bulgakov) and *loshadj*. Their etymology, together with that of Indo-European, Turkish and Finno-Ugorian terms is a most fascinating subject, as all of them are closely linked – a connection linguists cannot explain.
4. Strangely enough, this word is etymologically rooted in *sad* 'garden', a connection Bethea (1982) explores in detail. The word used for Don Quixote as knight was different (*rytzar'*).
5. A possible model for 'Homeless' the poet, intriguingly, is Peter Altenberg, one of the main figures of Vienna modernism, widely considered as epitomising a 'homeless poet' (Magris 1986: 20).
6. The famous Rolling Stones song 'Sympathy for the Devil', recorded June 1968, was inspired by Bulgakov's novel. The song, by the way, itself contains an excellent analysis of the Trickster figure. For details, see Horvath (2000).
7. It should be added that *korovka* means 'ladybird', while the phonetically similar pair of words *korolj* and *koroleva* mean 'king' and 'queen'.

11 Heimito von Doderer
Demons

Novels and the Sociology of the Contemporary offered a sociological-genealogical analysis of classic works by some of the best-known figures of European culture. The first two parts of this book, even adding Chapter 7, which is closely connected to Chapter 3, still discussed some of the best-known figures of twentieth century culture, though works that had an incomplete character. In the rest of Part Three, unpublished works of much less known figures dominate – culminating in the last two chapters, devoted to extremely long books by an Austrian and a Hungarian writer that are hardly known outside their local context. Yet, no paradox is intended to finish a project focusing on European culture by them; and perhaps the best way to introduce their proposed centrality is to present the truly striking parallels between these two books.

Doderer worked on a first version of his novel, entitled 'Die Dämonen' after his reading of Dostoevsky's *Demons* in 1931, between 1929 and 1936 (Hesson 1982: 20–1). Hamvas started to write 'Ördöngösök', similarly derived from the Hungarian title of Dostoevsky's *Demons* ('Ördögök'), between 1928 and 1931. A major source of inspiration for both, just as for Dostoevsky, was the highly negative experience gained about the press, for which they actually worked. Setting aside their novel, they both returned to it after World War II, about 20 years after they started it;[1] and finished about 20 years after they first abandoned the draft.[2] Even further, before setting out to complete the novels, both wrote a crucial theoretical essay as a springboard for completion. For Hamvas, it was his 'Fragments for a Theory of the Novel' (*Regényelméleti Fragmentum*, Hamvas 1994; see Szakolczai 2012), based not only on his reading of novels but on his extensive work about the history of religions and philosophies. For Doderer, it was 'Sexuality and the Total State' (*Sexualität und totaler Staat*), a kind of mental preparation for resuming work on the novel, based on his efforts to overcome a personal obsession with sexuality, the central argument being that 'totalitarian regimes find their sustenance in any form of deviant sexual behaviour' (Hesson 1982: 11, 37–8).[3] Finally, both works turned out to be quite bulky; depending on the edition, they are 1200–1500 pages long. Doderer's novel was immediately published and hailed as a masterpiece, still widely considered as the most important Austrian novel of the twentieth century; Hamvas's remained a manuscript for 34 years, only published 17 years after his death, but then instantaneously hailed as the key novel of Hungary for the twentieth century, and still considered by many as such – though, just as Doderer's novel, and for a variety of reasons, it also has its detractors.

Apart from such parallel genesis, the central themes and methods of the novels are also closely related. They capture the demonic features of a society, even culture, in which the sense of reality is increasingly lost, human beings play roles and cover their faces by masks which they take as their own life, thus replacing the first reality with a second. This is a situation where the power of reasoning is irrelevant, thus Kantian rationality, far from promoting maturity, rather becomes an instrument of massive, by now globalised infantilisation, promoted by the mirage world conjured up by the increasingly omnipotent medias. Based on their unique life experiences, covering the two World Wars and various totalitarian regimes, *Die Dämonen* and *Karnevál* offer still unparalleled, and possibly unsurpassable, analyses of modern permanent liminality as a sacrificial carnival.

Life and work

Just as Broch, Heimito von Doderer (1896–1966) did not dream about becoming a writer. He became one due to circumstances, by accident or rather misfortune: a consequence of living through much of the most turbulent times of the twentieth century, and at a particularly exposed place. He became a writer in order to come to terms with his life, including his own stupidity (Hesson 1982: 38; Shillabeer 2008: 77).[4] He did not just live through the times, rather he plunged headlong into them. Still, he had the presence of mind to react to his own actions and mend his ways. As a result, he became one of the most important twentieth century novelists in Austria (Arens 1996: 15), and not only there; his work having particularly close links to his life (Hesson 1982: 7).

Born on 5 September 1896, he turned 18 just a few months after the start of World War I, thus he was at the front in the first war year, becoming a prisoner, spending four years in a POW camp, then staging a spectacular escape back home. In the 1920s, apart from finishing academic studies as a historian, as member of the first Freud generation he not simply experimented with various erotic experiences, but became obsessed with sexuality, describing his experiences in excruciating detail, so that people close to him considered him as a fool estranged from the world (Shillabeer 2008: 75). Married in 1930 but soon divorced; his wife being Jewish, yet joining the Nazi party and living in Munich after 1930; yet again, increasingly disenchanted from Nazis, he published in 1938 back in Austria a novel that would be banned soon after the Anschluss, and converted to Catholicism in 1939/40. While prohibited to publish for a time after World War II, in 1951 his novel *Die Strudlhofstiege* appeared, with great success, and the 1956 publication of *The Demons* also generated substantial echo. In a letter written in 1957, thus shortly after publication, Doderer characterised the nature of his work as swimming 25 years against the stream (Hesson 1982: 52–3).

While borrowing his title from Dostoevsky, he followed less the dialogical method of the Russian writer as Goethe's and Nietzsche's insights concerning self-overcoming. *The Demons* contained no less than three autobiographical characters; yet, far from simply serving as the mouthpieces of the author, they rather represented what Doderer has overcome. Kajetan von Schlaggenberg wrote a manuscript entitled 'Fat females' about the subjects of his sexual obsession; René Stangeler was a historian, the career Doderer abandoned in order to become a writer;[5] while Georg von Geyrenhoff started to write a mere chronicle about the group of people around him, an undertaking which at a point stopped being a mere document, precipitating his involvement (Doderer 1961: 14–15); still, the narrator insinuated that it was only possible to incorporate little of this chronicle into the final novel. It is through such Goethe-Nietzschean ways of self-overcoming that the novel could become much more than a mere 'critique' of post-war Vienna, and – through this – of the rising modern world. Far from proclaiming immunity, central for the pretence of a critical position, Doderer acknowledged his manifold involvement, thus gaining the force to detach itself, gaining unique penetration into the root causes of the 'modern illness' (Shillabeer 2008). Such method is explicitly contrasted with the presumed 'objectivist' method of watching people from a distance, as if covered in darkness, a position identified as a 'second reality'; a metaphor with evident theatrical analogies.

Questions of method

Doderer developed in the novel a series of further methodological tools, closely compatible with the anthropological concepts developed previously: some being simple techniques of writing, while others containing insights alluding to true metaphysical depth. They include the idea of a 'total novel' exposed in the *Overture*. According to this, it is enough to draw a single thread at any point

> out of the fabric of life and the run will make a pathway across the whole, and down that wider pathway each of the other threads will become successively visible, one by one. For the whole is contained in the smallest segment of anyone's life-story; indeed, we may even say that it is contained in every single moment.
>
> (Doderer 1961: 7)

This is because

> the past masses like clouds to the right and left of your head, as it were, and the sharp and sweet tooth of memory sinks to the heart's core. Out of that past there floats toward you, as though composed of mists, all that combines to form the truth; things we were scarcely aware of now join themselves together, one related image to another. They form a bridge across time, although in life they may never have touched.
>
> (Ibid.: 13)

This perspective implies a revalorisation of the given. In modern thinking the 'taken for granted' became something to be overcome at any cost, enshrined at the heart of modernist orthodoxy, neo-Kantianism, where transforming the 'given' (*gegeben*) into a 'task' (*Aufgabe*) became a central slogan. Doderer, just as Ortega and Bakhtin, managed to see through this trick, recognising the gift-like value of the given: 'What is most significant about every situation is the aspect of it that is taken for granted [*was dabei als selbstverständlich gilt*]' (Doderer 1956: 33; 1961: 30). Thus, instead of generating a 'clear slate' (*tabula rasa*), and constructing 'second realities' that purport to be realer than the real, the task of a genuine novelist of truth is the opposite: to penetrate, with the purpose of understanding, the extremely complex web of the first reality.

Doderer's approach explains the length and meander-like structure of the novel, almost devoid of a plot in the classical sense. Yet, the method works, as the novel skilfully blends a single micro-historical event, a chance encounter of the chronicler with an acquaintance, Levielle the financier, dated to 24 March 1927, and the popular revolt against the Palace of Justice in Vienna on 15 July. Both events are marked by a series of further coincidences, which by the end of the novel gain their full meaning. It was also a coincidence that this meeting fell on the day before Annunciation Day, thus 'announced' something for the novel. While this was an invention of Doderer, 15 July 1927 indeed fell on a full moon, a strangely significant coincidence, given the symbolic significance of the full moon, with its round face, for modernism.[6]

Doderer calls attention to the potential significance of 'mere' coincidences at the closing page of the Overture, claiming to 'discern a gigantic hand', just after he described a gothic cathedral as a finger pointing to the sky, 'beyond the ridiculous boundaries of an individual life', compared to 'the outstretched hand of a gigantic clock', which is further compared to the booming sound of a canon. The sign-like character of coincidences is taken further in another crucial aside, a few pages before about dreams, visions and insights (a crucial Shakespeare theme): dreams that have a validity for life, thus which are more insights than dreams, and which gain their compelling power by alluding to a vital presence (1961: 13).

This combination of the indicative power of vision-insights and coincidences further valorises taking up a single thread of life, cutting across the whole, as the three terms are brought together by the word 'revelation': a prophetic vision-insight reveals the future, just as a single thread across life reveals the present or the past.

The effective power of coincidences and the formative power of events also bring in liminality. The idea is prominently present through one of Doderer's alter-egos, the historian René Stangeler. Stangeler works jointly on the Merovingians and the later Renaissance – a choice most peculiar for mainstream historians, as the two periods are separated by almost a millennia; yet, justified by René through the two periods being joined by 'their evident inchoateness' (Ibid.: 207); an argument all the more interesting as it brings into view contemporary times. The tissue of coincidences is thick, as René means 'reborn', evoking the Renaissance, one of the central interests of René.

The evocation of liminality extends to 15 July 1927 as a formative liminal event, or the metaphor of windows or glasses being so clear and transparent that, exactly by becoming nothing, they could gather everything and discolour nothing (Shillabeer 2008: 100). Doderer also combined a situation of time being out of joint with the need to preserve oneself (Doderer 1961: 260), arguing that the extreme fluidity of Austrian law after World War I contributed to the rising totalitarianism (Ibid.: 1082).

Moral purpose

The idea that novels serve a moral purpose is not new. Apart from Bakhtin on Plato's dialogues and Menippean satire, it also relied on a strong local tradition, including Hofmannsthal and Broch. Yet, Doderer adds a series of steps, relying on his own problematic personal experiences. To begin with, he was clearly aware that such moral concerns developed in schismatic tandem with their opposites: a play with inciting emotions and desires on the one hand, and the proclamation of pure value freedom on the other. It is no accident that such focus on morality by Viennese writers, becoming especially pronounced after World War I, went hand in hand with the similar Viennese focus on the rejection of conscience, even the self, proposed by Mach, or the declaration of neutral, value-free science, professed both by neo-Kantians and the Vienna school. Such intellectual escape into value freedom and positivism directly supported social corruption. Doderer singled out for attention the declining morals in finance – through one of his heroes, the Jewish banker Altschul, descendant of a long-standing merchant family (Ibid.: 363–4); or the promotion of indecency in the press and in art. Here Doderer mentions the trick of promoting ever shorter skirts, through fashion (Ibid.: 276), and legitimating indecency through the label of art – where he singled out for attention the *Rosenkavalier*, the most famous work of Hofmannsthal (Ibid.: 212). The consequence of such schismatic practices is the rise of anti-intellectualism, on the one hand, reflecting the recognition of the problem caused by the prevailing corrupt notion of the intellect (Ibid.: 327); but which, on the other hand, renders impossible to counter such trends, as real intellect is only the outer extension of the inner strength necessary to stand up against publicly dominant trends (Ibid.). Such schismatic processes help the construction of second realities and undermine the perception of such constructs as mere constructs – while the purpose of novels is not simply to present such constructs as 'second realities', but to see in ourselves the capacity both for constructing such second realities *and* for failing to see that we are doing so (Shillabeer 2008: 97).[7]

Conversion

This directly brings in the concern with conversion. While the term is usually considered to have a religious meaning and over time has become associated with a shift from one set of religious belief to another, recently it gained wider significance.[8] This concern has a particularly strong 'imperial Austrian' focus: the concluding lines from Rainer Maria Rilke's 'Archaic Torso of Apollo', 'You must change your life', close the last chapter on Pascal in the classic book of Borkenau (1976: 559), just as the chapter on Doderer in Shillabeer's (2008: 101) thesis.

According to Shillabeer (Ibid.: 80–1), Doderer thematises the process of conversion in three steps. To begin with, in line with Foucault and in contrast to Descartes and Kant, nobody can be the source of his or her conversion: one cannot 'autonomously' 'will' to change one life; such change requires an accident, a chance event, a coincidence, which sets one on the road to recovery. Second, however, this only provides the starting point, where one then must proceed unwaveringly. In particular, one must fight one's own double, or the self-image created and sustained by one's own 'second realities', or assumed masks. Finally, engaging such a process assumes humbleness, instead of pride.

Conversion is a central way of exiting from 'second realities' produced by the 'failure to perceive'. These two concepts are central for Doderer, the point at which he becomes from a simple novelist an important and innovative thinker.

'Second reality'

The term 'second reality' is the best-known and indeed central invention of Doderer. Its importance was recognised by Eric Voegelin, who in his lectures *Hitler and the Germans* and *Anamnesis* placed a considerable importance on the word (see also Wydra 2008). It was central for his essay 'The Eclipse of Reality' (Voegelin 1990b), originally published in a Festschrift for Alfred Schutz. However, Voegelin never offered a detailed discussion of the term, and even conflated Doderer's ideas with Musil's (Shillabeer 2008).

Doderer's concern with second reality is particularly helpful to revisit the contemporary version of neo-Kantianism called 'social constructivism'. Second realities emerged due to our efforts to surround ourselves with constructs (Ibid.: 78): hobbyhorses, fabrications of our imagination (Doderer 1961: 836–7, 844). Such fabrications recall a spider-web (Ibid.: 963), with the fantasy-dreamer at the centre of his world – a position evoking that of a novel-writer, further explaining why novels are not only primary examples for fictioning reality, but also offer privileged tools to understand the modalities of such fictioning. In his early novel Doderer presents a position central for creating such fictions: it is watching people from darkness (Shillabeer 2008: 78), identical with the position of a spectator in a modern theatre, and also the privileged position of modern 'rationalist' philosophy. Examples for such fabrications include the obsession with the 'fat females' of Kajetan, leading him to write a book-length diary, which contained nothing but 'asininity' (*Popanzerei* 1956: 670), an 'idiotic doctrine' and 'grotesque nonsense', rooted in resentment,[9] based on the principle that '"Everything has to be carried to extremes"' (Ibid.: 671: *Es muß alles auf die Spitze getrieben warden*), but meaning only that 'he was clowning over the ruins of his own life', camouflaged as 'the dawn of a "new era"' (Doderer 1961: 685); or Jan Herzka's strolls (Ibid.: 1024).

The creation of second realities implies the taking up of a mask, but also something much more sinister: one 'enter[s] the danger zone of self-deception'

(Ibid.: 181); the 'honest dishonesty' of identifying ourselves with our own constructs, and the belief that the second reality is the only reality (Shillabeer 2008: 77) – a situation where it is difficult to establish the degree of consciousness about the distortion, but from which eventually it becomes all but impossible to turn back (Ibid.: 79–80). Such constant self-falsification leads to utter vulgarity (Doderer 1961: 1138–9), a point analysed through Paul Valéry, also reached by Broch (1985) through the figure of Bertrand. The direct outcome is a permanent friction between two realities (Doderer 1961: 1019), which renders everybody in this state particularly delicate, as if the balance of life could topple at any minute (Ibid.: 191), and which indeed often happens through the central modern experience of a split self; the creation of our own doubles that we then have to fight (Shillabeer 2008: 81).[10]

The failure to perceive

The central means to reach a stage where one becomes imprisoned in his or her own construct is *Apperzeptionsverweigerung*, or the failure to perceive reality as it is; a resistance to reality itself, which directly produces false realities (Voegelin 1978; Arens 1996: 15–16, 20); an act of stupidity that leads to the construction of second realities (Shillabeer 2008: 79).

Doderer exposes his idea in a dialogue about recent psychological discoveries (Doderer 1961: 456–8). According to these, perception through senses is not 'objectively' given, but involves a creative, productive component. This can be twisted around and turned into a denial of reality – meaning that we have the inalienable human right, due to our gift of creative imagination, to destroy our ties with reality by making a fool out of ourselves.

Failure to perceive reality as a 'human right' and the root of constructing second realities is directly connected to the nature of the demonic. The word is brought in through the interest in the late Middle Ages by Stangeler, Doderer's most important alter ego (Ibid.: 1018–19). While technically only relevant to that period, through his characters Doderer argues about the literal significance of the term for modernity as well. Details are again of utmost relevance, thus Doderer's argument must be reconstructed, with abundant citations. In the context of the narrative, the demonic appears in a late fifteenth manuscript about witch-hunts. Nothing could be further from our enlightened present – but Doderer begs to differ. The story, he relays through Stangeler, 'exemplif[ies] the dominant factor of our time: a second reality [*zweite Wirklichkeit*]. This is something which is set up alongside the first, actual reality' (1956: 1021; 1961: 1018). In particular, the *idées fixes* of the fifteenth century stand direct parallel with the sexual ideologies of our epoch.[11] As an example, he brings up a protagonist of the witch-trials who imagines that he consists of two halves, with half of his body made of wood. Far from being an obscure medieval oddity, this has vital relevance for the modern age of ideologies, as it evokes 'the modern experience, the clash between a first and a second reality, between which no bridge exists, and no common language', even though they may use the same words (1961: 1019). In the medieval language of the novel-within-the-novel this experience is expressed in the following terms: 'A dreme, when that overcometh thee and thou art alone wyth it, wyth thy dreme and vision, alle els escapeth thee and thou art loste'. It is identified with the demonic; this is what '[t]oday is falsely called a philosophy [*eine Weltanchauung*]' (1956: 1023; 1961: 1019). Thus, following Thomas Mann and Broch, but going further, Doderer does not shy away from identifying Kant's rationalist constructivism with the affirmation of the demonic. In the directly ensuing sentences he makes his meaning plain, going back to the experiential roots of the debates around 'critical philosophy':

> As if it were of rational origin! But the mutual hatred that constantly breaks out between these rival philosophies [*Weltanchauungen*] should tell us something. That alone should indicate that their real source has nothing to do with the divergent opinions on how 'humanity' can be helped, or on this class or that race, six of one and half dozen of the other, and suchlike idiocies.
>
> (Ibid.)

Yet the demonic, irresistible as it becomes when it suddenly enters the scene, transforming reality into the image of its phantasmagorical constructs, disappears just as quickly, and – apparently – without a trace: 'it is characteristic of all matters connected with the demonic that although they create a tremendous stir and a great deal of motion, they never leave anyone with anything substantial in his hands afterwards' (1961: 1024).

Modes of creating second realities

As prime examples for creating second realities, Doderer offers four cases: the press, coffee-houses, the world of finance and the revolutionary.

The coffee-house

Coffee-houses were omnipresent in *fin-de-siècle* Vienna, this third Constantinople (after Venice and Moscow or St Petersburg), or perhaps more appropriately second Istanbul, central for the social elite and the avant-garde, playing a key role in the gestation and promotion of modernism. Doderer's angle on coffee-houses, however, is quite different from Habermasian celebration; for him, these play a central role rather through creating second realities.

The description of activities in these establishments is preceded by the first occasion where one of the most famous statements of the book is made: *primum scribere, deinde vivere*, or 'first write, and only then live': a distortion of the Latin claim about first live, then philosophise, attributed to Cicero or Seneca, and used by Cervantes, Hobbes and Nietzsche; certainly an ironic take on Viennese modernism. The coffee-house is introduced through a three-floor building on the Franz-Josephs-Kai (1961: 53). The enormity of the building indicates the amount of people who can turn up in the place at one time, and the amount of time and money they spend there. Their activities are captured in a particularly revealing passage, initiating into the environment:

> The instant you entered this café you obtained a true picture of the real nature of social intercourse among people of the day, a picture of visionary clarity precisely because of its exaggeration. For so deafening was the clamor that you could only leap to the conclusion: everyone is talking and no one listening.
>
> (Ibid.: 86)

Doderer continues with capturing the central 'second reality' generated in coffee-houses, shifting emphasis from the Vienna of literary modernism to the Vienna of Freud. During late morning hours four-fifth of the costumers were women. Their position in the room followed their weight, the heavier ones taking up the velvet seats alongside the walls. Fatness in this time and place was not considered negative, rather a privilege, a sign of being bred in the best coffee-houses; and most women were not excessively fat, rather plump, so even more sexually desirable – an opportunity which most were systematically using, considering having a lover as within their 'perfect right', though this was not openly acknowledged, contributing to the utter hypocrisy of Vienna society (Ibid.: 97).

The book also introduces in detail another, quite different coffee-house. For this place, while open during day-time, real business came during the night. As in all coffee-houses, by the late afternoon customers left; but instead of evening closure only the personnel changed, the nature of the place becoming altered. Customers now drank beer and hard liquor, the main activity was dancing and card games, with crowds assisting players through kibitzing – another interesting metaphorical take on the 'public sphere'. The place, half-empty during the day, by 3:30 am was steaming with people and looked like a 'sheer hell [*die Hölle selbst*]' (1956: 138; 1961: 139).

Closely interwoven into the description of coffee-houses Doderer inserts an ethnographic description of another central aspect of modern social life, another modality of second reality building: morning phone calls (1961: 81–3). Far from arranging meetings or solving matters from distance, such phone calls were a ritual with its own etiquette. The central message, comparable to Kafka's capturing the pitfalls of letter writing, is that without mutual personal presence such conversations were only instruments for proliferating second realities.

The press

Apart from the coffee-house, the other central protagonist in Habermas's account on the rise of the public sphere is the press. Not surprisingly, the press also plays a prime and even more sinister role in generating second realities.[12]

A prime activity in a coffee-house is reading a journal, when one is not engaged in a dialogue of deaf – though reading a journal is quite similar, being a dialogue of the dumb, as one is only reading what somebody else wrote down; and when it is followed by a 'real' dialogue, people would only repeat and debate what others wrote down, thus miming their views while pretending them as their own – enacting an agenda set up in a rather obscure place, the press house, about which hardly anybody has a cue what is going on and how; a situation closely comparable to the seats of the communist party apparatus in Budapest (Horvath and Szakolczai 1992).

In one of the most fascinating chapters of ethnographic value, based on personal experiences, Doderer offers some in-depth insights. The place supposedly propagating freedom of opinion and creativity rather could have a Dantesque motto written over its entrance: 'Abandon hope all ye who enter here'. Insights are offered through one of the protagonists, Kajetan, who received a job offer from somebody not known to give free favours (Doderer 1961: 95–6); and the gift indeed turns out to be poisonous, as soon after joining the journal Kajetan perceives that he lost control over his life (Shillabeer 2008: 88).

The fictionalised ethnographic description captures the real *falsification* of reality promoted by the press in a manner not accessible to sociological description. The first surprising insight is that, while evidently a product of modernity, the running of newspapers represented a particular amalgam of old and new political and economic spirits (Doderer 1961: 334). This is because both managers of the press consortium were from Prague, old capital of the Holy Roman Empire, for long in privileged contact with the other main Empire of the medieval period, the Byzantine, embodying a combination of the carnivalesque features of fairground capitalism with a faceless bureaucratic machinery. The result was lethal, for life as well as for thinking:

> The air alone, with its machinelike, mineral quality, had the capacity to invalidate, to emasculate, any product of the intellect it touched. [. . .] A massive current flowed here in which all form, all quality, were drowned: drowned in oily smells, and already evaporating in the editor's hand, if only by the way that hand leafed through a manuscript. Nothing was needed here. Every individual contribution [*jedes einzelne*] [. . .] was expendable; only the total mixed quantum, taken all together, was essential.
> (1956: 330; 1961: 335)

The prime instrument for creating such a result was an atmosphere closely recalling coffee-houses: there was much talk, but nobody cared to listen; the corridors, in particular (see again Horvath and Szakolczai 1992: 105–6), were scenes of endless chatter (see Kierkegaard 1962) of utmost superficiality (Doderer 1961: 336). Far from distracting from work, a sign of idleness, this mode of activity was rather an integral part of the work 'ethic' characteristic of the press; an instrument of enforcing mechanised homogeneity. It was mimed in the work-style of the editorial office, in which always a meeting or a 'conference' took place: it was a 'permanent condition [*ein Dauerzustand*]' (1956: 340; 1961: 345), identical to the *modus operandi* of the Communist party (Horvath and Szakolczai 1992: 106–7), as well as contemporary manager 'culture'. Yet, some people were also working, and a lot. There were two main kinds of workers: the 'fathers' and the 'larvae'. 'Fathers' were senior writers with a degree of authority; while the 'larvae' – alluding both to Latin 'mask' and their insect-like place in the machinery – were junior employees with faces distorted from ambition, trying desperately to increase their contributions and move up on the ladder. Decisions, however, in spite of talks and meetings, were highly centralised, in the hand of the chief editors, thus highly personal. Doderer again renders us aware of this in a particularly striking way. Kajetan's articles were always approved by an editor-in-chief, so once he encountered a problem he went directly into his office. The editor approved his writing without making an effort to read it, telling the astonished Kajetan that he never ever read a word from him; simply by looking at him it was evident that his writings are good (Doderer 1961: 347–50).

Just as journals were intimately connected to coffee-houses, they also had tight connections to the third main force generating second realities, the world of finance.

Finance

The main villain of the novel, its par excellence 'demonic' figure, is Levielle, a businessman like Bertrand or Huguenau, a self-made and self-declared financial wizard like Mr Merdle. Doderer names him a 'manager', showing evident reluctance in uttering such a word (Doderer 1961: 317). Significantly, nothing is known about his background (Ibid.: 95); but his behaviour indicates extremely low birth (Ibid.: 11). His main counterpoint in the novel is Altschul, a different kind of bank director: heir of an old Frankfurt Jewish banking family (Ibid.: 1154), he does business in an ethical way (thus his name, 'old school'), and repeatedly laments the decline in the moral climate of the business world (Ibid.: 363–4). By his very being he becomes a natural enemy of Levielle, who conspires to sack him (Ibid.: 324–5, 480).

Levielle's character is revealed by his mode of behaving, repeatedly captured with the term 'insolence', mentioned twice in the first meeting that introduced him, setting up the central plot of the novel (Ibid.: 9–10). Such arrogance is written all over his face (Ibid.: 1059); but is particularly revealed in the tone of his speaking: he has a falsetto voice with an 'unpleasant penetrating quality (Ibid.: 244); 'piercing, penetrating' at its sharpest end (Ibid.: 324–5) that can reach a nearly screaming pitch when something angers him (Ibid.: 11). Yet, neither the voice, nor the person contains any human emotion or warmth, rather showing not fully explicable icy coldness against anyone who happened to be in his way, with claims like '[r]uin him'; '[t]he devil take him' or '[l]et him fall' (Ibid.: 324–5).

Levielle is not simply the villain, but the plot of the novel is woven by and around him. The novel is purportedly based on a chronicle compiled by Geyrenhoff, third alter ego of Doderer, which was started due to the peculiar circumstances of an encounter he had with Levielle. The coincidence has three levels: two chance encounters; a philosophical-novelistic level, where this coincidence allows Doderer to develop and illustrate his position about revealing the tissue of reality through a single event; and a theological/spiritual level, given that the chance encounter, first only assigned to early Spring (Ibid.: 8), is later dated to 24 March and explicitly identified as Annunciation Day (Ibid.: 52, 844).

The central significance of Levielle concerns the contribution of the world of finance to the falsification of reality, through the creation of second realities. Here again the fictional details of the narrative, the historical experience of Austria around the war, and general theoretical, even metaphysical concerns are tightly woven together. At the fictional level Levielle is a shaky wheeler-dealer who somehow gained the confidence of a war widow, obtaining the charge of executing the will but failing to do so, misleading the widow. Due to the liminal war times he managed to create the appearance of trustworthiness and generate the impression of being an indispensable man (Ibid.: 398), much similarly to Mr Merdle in *Little Dorrit*. After the war he continued to profit from the still liminal conditions, engaged in the transformation of a little-known bank, being engaged in obscure, parasitic, even jackal-like dealings (Ibid.: 399–407). Beyond merely revealing corruption and illegality, Doderer rather carefully exposes how liminal conditions are conducive for the rise of trickster figures to the top, which then alters the conditions of reality for others – including entire cultures. Such machinations destroyed the assets of the traditional European ruling strata, rendering possible the rule of ideologies and totalitarian movements over a massified population left without genuine and concrete, personal leaders – masqueraded, then as now, as a 'victory of democracy'.

Levielle handled most carefully his machinations of the Ruthmayr will, never releasing any document that could be held against him. Yet, eventually his bluff was pulled. This allows Doderer to offer two conclusive claims about 'second reality', concerning its effects and conditions of possibility. The first is tightly connected to Broch's concerns with sleepwalkers, especially their 'irrational rationality', arguing that '[t]he shallow stupidity of so-called "clever" people cannot be approximated by the deepest thinker' (Ibid.: 1137). The second offers, through a characterisation of Levielle, using Paul Valéry's book *Tel quel*, a conclusive take (Ibid.: 1138–9). Valéry defines as 'the height of vulgarity' arguments that only target the public, in the form of spectators, assuming the smallest common denominator, or the stupidest possible mode of existence for humans, and that would never work if tried in front of a solitary person who has the capacity to weigh arguments on their merit. Doderer goes a step further than giving the lie to the supposed objectivity and rationality of the 'public sphere', identifying the kind of person ready to offer such 'vulgar' arguments, tying together the 'public sphere' and the world of finance. Such mode of behaving is the opposite of a 'care of the self', the heart of European civilisation, according to Plato, Voegelin, Patocka and Foucault; a certain 'brazenness [that] is made possible by a life lived on its own inner surface, with constant falsification of the ego's accounts' (Ibid.: 1139). In order to build second realities for others, whether as engineer (technology), demagogue (public sphere) or financier (economy), one must first transform oneself into a mask, and then believe that this being is real.

The revolutionary

The ultimate figure of second reality discussed by Doderer is the revolutionary. The connection between revolutionaries and the coffee-houses, just as with the press, is evident, but Doderer also indicates that the world of finance is also deeply interwoven with the revolutionary falsification of reality. Doderer presents and discusses the figure of the revolutionary in two places of the novel – both fundamental. One is at the beginning of the culminating Chapter 11, about the historical riot against the Palace of Justice. The 'revolutionaries' are those who incite the crowds, recalling the agitator in Dickens's *Hard Times*, but much more caricature-like – insecure fakes, the most vexing being a journal editor, both by his behaviour and the fact of being there. The reasons for depicting them in this manner are offered at a similarly central point for the fictional texture of the novel (Doderer 1961: 488–95). The concrete occasion is a visit of the narrator to his former superior, Hofrat von Gürtzner-Gontard (Ibid.: 484–505), and the characterisation is offered by the latter, who appears only here. His role turns out to be puzzling, as at the end reveals that he took the ideas from a young man, René Stangeler. The conversation would have such a shattering impact in that the narrator disappears from the novel for 330 pages (Ibid.: 836–7); and at that point the financier villain also reappears, or rather its 'double', called the 'false Levielle' (Ibid.: 837).

This disappearance had to be just as significant as the much discussed disappearance of the narrator in Dostoevsky's *Demons*, and can be made sense of by recalling that the narrator and Stangeler are both Doderer's alter-egos. The shift from one to the other, through the mediation of the Hofrat as a master of ceremonies, is a staging of Doderer's own conversion to Catholicism that took place in 1939–40 (Hesson 1982: 32), evoked by the personal name of Stangeler (René, or 'reborn'); which evidently had something to do with overcoming the obsession with the 'revolution'. The characterisation of the revolutionary offered thus is a vital, perhaps *the* central point in the novel, underlined by a further stylistic device: in the middle of the speech the voice of the speaker left any tone of 'sacerdotal unctuousness' and became 'granite-like' (*körniger*) (Doderer 1956: 486).

So who is a revolutionary? The central feature, alpha and omega in recognising the figure is his obsession with generalities: 'a priori abstraction [*apriorische Unanschaulichkeit*] is the mother of all revolutionaries' (1956: 486; 1961: 493). A revolutionary always searches for schemas and rational classification; in fact, such 'rationalistic trait' is a central feature of all revolutions (Ibid.: 492–3). The explanation, in a fundamental way, must be searched in the (non)personality of the revolutionary – and here Doderer offers a point that might seem mere psychologisation: a revolutionary wants to change the world, because one cannot endure oneself – and cannot change oneself either. Thus, becoming a revolutionary is a flight from oneself, imposing the burden of endurance onto the others. Such personality flaw is due to a problem of perception: a would-be revolutionary is simply unable to perceive properly the world around him, and is thus forced to construct imaginary schemes and ideologies. This is the root of the 'revaluation of values', by which the revolutionary imposes his own erroneous perceptions on the others. A revolutionary is thus one who does not even have an inkling about the real world, about the daily joys of life, the 'permanent laws which life always spontaneously follows' (Ibid.: 492). He rather lives in permanent flux, as if half-blind, a wretched and degenerate existence under-ground, replacing concreteness with slogans. For him nothing is stable and permanent, existing in its rightful place, thus is always ready to alter everything in order to 'improve' it. Perfect example for revolutionaries are those promoting the rule of a particular demographic group (Doderer mentions race and class), which re-qualifies the wretched non-existence of the revolutionary into the vanguard, above and over those who fail to belong to his own group. In contrast to the revolutionary and his doctrine, combining abstract rationality and permanent alteration, there stands the concrete, stable person and the true community, which 'must rest upon what is not common, upon the singular, the personal, the noncommunicable [*Nicht-Mitteilbar*] qualities that each possesses; upon what makes him irreplaceable' (1956: 488; 1961: 494).

Doderer's unqualified rejection of the revolutionary is not limited to the Bolshevik or Nazi version of the type, but emphatically includes the economically, scientifically or technologically driven revolutionaries, based on his Thomist vision of the world, according to which any efforts to tamper with the created world imply a rejection of Divine Being (Hesson 1982: 4–5, 33, 97), but also on his long-standing interest in St Francis of Assisi, which goes back to the 1920s (Ibid.: 79).

Conclusion

The overcoming of second realities, due to their demonic formation, is both extremely simple and difficult. It is simple, as second realities do not have a real existence; they are artificial bubbles that, once burst, disappear almost without a trace. But it is also very difficult, as – in so far as they exert a hold – they require nothing less than a conversion, and no individual human being is capable of a conversion due to his own powers; even philosophical conversion, a central concern of Greco-Roman antiquity always requires somebody else (Hadot 1993; Foucault 2001). In *Demons* such external position is often provided by women: thus, Jan Herzka used his secretary, Agnes to lift himself from second into first reality (Doderer 1961: 1041); while the second reality of Kajetan, his obsession with 'fat females' was burst through a letter from his mother – a solution reminiscent of *Crime and Punishment*. Second realities are continuously, day by day, minute by minute confronted by the true reality of our concrete world: love, friendship, self-sacrificing devotion, collegiality. Yet, second realities produce real destructions and victims, and thus their effects may reverberate way beyond their remit. The collapse of Communism, taking place long decades after this novel was published, offers a perfect illustration for this position.

This is why the concluding image of the novel, seemingly so banal, waving goodbye on the platform of a train, is so perfectly appropriate and even deep: as it is about memory. Second realities only survive by the devastation they produce – while meaningful concreteness is preserved in memories that, for Plato, extend well beyond our concrete lives, and even this world.

Notes

1. Hamvas in 1948 (see Darabos 2002, III: 23), while Doderer on 17 April 1951 (see Hesson 1982: 39).
2. Between 1936 and 1951, Dodeder only added one, though crucial, chapter to the novel: the first chapter of Part Two, on the revolution (Hesson 1982: 38).
3. Such parallels are all the more significant, given that the centrality of its genesis for understanding the novel was singled out separately by Hesson (1982: 2–3) and Darabos (2002, III: 83–4).
4. According to Kundera (1986: 197–8), Flaubert's great discovery was human stupidity (*bêtise*) that cannot be analysed through the means of philosophical rationalism, and which in itself promotes novels for in-depth social analysis. The term etymologically is rooted in *bête* 'animal, beast', so 'stupidity' in French is literally identical to 'bestiality'.
5. Doderer studied first law, then history and psychology, and in 1925 defended at the University of Vienna a dissertation about the fifteenth century (Hesson 1982: 8).
6. For details, Szakolczai (2013a: 271–2, 88).
7. 'Second reality' emerged as a central theme, concerned with assessing the damage created by obsessive thinking, in 1951, after the long review and correction of Part One (Hesson 1982: 39).
8. See Hadot (1993) and Foucault (2005); for an overview, see Twomey (2006).
9. This represents Doderer's experientially based settlement of accounts with Freud.
10. The affinities of these ideas with Dostoevsky's *The Double* are evident.
11. This is how Girard would argue against Freud: all what Freud considered as 'objective reality' is merely the product of mimesis, thus – in Doderer's language – phantasmagorical second reality building.
12. Habermas's study was inspired by the work of Hans Speier, an exile under Nazism who worked for the Rand Corporation, an organisation helping US military strategy (Ellis 2006).

12 Béla Hamvas
Carnival

Karnevál (Carnival) is a novel written by the Hungarian philosopher, essayist and historian of religions Béla Hamvas.[1] Written between 1948 and 1951 (Darabos 2002, III: 23), when its author was thrown out of his library job – courtesy of Georg Lukács – and lived literally like a hermit in the scenic town Szentendre in the Danube Bend, it remained in manuscript until 1985, when – still under Communist rule – it was published, with minimal censorial cuts. Though 1184 pages long in two volumes, the novel was sold out within days, becoming a treasure and hailed as the key novel of its time and place. Yet, until today, awareness about it outside Hungary is practically nil, and even inside it is more known about than read, let alone discussed.

The book presents evident challenges for understanding. This starts by its size: in the pocket-size collected works edition, it runs to three volumes, about 500 pages each, containing about 400,000 words. Beyond sheer size, it is not an easy read: it covers three generations and almost a century (the book starts in 1884 and ends in 1950, but the origins of the protagonist are traced back to the 1850s); the list of its characters, appended to the third volume, runs to ten footnote-sized pages; the protagonist of the first part is introduced surreptitiously, and is not named until p.183, where he is revealed as Virgil Bormester, a clearly Dantesque name, and identified as the father of the novel's author, Mihály Bormester.[2] The stylistic devices employed in the book are also taxing: the dialogues are systematically interspersed with unfinished sentences, each section starting in the middle of sentences, containing innumerable episodes, often running to tens of pages, which seem to make no sense whatsoever. As the book's editor remarks in his short Afterword, it is advisable that we re-read the novel immediately for a second time; while within the novel the presumed author, Bormester adds the even more taxing advice that if someone is not prepared to read it three times, it is better not to touch it. As translating this work would be a nightmare even to the most experienced, by now it should not be surprising that most people took up the suggestion and saved themselves the trouble of immersing in it.

It is difficult to characterise the genre of the novel. Though it extends to three generations and almost a century, and daily aspects of Hungarian life – especially the 1944 siege of Budapest – are vividly evoked, it is by no means a historical novel nor a family saga. In its first pages the author defines his work as a 'confession' as well as a 'catalogue of fates' (*sorskatalógus*), terms that are by no means easy to reconcile. In his monograph Pál Darabos, who knew Hamvas, calls the work a 'novel of initiation', whose seven parts were consciously modelled on the seven stages of ancient initiation ceremonies. However, its most appropriate short characterisation is probably contained towards the end of the book, where it is repeatedly described as a 'comedy of fates' (*sorskomédia*) (Hamvas 1997, III: 426). This brings out the intensely comic, often hilarious aspects of the novel, while giving a proper due to its theatrical character. The seven parts, even main sections, are separated by a gong, literally cutting sentences in half, making the reader all but 'hear' the sound; and these parts are also introduced or concluded – in the first three parts even interrupted – by so-called 'curtain lectures' (*sic* in original), in which the presumed author discusses its content with one or more interlocutors (also alter-egos of Hamvas), and occasionally even an unspecified 'voice'. The novel also makes explicit links to cinema, and – more metaphorically, but close to the main substance – the circus.

Hamvas wrote the novel during the worst Stalinist period in Hungary, in his early fifties, a most productive period for a thinker, but it was by no means a simple reflection on Communist terror and nonsense. Readers expecting passionate denunciations of sordid Stalinist crimes must have been deeply disappointed. The book is indeed about Hungary – and the world at large – going desperately wrong, even becoming utterly mad, but for Hamvas the reasons go way back, before the Communist takeover, and his interest focuses on these reasons, rather than the intellectually trivial details about the Communists and their cronies. The basic ideas go back to a 1924 story 'The Error', while a 1928–9 draft even contained main characters with identical names (Darabos 2002, III: 83–4). However, Hamvas then thought he should wait until fifty in order to write the novel properly. Lukács and the Communist regime unwittingly procured him the best opportunity to do his job.

Hamvas's most obvious predecessor is Dostoevsky, the early draft title (*Ördöngösök*) rhyming perfectly with the Hungarian title of Dostoevsky's *Demons* (*Ördögök*).[3] Affinities are clearly revealed in the three-generational structure and the harrowing capturing of internal decay in single persons and even families. Girard's argument that the hysterical features of Dostoevsky's characters cannot be reduced to the 'Russian soul' gain further confirmation from Hamvas's novel, while at the same time it poses the tricky question of what rendered Hungary susceptible, already in the late nineteenth century, to such a pervasive and penetrating social and spiritual decay.[4] However, the bracketing of the reference to Dostoevsky in the final title is relevant, as Hamvas explicitly shifted his focus from demons to the mask. With this shift theatricality became more pronounced, reflected in the fact that the single most cited author is Shakespeare, evoked especially by the figures representing the author. Emphasis is on the great tragedies, especially *Hamlet*, *Macbeth* and *King Lear*, and even more on the two most enigmatic plays, *A Midsummer Night's Dream* and *The Tempest*. The basic experience of the novel became the carnival night (Kemény 1990: 10–11), bringing out – beyond the evident parallels with Doderer – the close affinities with Thomas

Mann, Blixen and Bulgakov, each recalling (beyond Dostoevsky) Goethe, and also with Kafka's night-writing, evoking the link between Hermes the trickster, the night-experience and the *unheimlich* (Kerényi 1986). In Hamvas's novel the extension of the carnival atmosphere to the entire year, thus abolishing the difference between feasts and everyday life, is particularly clear (Kemény 1990: 12). Permanent mask-wearing and permanent carnival are two sides of the same thing, generating the world of *Karnevál* whose central features are its labyrinthine and swirling character (Kemény 1990: 10, 19, 33).

If there was an initiatory work of art in European literature, it was certainly Dante's *Commedia*, recurring in central moments. The most significant reference, however, establishes a distance: the hero's father is called Virgil, but does not guide anybody, rather at the beginning sets out to find himself – only to become lost.

Concerning other references to main figures of European culture and thought only two comments will be made. First, at an important junction and with some malice Hamvas uses a mask to present, half-mockingly, a short list of his most and least liked writers within the European tradition. Thumbs up are given to the great writers of comedies, who thus help proper digestion: Aristophanes, Lucian, Plautus, Boccaccio, Rabelais, Sterne, Cervantes, Shakespeare and Molière (the link between culture and proper body functioning alludes to Nietzsche's *Ecce Homo*); while thumbs down to Kant, Hegel, Schopenhauer, Descartes, Victor Hugo, Voltaire, Corneille, Racine, Balzac and Zola. Both lists are interrupted, as usual, so we can't draw conclusions about omissions; and while the second list speaks for itself, concerning the first one should remark that the modern list contains *the* most important literary figures of their time and place, rendering evident the strange intellectual dominance of comedy over tragedy in the modern scene.

Second, the novel 'unmasks' – a term of considerable importance for the book – some major European luminaries. Thus, as part of an imaginary walk around Venice, both Tintoretto and Wagner are identified as fakes (Hamvas 1997, II: 71–3).[5] Tintoretto's paintings are overcrowded with countless inexpressive faces, all made by his assistants; they are not carefully composed portraits, rather masks imitating the style of the 'master', recalling the windows of a hairdresser or a department store. His art is pure bluff. The music of Wagner is alike, which one should try *not* to understand. It is not even real music, rather entertainment belonging to the fairground (*vásár*), recalling 'football games, weekend, international fair, world exhibition, organised tour, newsboys, the clattering [of trains], ringing [of alarm clocks], bellowing [*bömböl*]'; in one word, a music for lemurs, with Siegfried as newsboy or fairground barker (Ibid.: 72). Still, and due to this his music is popular, effective and will transform the world, making it into its own face:

> Soon the Siegfrieds, and not in the last the Walküres will gain power, and then you will be sorry, but remember, that all this was unleashed on us by Wagner. The theatre always goes out into the street. The power of theatre is greater than the Parliament. *Je suis fatigué de répéter la même chose*

[*sic* – I'm tired to repeat always the same thing]. Then we'll all be nibelungised. This article, I must write it. Siegfried, or the victory of the barker.

(Ibid.: 73)

Hamvas's view of Hegel is also scornful, but with a difference. Paraphrasing Kierkegaard, he identifies in Hegel's problem the typical Nordic problem of losing the balance and measure of playfulness, and thus taking himself too seriously:

> if in the Preface and Postface of his *Logic* Hegel had written that all this is a thought experiment and improvisation, he would have been the greatest thinker who had ever lived. In this way, however, presenting this logic as eternal and absolute, he is at best comic.

(Ibid.: 184).

The discussion continues about the difference between an experimental work and a scandal, implying that Hegel's work is one of the greatest scandals in Western thought.

Hamvas returns to Hegel by contrasting him with Proust concerning temporality. For Hamvas, Hegel has no understanding of the time dimension of history, as he 'constructed in his *Logic* a colossal mechanism to freeze time' (Ibid.: 416) – a stunning claim about the philosopher who is supposed to have rendered dynamic the 'static' categories of Kant's idealism.

A further reference to Hegel is part of a particularly important 'curtain lecture' which also identifies, in the next paragraph, the two works of fiction whose attitude with respect to time most closely correspond to *Karnevál* (Ibid.: 417). One, to be sure, is Dante; but the other is not part of the European tradition: *1001 Nights*. References recur in the book, and always in a charged context; first in the first 'curtain lecture' interrupting the first part of the book (I: 128), at a moment when the bewildered reader is desperately looking for a clue about what is going on. The curtain lecture indeed wonders about the situation of such a first reader, and as similar works it mentions, two lines even before Dante, the *1001 Nights*. The 'Arabian tales' are evoked again at a crucial moment in Part Five, the initiatory vision, and even twice, in both cases at the start of the Dantesque travel of the hero, Mihály Bormester, to the otherworld. The *1001 Nights* are thus not simply evoked, but set out the hero to his initiatory trip. On the first occasion there the *1001 Nights* captures the central feature of our world as 'world circus' (III: 23). This is not followed by the trip, only its premonition, starting with a reflection on the magic nature of a tale and the initial experience of the void (*űr*) as an immersion. The work is evoked just a few pages later (III: 31), and this time the trip indeed starts, with the same experience of a 'grey and damp void', and the attempt, with the hero's last remaining force, to resist annihilation (III: 32). Then comes another allusion to Dante, through evoking the Virgin Mary; though everything has perished, names are still there, the only remaining things to hang on to.[6]

At this point, the story must be told in the minimal necessary detail, as the work is not available in translation.

The storyline

The novel starts with a short 'curtain lecture' offering a modicum of guidance to the reader (I: 7–11). It contains three precious hints. It identifies the protagonist, Mihály Bormester, also wearing the mask of the writer, although his name would not appear again for hundreds of pages; it reveals that the novel would contain a high degree of reflexivity and playfulness at the same time; and finally, it makes it evident that this is not a technique of ironic distancing, as the writer, just as readers or critics, cannot presume a position of exteriority: though the figures depicted look as if taken out of an 'infernal catalogue', so many members of a zoo, nobody can presume immunity and innocence: 'the basic thesis is that all of us are deeply inside the pickle [*pác*]' (I: 10).

The novel starts in 1884 with the protagonist of the first generation, Virgil Bormester, presumed father of Mihály Bormester,[7] though only identified as 'the red-haired assistant editor' (I: 16), encountering a puzzle in his workplace in the form of the evident madness of his newly appointed director, and as a result decides to search out himself, travelling to his native city. Here we are introduced to a series of extremely peculiar characters, each not simply wearing but identifying themselves with a mask. The most peculiar and most atrocious of these is Mihály Hoppy, who best embodies the new breed of human beings, and who is indeed the first person Virgil encounters, already on the train.[8] This figure has already debased himself so deeply that he has lost all self-respect and thus became impossible to change, as he only responds to any negative characterisation of his outrageous and revolting antics – even offences by which any normal human being would be deeply hurt – by seconding the proposition. His attitude is characterised by 'a combination of impertinence, affection, impudent roguery (*ripőkség*) and shameless indelicacy', adding that 'it is impossible to defend against it' (I: 33). Virgil Bormester then arrives and starts his quest. The results are inconclusive and deeply disturbing: according to some, he was the son of a general, hero of the 1848 uprising; but, most probably, he was simply an exposed child, brought up in a poorhouse. However, before further results could be reached, there is a knock on the door: the police come to arrest him, charged with murder.

The charge is improbable, and indeed turns out to be deeply absurd, as the occupation of the presumed victim is non-sensical (he is a *paté*-griller), and neither the presumed village in which the deed was committed nor the victim exist. This, however, bothers neither police nor judge, so Virgil is duly condemned to four years for murder.

Part I ends with a feast – only appropriate for a book titled *Carnival* – a silver wedding anniversary that has three points of interest. First, its participants occasionally mention 'the red-haired assistant editor', but only as a butt of jokes, failing to acknowledge even minimally the tragic absurdity of his condemnation. As an aside, it is also mentioned that in the prison he had a vision that he is the archangel Michael. Second, the happy wife, Laura Kankalin, is one of the most bizarre masks of Part I: a woman spending 25 years of marriage preparing for this anniversary.[9] Laura forced her husband to save every penny, drinking nothing but water and having meat only once per week so that this great feast could be perfect, now feeling redeemed (I: 180). Still, after the feast she starts to save again for the golden wedding anniversary – except that something now clicks in the husband-judge and he starts squandering money in every possible way.

The third point is the high moment of the feast, the toast during the dinner, in which the cavalier Raimund Herstal, Chief Advisor of the State Chancellery and future Chancellor, greets the couple and – beyond a toast – offers a prophecy to their health. In his vision by the time of their golden anniversary the world would be completely changed: the power and authority of the State will increase, the life and prosperity of citizens will be safeguarded and world peace realised; a genuine, new golden age is upon us (I: 178–9). Instead, World War I came.

This 'prophecy' was preceded by two other forecasts. One is offered by a main representative of scientism,[10] Maximus Barnabás, who declares that on the basis of 25 years' work and the reading of 84566 books he can safely pronounce that the 10000–years-old problems of humankind are about to be solved, and by 30 years, in 1914, 'science will celebrate its complete victory on the entire planet', generating a new golden age (I: 139–40). A third, apocalyptic vision is offered by Father Ágoston, not at all surprised by the miscarriage of justice, and forecasts that 'soon such legal processes would be everyday events', as the decay will become accelerating, leading to the outbreak of terrible wars, destroying millions (I: 155). 'There has never been the kind of slavery that is upon us. Today we are in 1884, but you'll see, thirty years won't pass and the world will be shaken in its grounds. We're on the eve of destruction' (I: 156). Still, Father Ágoston does nothing either about the miscarriage of justice, or about the implications of his prophecy, so in Part II we encounter him destroying a pub during a brawl, once he quit the Church and became a barman (I: 192, 211–13).

The narrative of Part II starts with Virgil leaving the prison, in late 1887. He is introduced to the 'new world' again by Hoppy. Behind the motif of repetition there are striking changes: 'nothing is the same as it was before' (I: 191). However, while many of the characters have indeed changed their masks, things did not become 'better' by that; though modernised, the masks became only madder. Among them, the outrageous antics of Hoppy no longer looked so exceptional.

In due time Virgil gets married, to Améline who in Part I formulated a utopia about the emancipation of women, including complete and radical separation of sexes, and female rule (I: 106–8). The marriage transformed both of them, making them somewhat less peculiar, though by no means simply normal. Years passed, and their presumed son Mihály – named after the archangel – was already six years old when suddenly there was a loud knocking on the door: Virgil was again arrested for murder (I: 251). The same old story, yet radically different; not only because this time there was a real murder, but as this new turn of the story produces a genuine emotional shock: while the first time everything was burlesque, unreal, the experience now is heart-rending. This is because Virgil's status changed: he is no longer an intruding outsider, and the episode is presented through the eyes of his six-year-old son. Améline also gained existential weight, and intuits the right course of action: she goes to the police and 'confesses' the murder (I: 255). This act of self-offering forces the police inspector to send both home.

The policeman, however, fails to draw the further implications. He persists with his fixed ideas and keeps accusing all kinds of unlikely people with committing the crime. He even develops a bullet-proof theory for his way of proceeding, called 'the improbability factor': the more improbable it seems that a particular person committed the deed, the more likely it is that he actually did so (I: 267–74). His mania becomes contagious, and the novel descends into burlesque, with various people denouncing themselves as the culprit, so when the actual killer presents himself at the police headquarters, the outraged police inspector does not let himself to be misled by the evidence presented and throws him out (I: 337–46). Burlesque becomes widespread and general, with the monomaniac characters of the previous generation who pursued, rigidly and mechanically, their single fixed idea being replaced by figures incapable of any sense of judgement. Pure hilarity reigns, the novel generating irresistible laughter; yet, the reader cannot hide a certain unease, as he was already averted to the threat of farce becoming a force to transform the world. The corresponding term, closely related to the 'improbability factor' (I: 335–7), is nothing else but *scape-goat*; the last word of substance at the end of Part II (I: 352), followed only by noise and then by silence: 'and then there was silence, the silence of men and of places and of words and of names –' (I: 353).

Part III shifts the perspective from men to women. Hamvas acknowledges that so far his work was imbalanced: female figures only played a minor role. However, given the character of male 'heroes', the statement must be read tongue in cheek. This is the most Dostoevskian of all parts, presenting an at once extremely realistic and totally absurd psycho-drama of family life in Hungary, where males are dominated by contagiously hysteric women playing razor-sharp and irresistible Machiavellian power games. The central character is Lala, another stunning take on the same Lilith-Lola-Lulu motive; a figure at once opposite and alterego of Lolita. Lala is not an irresistibly, corruptively attractive nymph, rather a fifty-something virgin spinster; just as lethal for men, and without any redeeming features. She is the schismogenic pair of Lolita: the more women turn into Lolitas or Colombinas, the more they generate a new breed of Lalas.

Lala is not an exceptional person, and is not even bad (I: 476); she could even be considered as 'average' (II: 153, 5). The only problem is that somehow she remained virgin (I: 443). This fact completely transformed her being, rendering her a 'bloodthirsty Amazon, who would take vengeance on any woman and would butcher every man' as a compensation; a terrifying beast, only comparable to Medusa the Gorgon (I: 443–4), though one who transforms not only by the glimpse of her dead eyes, but with her entire being everyone into a stone. In order to hide she chose a lethal double mask: a victim with a big heart who sacrifices herself for her loved ones (II: 7, 103); and the champion and guardian of virtue and morality (I: 470–4, II: 34–7). The first mask is sheer lie, Lala is incapable of loving anybody; her lovelessness is contagious and totalising, destroying any human warmth around herself, thus rendering the life of those forced to share her living space an utter misery (II: 17). The second mask is mere fake, as Lala only acts in the name of morality, but is not an ethical being. An ethical life implies benevolent activity and innocent simplicity, while

> nothing is further from Lala than activity and simplicity. She is aggressive and solemn. For this reason her talents reside in the field of moral pedagogy and indiscretion. Lala only sees what is under the blanket. She is lifting the blanket of everybody around her, and looks under it.
>
> (I: 477)

While her self-image as victim and guardian is an absurd joke, it is irresistible and eventually, through her aggressive insolence, she forces everybody into defensiveness, thus gaining dominance, instigating a 'revaluation of values'. In the end everything around her is 'turned upside down', coloured with 'the blood-chilling comedy of faces that are distorted by pain' (II: 153).

The final characterisation of Lala, towards the end of a long 'curtain lecture' closing Part III, captures as if in a distilled essence a crucial aspect of the ridiculous and the comic. The central feature of Lala is that she

> not only takes herself seriously, but even takes seriously her own seriousness as well. For this reason humour-mystically she is comic in an exemplary way, as humour-mysticism starts with laughter, more precisely by laughing at oneself. Lala is humourlessly idiotic. She does not tolerate any criticism, and is thus irreligious.
>
> (II: 154)

Here we are getting close to one of the central ideas of Hamvas's book, the tight link between religion (the sacral) and humour. For Hamvas, the heart of religious ethic does not lie in strained seriousness, but in sacral serenity: an at once calm and cheerful conduct of life. Lala considers herself the bastion of morality, and goes to church every Sunday, but 'her religion is a clerical atheism. She is faithless while adhering to all the ceremonies' (II: 156). Her seriousness, and lack of sense of humour, is daft and cracked, but also tragic and shocking. This is best visible in her voice, which is 'existentially false. Lala is not lying. No, it is the basic tone of Lala that is false. It is the intonation of the seriously mad persons – not of the smaller kind, who are closed into asylums, but of those who rule the affairs of mankind in their monomaniac aggressivity' (Ibid.). But the same falseness animates all her movements, 'with fake dignity and mindless stiffness [*kimértség*]'. Hers is a 'magical' kind of movement, which is 'completely ridiculous. It is ridiculous, as it separates itself from other human beings. What she does is inacceptable, and is thus grotesque' (Ibid.).

Lala in action can be seen through one of the most absurd and also most harrowing scenes of the novel. Lala lives with her two sisters, one of whom

(Gitta, close to 'Gretchen') is married to a colonel, Antal Kanavász, who has a daughter (Angela) from his first marriage. At one night, at half past twelve, the family is woken up by a notorious lunatic character of the town, who systematically, one by one, accuses the male population of the town to have seduced his wife (II: 75–83). Nobody ever takes him seriously – except, of course, Lala, who uses the occasion to go into a frontal attack against her brother-in-law, with the situation turned into such an absurd row that Kanavász is forced to move out of his own flat with his family. Needless to say, a few month later wife and daughter would return, slinking home, leaving the hapless colonel utterly destroyed and robbed.

A similar scene takes place after Angela's wedding to Mihály Bormester the moment they are leaving for their honeymoon (II: 24–7). Lala feels she is losing power, so must insinuate herself at the centre of action. She discovers that Angela forgot to pack her wedding gift for the honeymoon. She forces the family into a meaningless and mad rush home, to retrieve the 'gift'.[11] The trick works: she manages to spoil the moment, infecting with her poison the trip to Italy, the honeymoon and then the couple's whole life. This is one of the most desperate parts of the book, but only because it demonstrates the futility of romanticism: Mihály Bormester marries Angela in order to save her from Lala; but the moment Angela is freed, she transforms herself into Lala's double, poisoning the new family with her inability to love.

At the end of Part III, just before World War I, an important meeting takes place between Bormester and Herstal (II: 111). Upon learning his age Herstal almost recognises in Bormester his own son, so different from his own red-haired son. Aware about the imminent war, he also recalls the prophecy he made 30 years before, but instead of learning from his mistake, after a few drinks he ventures to make another prophecy, predicting that this war will be the last, and again thirty years later – i.e. in 1944 – prosperity and world peace will reign full (II: 113–17).

World War I was an event of utmost importance for Hamvas, including long front experience. At this moment the protagonist becomes split, thus realising what Hofmannsthal failed to complete, and Part IV contains his 'parallel autobiographies'. One of his 'halves' goes to the Italian front, then escapes to Latin America, and as Mike Winemaster will familiarise himself with all the modern American 'life technics' (*élettechnika*), by which Hamvas means a quite Foucaldian apparatus of power/knowledge, deployed to transform and disfigure the planet, and first of all to manipulate human beings. His other half, Michail, becomes a prisoner in the Russian front, and through a series of quite different life experiences becomes thoroughly immersed in various forms of Asian spirituality and mysticism; first of all, Tibetan Buddhism.

The high moments of this part are contained in three conversations taking place in high mountains and modelled on the Sermon on the Mount. The first is in the Cordilleras, between Mike and his American friend Mr Pen. This discussion is in a comic key, exposing the principles of a 'cacocentric' philosophy, and includes the already mentioned distinction between strands in European philosophy and culture (II: 190–3). The first Tibetan discourse on the mountain (II: 296–301) is delivered by a monk, Yubainkan, who intimates to Michail that given the current state of the world, one must tolerate suffering and endure the crisis. It is impossible to do anything more, as 'nobody can be saved before he is mature for it' (II: 297). The second (II: 325–32) is clearly the most important of all, taking place in the Himalayas but delivered by a Christian monk, père Manouel. He offers a strange apology of Christianity, identified explicitly as *not* a missionary speech (II: 326). According to père Manouel, the current state of crisis has two sides. One is the crisis outside Christiantity, which is hopeless and futureless, full of aimless and meaningless suffering, waiting for the annihilation. This world-view pretends that we do not have any other duties than to fill our stomach and rule over others, as if the world had no centre and meaning, but really knows that this is not so, and rather tries everything to suffocate this centre (II: 327). This part of the world is still fighting, mindlessly, 'against Christianity which today, not less than two thousand years ago for the Greeks, or the intellectualists was foolery, while for the Jews, or the moralists, the Puritans, was scandal' (the text verbatim refers to 1Cor 1: 22), yet with no avail.

The other crisis takes place inside Christianity. In fact, this crisis lasts since 2000 years; it is an apocalyptic crisis, as Christianity is nothing but a crisis and a judgement, and it can only end with the realisation of the kingdom of God (Hamvas 1997, II: 328). For this reason even the holy man of Tibet, though he knows well that we live in a crisis, has lost all touch with reality; as 'the historical fact of salvation lasts since 2000 years, and whoever fails to take notice of this is hanging in the air. Who does not order his life accordingly, is dispersing his life into the nothingness –' (II: 329).

This gives a measure: the question of 'good faith'; a problematic measure, as just when we thought to have gained clarity, at least concerning the position of père Manouel, another mask of Hamvas, it again escapes from our grasp. As not only the Asian holy men, including Yubainkan, fail this test, but every single person so far encountered by père Manouel. This is – and here, indicates Hamvas, the tone of père Manouel became more declamatory – because Christianity is not exempt from the general bankruptcy of all doctrines:

> I am also outside Christianity as everybody else, as you yourself. I do not believe more in it, though I would like to believe, but I don't know whether I really believe in it. I would like to remain in good faith, and not proclaim something of which I don't consider even a word as true. I don't like to lie. Therefore I cannot say that I'm a Christian.
>
> (I: 330)

In this way père Manouel's speech became, in the analogy of Weber's 'anti-prophetic prophecy' (Szakolczai 1998: 179–88), an anti-missionary missionary speech, due to the fact that we became too modernised, meaning the impact of Nietzsche (Hamvas 1997, I: 331). So it became impossible to assert conviction; it is even meaningless to hope in miracles (I: 332). The full meaning of this point will only become visible in Part VI, when the novel presents an actual miracle, produced by a Hebrew sage (*cadik*) during the siege of Budapest, but it has no effect on anything. It intimates the central message of Hamvas: the crisis is first of all internal; what matters is to recover, from inside, the whole person.

Mike Winemaster and Michail meet each other at the end of Part IV; and at that meeting something truly remarkable takes place. The two doubles manage to do what human beings forgot in the past centuries, to recognise the saint in the other and the fool in themselves, while both were fools and saints at the same time, being two halves of the same split person. Due to this act of recognition they can now be united, and Mihály Bormester is now ready to turn home. As the crucial 'curtain lecture' at the end of Part IV renders it evident, he now carries in himself the promise of a new kind of human type, the man with a 'double consciousness' (*schismotimia*), who incorporates the knowledge of American 'life techniques' with full awareness about Eastern spirituality, and is thus able to overcome the difficulties before which the great heroes of Western culture had to yield (II: 378–84). Hamvas lists here four such heroes: Prince Myshkin from Dostoevsky's *Idiot*; Lawrence Sterne's Tristram Shandy; but especially the great 'romantic' pair of European culture, Hamlet and Don Quixote (II: 378–84). Hamvas uses to the full the double reference points of Hamlet and Don Quixote, including the striking coincidence that Shakespeare and Cervantes died on the same day (I: 19).

At the start of Part V, in 1921, from the top of the Cordilleras and the Himalayas, so literally from the top of the world, Bormester returns to the plain reality of Budapest, where Angela is just as hysterically abusive as ever, and in a fit of rage Bormester almost suffocates her – for a time he even thought her dead. In his escape he ends up in a cemetery, where he happens to meet the Master, Márkus, who sets him out on an out-of-body vision-experience-trip, though at first Bormester suspects him of black magic. In this vision-trip he encounters, in various forms, the different characters that were the subject of the long, seemingly endless and pointless story-telling sessions he had with Márkus, leading him to recognise their identity. In this trip he is helped by three beings: Henoch, author of the best-known Jewish apocryphal apocalypse, his guide in the first part (III: 30, 33, 40);[12] St John the Baptist (III: 51–9); and finally the Virgin Mary, whose name first appeared to Bormester in the moment of void and imminent annihilation experienced at the start, about which Márkus would say after his return that he was 'touched' (*megérintett*) by her (III: 32, 66–7). The Dantesque trip ends with a vision of the golden city, where he also sees a stone house, without mortar, with a smoking chimney (III: 62).[13] Thus, even at the heart of the present as the permanent apocalyptic carnival, Hamvas never loses sight of the presence of the idyll, the only and eternal normality, and the possibility of a return to the Golden Age, given the 'indestructible consciousness of the Golden Age [*eltörölhetetlen aranykortudat*]' (Kemény 1990: 12). The indestructible never disappears, but can be covered, by the shade-phantasm (*árny*) or the mask; this is why the central feature of the great, sacral novels is to liberate from the mask, focusing on seeing and not reasoning (Ibid.: 12–13, 53), also singled out for attention in particular by Rilke, Broch and Doderer.

After this initiation Bormester is ready to return home to his three sons. Angela no longer has power over him; we won't meet her again. At this point the narrative jumps over two decades, and Part VI is devoted to the 1944–5 siege of Budapest, during World War II. This is a kind of initiatory experience for an entire nation, but there is little sign of genuine reckoning. Bormester, who is only in his mid-fifties, plays a minor role in this part, emphasis shifting to his sons, Gergely, Máté and Jusztin, and at the end of the siege he even dies – so the presumed author disappears before the last part of the novel. Even the miracle performed by the Jewish sage on the left foot of Máté, the cynical son of Mihály, born with a hoof, has no effect; Máté even claims that his life philosophy was thus destroyed, as he no longer can justify himself through misfortune.

Part VII moves to the time of writing, 1948–50. By jumping over the 1945–8 period, Hamvas did not want to ignore its importance; but he thought that the opportunity that presented itself in 1945 to Europe, and the world, was simply missed. The novel has surprisingly little connection to everyday (un)reality under Communist rule.

In this part the role played by the Bormester family is minimal. The emphasis shifts on the family of Raimund Herstal Jr., and Vidal, a Frenchman, whom Raimund invites to Budapest in order to rearrange his library. We have to be careful here, though, as the fate of the two families has been intertwined at the moment when in 1890 the two newborn babies were mistakenly exchanged. Furthermore, we'll come to know that the youngest Raimund Herstal in fact is the son of Mihály Bormester, who had a short affair with the wife of Raimund Herstal Jr. in 1924 (Hamvas 1997, III: 423). Thus, in opposition to his father, he is a real Herstal, but this only further confuses things, as the type of contrast between his father and himself, quite different in quality from the mismatch between his grandfather and father, turns him into a genuine monstrosity.

When ordering the library Vidal finds the notes of Virgil Bormester, just as the manuscript of Mihály Bormester, together with other bits and pieces. He thus starts to understand the story, and one by one pulls down everyone's masks. In this way he tries to perform the task that was missed in 1945, to put things finally into their place, but fails, as he ignores a most important truth: it is not enough to unmask others; one also has to keep an eye on the *Vita Nuova*, which for Hamvas is nothing else but the way of love. Vidal – whose name evokes the Indo-European root **vid* 'see' – manages to see beyond the masks, but misses the opportunity to commit himself to Flóra, Raimund Herstal Jr's daughter, in spite of their mutual attraction. Even here the novel evokes Dostoevsky's *Idiot*, which similarly has the failed marriage between Myshkin and Aglaia at its centre.

The problem is discussed during a conversation between Vidal, Flóra and her mother, Adelhaide baroness, wife of Raimund Herstal Jr, easily the highest moment of the novel. Vidal should have used the opportunity to commit himself; but instead he quotes, from the novel that he is reading (and which is presumably the book we are reading as well), a sharp and acute diagnosis of the modern condition:

We live under a curse. This curse is called mask. I cannot reach the other human being. His illness and madness and sin become dense, and turned into a form – a false form [*álforma*]. This dense false form is the mask. In most cases it pushes the living being out of its place and tries to live in its stead. This is the mask; this is the larva, the madness. The mask is the devil. The devil is not a face [*arc*], but a mask [*álarc*]. Larva. This is why the devil always lies. It cannot even be real. It cannot live. The devil has no real existence on its own, only to the extent in which it sucks the vital force of others. It has no reality; only as much reality as it can take away from the others.

(III: 369–70)

This recognition gives a task: to take away the mask, to unmask, literally to 'flay' the mask and thus 'at any price to stick to the naked, living, real being, and to touch her, to live directly with her' (III: 370). But – as there is always a but – this is not enough, because at the same time the mask is also the female, and thus at the same time it is sacred, it is the great mystery; it cannot be taken of, this is strictly forbidden, as we have to play the game, and in a mask. It is this identity between the madness and sacredness of the mask that is called humour-mysticism, revealing the 'unheard-of comicity and the hair-raising beauty of existence' at the same time (III: 370–1).

Vidal reads this insight; applies to himself, as it confirms the bad feelings he had about taking off everybody's mask; even utters the key phase that 'it is only in the greatest moments of love that we are not covered' (III: 371) – but still fails to make a move. The baroness realises that the occasion is missed, but cannot help it – also because at this moment an intruder arrives, the doctor Ábsalom, a particularly dubious trickster character of medical scientism, and the opportunity is forever closed. Vidal would soon leave Hungary, but neither he, nor any of the characters find a real way out.

Vidal is talking about the need to reach out and touch somebody, instead of merely talking about it – but he fails to do so actually. But, of course, we can only read about it if somebody writes this down. So here we have reached something like an ultimate level of self-reflexivity, close to Plato's *Phaedrus* and *Philebus*, the writer making us aware of the difference between life and literature by rendering the main character *fail* to do what he preaches, so that it could inspire us to *really* do what we think must be done, and not simply resigning ourselves to the 'elevating' experience that the hero did the right thing – and then return to our everyday banal denial of this experience.

The novel closes with a few sentences Vidal uttered, before he left, in a shop, in the context of a discussion about the imminence of World War III, about the need for waking up, closely paraphrasing the last words of Dostoevsky's *Karamazov Brothers*, the same passage quoted by Girard at the end of his book on the novel: 'prepare for the wonderful waking up. I wish I could be there. If at least I could reach the gate, so that I could cast a glance at the Promised Land, just a single one –' (III: 461).

The importance of writing/the significance of novels

In contrast to the other authors discussed in this part, Hamvas was not primarily a novelist, but a thinker. Yet, writing a novel for him was not a mere *divertissement*. He reflected upon the activity, explaining his perspective both in a separate work and within the body of the novel.

In his *Fragments of a Theory of Novel* (Hamvas 1994), written in 1948, just before embarking on writing *Karnevál*, he attributes utmost significance to this genre, recalling Girard. According to this by the twentieth century the novel became a general and universal interpretation of existence, incorporating all similar attempts from science and art (see also Darabos 2002, III: 36; Hamvas 1997, III: 253–4).

In the novel Hamvas discusses the activity of writing in the last part, through Vidal (III: 334–6). Our world was created by wars and revolutions, and by the mid-twentieth century these 'have reached their worst stage, where they have become meaningless, and yet the machine set in motion keeps working', by itself (III: 334). Under such conditions the central issue becomes the freedom of stepping outside; a possibility that presented itself in 1945, but which was lost. This renders writing an almost unique mode for gaining access to this state of freedom, as 'writing has a primordial state. It can be done under direct spiritual inspiration. Besides revelation, I have never encountered this inspiration' (III: 334). It has a clear ringing, comparable to singing; any mistake and misunderstanding is excluded. This kind of writing 'makes no use of stylistic tricks. Abandon oneself to it, so that your entire existence would sing with it. I know how a choir of angels sing, though have never heard it' (Ibid.). This writing is a kind of passion, though not the sick intoxication characteristic of monomania and fixation; and is only possible if one does not pay any attention to effects (III: 336–7). Here again a schismogenic pair is identified, where the obsessive compulsion of 'realising oneself' and 'generating effect' go hand in hand, as illustrated paradigmatically through 'the case of Wagner'. Writing as genuine passion is a 'sacred authority', as 'a beautiful life and a great work go together' (III: 337). Hamvas helps to understand why some great novels of the twentieth century after World War I and the Bolshevik revolution were written by figures who were not only ignored but wrote without any hope of success, even outright without any hope of publication within their lifetime, and yet kept working.

The irony is that Vidal does not write at all, only makes an order among the writings of others, and even tries to justify his own ineptness (III: 337–40). The novel can be *sui generis* interpretation of existence only if it is reflexive and playful at the same time: if it neither searches involvement at any price – though it can have heart-smothering moments; nor descends into parody and farce – though can present outrageous hilarity; rather is fully aware of the activity of writing and reading and its responsibilities, rendering it evident as well. The novel of the twentieth century therefore must be a philosophical novel, but only to the extent that it is a spiritual novel as well. Hamvas here works towards re-uniting not only art and science, sociology and literature, but philosophy and spirituality, *the* project of our times.

Out of joint

The novel, just as Hamvas's philosophical essays and historical writings, addresses the condition of mankind in the twentieth century, the ever deepening and painfully acute sense of crisis, with a degree of freedom that is hardly available in our publicised world, maintaining full responsibility for every word, once liberated from the irresponsibility of having to address the 'public' as 'judge'.

The starting point is the joint recognition by Hamlet and Don Quixote: time is out of joint; stabilities no longer hold; a vortex has been opened under our feet – an experience that in *Scientia Sacra* Hamvas would trace back about 2500 years and which could even be moved further back, the at once mythical and extremely real time of the Trojan War, which leans back even to the sack of Arslantepe/ Meliddu around 3000BC (Szakolczai 2016b). This is what Hamvas calls the 'original disjoining' (*principiális kizökkenés*), a singular event of which everything else is the 'self-evident consequence' (Hamvas 1997, I: 145). This tragic event involved and involves everyone, from which nobody can withdraw oneself, pretending a position of exteriority. Any such pretence, like 'scientific objectivity' or the posture of 'critic' is merely comical.

But the state in which the world and we all are as a consequence of this tragic disjoining can also be described through the means of humour and comedy. So it can only be captured by jointly using tragic and comic expressions and means, while fully preserving the involved position of sacral playfulness; or of the sacred clown.

Carnival society

Hamvas locates the origins of 'carnival society' in the sixteenth century, and connects its gradual progress to every new war and revolution, 'progress' being identical to the deepening of the crisis, which by the twentieth century took apocalyptic proportions. In a summary but incisive passage Hamvas characterises the seventeenth and the eighteenth centuries as the time of the hypocrites, who are 'a mixture of pietised miser and womaniser'; this is followed in the nineteenth century by the age of the dandy and the snob; while the twentieth century is the period of saints and fools (III: 360).

Hamvas is interested not in historical facts, rather the underlying logic of this process, and traces this to spiritual factors, moving forces of life-conduct. Here over the centuries a double movement was taking place. Negatively, through Puritanism, absolutistic court and radical Enlightenment intellectuals it resulted in the elimination from human life of love – this most simple and basic of feelings, which exists within families and circle of friends, between generations, between a mother and a child, between a husband and a wife, and without which it is simply not possible to live; while positively, love as the basic principle of human life was replaced by the struggle for survival, regressing human beings below the level of animal life.

Such reductionist regression concerning one's moving forces entailed corruption in everyone's view of the other. If everybody only tries to secure survival and maximise pleasures during our short lifetime, then certainly this is what everybody else is doing. Deprived of the possibility of trust, everyone's attitude towards others is motivated by deep-seated suspicion, and a search for hidden motives behind anything done:

> these people don't know each other, as they have never met each other [...]; in the struggle for their own salvation they did not have time for this; [... so] in the heat of their raging, as they don't have a clue about each other, these people think all kind of mad things about the others.
>
> (II: 133)

Thinking leads to acting, so they ceaselessly try to push the others under the water. Still, the basis of these acts are psychological games:

> They desperately try to guess each other's thoughts, as they know that the danger lies not in what is said but what is unsaid. The real danger is what is assumed. Against this it is not possible to defend oneself. The winner is the one who guessed the thoughts of the other. This is the back-stairs drama. This is called psychology. This is cowardice. Living in backdoor thoughts. Counting upon what the other does not say. But of course it is not our fault that things are like that. This is the immanent (or transcendent) unreality of things, that it is like that, and yet it isn't.
>
> (II: 133–4)

A climate of mutual suspicion permeates human relations, rendering a meaningful, gracious, noble life based on giving, compassion and love impossible. As Dostoevsky indicated, in a world dominated by 'demons' generous human beings are turned into 'idiots'.

Hamvas, however, went a step further than Dostoevsky, replacing 'demon' as the central term with 'mask'. The modern world is not so much a demonic world agitated by dark forces, rather a masked ball, a carnival, in which the comic element, which remained an undercurrent in Dostoevsky, becomes dominant – though by no means exclusive, as the tragic character of this comedy repeatedly becomes transparent at the greatest moments of hilarity.[14]

Hamvas offers a series of characterisations of carnival society which in themselves seem simplistic and misleading, especially if hypostasised into 'concept' and 'definition', but taken together convey a coherent and thought-provoking picture. The world of carnival society at a first instance is a 'zoo' (I: 9), and 'panopticon' (I: 130, 412), also resembling a marionette show (I: 10), or 'puppet theatre' (II: 187). Most of all, it is a circus (I: 301, 365; II: 374), even 'world circus' (III: 23), 'the castle of madness' about which it is easy to write a satire (I: 386). But what kind of beings populates this zoo or circus? They are first of all 'Protean' (III: 88), capable of permanently changing their shape, so 'it is in vain to fight against them, it is not possible to capture them, as the moment one catches them they take up a different shape' (III: 88). They most recall lemurs, 'a small rodent-like animal with tiny and restless eyes' (I: 455), as 'the age of lemurs is starting. Here, *devant les yeux* (*sic*; before our eyes)' (I: 435).[15] The perfect illustration of lemur age is the movie theatre, where art becomes 'non-art, or pure entertainment, aiming to liberate human beings from themselves. It is a matter of nerves, nothing to do with the spirit. An introduction to Lemuria: they sit inside the dark and let themselves be titillated' (I: 435). This means that the twentieth century is 'the century of madmen' (I: 357), which will lead to a situation where fools 'will actually take over power above the world' (II: 424). Concerning the circus metaphor, there are two emblematic figures: the animal trainer and the clown. Here the situation is a bit more complex, less a mere caricature, as we enter the heart of the 'social structure' of carnival society.

This society is populated by three kinds of humans. For its leaders, Hamvas uses expressions like circus master, animal trainer (II: 374–82) or dancing master (III: 360–2). The dancing master is identical to the animal trainer (*idomító*), as both teach us 'to perform fantastic tricks – needless to say, only in our own interest' (III: 361). For the population at large, Hamvas uses an even more striking word: aborigines (*bennszülött*). The term is derived from Hamvas's interpretation of the modern colonisation experience: far from elevating the colonised to the civilisational level of colonisers, as it was supposed to happen, rather techniques experimented over colonies were taken over and regularised in treating the population of coloniser countries. The colonial wars of the nineteenth century were thus field of experiments for the World Wars, eventually reinvested into the periphery wars of containment.

The normal state of being of an aborigine, meaning all of us, is sleepwalking (III: 101). Having accepted the doctrines of struggle for survival and pleasure principle, they can easily be trained by circus directors. In order to characterise the logic by which 'carnival society' functions, Hamvas invents two terms by modifying slightly, to great comic effect, two ordinary Hungarian words: 'lunyacska' (rendered into English as *barrit*) (II: 395; III: 23, 133, 243–5) and 'kenyőcs (*creem*)' (II: 266–70, 374–6). 'Lunyacska' is from *nyulacska*, Hungarian diminutive for 'rabbit' (*nyúl*). It represents the ever elusive ideals circus directors promise the aborigines, the cornucopia or golden-egg-laying-hen of the bright future of peace and prosperity:

> Barrit. Run and hide among the bushes. Are you the golden rabbit whom everyone is searching for? Eat. You think I have the barrit? I think you have it. You want to kill me as you think I have it and am hiding it [. . .] Everybody is searching for the barrit. The Chinese believe that the Mongolians have it, the Japanese believe that the Chinese have it, and the Jews believe that the Babylonians have it. And they say it in vain that well, sorry, but we don't have it, we are also looking for it. But then the Chinese and the Japanese and the Romans and the Jews and the English and the Spanish become ever more angry, and they believe that surely it must then be with the Afghans and the Indians and the Hindus. They kill them, and then it turns out that it is not

there, and has never been. It's all gone. I don't have the barrit, no matter how much I would like to have it, but no –

(II: 395)

The barrit not only underlies the logic of modern warfare, but also the scapegoating mechanism. Hamvas applies this idea for the Nazi logic: to be sure, the barrit must be with the Jews (III: 133).

'Kenyőcs' comes from 'lubricating cream' (kenőcs). It is the ideology by which 'things can be palmed so that they would slide down smoothly' (II: 266). It is used to keep the 'machine' running; perfect for mobilising a large number of people for action and at the same time justify as inevitable what they do; especially that they squander their lives, sacrificing it in pursuit of chimeras. It is outright the Bible of our world, replacing the Gospel of John: 'At the beginning there was the creem and the creem was with the animal trainer and the animal trainer was the creem' (II: 374).

While the reality to which these terms allude is serious, even deadly serious, they are also comic, even playful. Most metaphors and terms used to analyse 'carnival society' have comic affinities. This is only natural for a book that takes the circus as main metaphor for modernity. Still, the comic nature of this 'new world order' must be analysed in detail – never forgetting the proviso by which Hamvas started his book: we might ridicule and denigrate this comic world circus, yet we are part of it, even deeply so, and can't pretend outsider status and immunity.

Not surprisingly, the comic is omnipresent in a book whose genre was defined a 'comedy of fates'. The book is full of outrageously hilarious comic elements, as carnival society is a permanent comedy. Thus, comedy is the par excellence genre of our age, which is not able to produce a proper drama, a tragedy (II: 154). Still, the comedy of our times, the age of comedy cannot bring much relaxation, as it is 'apocalyptic comedy' produced by 'raging lovelessness' – a comedy that chills the blood (III: 89–90). Far from magnifying this comic element, the book generates a reflexive attitude about it – which is itself comic (I: 10). The presumption of an external position is even more comic (I: 129), though the most comic position of all is to take oneself deadly seriously (I: 359). We should neither laugh with the world, nor laugh at the world, but should first of all be able to laugh at ourselves – as parts of this world (I: 131).

Yet, even this is not enough, and for three reasons. First, most evidently, this can be itself a sophist trick: laughing at oneself may be a way to avoid becoming truly comic (I: 373), just as Lala, who is without any sense of humour, becomes exemplarily and utterly comic, in spite of her terrifying character (II: 154). Second, there are serious problems with laughter, as it is a form of rage, produced by recognising the absence of love (II: 140–1). This is connected to the 'basic humour-mystical stand', to be discussed later. Finally, it is not enough, as self-distancing has two different methods: one 'timed at zero' (the method of Kierkegaard, the basis of existentialism), and the other oriented towards infinity (the method of Shakespeare, taking the entire mankind as a mirror). Only taken together do they constitute the genre that can be called satire, irony or humour, and whose greatest masters, among others, are Socrates, Zhuang-Zhou, Molière, Dickens and Joyce (I: 413).

Still, this humour is a last veil, even last mask (III: 87). Here we again reach the core concept of Hamvas's novel, his political anthropology of the modern world. The metaphors of carnival and circus culminate in the idea that its inhabitants are first of all *masks*.

Demons and masks

The mask is first of all what is abstract and impersonal; which can be taken up and exchanged; a pure role (I: 358). A human being who becomes a mere mask no longer has passion and concreteness, even loses the sense of reality, 'living in an unreal world imagined by oneself a life that is arbitrary and without any human contact, detached from the community; he does not count, is despised and idiot' (II: 433). Most importantly, such a person loses his unique, single personality, giving rise 'not to freedom but madness' (I: 359). This is not an idiosyncrasy, rather central aspect of the processes that gave rise to the modern world:

> at the end of the nineteenth century the germs of the current madness were already present in social life. They wanted freedom, but it became madness, as they started not from the unique concrete person, but from the mask. Human beings are not living their own passions, but the madness of their demon.
>
> (I: 359–60)

Such demons are set free through the impersonality generated through the mask, as the demonic, the impersonal and the mask are identical: 'the impersonal is demonic power', nothing but a work of 'demiurgic phantasmagoria' (I: 299).

Hamvas gives a harrowing description of the way a concrete human being is transformed into a mask (I: 145–50), taking a cue from the fact that in Hungarian there are two words for mask: *maszk* and *álarc* (false face):

> Look at one of these faces. It does not matter which [. . .] You name it. So let it be Laura [Kankalin]. I knew her when she got married 25 years ago, and even fell in love with her a little bit; she was a disarmingly beautiful and vain woman [. . .] and look at her now, what a pale and waxed face she has, it is almost revolting and depraved. You cannot say that this face was destroyed by her husband, or by somebody else, by troubles, disasters, poverty, the environment, disappointment, illness; no, even she would not dare to say so. Beside herself, nobody is responsible for this face, solely she alone, yes, she herself. Look at this sly terror in her eye, what became of this face, look at that embittered pain under her nose, the tired and depressed inclination in her chin [. . .] the so-called circumstances can never deform and ravage a face in this manner, never ever, she impaled herself.
>
> (I: 145–6)

228 *After World War I*

These faces are immensely comic; yet, at the same time fill the observer with deep sorrow.

Hamvas even offers a reason why human beings willingly turn themselves into masks – the masks of themselves. The explanation closely evokes Girard. The central idea is the belief that one is an *exception*; that one is 'different'. In this way one's singular individual personality is traded into a relative concept: we are individuals in contrast to the 'other'. This is the central ideology of the modern world, the lie of modern individualism and autonomy. As a result everyone is permanently offended, carrying a reproach against the whole world, because their fantasies were not fulfilled. All this is a comedy, but 'a base and ignominious comedy' (I: 149), with a lethal ending: the person becomes

> irritable and rude, indifferent and monomaniac, which of course makes him stupid, and then would not like to hear about anything else but that he is always hurt, and then come the deep and sour wrinkles, the loss of appetite, the bad digestion, the hair starts to fall out, the nose becomes swollen, the eye frightful, the mouth mean, and no matter how much powder is wasted on it, the face will be full of viciousness and suffering, increasingly becoming a clown and a death mask and chimera and inhuman and ugly and tragic and monstrously comic.
>
> (I: 150)

A central aspect of the human face is the eye, never covered by masks. However, when a human face is turned into a mask, the eye is also transformed, condensing the process in an extremely succinct manner: 'the same voluptuous eye, that ice-cold brilliance, that touch which provokes fainting, even in this manner, through a photo. It is demonic –' (III: 343).

The central feature of a person transformed into a mask is to lose all contact with reality: 'the great question of the century of fools is the question of reality' (I: 357). One of the masks, Episztemon, mistakes the mask for reality, thus cannot even imagine what it means to be real (I: 375–6). This has a concrete and timely anthropological and sociological bearing concerning the difference between person and identity. 'Identity' is a mask through which humans are encouraged to give up their concrete personality, the possibility of genuine living, for the pursuit of a 'construct' – in the company of similarly fooled fools.

Concrete persons are moved by passions, involving spirituality. Masks no longer have genuine passions, but they also need to move themselves. Hamvas uses two terms to describe the masked existence of 'carnival society', fixed idea (*rögeszme*) and monomania. They represent a parodic take on the presumed unity of theory and practice. A 'fixed idea' is something a carnivalesque human invents as his aim and essence, *the* purpose justifying his 'identity'; mere fancy, with no relationship to reality. 'Monomania' refers to the dogged, maniacal persistence by which such masks set out to real-ise their folly, transform themselves – and the world around them – into their mirror mirage.

A crucial feature of carnival society is that marriage becomes an impossibility. Any *bona fide* anthropologist and sociologist knows, deep in their heart, that genuine marriage is the foundation of social life. Even Dionysian ritual was a feast for celebrating marriage. In carnival society marriage implies the unbearable burden of becoming tied for life to a monomaniac – to *another* monomaniac – clearly intolerable in the long run. A marriage only lasts until one realises that the fixed idea gained about the other does not correspond to reality, and the two monomania become incompatible.

A human being turned into the mask of his own identity becomes blocked, as if arrested in time (I: 417). He will no longer be able to develop, becoming a mummy, practically ceasing to be human: unable to live, to love, to suffer (III: 434). Hamvas argues that for this state of (non-)being there is an even better word than 'mask'; it is 'larva' (I: 388–9). This establishes direct contact to the core human element, which is not reason – as reason can easily entrap humans in fixed ideas and then in monomania – rather *imagination*: 'imagination is the primordial power of the soul, which is nothing else but faith, or the kind of magic that takes fire from the passion of will' (*akarat szenvedélye*; I: 388). It can arrive there, the realm of mystery, where reason, being too much rooted in the material world, cannot reach. Due to its limits reason is forced to form opinions, thus 'places its will under the sign of madness' (III: 388). However, 'larva' is indeed a Venetian mask, and one of the most powerful: a completely white mask, also called *volto* (which means 'face' in Italian) usually worn with a black dress, as in the cover of the Penguin edition of Thomas Mann's *Death in Venice*. Another circle is closed around masks, carnival, circus, theatre and clowns.

In the modern world, from the sixteenth century, masks were only worn in the theatre. In the contemporary world even this has disappeared, the only masked figures still around are clowns. It is this metaphor of clown or fool that Hamvas applies to the inhabitants of carnival societies (I: 8, 129, 260, 341, 475; III: 98, 105–7); occasionally even using the word 'Harlequin' (II: 375, 380). In such world a most important element of human life, the sense of judgement is fatally undermined: 'It is getting increasingly more difficult to recognise fools. Just a few years back it was relatively simple. Soon it will be impossible. World history is reaching levels that it will be no longer possible to distinguish a sane mind from a mad one' (II: 424). The logical outcome is that this will extend to leaders, resulting in a situation formulated earlier in the novel as a forecast, with a desperate scream: 'What will happen if this caducity will inundate the world? What will happen if sheer foolery will govern the world, and mankind will be ruled by clowns?' (I: 260).

The question is not purely rhetorical, and the answer offered by Hamvas is quite stunning. Making use of one of his favourite quotes, from Hölderlin, 'But where danger is, there grows the saving power as well', also central for Heidegger, he argues that world madness can only be cured by fools of a special kind: sacred fools. His main source is Shakespeare, especially *Hamlet* and *King Lear*; but in order to understand the point we need to revisit his ideas about imagination and mirage (*káprázat*).

According to Hamvas, for the soul imagination is more important than reason. This is because reality itself is created through imagination (I: 387–9; III: 249).

Imagination is the product of sight, the eye, and not of reason, the mind, so to see is more important than to think (II: 430, 5). This point is resumed, after the initiatory vision experience of Bormester, in a striking passage by the Master: 'What do you want to solve? What do you want to comprehend? You must see. The eye is more than the mind. Nothing is more sensitive and delicate, than reality' (III: 63). But we can only see, and imagine, if our imagination is fuelled by the fire of real experience, through the soul (I: 387), as 'the soul is fed by experiences; and in the absence of experiences the soul perishes' (III: 277). Personality is rooted in concrete experiences. Otherwise, our power of imagination becomes damaged, as it happened in the modern world: 'such corrupted imagination is called madness, and this imagination running amok creates what we call – in a manner that cannot be condemned enough – the world' (III: 250); so we are ruled by illusion and mirage. This type of imagination is pure fantasy, and is the opposite of reality (II: 432), and yet we live inside this, as 'all of us are living this peculiar life, in stunning confusion, in the midst of mirages' (II: 147), given that 'the present is pure, condensed mirage' (III: 253). We don't simply 'live' in it, but fell into it and were captivated by this mirage, caught as if in a tempest, and 'whoever steps into the maelstrom of mirage loses his common-sense [. . . as there] it is not possible to stop' (I: 275). The result is quasi-alchemic transformation: 'the man who lives in such a dream-world begins to lose his genuine being, and very slowly starts to become a mirage himself, and is not a man anymore but a phantom or monster or mask or mirage, but in no way a human being' (III: 114).

Yet again, mad acting also has saving power; the act of a fool, but a sacred fool. The favourite example of Hamvas is the story of Mary and Martha, the Mary who anointed the feet of Jesus with an expensive cream, wasting a great amount (e.g. II: 341, 387; see Jn 12: 1–8). According to the logic of the world, this was an act of madness; and the disciples – who always sided with the logic of the world, until the cock crew thrice, and even beyond – duly reproach her, according to the blackmail logic of hypocritical charity, that it could have been given to the poor. Yet, Jesus defends her, knowing that anything valuable in the world is a product of sacred folly.

In order to understand how illusion, fantasy and mirage, or the corruption of imagination, can turn into divine folly, and how the clown, this most decayed form of human mask can become a sacred fool, we need to discuss the term *humormisztikai alapállás* (humour-mystical basic stand) (I: 131; II: 139–41, 154; III: 87, 371).

This creates considerably difficulties, first of all because according to Darabos (2002, III: 52, 66) both published versions of the novel misread in the manuscript *humormisztikai* as *humorisztikai* (humouristic, a much lighter meaning). The reading of Darabos certainly makes more sense, as it combines the two central aspects of the last position in the novel: the comic effect or humour and mysticism.

'Humour-mysticism' is based on a moral stand: it is ethically forbidden to laugh at others; genuine laughter means that we laugh at ourselves (Hamvas 1997, I: 131). 'Humour-mystical basic stand' is the reflexive elaboration of the meaning and significance of the comic as the core ethical stance in the modern world (II: 139–41). It starts with the recognition that without love, we cannot live, we can only go mad (II: 139; also III: 89); but as genuine love is absent from the modern world, we are all mad – so I am mad as well – and thus we must go mad, as if on the second power, due to this recognition. All this gives rise to a mad raving, which is laughter. So, 'humour-mystical laughter is the real and genuine laughter, a laughter due to the maddening recognition of the madness of living a life without love, which is the basic stand of real comedy' (II: 141). But even this must be taken to a further level of reflexivity, as this genuine laughter – a mad laughter, sign of a second order madness – reflecting on itself can become a third order madness, which is sacred madness, where sage and fool, saint and madman become identical. This leads to the idea that life, in its most profound sense, is play, and a sacred play: life is 'saint madness' (*szent őrület*) or 'sacral folly' (II: 379; see also III: 253).

The last surprise is that, according to Hamvas, this human being, apparent product of a complicated modern mental game, is identical to the man of the Gospels (*evangéliumi ember*) (II: 341).

At this level not just the fool with his manias and mirages, but even the mask is redeemed, again in a most surprising way, explaining why we cannot restrict ourselves to the endless task of removing masks. According to Hamvas, the mask is not gender neutral:

> The mask is a very strange thing. The author says quite peculiar things about it. He says that the mask is woman [. . .] He means that among human beings it is the female, or the body, the shape, the form, the mirage, which is the great mystery. The mask is sacred. It cannot be taken down. This is strictly forbidden. We must play the game in a mask. We should not fully awaken [*kijózanodik*] from our folly. Folly is our natural state. The mask is the sign that we live in a sacral madness [. . .] This is called humour-mysticism. He is laughing and trembling at the same time at the madness and sacredness of mask, at the incredible [*hallatlan*] comicity and hair-raising beauty of existence.
>
> (III : 370–1).[16]

Those who manage to reach this 'humour-mystical basic stand' constitute a third human type inhabiting 'carnival society', showing the way out of its madness and monomania. They no longer respond to the tricks of animal trainers, though they do not pretend an exterior position in the form of criticism either; they do not preach the revolution (for them this is the height of demonic madness), and do not form a sect of the elected. Their central characteristic is double consciousness. They represent the threshold towards the *Vita Nuova* (II: 22–3, 384; III: 93).

This is another Dantesque term, only too appropriate for an 'initatory novel', with a visionary trip at its centre. About this, Hamvas only gives glimpses, of which the most important elements have already been discussed: this is love,[17] rooted in the heart, the central value, in contrast to goodness or justice (II: 99; III:

105–6, 396), which are based in the mind. This is based not on self-love, self-knowledge and the pursuit of self-realisation – all this only results in closing the human being into a preoccupation with oneself (III: 291) – rather knowledge of the other; and not any such 'knowledge', but the recognition of the other in its essential humanness, which is not simply a Christian value but – in contrast to the will to domination – is the original basic stand of mankind (I: 247). It is itself power (III: 291), and freedom, even free choice (I: 141; III: 335), which can only be based on the readiness to serve (II: 238), or intactness (*épség*) (I: 411), which is always concrete, in contrast to purity, which is always abstract; and finally on the 'ocean of faith' (III: 397–8), which is not the same as an immersion in the nothingness, a product of desperate egoism (III: 414), due to atheism and secularity (III: 398), rather a sacred form of madness, 'the madness of religion', which is the fermenting 'wine of existence', a form of existence which is no longer purely human, as it belongs to the realm of the Holy Spirit, beyond good and evil; this is 'the *Pneuma* [of the Gospel according to John], which thunders but also rustles among the leaves of the trees. This is the passion of madness, and the humility of meekness' (III: 398).

The 'ocean of faith' identifies secularisation as a main problem. There is indeed a peculiar correspondence between comedy and secularisation, as the three major periods of secularisation in history – (post-)classical Athens, (post-)Republican Rome and the contemporary modern world – are also the periods when comedy gained dominance. These were also the three main instances of democratic government in world history, just as three main instances of unlimited political expansion, globalising wars and the rise of power/knowledge complexes, driven by 'vaulting ambition' – all this cannot be mere coincidence. Secularisation leads to a loss of weight, the 'unbearable lightness of being', an internal emptying to be compensated by external expansion and 'concupiscential conquest'.[18] It can also be related to the Platonic life cycle of forms of governments, according to Voegelin, taken in a Nietzschean key. Like all things, democracies also perish by their own success: the ability to rely on the positive, active contribution and worth of every single citizen, also leads to hubris, and intoxication with success and with one's own worth can easily become destructively contagious.

Notes

1. About Hamvas, see Szakolczai (2005a, 2005b, 2012, 2014b) and Szakolczai and Wydra (2006).
2. This translates as Michael Winemaster, as he would indeed be called in Part IV.
3. This was published in July 2015 as vol.28 of the collected works of Hamvas.
4. For an important sociological fact, see the pioneering of single childhood (*egyke*) and childlessness in Europe (see Poston and Szakolczai 1986). The answer certainly has to do with the extremely liminal position of the country.
5. Jacopo Tintoretto (1518–94) was a Venetian painter, while Wagner was obsessed with Venice.
6. This is strikingly close to the Hindu idea of indestructible as *aksara* (syllabe).
7. Only presumed, as two babies were mistakenly exchanged at birth in the hospital.
8. 'Hopp' is the Hungarian word by which trainers induce animals to do a jump.

9. The husband is the judge who condemned Virgil.
10. Another representative of scientism is doctor Vermerán, the forensic psychiatry expert of the court, talking in a jargon recalling the *Dottore* of *commedia dell'arte*.
11. So, just as the feast before, another founding element of human life becomes emptied of meaning.
12. Hamvas published his version of Henoch's *Apocalypse* in 1945.
13. An interesting aspect of the trip is the reference to the configuration of the Centaur (III: 38, 66–7), other name for the Sagittarius in the Zodiac, the constellation closest to the Southern Star; strangely enough, in both cases shortly after the evocation of Virgin Mary. The house at the end of the vision is remarkably close to the eternal refuge of at the end of *Master and Margarita*.
14. This is close to the characterisation of the demonic in the classic work of Gerhard Ritter, according to which demonic power, like the head of a Gorgon 'stiffens a human face into a mask and grimace' (Ritter 1997: 194).
15. Lemurs are 'prosimians', a group of mammals that includes all primates except monkeys and apes, considered more 'primitive' than monkeys. The word is from Latin *lemures*, meaning 'spirits of the night' or 'ghosts'. Apart from hyenas, they are the only mammals that live in matriarchy. Ovid suggests that lemurs are shadows of the dead (*Fasti*, V: 419–92; see O'Connor 2016). Hamvas might have confused lemurs with lemmings, which are rodents.
16. This link between women and the highest pitch of divine folly has already been alluded at with the story of Martha and Mary, and is underlined in two other crucial moments of the New Testament: the resurrection was first experienced by a woman, and quite 'sinful' one, Mary Magdalene; and the single most important human being in the Catholic tradition is also a woman, Virgin Mary.
17. This is the last word of Thomas Mann's *The Magic Mountain*; though he later, in his liberal period, came to forget it.
18. For details, see Szakolczai (forthcoming2).

Conclusion

> Step by step, peace shows itself a bit everywhere. It is not a well-designed peace that usually succeeds wars definitely finished by peace treaties, heralding a new stage of history. This age has no name; it is the end of all things. An end that will never end ending. A swamp that consumes any dynamism. We don't feel the approaching of a good or bad conclusion. Quite on the contrary. We are sinking deeper and deeper into the putrefaction of a temporariness that resembles eternity.
>
> Nothing can be concluded [. . .] Everything is dissolved [. . .]
>
> The approaching peace is not the fruit of human decisions.
>
> It spreads like leprosy.
>
> Antoine de Saint Exupéry, *War Pilot*, 1942

The modern world has come into being by offering the strongest and broadest promises possible. Using the language of the French Revolution, it promised freedom, equality and fraternity, for each and all; in the terminology of the American constitution, it proclaimed the unalienable right to life, liberty and the pursuit of happiness; according the United Nations Declaration of Human Rights, everyone has the right to life, liberty and security.

Underlying such promises is a certain vision of power: actually enabling everyone to reach such goals, beyond merely sketching a future utopia, thus power as universal *empowering*. Yet, the actual reality of our days demonstrates the exact opposite. The problem is not simply that not everyone is free, wealthy and happy, that inequalities and poverty persist, but that we as human beings, alone and together as members of any political community, are increasingly and radically disempowered in face of three anonymous forces: the 'markets', supposedly objective and irresistible, escaping the control of any political entity, and through globalisation dictating the agenda of human existence; 'technology', similarly developed beyond human control, purportedly serving the interests of mankind, yet already drafting the radical vision of the 'post-human'; and mediatised mass 'democracy', through the omnipotent 'public sphere', including anybody and caring for nobody in particular, combining infinity and zero in the flux of the void. We are not simply facing a prolonged economic crisis, but must revisit the very foundations of the project 'modernity'.

As a first step towards settling the accounts of modernity, it was indeed a project, close to the 'Enlightenment project' of Habermas, even the project of 'Radical Enlightenment', as analysed by Margaret Jacob (1981) and Jonathan Israel (2001), but that, considering its (Byzantine) sources and orientation, can arguably be best called as 'secular politicised humanism' (hereafter the 'Project'). This is because, apart form offering a series of promises, the 'Project' distinguished itself, from about the fifteenth century onwards, by waging a systematic warfare against three targets: Nature, God and Tradition. It declared a war against Nature, in the name of science and technology (following the logic of alchemy), to pacify natural forces by subjugating them to human control; against God, or the divine, and all its 'servants', in the name of liberating mankind from the slavery of such imagined powers; and against Tradition, which supposedly merely combines the proliferation of ignorance with the defence of vested interests, captured through the metaphors of chains and cage.

Destroying tradition indiscriminately, destroying any belief in the divine, and destroying nature in the form in which it was given to us as reality was the precondition for proclaiming the existence of a truer reality, unavailable for the human senses but discoverable through scientific instruments and confirmable through mathematics and logics and serving *then* as a model for human life implies that modernity is first and foremost based on *destruction*. As the idea of creating by destruction is alchemic, generalising from metallurgy, the modern mentality is fundamentally alchemic (Horvath 2013a, 2015; see also Yates 1964, 1966, 1975). Yet, such destructiveness was hidden by the same forces that rendered the operation possible, the widespread belief in science, knowledge, technology, economic development, in one word Progress, replacing – literally – belief in God; a quite absurd idea, as Kafka realised. The inherent destructiveness of modernity was paradoxically rendered visible, jointly, by its most extreme apologues, Joseph Schumpeter (1883–1950), theorist of entrepreneurship and capitalist economic development, and Leon Trotsky (1879–1940), theorist of the permanent revolution, exact contemporaries. According to both, revolutionary change progresses in two steps. In the first, the power of 'tradition' must be broken: human culture, the set of skills and ways of doing that was taken for granted, existing as a *gift* for millennia must simply be destroyed. In a second stage, a permanent terror of innovativeness must be inculcated, in which the logic of fragmentation and integration must be permanently maintained, until every single community, each human being and all natural objects are put into the service of an anonymous and omnipotent 'public', whether mediated by money or popular justice, the stock-market or the central committee; two versions of anonymity and void. The central principle of both is that no stone should be left untouched. Secular humanism, together with its schismogenic double and mirror face, religious fanaticism and fundamentalism, animated by the 'people of god' delusion are on their way to jointly destroy the planet.

Such destructivity received a boost by a particular socio-historical condition for which the anthropologically developed term 'liminality' can be applied. Every step in the rise of the modern world involved a situation of transition or crisis, where the taken for granted order became shaken, even turned upside down, requiring a new solution. Here again, the condition that rendered the progressive emergence of the modern world possible at the same time hid its specific features, dressing up, even transmogrifying emergency measures into something that is necessary, even inevitable. Transitions imply the temporary lifting of limits, suspending accepted rules, values and measures, thus weakening the powers of judgement, even of perception. This has three basic implications. To begin with, situations of transition, or crisis, could be artificially provoked; second, a central means for such provocation is to play with boundaries, even proclaim that boundaries don't exist, as any boundary is an artificial constraint on infinite human freedom; finally, a persistent provocation of liminality and playing with limits might culminate in a most paradoxical situation where the temporary and transitory become enduring and lasting, or a situation of permanent liminality. Permanent liminality as borderlessness, resulting both in eternal flux and complete void, is the ultimate horizon of modernity, understood as a project of unlimited destructiveness, capturing the core of globalisation. Modernity, through the discreet charms of its smooth automatisms, the free market (or fairground capitalism), scientific knowledge (or alchemic technology) and democracy (or mass-mediatised public sphere), had more success in inflicting damage on the planet than any purposeful conspiracy could possibly have achieved.

If modernity, or the 'Project', is identical to destructiveness, then the question is what can actually stop it; what is indestructible. Not surprisingly, the concern with the 'indestructible' was central for most main figures launching the hypermodern novel, starting with Rilke, Hofmannsthal and Kafka. What is surprising is that they failed to give a proper weight to their own discovery, leaving it out of their – mostly incomplete – novels, even cancelling it out from publications, as if they were surprised and frightened by their own idea. Still more surprisingly, given the suggested connections with modernity, the 'indestructible' was a central concern for two of the most ancient and classical traditions of thought, the Vedas and Plato.

For Plato, the indestructible (*adiaphthoros*) is a crucial feature of the soul, whether in the sense of immortality or incorruptibility (see *Phaedrus* 245D, 252D, *Phaedo* 106E, and *Laws* 768B, 918E, 951C). It means that the inner essence of any human being simply cannot be changed, altered or transformed by any external force. In the Vedas indestructible (*aksara*) similarly implies that something cannot be liquefied, reduced to a flux, as *ksara* means 'to flow' as a liquid (see Calasso 2001, 2010; see also Turner 1989: 190). The term was also connected to the soul, the *atman* being defined in the *Upanishads* as both intangible and indestructible: '"it is intangible, for it cannot be grasped, indestructible, for it cannot be destroyed"' (as in Parrinder 1973: 30). It is also the etymological root of the word used by Plato. Thus, reaching a degree of surprise that can hardly be surpassed, the meaning of the indestructible in the Vedas, Plato, Rilke, Hofmannsthal and Kafka is identical: it captures the inner essence of any human being. We are all indestructible. In this way, the hopelessness of the modern world is suddenly transfigured into literal bliss.

However, before drawing hasty inferences, one must note that indestructibility refers to the application of external forces. What all these works of thought assert is that external forces cannot destroy the indestructible in us, even though they can threaten us in all kinds of ways, even kill us. The indestructible, however, *can* be destroyed: if we can be enticed to give up our own inner essence. Such an act might seem irrational and un-modern, yet one of the most important modern works of art, indeed the only modern myth, *Faust*, is exactly about such an eventuality: a selling of one's soul to the devil. Read from this perspective, much of contemporary 'avant-garde' thinking is nothing else but an invitation for such an act, and since quite a long time: there is no essence, no nature, especially no human nature, it whispers into our ears, so follow your dreams and fantasies, be whatever *you* want to be, realise yourself, chose your identity, construct yourself. From the perspective of the 'indestructible', this is identical to a leap into the void, as discussed by Kierkegaard. Modernity is individualistic only in the Machian sense of reducing the self to a bundle sensations, maximising pleasures through 'rational' choices, which however does not offer a 'real, scientific truth' about us humans, rather is identical to our luring into destroying the indestructible in us, rendering us accomplices in our own (self-)destruction. Such acts, as Dostoevsky analysed it, spread contagiously: whoever took the leap would eventually realise the terrible mistake made but cannot face up his own act, in a manner strikingly recalling the way Girard analyses the logic of the sacrificial mechanism, and can only keep going on by luring others into the same leap – unless coming to follow Rilke's dictum about conversion, which however requires something beyond the concrete person, an act of grace.

In order to resist, or literally persist, not by doing a heroic act, rather by standing up to the storm and staying *what one is*, one needs inner guidance that is strong enough not to be liquefied and liquidated by the chemical dissolvent of permanent liminality. Such guidance, as Pascal and Kierkegaard advise us, cannot be offered by reason, which is weak, being easily exposed to fantasy, imagination and whimsical feelings, rather by the *heart*.

Far from being subjective, flimsy and overall unreliable, it is the heart that offers humans a unique guidance towards inner stability, the sole way to counter a situation of (permanent) liminality (see Szakolczai forthcoming1). This is because the heart, both metaphorically and in its most concrete reality, offers a unique combination of body and mind, spirit and soul, transcending any dualism, partition and split. To begin with, the heart is certainly part of the body, being its central organ, controlling blood circulation, literally the gatekeeper between life and death. Furthermore, through its regular beating, it gives a rhythm to human life, functioning as a signal for any internal or external disturbance, marked by an immediate acceleration of the heartbeat, spurring to work not simply the mind or the spirit, but our inner essence, named soul. It is no doubt for these reasons that in most languages, beyond the modern dualisms of reason and emotion or body and mind words capturing feelings, reasoning and perceiving are etymologically connected, as shown by derivatives of Latin *sent (see in English 'sentiment', 'senses', 'sensuality', 'sense of judgement'; a connection better visible in Italian *sentire*), Greek *penth/ pont/ pat, or Hungarian *ér, testifying the fundamental unity of human experience.

The heart our stabiliser occasionally also needs to be stabilised. This can be done by another main source of regular rhythm in human life, walking. The rhythm of our heartbeat and of our walking coincide in a most natural way, also with an important technique of enchantment, music, each having a 60 times per minute beat, thus at the same time attuned to the cosmic rhythm of the movements of the sun and the Earth. It is this rhythm that is used and abused, to perfection, by two of the most characteristic and disgusting instruments of the modern destruction of body, mind and soul, the Muzak music of shopping malls and the soldiers' march during a military parade, distant echoes of the drums beaten by prehistoric shamans. The proper way of attuning the heart rather lies through long-distance walking, which still survives in pilgrimages and in mountain trekking, and which – according to the testimony of Palaeolithic painted caves, and the frequencies and manner of their visitation – played a major role in the rise of human culture, certainly in Europe.

But there is an even more basic stabiliser of the individual heart, and this is the mother's heartbeat. Each of us spent about nine months in the womb of our mother, and this is when her heartbeat, with its stability just as through the occasional acceleration, prepares us in a unique manner for living. This is why the various means conjured up by modernist ideologies to replace the mother's womb by technological means are among the most lethal instruments of modern nihilism.

There is a term for the times in which human experiencing was still united, where each and every human being was guided by the indestructible inside, and this is the Golden Age; a memory that is present, in one form or another, in most human cultures. The modern world never promised anything less than to bring about a new golden age, whether in the form of liberalism or socialism, the American dream, the welfare state (*l'État-providence* in French) or communism, best visible in the at once visionary and lunatic writings of Henri de Saint-Simon (1760–1825), joint source of industrialism and entrepreneurship, socialism and sociology (see Szakolczai 1987). But the theme of the Golden Age is also one of the most important, perhaps *the* most important threads connecting all main modern novelists, from Rabelais and Cervantes through Goethe and Dostoevsky up to Bulgakov and Hamvas. They also univocally attribute a fundamental role in the possibility of a new Golden Age to women – perhaps acknowledging the role of maternal heartbeat in forming the indestructible.

The Golden Age is one of three central historical memories of mankind. The second is its opposite, the Fall, ending the Golden Age, much less remembered, partly for obvious reasons concerning forgetting bad events, partly because the effective functioning of the sacrificial mechanism, central instrument of human cultures for maintaining order after the Fall, is based on forgetfulness, as Girard analysed it so well.

The third concerns the triple events of Incarnation, Crucifixion and Resurrection, resumed in the doctrine of the Trinity, core and culmination of Christian faith, at the origins of contemporary European culture (the sources of European culture can be traced back, through the Upper Palaeolithic, Neanderthal and Heidelberg cultures to the Atapuerca 'homo antecessor' culture, about a million years ago), promising to redeem the Fall. This is why the mass is not a ritual, as it is not connected to myths – whatever condensed wisdom myths might contain – rather it perpetuates the memory of concrete events. It is thus the direct model for the contemporary, vastly exaggerated and misdirected culture of memorials, which centres on death and suffering and not on its (self-)overcoming. From the perspective of these triple events, which define the central values of the culture into which most of us brought up in Europe were born, modernity represents not so much the promise of a new Golden Age, rather a second Fall.

Yet, the modern world still came out of Europe; yet, it is still coloured and moderated by the rock-solid values of our culture, of *culture*; yet, the indestructible is indestructible, unless we resign and give up.

So not only there is no reason for giving up, neither is for doubting the coming of a new 'Golden Age', even though nobody is privy to the times (Mk 13: 32; Mt 24: 36).

Bibliography

Allen, Stewart L. (1999) *The Devil's Cup*, Edinburgh: Canongate.
Agnew, Jean-Christophe (1986) *Worlds Apart: The Market and the Theater in Anglo-American Thought, 1550–1750*, Cambridge: Cambridge University Press.
Appignanesi, Lisa (1975) *The Cabaret*, London: Studio Vista.
Arens, Katherine (1996) *Austria and Other Margins*, Columbia, SC: Camden House.
Ascarelli, Roberta (1992) 'Introduzione e Note', in H. von Hofmannsthal, *Ieri*, Pordenone: Edizioni Studio Tesi.
Augé, Marc (1992) *Non-lieux : Introduction à une anthropologie de la surmodernité*, Paris: Seuil.
Bakhtin, Mikhail (1981) *The Dialogic Imagination: Four Essays*, Austin: University of Texas Press.
Bateson, Gregory (1958) *Naven*, Stanford: Stanford University Press.
—— (1972) *Steps to an Ecology of Mind*, New York: Ballantine.
Batto, Bernard F. (1995) 'Behemoth', in K. van der Toorn, B. Becking, and P.W. van der Horst (eds) *Dictionary of Deities and Demons in the Bible*, Leiden: Brill.
Bauman, Zygmunt (1991) *Modernity and Ambivalence*, Cambridge: Polity.
Beck, Evelyn T. (1971) *Kafka and the Yiddish Theater*, Madison: University of Wisconsin Press.
Becker, Ralf et al. (eds) (2003) *Synoptische Konkordanz zu Franz Kafkas Nachgelassenen Schriften und Fragmenten*, Tübingen: Niemeyer.
Bemporad, Gabriella (1976) 'Nota', in H. von Hofmannsthal, *Andrea o i ricongiunti*, Milan: Adelphi.
Benjamin, Walter (1977) 'Franz Kafka', in *Gesammelte Schriften*, vol. II/2, Frankfurt: Suhrkamp.
Bennett, Benjamin (1988) *Hugo von Hofmannsthal: The Theaters of Consciousness*, Cambridge: Cambridge University Press.
—— (2005) *All Theater is Revolutionary Theater*, Ithaca: Cornell University Press.
Bernauer, James (1990) *Michel Foucault's Force of Flight*, London: Humanities Press.
Bethea, David M. (1982) 'History as Hippodrome: The Apocalyptic Horse and Rider in *The Master and Margarita*', *The Russian Review* 41, 4: 373–99.
Blanchot, Maurice (1981) *De Kafka à Kafka*, Paris: Gallimard.
Blixen, Karen (1975) *The Angelic Avengers*, Chicago: University of Chicago Press.
—— (1986a) *Out of Africa*, Harmondsworth: Penguin.
—— (1986b) *Ehrengard*, Harmondsworth: Penguin.
—— (1987) *Carnival: Entertainments and Posthumous Tales*, London: Grafton.
—— (1995) *Ultimi racconti*, Milan: Adelphi.

―― (2002) *Seven Gothic Tales*, Harmondsworth: Penguin.
Boland, Tom (2013) *Critique as a Modern Social Phenomenon*, Lewiston, NY: Edwin Mellen Press.
Bonfiglio, Thomas P. (2003) 'Dreams of Interpretation: Psychoanalysis and the Literature in Vienna', in E. Grabovszki and J. Hardin (eds) *Literature in Vienna at the Turn of the Centuries: Continuities and Discontinuities around 1900 and 2000*, Rochester, NY: Camden House.
Borkenau, Franz (1938) *Austria and After*, London: Faber.
―― (1976) *Der Übergang vom feudalen zum bürgerlichen Weltbild: Studien zur Geschichte der Philosophie der Manufakturperiode*, Darmstadt: Wissenschaftliche Buchgesellschaft.
―― (1981) *End and Beginning: On the Generations of Cultures and the Origins of the West*, ed. by Richard Lowenthal, New York: Columbia University Press.
Bradshaw, Steve (1978) *Café Society: Bohemian Life from Swift to Bob Dylan*, London: Weidenfeld and Nicolson.
Bridgwater, Patrick (1974) *Kafka and Nietzsche*, Bonn: Bouvier.
Broch, Hermann (1974) *Hoffmansthal und seine Zeit*, Frankfurt: Suhrkamp.
―― (1975) *Schriften zur Literatur*, Vol.1, Frankfurt: Suhrkamp
―― (1978) *Schlafwandler*, Frankfurt: Suhrkamp.
―― (1984) *Hugo von Hoffmansthal and His Time: The European Imagination, 1860–1920*, Chicago: University of Chicago Press.
―― (1985) *The Sleepwalkers*, San Francisco: North Point.
Bulgakov, Mikhail (1974) *Don Kikhot*, Letchworth: Prideaux.
―― (1986) *Black Snow: A Theatrical Novel*, London: Fontana.
―― (1988) *The Life of Monsieur de Molière*, Oxford: Oxford University Press.
―― (1997a) *Il Maestro e Margherita*, Milan: Rizzoli.
―― (1997b) *The Master and Margarita*, Harmondsworth: Penguin.
―― (2008) *Mast'er i Margarita*, St Petersburg: Azbuka-klassika.
Calasso, Roberto (1983) *La rovina di Kasch*, Milan: Adelphi.
―― (1993) 'La bella tenebra', in H. von Hofmannsthal and R. Strauss, *Die Frau ohne Schatten (La donna senz'ombra)*, Firenze: Teatro Comunale, available at www.rodoni.ch/FRAU-OHNE-SCHATTEN/calasso.html. Accessed 27 January 2015.
―― (2001) *La letteratura e gli dèi*, Milan: Adelphi.
―― (2003) *Cento lettere a uno sconosciuto*, Milan: Adelphi.
―― (2004) 'In margine', in F. Kafka, *Aforismi di Zürau*, R. Calasso (ed.), Milan: Adelphi.
―― (2005) *K.*, Milan: Adelphi.
―― (2010) *L'Ardore*, Milan: Adelphi.
Citati, Pietro (2000) *Il male assoluto nel cuore del romanzo dell'Ottocento*, Milan: Mondadori.
―― (2007) *Kafka*, Milan: Adelphi.
―― (2008) *La malattia dell'infinito*, Milan: Mondadori.
―― (2010) 'La nuova montagna di Thomas Mann: da "incantata" è diventata "magica"', *Repubblica*, 3 November.
Clayton, J. Douglas (1993) *Pierrot in Petrograd: The Commedia dell'Arte/Balagan in Twentieth-Century Russian Theatre and Drama*, Montreal: McGill–Queen's University Press.
Corngold, Stanley and Ruth V. Gross (eds) (2011) *Kafka for the Twenty-First Century*, Rochester, NY: Camden House.

Corngold, Stanley and Benno Wagner (eds) (2011) *Franz Kafka: The Ghosts in the Machine*, Evanston, Ill.: Northwestern University Press.
Crescenzi, Luca (2010) 'Introduction', in T. Mann, *La montagna magica*, Milan: Mondadori
—— (2011) *Melancolia occidentale: La montagna magica di Thomas Mann*, Rome: Carocci.
Curtis, J.A.E. (2012) *Manuscripts Don't Burn: Mikhail Bulgakov: A Life in Letters and Diaries*, London: Bloomsbury.
Darabos, Pál (2002) *Hamvas Béla: egy életmű fiziognómiája*, 3 vols, Budapest: Hamvas Intézet.
Decker, Hannah S. (1991) *Freud, Dora and Vienna*, New York: Free Press.
Diamant, Kathi (2003) *Kafka's Last Love: The Mystery of Dora Diamant*, London: Secker & Warburg.
Dobrenko, Evgeny (2008) 'Introduction: Writing Judgment Day', in M. Bulgakov, *The White Guard*, New Haven: Yale University Press.
Doi, Kiyomi (2011) 'Onto Emerging Ground: Anticlimatic Movement on the Camino di Santiago de Compostela', *Tourism* 9, 3: 271–85.
Doderer, Heimito von (1956) *Die Dämonen*, München: Biederstein.
—— (1961) *The Demons*, New York: Knopf.
Doyle, Peter (1983) 'Bulgakov and Cervantes', *The Modern Language Review* 78, 4: 869–77.
Dürr, Volker (2006) *Rainer Maria Rilke: The Poet's Trajectory*, New York: P. Lang.
Elias, Norbert (2000) *The Civilizing Process*, Oxford: Blackwell.
Ellis, Markham (2004) *The Coffee-House: A Cultural History*, London: Weidenfeld & Nicolson.
—— (2006) 'Introduction', to M. Ellis (ed.) *Eighteenth Century Coffee House Culture*, London: Pickering & Chatto.
Faber, Marion (1979) *Angels of Daring: Tightrope Walker and Acrobat in Nietzsche, Kafka, Rilke and Thomas Mann*, Stuttgart: Akademischer Verlag H.-D. Heinz.
Ferguson, Harvie (1995) *Melancholy and the Critique of Modernity: Soren Kierkegaard's Religious Psychology*, London: Routledge.
—— (2010) 'Comparing (Sick)-notes: Intercultural Reflections on Modernity and Disease in the Writings of Thomas Mann and Jun'ichiro Tanizaki', *International Political Anthropology* 3, 1: 29–53.
Ferreira, M. Jamie (1995) 'Review of Harvie Ferguson, *Melancholy and the Critique of Modernity*', *Religious Studies* 31, 4: 537–540.
Finucane, Brian (2011) 'Unmasking Nietzsche: Exploring the Symbolism of the Death of God', PhD thesis, University College Cork.
Foucault, Michel (1961) *Folie et déraison: Histoire de la folie à l'âge classique*, Paris: Plon.
—— (1966) *Les mots et les choses*, Paris: Gallimard.
—— (1978) 'Introduction', in G. Canguilhem, *On the Normal and the Pathological*, Dordrecht: Reidel.
—— (1984) *L'usage des plaisirs*, Paris: Gallimard.
—— (2001) *Fearless Speech*, Los Angeles: Semiotext(e).
—— (2005) *The Hermeneutics of the Subject: Lectures at the Collège de France 1981–1982*, New York: Picador.
Frankfort, Henri (1948) *Kingship and the Gods*, Chicago: The University of Chicago Press.
Francis, Mark (ed.) (1985) The *Viennese Enlightenment*, London: Croom Helm.

Freedman, Ralph (1996) *Life of a Poet: Rainer Maria Rilke*, New York: Farrar, Straus and Giroux.
Freud, Sigmund (1965) *The Interpretation of Dreams*, New York: Harper Collins.
Frisby, David (2011) 'Preface to the Third Edition', in G. Simmel, *The Philosophy of Money*, London: Routledge.
Galbraith, John K. (2004) *The Economics of Innocent Fraud: Truth for Our Time*, New York: Houghton Mifflin.
Ginsburg, Mirra (1988) 'Preface', in M. Bulgakov, *The Life of Monsieur de Molière*, Oxford: Oxford University Press.
Girard, René (1961) *Mensonge romantique et vérité romanesque*, Paris: Grasset.
—— (1972) *Violence et le sacré*, Paris: Grasset.
—— (1978) *Des choses cachés depuis la fondation du monde*, Paris: Grasset.
—— (1999) *Je vois Satan tomber comme l'éclair*, Paris: Grasset.
Goldman, Harvey (1988) *Max Weber and Thomas Mann: Calling and the Shaping of the Self*, Berkeley: University of California Press.
—— (1992) *Politics, Death and the Devil: Self and Power in Max Weber and Thomas Mann*, Berkeley: University of California Press.
Gray, Richard T. (ed.) (2005) *A Kafka Encyclopaedia*, Westport, CT: Greenwood Press.
Green, Martin (1986) *The Triumph of Pierrot: The Commedia dell'Arte and the Modern Imagination* (with John Swan), New York: Macmillan.
Griffin, Roger (2007) *Modernism and Fascism*, Basingstoke: Palgrave.
Guenther, Mathias (1999) *Tricksters and Trancers: Bushman Religion and Society*, Bloomington: Indiana University Press.
Hadot, Pierre (1993) *Exercices spirituels et philosophie antique*, Paris: Institut d'études Augustiniennes.
Hamvas, Béla (1989) *Henoch apokalypsise*, Budapest: Holnap.
—— (1994) 'Regényelméleti fragmentum', in *Arkhai*, Szentendre: Medio.
—— (1997) *Karnevál*, 3 vols, Szentendre: Medio.
Hatfield, Henry (1969) *Crisis and Continuity in Modern German Fiction*, Ithaca: Cornell University Press.
Heidegger, Martin (1977) 'The Question Concerning Technology', in *Basic Writings*, New York: Harper & Row.
Heilbut, Anthony (1996) *Thomas Mann: Eros and Literature*, London: Macmillan.
Hendry, J.F. (1983) *The Sacred Threshold: A Life of Rainer Maria Rilke*, Manchester: Carcanet New Press.
Hennessy, Elizabeth (2001) *Coffee House to Cyber Market: 200 years of the London Stock Exchange*, London: Ebury.
Hennis, Wilhelm (1988) *Max Weber: Essays in Reconstruction*, London: Allen & Unwin.
Hesson, Elizabeth C. (1982) *Twentieth Century Odyssey: A Study of Heimito von Doderer's Die Dämonen*, Columbia, SC: Camden House.
Hofmannsthal, Hugo von (1902) 'The Letter of Lord Chandos', accessed at http://depts.washington.edu/vienna/documents/Hofmannsthal/Hofmannsthal_Chandos.htm. Accessed 27 January 2015.
—— (1953) *Die Erzählungen*, Frankfurt: Fischer.
—— (1959) *Prosa II*, Frankfurt: Fischer.
—— (1964) *Prosa III*, Frankfurt: Fischer.
—— (1979) *Gedichte* and *Dramen I*, Frankfurt: Fischer.
—— (1992) *Ieri*, Pordenone: Edizioni Studio Tesi.
—— (1993) *The Woman Without a Shadow*, Lewiston, NY: Edwin Mellen Press.

244 Bibliography

—— (1998) *Andreas*, London: Pushkin Press.
—— (2008) *The Whole Difference: Selected Writings of Hugo von Hofmannsthal*, J.D. McClatchy (ed.), Princeton, NJ: Princeton University Press.
—— (2011) *Hugo von Hofmannsthal and the Austrian Idea: Selected Essays and Addresses, 1906–1927*, D.S. Luft (ed.), West Lafayette: Purdue University Press.
Horvath, Agnes (2000) 'The Nature of the Trickster's Game: An Interpretive Understanding of Communism', Ph.D. thesis, European University Institute, Florence, Italy.
—— (2008) 'Mythology and the Trickster: Interpreting Communism', in A. Wöll and H. Wydra (eds) *Democracy and Myth in Russia and Eastern Europe*, London: Routledge.
—— (2010) 'Tarde's ultimate paradox, or realism confronting erratic understanding', *International Political Anthropology* 3, 2: 221–5.
—— (2013a) *Modernism and Charisma*, Basingstoke: Palgrave Macmillan.
—— (2013b) 'The Fascination with Eros: The Role of Passionate Interests under Communism', *History of the Human Sciences* 26, 5: 79–97.
—— (2015) 'The Genealogy of Political Alchemy: The Technological Invention of Identity Change', in A. Horvath, B. Thomassen and H. Wydra (eds), *Breaking Boundaries: Varieties of Liminality*, Oxford: Berghahn.
Horvath, Agnes and Arpad Szakolczai (1992) *The Dissolution of Communist Power: The Case of Hungary*, London: Routledge.
—— (2013) 'The Gravity of Eros in the Contemporary: Introduction to the Special Section', *History of the Human Sciences* 26, 5: 69–78.
Horvath, Agnes and Bjørn Thomassen (2008) 'Mimetic Errors in Liminal Schismogenesis: On the Political Anthropology of the Trickster', *International Political Anthropology* 1, 1: 3–24.
Horvath, Agnes, Bjørn Thomassen and Harald Wydra (eds) (2015) *Breaking Boundaries: Varieties of Liminality*, Oxford: Berghahn.
Hughes, Ted (1992) *Shakespeare and the Goddess of Complete Being*, London: Faber.
Huizinga, Johan (1990) *The Waning of the Middle Ages*, Harmondsworth: Penguin.
Hutter, Manfred (1995) 'Lilith', in K. van der Toorn, B. Becking, and P.W. van der Horst (eds), *Dictionary of Deities and Demons in the Bible*, Leiden: Brill.
Huyssen, Andreas (2010) '*The Notebooks of Malte Laurids Brigge*', in *The Cambridge Companion to Rilke*, Cambridge: Cambridge University Press.
Israel, Jonathan I. (2001) *Radical Enlightenment: Philosophy and the Making of Modernity*, Oxford: Oxford University Press.
Jacob, Margaret C. (1981) *The Radical Enlightenment: Pantheists, Freemasons and Republicans*, London: Allen & Unwin.
Janik, Allan (2001) *Wittgenstein's Vienna Revisited*, New Brunswick: Transaction Publishers.
Janik, Allan and Stephen Toulmin (1973) *Wittgenstein's Vienna*, New York: Simon and Schuster.
Janowski, Bernd (1995) 'Azazel', in K. van der Toorn, B. Becking, and P.W. van der Horst (eds), *Dictionary of Deities and Demons in the Bible*, Leiden: Brill, 240–8.
Juvenal (1991) *The Satires*, trans. Niall Rudd, Oxford: Clarendon.
Kafka, Franz (1953) *Letters to Milena*, New York: Schocken.
—— (1958) *Briefe 1902–24*, M. Brod (ed.), New York: Schocken.
—— (1990) *Tagebücher*, Frankfurt: Fischer.
—— (1992) *Nachgelassene Schriften und Fragmente II*, 2 vols, ed. by J. Schillemeit, Frankfurt: Fischer.

Bibliography 245

—— (2004) *Aforismi di Zürau*, R. Calasso (ed.), Milan: Adelphi.
—— (2005a) *Das Urteil*, accessed as www.digbib.org/Franz_Kafka_1883/Das_Urteil. Accessed 16 September 2015.
—— (2005b) *Der Prozeß*, accessed as www.digbib.org/Franz_Kafka_1883/Der_Prozess. Accessed 16 September 2015.
—— (2011) *Das Schloß*, accessed as www/digbib.org/Franz_Kafka_1883/Das_Schloss. Accessed 16 September 2015.
—— (2013) *Amerika*, accessed as www.digbib.org/Franz_Kafka_1883/Amerika. Accessed 16 September 2015.
Kaufholz, Elaine (1986) 'Les somnabules d'Hermann Broch', in J. Clair (ed.) *Vienne, 1880–1938: l'apocalypse joyeuse*, Paris: Éditions du Centre Pompidou.
Kemény, Katalin (1990) *Ember, aki ismerte saját neveit: széljegyzetek Hamvas Béla Karneváljához*, Budapest: Akadémiai.
Kerényi, Károly (1986) *Hermes, Guide of Souls: The Mythologem of the Masculine Source of Life*, New York: Spring Publications.
Kierkegaard, Soren (1962) *The Present Age*, New York: Harper.
Kobry, Yves (1986) 'Ernst Mach et le "moi insaisissable"', in J. Clair (ed.) *Vienne, 1880–1938: l'apocalypse joyeuse*, Paris: Éditions du Centre Pompidou.
Koelb, Clayton (2010) *Kafka: A Guide for the Perplexed*, London: Continuum.
Koselleck, Reinhart (1988) *Critique and Crisis: Enlightenment and the Pathogenesis of Modern Society*, Oxford: Berg.
Kuna, Franz (1991) 'Vienna and Prague 1890–1928', in M. Bradbury and J. McFarlane (eds) *Modernism: A Guide to European Literature 1890–1930*, Harmondsworth: Penguin.
Kundera, Milan (1986) *L'art du roman*, Paris: Gallimard.
Latour, Bruno and Vincent A. Lépinay (2009) *The Science of Passionate Interests: An Introduction to Gabriel Tarde's Economic Anthropology*, Chicago: Prickly Paradigm Press.
Lemaire, Gérard-Georges (1997) *Les cafés littéraires*, Paris: Différence.
Lepenies, Wolf (1988) *Between Literature and Science: The Rise of Sociology*, Cambridge: Cambridge University Press.
—— (1992) *Melancholy and Society*, Cambridge MA: Harvard University Press.
Liddell, Henry G. and Robert Scott (1996) *A Greek-English Lexicon*, Oxford: Oxford University Press.
Lonergan, Bernard (1971) *Grace and Freedom: Operative Grace in the Thought of St. Thomas Aquinas*, London: Darton, Longman & Todd.
Luke, David (1998) 'Introduction', in T. Mann, *Death in Venice and Other Stories*, New York: Vintage.
Luft, David S. (2011) 'Preface' and 'Introduction' in H. von Hofmannsthal, *Hugo von Hofmannsthal and the Austrian Idea*, D.S. Luft (ed.), West Lafayette: Purdue University Press.
McClatchy, John D. (2008) 'Introduction', in H. von Hofmannsthal, *The Whole Difference: Selected Writings of Hugo von Hofmannsthal*, J.D. McClatchy (ed.), Princeton, NJ: Princeton University Press.
Magris, Claudio (1986) 'Le flambeau d'Ewald', in J. Clair (ed.) *Vienne, 1880–1938: l'apocalypse joyeuse*, Paris: Éditions du Centre Pompidou.
Mann, Thomas (1995) *Der Zauberberg*, Frankfurt: Fischer.
—— (1996) *Tod in Venedig*, Frankfurt: Fischer.
—— (1998) *Death in Venice and Other Stories*, New York: Vintage.

246 Bibliography

—— (1999) *The Magic Mountain*, New York: Vintage.
Masini, Franz (2010) *Kafka: la metamorfosi del significato*, Torino: Ananke,
Massino, Guido (2002) *Fuoco inestinguibile: Franz Kafka, Jizchak Löwy e il teatro yiddish polacco*, Rome: Bulzoni.
Mauss, Marcel (1992) 'A Sociological Assessment of Bolshevism [1924–5)]', in M. Gane (ed.) *The Radical Sociology of Durkheim and Mauss*, London: Routledge.
—— (2002) *The Gift*, London: Routledge.
Metzger, Rainer (2006) 'Vienna around 1900: The Duration of Denial', in C. Brandstätter (ed.) *Vienna 1900: Art, Life and Culture*, New York: Vendome Press.
Miles, David H. (1972) *Hofmannsthal's Novel Andreas: Memory and Self*, Princeton: Princeton University Press.
Milne, Lesley (1990) *Mikhail Bulgakov*, Cambridge: Cambridge University Press.
Musil, Robert (1982) *On Mach's Theories*, Washington: Catholic University of America Press.
Neumann, Michael (2010) 'Discesa agli inferi', in T. Mann, *La montagna magica*, Milan: Mondadori.
Nietzsche, Friedrich (1967) *The Genealogy of Morals*, New York: Vintage.
—— (1988) *Sämtliche Werke: Kritische Studienausgabe*, G. Colli and M. Montinari (eds), Munich: Deutscher Taschenbuch.
O'Connor, Paul (2016) 'The Sacred Centre: Home, Meaning, and Modernity', PhD thesis, University College Cork.
Ortega y Gasset, José (1932) *The Revolt of the Masses*, London: Allen and Unwin.
Parrinder, Geoffrey (1973) *The Indestructible Soul*, London: Allen and Unwin.
Pascal, Blaise (1972) *Pensées*, Paris: Librairie Générale Française.
Pearce, Richard (1970) *Stages of the Clown*, Carbondale: Southern Illinois University Press.
Pevear, Richard (1997) 'Introduction', in M. Bulgakov, *The Master and Margarita*, Harmondsworth: Penguin.
Pevear, Richard and Larissa Volokhonsky (1997) 'A Note on the Text and Acknowledgements', in M. Bulgakov, *The Master and Margarita*, Harmondsworth: Penguin.
Pizer, John (2003) 'Venice as Mediator between Province and Viennese Metropolis: Themes in Rilke, Hofmannsthal, Gerhard Roth and Kolleritsch', in E. Grabovszki and J. Hardin (eds) *Literature in Vienna at the Turn of the Centuries: Continuities and Discontinuities around 1900 and 2000*, Rochester, NY: Camden House.
Poston, Dudley L. and Arpad Szakolczai (1986) 'Patterns of marital childlessness in Hungary, 1930 to 1980', *Genus* 42, 1–2: 71–85.
Prater, Donald A. (1986) *A Ringing Glass: The Life of Rainer Maria Rilke*, Oxford: Oxford University Press.
Proffer, Ellendea (1996) 'Bulgakov's *The Master and Margarita*: Genre and Motif', in L.D. Weeks (ed.) *The Master and Margarita: A Critical Companion*, Evanston, Ill.: Northwestern University Press.
Radkau, Joachim (2009) *Max Weber: A Biography*, Cambridge: Polity.
Riedl, Joachim (2005) 'The City Without Qualities', in M.-A. zu Salm-Salm (ed.) *Klimt, Schiele, Moser, Kokoschka: Vienna 1900*, Aldershot: Ashgate.
Riedl, Matthias (2010) 'Living in the Future – Proleptic Existence in Religion, Politics and Art', *International Political Anthropology* 3, 2: 117–34.
Rilke, Rainer M. (1952) *Briefe über Cézanne*, C Rilke (ed.), Wiesbaden: Insel.
—— (1966) *Sämtliche Werke*, vol 6, Frankfurt: Insel.

—— (1979) *Die Aufzeichnungen des Malte Laurids Brigge*, Frankfurt: Suhrkamp.
—— (2007) *Verso l'estremo: Lettere su Cézanne e sull'arte come destino*, F. Rella (ed.), Bologna: Pendragon.
Rella, Franco (2007) 'Il mondo come destino', in R.M. Rilke, *Verso l'estremo: Lettere su Cézanne e sull'arte come destino*, Bologna: Pendragon.
Ritter, Gerhard (1997) *Il volto demoniaco del potere*, Bologna: Il Mulino.
Robertson, Ritchie (1985) *Kafka: Judaism, Politics and Literature*, Oxford: Clarendon.
—— (2011) 'Kafka, Goffman and the Total Institution', in S. Corngold and B. Wagner (eds) *Franz Kafka: The Ghosts in the Machine*, Evanston, Ill.: Northwestern University Press.
Saint-Exupéry, Antoine de (1942) *Pilote de guerre*, New York: Éditions de la Maison française.
Salm-Salm, Marie-Amélie zu (ed.) (2005) *Klimt, Schiele, Moser, Kokoschka: Vienna 1900*, Aldershot: Ashgate.
Scaff, Lawrence (1989) *Fleeing the Iron Cage: Culture, Politics, and Modernity in the Thought of Max Weber*, Berkeley: University of California Press.
Schoolfield, George C. (2001) '*Die Aufzeichnungen des Malte Laurids Brigge*', in E.A. Metzger and M.M. Metzger (eds) *A Companion to the Works of Rainer Maria Rilke*, Rochester, NY: Camden House.
Schorske, Carl E. (1981) *Fin-de-siècle Vienna: Politics and Culture*, New York: Vintage.
Scott Haine, W. (2013) 'Introduction', in L. Rittner, W. Scott Haine and W.H. Jackson (eds) *The Thinking Space: The Café as a Cultural Institution in Paris, Italy and Vienna*, Farnham: Ashgate.
Sebald, W.G. (1976) 'The Law of Ignominy: Authority, Messianism and Exile in *The Castle*', in F. Kuna (ed.) *On Kafka: Semi-centenary Perspectives*, London: Elek.
Segel, Harold B. (1987) *Turn-of-the-century Cabaret: Paris, Barcelona, Berlin, Munich, Vienna, Cracow, Moscow, St. Petersburg, Zurich*, New York: Columbia University Press.
—— (1995) *The Viennese Coffee-House Wits 1890–1938*, West Lafayette: Purdue University Press.
Shillabeer, James (2008) 'Self-knowledge, Immunity and Conversion', PhD thesis, University of Kent at Canterbury.
Simmel, Georg (1994) 'Bridge and Door', *Theory, Culture & Society* 11, 1: 5–10.
Sokel Walter H. (1980) 'The Devolution of Self in *The Notebooks of Malte Laurids Brigge*', in F. Baron et al. (eds) *Alchemy of Alienation*, Lawrence: Regents Press of Kansas.
—— (ed.) (1984) *Anthology of German Expressionist Drama: A Prelude to the Absurd*, Ithaca, New York: Cornell University Press.
—— (2002) *The Myth of Power and the Self*, Detroit: Wayne State University Press.
Springer, Käthe (2006a) 'Theatre and Cabaret', in C. Brandstätter (ed.) *Vienna 1900: Art, Life and Culture*, New York: Vendome Press.
—— (2006b) 'The Secret of Dreams', in C. Brandstätter (ed.) *Vienna 1900: Art, Life and Culture*, New York: Vendome Press.
Stach, Reiner (2013) *Kafka: The Decisive Years*, Princeton: Princeton University Press.
—— (2015) *Kafka: The Years of Insight*, Princeton: Princeton University Press.
Starobinski, Jean (2001) 'Franz Kafka: Regards sur l'image', in M. Gagnebin and C. Savinel (eds) *Starobinski en mouvement*, Seyssel: Champ Vallon.
Steinberg, Michael P. (1984) 'Translator's Introduction: Hermann Broch', in H. Broch, *Hugo von Hofmannsthal and His Time*, Chicago: University of Chicago Press.

Szakolczai, Arpad (1987) 'Concerning the Grounds of Modern Economic Society and Political Economy: An Analysis of the Writings of Say, Saint-Simon, and Sismondi, Using the Works of Michel Foucault', PhD thesis, University of Texas at Austin.
—— (1998) *Max Weber and Michel Foucault: Parallel Life-Works*, London: Routledge.
—— (2000) *Reflexive Historical Sociology*, London: Routledge.
—— (2003) *The Genesis of Modernity*, London: Routledge.
—— (2005a) 'Moving Beyond the Sophists: Intellectuals in East Central Europe and the Return of Transcendence', *The European Journal of Social Theory* 8, 4: 417–33.
—— (2005b) 'In Between Tradition and Christianity: The Axial Age in the Perspective of Béla Hamvas', in J. Arnason, S.N. Eisenstadt and B. Wittrock (eds) *Axial Civilisations and World History*, Leiden: Brill.
—— (2007) *Sociology, Religion and Grace: A Quest for the Renaissance*, London: Routledge.
—— (2009) 'Liminality and Experience: Structuring Transitory Situations and Transformative Events', *International Political Anthropology* 2, 1: 141–72.
—— (2011) 'Eric Voegelin and neo-Kantianism: Early Formative Experience or Late Entrapment?', in L. Trepanier and S. McGuire (eds) *Eric Voegelin and the Continental Tradition: Explorations in Modern Political Thought*, Columbia, MO: University of Missouri Press.
—— (2012) 'Dreams, Visions and Utopias: Romantic and Realist Revolutionaries, and the Idyllic', in M.H. Jacobsen and K. Tester (eds) *Utopia: Social Theory and the Future*, Farnham: Ashgate.
—— (2013a) *Comedy and the Public Sphere: The Re-birth of Theatre as Comedy and the Genealogy of the Modern Public Arena*, London: Routledge.
—— (2013b) 'In Liminal Tension Towards Giving Birth: Eros, the Educator', *History of the Human Sciences* 26, 5: 100–15.
—— (2014a) 'Living Permanent Liminality: The Recent Transition Experience in Ireland', *Irish Journal of Sociology* 22, 1: 28–50.
—— (2014b) 'Theatricalised Reality and Novels of Truth: Respecting Tradition and Promoting Imagination in Social Research', in M.H. Jacobsen, K. Keohane, A. Petersen and M.S. Drake (eds) *Imaginative Methodologies: The Poetic Imagination in Social Science*, Farnham: Ashgate.
—— (2015) 'The Theatricalisation of the Social: Problematising the Public Sphere', *Cultural Sociology* 9, 2: 220–39.
—— (2016a) *Novels and the Sociology of the Contemporary*, London: Routledge.
—— (2016b) 'Processes of Social Flourishing and their Liminal Collapse: Elements to a Genealogy of Globalisation', *British Journal of Sociology* 67, 3.
—— (forthcoming1) 'Permanent (Trickster) Liminality: The Reasons of the Heart and of the Mind', *Theory and Psychology*.
—— (forthcoming2) 'Empires: Rise, Decline and Fall', in B.S. Turner (ed.) *The Encyclopaedia of Social Theory*, Oxford: Wiley-Blackwell.
Szakolczai, Arpad and Bjørn Thomassen (2011) 'Gabriel Tarde as Political Anthropologist: The Role of Imitation for Sociality, Crowds and Publics within a Context of Globalization', *International Political Anthropology* 4, 1: 43–62.
Szakolczai, Arpad and Harald Wydra (2006) 'Contemporary East Central European Social Theory', in G. Delanty (ed.) *Handbook of Contemporary European Social Theory*, London: Routledge.
Szelényi, Ivan (2015) 'Entzauberung: Notes on Weber's Theory of Modernity', *International Political Anthropology* 8, 1: 5–14.

Thomassen, Bjørn (2009) 'The Uses and Meanings of Liminality', *International Political Anthropology* 2, 1: 5–27.
—— (2014) *Liminality, Change and Transition: Living through the In-between*, Farnham: Ashgate.
Thomassen, Bjørn and Harald Wydra (eds) (forthcoming) *Handbook of Political Anthropology*, Cheltenham: Edward Elgar.
Thurman, Judith (1984) *Isak Dinesen: The Life of Karen Blixen*, Harmondsworth: Penguin.
Traubner, Richard (2003) *Operetta: A Theatrical History*, London: Routledge.
Turner, Ralph L. (1989) *A Comparative Dictionary of the Indo-Aryan Languages*, London: Oxford University Press.
Turner, Victor W. (1967) 'Betwixt and Between: The Liminal Period in *Rites de Passage*', in *The Forest of Symbols*. New York: Cornell University Press.
—— (1969) *The Ritual Process,* Chicago: Aldine.
Twomey, Pat (2006) 'Conversion as Transformative Experience: A Sociological Study of Identity Formation and Transformation Processes', PhD thesis, University College Cork.
Van Gennep, Arnold (1981) *Les rites de passage*, Paris: Picard.
Voegelin, Eric (1978) *Anamnesis*, Illinois: University of Notre Dame Press.
—— (1990a) 'Wisdom and the Magic of the Extreme', in E. Sandoz (ed.) *Published Essays, 1966–1985*, Baton Rouge: Louisiana State University Press.
—— (1990b) 'The Eclipse of Reality', in T. A. Hollweck and P. Caringella (eds) *What Is History? and Other Late Unpublished Writings*, Baton Rouge: Louisiana State University Press.
—— (1999) *Hitler and the Germans*, D. Clemens and B. Purcell (eds), Columbia: University of Missouri Press.
Wagenbach, Klaus (2011) *Kafka: A Life in Prague*, London: Armchair Traveller.
Wagner, Peter (1994) *A Sociology of Modernity: Liberty and Discipline*, London: Routledge.
Weeks, Laura D. (1984) 'Hebraic Antecedents in *The Master and Margarita*: Woland and Company Revisited', *Slavic Review* 43, 2: 224–41.
Weinzierl, Ulrich (2005) *Hofmannsthal: Skizzen zu seinem Bild*, Zsolnay: Wien.
Whalen Robert W. (2007) *Sacred Spring: God and the Birth of Modernism in Fin de siècle Vienna*, Grand Rapids: Eerdmans.
Wydra, Harald (2008) 'The Power of Second Reality: Communist Myths and Representations of Democracy', in A. Wöll and H. Wydra (eds) *Democracy and Myth in Russia and Eastern Europe*, London: Routledge.
—— (2015) *Politics and the Sacred*, Cambridge: Cambridge University Press.
Yates, Frances (1964) *Giordano Bruno and the Hermetic Tradition*, London: Routledge.
—— (1966) *The Art of Memory*, Chicago: University of Chicago Press.
—— (1975) *The Rosicrucian Enlightenment*, London: Paladine Books.
Yates, W. E. (1992) *Schnitzler, Hofmannsthal, and the Austrian Theatre*, Haven: Yale University Press.
Zilcosky, John (2004) *Kafka's Travels*, Basingstoke: Palgrave.
Ziolkowski, Theodore (2005) *Ovid and the Moderns*, Ithaca: Cornell University Press.

Name index

Agnew, Jean-Christophe 5, 87
Alexander the Great 19
Altenberg, Peter 17, 18, 193
Aragonian family 8
Ariès, Philippe 43
Ariosto, Ludovico 50
Aristophanes 211
Aristotle 19
Auden, W.H. 120, 159, 164
Augé, Marc 1
Augustine, St 92, 128

Bahr, Hermann 18, 21, 24, 25
Bakst, Leon 163
Bakhtin, Mikhail 5, 18, 58, 165, 180, 197, 198
Balzac, Honoré de 57, 211
Barthes, Roland 69
Bateson, Gregory 150
Baudelaire, Charles 7, 28, 39, 42, 43, 116, 157, 165, 191
Bauer, Felice 66, 69, 70, 78, 82, 121
Bauman, Zygmunt vii
Beckett, Samuel 21, 59, 101
Beethoven, Ludwig von 5, 11, 22
Benjamin, Walter 65, 66, 85, 100, 101, 115, 129
Bennett, Benjamin 25, 28–36 *passim*
Bernhardt, Sarah 152
Bertram, Jeremy 126, 130
Bethea, David 185, 193
Blanchot, Maurice 84, 106
Blixen, Karen 150, 151–64, 175, 192, 211
Blumenberg, Hans 106
Boccaccio, Giovanni 211
Boland, Tom viii
Bonaventure, St 54, 158
Borkenau, Franz 1, 11, 13, 14, 22, 178, 199

Brand, Sebastian 126
Brandeis, Georg 151
Brecht, Bertold 17
Broch, Hermann 6, 13, 36, 37, 165–79, 195, 198, 200, 201, 205, 220
Brod, Max 22, 64, 65, 66, 71, 75, 78, 83, 86, 95, 101, 108
Brontë, Charlotte 57, 164
Brontë, Emily 57, 164
Browning, Robert 59
Bruant, Aristide 16, 17
Bulgakov, Mikhail 77, 150, 156, 157, 162, 165, 180–93, 211, 238
Burckhardt, Jacob 9
Burke, Edmund 94
Burton, Robert 128

Calasso, Roberto 2, 24, 25, 26, 28, 33, 36, 64, 67–83 *passim*, 92, 98, 99, 101, 102, 103, 104, 106, 108, 112, 113, 119, 121, 159, 162, 236
Callot, Jacques 63
Calderón, Pedro 2, 53
Canetti, Elias 5
Canguilhem, Georges 90
Carnap, Rudolf 19
Cervantes, Miguel de 1, 50, 127, 181, 201, 211, 219, 238
Cézanne, Paul 42
Christ 34, 78, 94, 109, 112, 179, 230
Chudakova, Marietta 191
Cicero 201
Citati, Pietro 2, 25, 65, 67, 69, 76, 77, 78, 81, 83, 85, 88, 89, 90, 92, 96, 98, 100, 102, 103, 105, 106, 113, 116, 121, 152, 158, 162, 163
Comte, Auguste 111
Conrad, Joseph 152
Copernicus, Nicolaus 101

Corneille, Pierre 211
Crescenzi, Luca 121, 126, 127, 128, 130, 131, 150
Cusanus 129, 150

Dante, Alighieri 41, 150, 184, 203, 209, 211, 212, 219, 231
Darabos, Pál 208, 209, 210, 222, 230
Darwin, Charles 77
Defoe, Daniel 57
Delvard, Marya 16, 17
Descartes, René 90, 199, 211
Diaghilev, Sergei 12, 59, 135, 152, 155
Diamant, Dora 76, 79, 83, 84, 94, 121
Dickens, Charles 1, 37, 57, 64, 65, 95, 96, 125, 184, 206, 227
Diderot, Denis 59, 71, 72
Dinesen, Isak *see* Blixen
Dobrenko, Evgeny 183
Doderer, Heimito von 36, 165, 194–208, 210, 220
Dörmann, Felix 12
Dostoevsky, Fyodor M. 1, 37, 45, 57, 64, 71, 76, 83, 88, 94, 95, 100, 125, 127, 155, 162, 164, 175, 182, 184, 194, 195, 208, 210, 211, 215, 219, 220, 221, 224, 237, 238
Dubarry, Madame 156
Dürer, Albrecht 126–7, 129, 130–1, 182, 185
Duse, Eleanor 45

Einstein, Albert 18, 100
Eliade, Mircea 91
Elias, Norbert 92, 150
Eliot, T.S. 41
Epimenes the Cretan 79
Erasmus, Desiderius 126, 150
Escher, M.C. 90

Faber, Marion 64, 65, 105, 106
Ferguson, Harvie 128–30
Fielding, Henry 57
Finucane, Brian 121
Flaubert, Gustave 57, 208
Foucault, Michel 21, 29, 53, 54, 68, 69, 79, 84, 90, 110, 112, 114, 126, 129, 130, 169, 199, 205, 207, 208, 217
Fourier, Charles 22
Francis I (Emperor) 9
Francis, St 54, 153, 155, 207
Frankfort, Henri 176
Frederick the Great 133
Frederick III (Emperor) 8
Freud 18, 19, 20, 22, 23, 111, 112, 153, 170, 195, 202, 208

Galbraith, Kenneth 179
George, Stefan 25
Giehlow, Karl 126, 130–1
Gielgud, John 153
Girard, René 1, 18, 71, 78, 138, 150, 183, 188, 208, 210, 221, 222, 228, 237, 238
Goethe, Johann W. 1, 17, 23, 24, 27, 34, 40, 49, 55, 57, 58, 63, 64, 65, 69, 71, 76, 83, 84, 88, 100, 104, 112, 125, 127, 131, 132, 181, 184, 195, 196, 211, 238
Gogol, Nikolai 181
Goldman, Harvey 60, 125, 132, 148
Gossen, Hermann Heinrich 19
Gothár, Péter 100
Goya, Francisco 13
Griffin, Roger 59
Grillparzer, Franz 22
Grünewald, Matthias 126

Habermas, Jürgen vii, 14, 201, 202, 208, 235
Hadot, Pierre 53, 207, 208
Hamvas, Béla 26, 129, 131, 150, 156, 157, 159, 162, 164, 165, 175, 190, 194, 208, 209, 238
Hašek, Jaroslav 22
Haydn, Joseph von 5, 11
Hayek, Friedrich von 19
Hebbel, Friedrich 102
Hegel, Georg W.F. 22, 117, 211, 212
Heidegger, Martin 22, 32, 111, 117, 229
Heine, Heinrich 151
Heller, Erich 65
Hennis, Wilhelm 148
Henry VIII 8
Heraclitus 89, 102, 165
Herzl, Theodor 14
Hitler, Adolf 11, 36, 37, 159, 175
Hobbes, Thomas 101, 128, 201
Hofmannsthal, Christine 25
Hofmannsthal, Franz 24, 25
Hofmannsthal, Hugo von vii, 2, 6–7, 17, 18, 21, 23–36, 37, 38, 39, 46–56, 57, 59, 60, 100, 101, 125, 126, 129, 179, 198, 217, 236
Hölderlin, Friedrich 22, 23, 27, 39, 40, 229
Horváth, Ágnes viii, 1, 12, 59, 60, 63, 84, 111, 112, 128, 129, 140, 145, 150, 169, 193, 203
Hughes, Ted 69, 74
Hugo, Victor 133, 135, 211
Huizinga, Johan 60, 126
Husserl, Edmund 5
Hutton-Finch, Denys 154

Name index

Ibsen, Henrik 6, 71
Isaiah (prophet) 142, 165, 191;
  Deutero 142
Israel, Jonathan 235

Jacob, Margaret 235
James, Henry 152
Janik, Allan 5, 10, 11, 12, 13, 14, 18, 20, 21, 23
Janouch, Gustav 65
Jean-Paul (Johannes Paulus Richter) 21, 77
Jeremiah (prophet) 98, 165
Jesus *see* Christ
John the Baptist, St 219
John Scotus 102
Joseph II (Emperor) 9
Joyce, James 2, 39, 59, 134, 152, 227
Juvenal vii

Kafka, Franz 2, 5, 16, 22, 37, 38, 52, 53, 55, 56, 57, 58, 59, 63–121, 125, 126, 152, 165, 179, 182, 211, 235, 236
Kafka, Hermann 65
Kafka, Ottla 102
Kant, Immanuel 13, 21, 45, 141, 144, 165, 175, 188, 199, 201, 211, 212
Kemény, Katalin 210, 211, 219
Kerényi, Károly 101, 211
Kierkegaard, Søren 26, 36, 45, 46, 93, 102, 108, 128, 129, 151, 155, 156, 163, 182, 203, 212, 226, 237
Kleist, Heinrich von 29, 32, 64, 65, 105, 157
Kokoschka, Oskar 13, 17
Koselleck, Reinhart 63
Kraus, Karl 6, 17, 24
Kundera, Milan 165, 172, 182, 208

Laforgue, Jules 88
Latour, Bruno 129
Lautensack, Heinrich 17
Leibniz, Gottfried W. 128
Leitich, Ann Tizia 9
Lenin, Vladimir I. 18
Leonardo da Vinci 67, 79, 126
Leopold II (Emperor) 9
Lepenies, Wolf 128–9
Lessing, Gotthold E. 59, 71, 72
Levetzow, Ulrike von 132
Levinas, Emmanual 29
Lonergan, Bernard 27
Loos, Adolf 10
Loris 24, 34 *see also* Hofmannsthal, Hugo von

Louis XIV 181
Louis XV 156
Lowy, Yitzchak 67, 68, 69, 71, 72, 78
Lucian 211
Lueger, Karl 11, 22
Lukács, Georg 53, 146, 209, 210
Lun 175
Luther, Martin 120, 126

Maack, Ferdinand 28
Mach, Ernst 5, 18–19, 29, 36, 53, 198, 237
Machiavelli, Niccolò 126, 215
Magris, Claudio 6, 17, 193
Magritte, René 26
Mann, Thomas 2, 37, 38, 47–60 *passim*, 92, 100, 121, 125–50, 154, 171, 184, 192, 201, 210–11, 229, 233
Mannheim, Karl 129
Marx, Karl viii, 85
Mary, Holy 37, 100, 162, 212, 219, 233
Mary Magdalene 233
Masini, Ferruccio 64, 76, 78–9, 81, 82
Matthias Corvinus 8
Mauss, Marcel 1, 34
Menger, Carl 18, 19
Metternich, Klemens von 9
Meyerhold, Vsevolod 186
Michelangelo 131
Miles, David 36, 51, 52, 56, 60
Milton, John 184
Mises, Ludwig von 19
Molière 150, 181, 211, 227
More, Thomas 126
Morgenstern, Willie 16
Mozart, Wolfgang A. 5, 11
Musil, Robert 5, 18, 22, 199

Nabokov, Vladimir 157
Nerval, Gerard de 39
Neumann, Michael 130
Newton, Isaac 13, 45, 63, 90, 101, 121
Nicholas of Cusa *see* Cusanus
Nietzsche, Friedrich vii, 6, 7, 13, 24, 26, 27, 31, 54, 59, 65, 69, 77, 91, 93, 95, 102, 104, 105, 107, 110, 119, 126, 130, 151, 156, 157, 163, 168, 176, 179, 191, 195, 196, 201, 211, 219, 232
Nijinsky, Vaslav 152
Novalis vii

O'Connor, Paul 233
Ortega y Gasset, José 1, 30, 197
Ovidius 233

Name index

Panofsky, Erwin 130, 131
Pascal, Blaise 36, 41, 102, 128, 129, 161, 163, 198, 237
Pasternak, Boris 182
Patocka, Jan 29, 205
Pearce, Richard 88
Pericles 182
Picasso, Pablo 155
Pilate 5, 183, 188
Pirandello, Luigi 155
Plato 26, 29, 40, 49, 50, 51, 54, 65, 69, 81, 89, 98, 100, 101, 105, 108, 111, 115, 117, 121, 132, 139, 154, 169, 178, 198, 205, 208, 221, 232, 236
Plautus 211
Pocock, J.G.A. 69
Poe, Edgar Allan 129
Popper, Karl 19
du Prel, Carl 130
Price, Morton 48
Propp, Vladimir 159
Protagoras 147
Proust, Marcel 39, 152, 212
Pushkin, Alexander 192

Rabelais, François 1, 211, 238
Racine, Jean 211
Raphael 59, 126, 127
Ravel, Maurice 12
Redford, Robert 151
Redl, Alfred 13
Reventlow, Eduard von 152
Reventlow, Fanny 152
Richardson, Samuel 57
Rilke, Rainer M. 2, 5, 37, 38, 39–46, 47–52 passim, 56–60 passim, 86, 101, 105, 121, 131, 152, 179, 198, 220, 236, 237
Ritter, Gerhard 233
Roth, Joseph 5, 11, 14
Rubinstein, Ida 163
Rudolf (Prince) 19
Rudolf IV (Emperor) 8

Saint-Beuve, Charles A. 157
Saint Exupéry, Antoine de 234
Saint-Simon, Henri de 111, 238
Salomé, Lou 39
Salten, Felix 17
Sappho 46
Saxl, Fritz 130
Schmoller, Gustave 19

Schnitzler, Arthur 20–21, 24
Schönberg, Arthur 11, 24
Schopenhauer, Arthur 211
Schorske, Paul 12, 20, 21, 23, 24, 25
Schumann, Robert 153
Schumpeter, Joseph 131, 235
Schutz, Alfred 199
Sebastian, St 133
Segel, Harold B. 15, 16, 17
Seneca 201
Shakespeare, William 7, 20, 63, 69, 74, 75, 76, 88, 127, 149, 150, 151, 153, 154, 155, 157, 159, 184, 189, 197, 210, 211, 219, 226, 229
Shillabeer, James 196, 198, 199, 200, 203
Simmel, Georg 60, 74
Skinner, Quentin 69
Socrates 40, 137, 227
Sokel, Walter 45, 65, 71, 84
Speier, Hans 208
Stach, Reiner 102, 103, 108
Stalin, Joseph 22, 181
Starobinski, Jean 64
Stendhal 57
Sterne, Laurence 60, 211, 219
Straus, Oscar 12
Strauss, Johann 12
Stravinsky, Igor 153, 155
Strindberg, August 71
Symons, Arthur 16
Szelényi, Iván vii, 60

Tarde, Gabriel 165
Tarkovsky, Andrei 162
Tati, Jacques 96
Thackeray, William M. 57
Thomas Aquinas, St 27
Thomassen, Bjørn viii, 143, 150, 165
Thucydides 182
Tieck, Ludwig 21
Tiepolos 28, 101
Tiepolo, Giandomenico 28, 95, 103, 104
Tintoretto, Jacopo 211, 232
Tolstoy, Leo 1, 37, 57, 89
Toulmin, Stephen 5, 10, 11, 12, 13, 14, 18, 20, 21, 23
Trakl, Georg 13
Trotsky, Leon 131, 235
Tschissik, Maria 67
Turgenev, Ivan 57
Turner, Victor viii
Twomey, Pat 208

Name index

Valéry, Paul 41, 102, 200, 205
van Gennep, Arnold viii, 36, 42, 143
Veinberg, Piotr I. 189
Villon, François 16
Virgil 19, 211
Voegelin, Eric 11, 22, 36, 104, 179, 199, 205, 232
Voltaire 211
Vulis, A. 180

Wagner, Peter 114
Wagner, Richard 59, 126, 152, 211, 222, 232
Watteau, Antoine 152
Weber, Alfred 22
Weber, Max vii, 19, 50, 60, 92, 103, 114, 118, 126, 130, 148, 174, 218
Wedekind, Frank 16–17
Weeks, Laura 188, 191
Weigel, Hans 10
Weltsch, Felix 119
Wilhelm II (Emperor) 167
Wittgenstein, Ludwig 11, 18, 22, 23, 25, 32
Wölfflin, Heinrich 131
Wohryzek, Julie 70
Wydra, Harald viii, 199, 232

Yates, Frances 130
Yeats, William B. 39, 51, 56, 59, 71, 101, 152

Zhuang-Zhou 227
Zola, Émile 57, 211
Zweig, Stefan 23, 25

Subject index

aborigines 225
Abraham 71, 85, 92, 93; anti- (Kafka) 93, 100
Absolute 175, 176, 177, 178
absolutism 2, 10, 223
absorption 145, 176
abstraction 176, 177, 178, 206, 207, 227, 232
absurdity 6, 30, 35, 41, 57, 69, 71, 73, 75, 79, 80, 82, 89, 93, 94, 95, 96, 100, 120, 175, 181, 182, 213, 215, 216
abyss 26, 82, 83, 94
Adam 191
adynaton *see* powerlessness
Aeneas 20
Aeneid (Virgil) 19
Africa 154, 158
air, thin: out of 161, 189; vanishing into 67, 134, 181, 186, 189
'Albatross' (Baudelaire) 28
Alchemists' Street (Prague) 103
alchemy 2, 19, 28, 39, 49, 54, 68, 83, 140, 145, 148, 149, 176, 230, 235, 236
alienation 26, 31, 44, 67, 135, 176
Alkmene 48
allomatic (Hofmannsthal) 28–9, 31, 33, 48, 55
alteration *see* metamorphosis
Amazons 215
ambiguity vii, 8, 177
ambivalence vii, 5, 12, 14, 26, 39, 47, 50, 52, 85, 91, 103
America(n) 57, 95–7; constitution 234; dream 95, 238; 'life techniques' (Hamvas) 217, 219; way of life 95–6
Amerika (Kafka) 39, 57, 64, 68, 90, 94, 95–7, 125; 'electoral canvass' 68, 96; Great Theatre of Oklahoma 68, 95, 96–7; 'hotel reception' 68, 96; Karl Rossman 64, 95

Anamnesis (Voegelin) 199
'anamnetic exercises' (Voegelin) 104
anarchism 16, 166
Anatolia 190
Anatomy of Melancholy (Burton) 128
Andreas (Hofmannsthal) 2, 29, 33, 38, 39, 46–56, 57, 58, 101, 125; Andreas 47–56 *passim*, 57, 58; Maria 47, 48, 52, 53; Mariquita 52, 53; Nina 52; Pater Aderkast 53; Romana 51, 53, 54; Sacramozo 52, 53, 55; Zorzi 52; Zustina 52
angel(s) 39, 40, 83, 89, 97, 98, 103, 159, 222; arch- 214; fallen 190
Angelic Avengers (Blixen) 158–62; Lucan 159–61; Olympia 160, 161; Zosine 160–61
anhedonia 53
animal trainer 225, 226, 231, 232
Anna Karenina (Tolstoy) 89
annihilation *see* destruction
Annunciation 72, 152, 197, 205
Anschluss 175, 195
anthropology 2, 58, 91, 108, 228; concepts viii, 42, 103, 196, 235; political 227
Antichrist 93, 117, 178
anti-Mach 130
anti-missionary missionary 218
Antiquity 11, 27, 45, 207
anti-Semitism 11, 149
anxiety 26, 82
apocalypse 6, 12, 77, 89, 97, 114, 115, 126, 134, 138, 142, 146, 149, 182, 183, 184, 185, 186, 187, 191, 214, 218, 219, 223, 233; four horsemen 185, 191; joyful 6; operetta mode 183
'Apocalypse' (Dürer) 126
apocryphal 189, 190, 219
aporia 26, 120

256 Subject index

apparition(s) 83, 106; Marian (Fatima 103, 121); *see also* epiphany
Arabic 15
'Archaic Torso of Apollo' (Rilke) 198
architecture 17
aristocracy 39, 49, 50, 136, 148, 151, 152, 158, 162, 166
Arlecchino *see* Harlequin
arrogance 98, 106, 204
ars poetica 105, 106, 121, 153
Arslantepe 223
Art of the Novel (Kundera) 165
As You Like It (Shakespeare) 189; Jaques 189
asceticism 39, 82, 172
Ash Wednesday 14
Asia 7, 13, 35, 91, 217
Assisi 155, 207
astrology 190
Atapuerca 239
atheism 18, 232
Athens 137, 232
Austria 1, 5–12 *passim*, 35, 39, 194, 195, 198, 205; Monarchy 47
'Austrian idea' (Hofmannsthal) 22, 35–6
authenticity 18, 26, 45, 68, 131, 138, 181
authorial intentions 69, 85
autobiography 14, 26, 40, 47, 53, 58, 64, 132, 133, 140, 142, 153, 182, 191, 195, 217
automatism 28, 29, 55, 95, 236
avant-garde 6, 15, 16, 63, 201, 207, 237
Avignon papacy 42
Azazel 190, 191

Babylon 185; whore of 191
ball(s) 13–14, 160; masked 13, 139, 161, 224; Satan's 192
Ballets Russes 12, 152, 163
barbarism 9
barrit (Hamvas) 225
battle of Tannenberg 175
Bavaria 22, 133
beauty 49, 51, 71, 89, 115, 136, 137, 153, 154, 221, 229; of nature 89; of the world 51, 150, 154
Behemoth 185, 190
believing 94, 102, 108, 109, 162, 176, 178, 198, 218, 225, 228, 235; *see also* faith
'Beloved Returns, The' (Mann) 131
Berlin 176, 179
bestiality 22, 119, 208
Beyond Good and Evil (Nietzsche) 156
Bible 44, 66, 104, 142, 157, 184, 190, 226

Bildung (education) 25, 26, 36
Bildungsroman (novel of formation) 49
Billy Budd (Melville) 132
bipolarism 2, 127, 128; *see also* schismatic personality
bird(s) 51, 189; canary 160–1; crow 77; eagle 51, 101; falcon 56, 59; owl 191; raven 77, 83; vulture 83
Birth of Tragedy (Nietzsche) 31, 65
Black Snow (Bulgakov) *see* *Theatrical Novel*
blasphemy 86, 92, 148, 190
Bohemia 35
Bolshevism 1, 53, 207
Book of Enoch 189, 232
Book of Friends (Hofmannsthal) vii, 129
Book of Hours (Rilke) 48
Book of Revelation 97, 182, 183, 191
book-keeper(s) 172
boredom 43, 91, 129, 183
boulevard(s) 9; Paris 9; Vienna 9, 10
bourgeois drama *see* tragedy, domestic
Boy Extracting a Thorn (Greek statue) 136
bridge 31, 74, 86, 104, 192, 196, 200
Budapest 5, 38, 203, 219, 220
Buddenbrooks (Mann) 59, 125, 132
Buddhism 217
buffoonery 67, 185, 189
bureaucracy 7, 8, 9, 22, 203; Austrian 7–9, 52; Byzantine 7, 9; Ottoman 7; Prussian 9
Burgundy 8
burlesque 98, 184, 214, 215
'Burrow, The' (Kafka) 76
businessman 159, 167–8, 171, 204
Byzantium 8, 52, 67, 89, 134, 150, 235

cabalistic: literature 191; spirit 15, 22
Cabal of Hypocrites (Bulgakov) 181, 191
cabaret 6, 9, 11, 15, 16–18, 21, 36, 189, 190; mania 16, 17
Cafe Savoy 67
cage 113, 114, 161, 235; iron 55
camp(s) 174
candelabra 189
cannibalism 161
capitalism 235; fairground 121, 203, 236
caravan carousel 184
care 29, 127
care of the self (Plato) 29, 205
Carinthia 50–2, 53, 56, 57, 58
Carnaval (Ballets Russes) 152
carnival 1, 2, 16, 97, 104, 139, 142, 145, 146, 149, 203, 210, 211, 224, 227, 229; apocalyptic 97, 142, 175, 185, 188, 219;

Subject index 257

global 2; permanent 1, 165, 211, 219; sacrificial 83, 162, 195; society 156, 223–7, 228, 229, 231
'Carnival' (Blixen) 151, 155–8, 163, 165, 175; Rosenthal 156; Zamor 156
Carnival (Hamvas) 164, 165, 175, 195, 209–33; doctor Ábsalom 221; Father Ágoston 214; Améline 214, 215; Angela 217, 219, 220; Maximus Barnabás 214; Bormester (Gergely 220; Justin 220; Máté 220; Mihály 209, 212, 213, 214, 217–20, 230; Virgil 209, 211, 213, 214, 233); Episztemon 228; Gitta 217; Herstal (Adelhaide baroness 220–1; Flóra 220; Raimund 214, 217; Raimund Herstal Jr 220); Mihály Hoppy 213, 214; Antal Kanavász 216; Lala 215–7, 226; Laura Kankalin 214, 227; père Manouel 218; Márkus (Master) 219, 230; Mr Pen 217; Yubainkan 218; doctor Vermerán 233; Vidal 220–1, 222; Michael Winemaster *see* Bormester, Mihály
carnivalisation 57
Castle, The (Kafka) 52, 58, 65, 74, 85, 86, 87, 89, 94, 98, 125; Arthur 88; Barnabas 87; Bürgel 89, 90, 98, 99; Erlangen 98, 99; Frieda 87, 98; innkeeper 87, 98; K. 52, 64, 85, 87, 88–101 *passim*; Jeremiah 88, 98; Klamm 87, 101; Momus 87, 101
cat 16, 185, 189, 190
Catholicism 9, 22, 39, 74, 89, 153, 162, 175, 195, 206, 233
cave 143; painted 238
centaur 158, 164, 233
'Chandos Letter' (Hofmannsthal) 25, 26–8, 32, 34
Change Alley (London) 15
chanson 16
chaos 11, 13, 100, 143; freedom of 138
charisma 50, 148
Chat Noir, Le 16, 190
chatter 85, 155, 203
'chosen people' 177
Christian Prince (Erasmus) 126
Christianity 70, 72, 74, 75, 92, 115, 175, 186, 218, 232, 238; Eastern Orthodox 39, 100; Germanic 48; Platonic 49, 177
Christmas 14
chronotope 5, 26
Church 177, 178, 214; anti- 178
cinema 131, 133, 145, 146, 148, 149, 151, 210, 225

circle(s) 51, 82, 141, 142, 229; of absurdity 100; birds (crow 77, 185; eagle 51, 101; falcon 56, 59, 101; raven 77, 83; vulture 83); blood- 73; infinite 91
circus 16, 17, 105, 169, 185, 210, 224, 225, 226, 227, 229; Moscow 185–6; world 212, 224
civilisation 147, 178; Akkadic 191; European 205; pathology 127, 130, 131; Western 130, 131
civility 126
classical age (Foucault) 21–2
classification 21, 206
clown(s) 17, 53, 88, 129, 132, 177, 225, 228, 229; circus 16; demonic 88; sacred 223
clownification 88
cobold 88
coffee 15–16; discovery 15
coffee-house 14–15, 16, 17, 22, 201–2, 203, 206; culture 14, 15, 17
coincidence 2, 8, 12, 15, 40, 48, 51, 57, 66, 68, 84, 99, 133, 134, 152, 158, 197, 199, 204–5
collapse 6, 64, 150, 175; empires 1, 2, 5, 8, 22, 34, 35, 36, 38, 47; Antiquity 11; Communism 207; imminent 17
colonialisation 225
Columbine *see commedia dell'arte*
comedy 95, 99, 137, 152, 156, 173, 211, 216, 223, 228, 231, 232; age of 226; apocalyptic 226; of fates 210, 226; permanent 226
commedia dell'arte 67, 87, 134, 151, 155, 171, 189; Columbine 87, 152, 215; Dottore 233; Franceschina 87; Harlequin 153, 155, 156, 157, 189, 229; Pierrot 16, 17, 89, 152, 153, 155, 156, 157, 186; Pulcinella 104, 153, 186
commedification 87
communication 80, 188; authentic 18; concrete 81; distorted 63, 78, 80, 82, 96, 107, 109; e-mail 81; mass 2, 80; non- 90, 129; non-personal (illusory) 80–2; non-verbal 33, 80; theories (critique) 81
communism 1, 87, 146, 180, 185, 186, 191, 192, 203, 207, 209, 210, 220, 238
communitas 68, 75
community 31, 33, 207, 227, 235
compassion *see* pity
complain(ing) 78, 148
complicity 50, 137, 138, 146

Subject index

concreteness (of being/s) 29, 41, 43, 44, 55, 80, 109, 128, 178, 207, 227, 228, 232
'concupiscential conquest' (Voegelin) 232
condemnation 28, 69, 89, 91, 92, 190, 191, 213, 233
condition(s) 12; of artist 105; authentic 131; democratic 150; of emergence 2; of exile 82; existential 46, 79; human 26, 31, 80, 104, 105, 165, 223; liminal 63, 136, 143, 170, 205; modern 64, 75, 77, 114, 127, 185, 187, 220; natural 32; of permanent liminality 28, 57; of possibility 32, 90, 91, 205; permanent 99, 203; universal 130
confession 26, 79, 210; self- 82; shamanistic (Calasso/ Kafka) 76
confusion 72, 82, 143, 144, 147, 165, 176, 230; theological 72
consciousness 29, 31, 32, 33, 35, 40, 68, 110, 127, 200; altered states 143; bad 12; double 231 (*see also schismotimia*); unhappy 130; modern vii; self- 5, 29–35
conservativism 11; Catholic 35; reactionary 9
Constantinople 15, 201; sack 8
constructivism 9, 32, 42, 54, 94, 176, 198, 200, 201, 228, 237; social 199
contagion 12, 21, 68, 128, 137–8, 149, 154, 167, 191, 215, 216, 217, 232, 237
conversion 53, 54, 74, 182, 198–9, 207, 237
Copenhagen 155, 162
Cordelia *see King Lear*
Cordilleras 217, 219
corruption 21, 144, 175, 198, 205, 230
corruptness 93
cosmopolitanism 96, 157
cosmos 111, 115–16, 118, 120
courage 53, 182, 192; moral 53
court society 2, 161, 223
cowardice 180, 224
Creation 34, 207
creative process 39, 70, 74, 76, 77, 79, 85, 180; *see also* inspiration: external
creem (Hamvas) 225
Crime and Punishment (Dostoevsky) 207
crisis 17, 28, 132, 143, 218, 219, 223, 234, 235, 236; apocalyptic 218; creativity 25–6, 32, 38, 40, 48, 59, 132; of language 25; spiritual 53
critic 196, 213, 223
critical theory vii, 85
crow *see* bird(s)

crowd(s) 202, 206
Crucifixion 184, 185, 238–9
culture 178, 205, 238; Austrian 2, 5, 27; cabaret 17; Central-European 2; Christian 111; coffee-house 14, 17; English 63; European 5, 7, 25, 27, 70, 72, 91, 127, 172, 179, 194, 211, 218, 219, 238, 239 (crisis 35, 49); German 27, 34, 37, 63; Greek 74, 115, 136; manager 204; of memorials 239; modern 5, 17, 34, 49, 127, 179; Roman 74; sexual 15; Viennese 6; Western 131, 219
cynicism 12, 16, 119, 170, 220

daimonic 69, 169
dance 33, 139, 146
dancing master *see* animal trainer
dandy 223
Danube Bend 209
Davos 140, 141, 145
daydreaming 53
Days of the Turbins (Bulgakov) 181
Dead Souls (Gogol) 181
death 14, 17, 30, 43, 69, 77, 90, 105, 107, 112, 127, 131, 136, 137, 139, 146, 147, 150, 172, 239; dance of 20, 145; experience of 30; world of 46
Death in Venice (Mann) 2, 38, 51, 57, 58, 59, 125, 131–9, 140, 144, 148, 229; Aschenbach 51, 57, 58, 132–9, 147, 149; Tadzio 136, 138
debauchery 138; self- 139
decadence 7, 13, 15, 17, 41, 100; fin-de-siècle 7, 10, 15, 16
decay 7, 12, 13, 158, 167, 175, 210, 214, 230
deceit 81, 110, 116, 117, 183; divine 65, 86; self- 199, 200
deception *see* deceit
decontextualisation (Kafka) 99, 103, 107, 112, 113
degradation 88, 90
'Deluge' (Leonardo) 126
demagogue(s) 170, 176, 178, 205
democracy 97, 150, 153, 176, 182, 205, 232, 236; mass 96, 234; social 11, 166; spirit 14
demon(s) 75–82, 83, 103, 104, 117, 119, 120, 149, 162, 190, 191, 210, 224, 227–32; of Gadarenes 162
demonic 12, 19, 58, 69, 76, 85, 88, 117, 119, 169, 175, 188, 195, 200–1, 204, 207, 224, 233; forces 21; pact 79; power 149, 233

Demons, The (Doderer) 165, 194–208; Agnes 207; Altschul 198, 204; Georg von Geyrenhoff 196, 204–5, 206; von Gürtzner-Gontard 206; Jan Herzka 199, 207; Kajetan von Schlaggenberg 196, 199, 203, 204, 207; Levielle 197, 204–5 ('false' 206); René Stangeler 196, 197, 200, 206; Ruthmayr 205
Demons, The (Dostoevsky) 71, 76, 125, 164, 165, 175, 194, 206, 210; Stavrogin 167
Denmark 43, 152, 158, 159, 162
depersonalisation 174, 179, 203, 227
depression 127, 130, 152
desert 82, 155, 190
desire 21, 70, 81, 82, 112, 147, 198; killing as 147; metaphysical (Girard) 81; mimetic 169
despair 106, 129
destruction 35, 139, 207, 212, 214, 217, 218, 232, 235, 237; of distance 172; of limits 141; self- 72, 82, 106, 227, 237
devil 76, 111, 116, 160, 181, 184, 188, 189, 204, 221, 237; pact with 157, 237
dialogue(s) 29, 174, 195, 200, 202–3, 209; Plato's 40, 65, 105, 111, 178, 198
diaries 65, 66, 67, 68, 69, 70, 73, 77, 83, 112, 152, 199
Dionysus 32, 86, 139, 229
Diotima 40, 41
disciplinary network (Foucault) 2
disempowering viii, 234
disenchantment (Weber) 50
disgrace vii
disintegration 14, 31, 167; inner 55; of values (Broch) 167, 171, 172–9
Disneyland 151
'Dispersed One, The' (Kafka) *see Amerika*
disproportionality 73, 115
divertissement 34, 36, 129, 222
divine 26, 28, 34, 55, 58, 86, 88, 108, 117, 207, 235
Divine Comedy (Dante) 211
divinisation of man 28
Dnieper 183
Doctor Zhivago (Pasternak) 182
dog 121, 127
Don Quixote (Bulgakov) 181, 182, 193
Don Quixote (Cervantes) 30, 50, 100, 172, 181, 219, 223
Door and Death, The (Hofmannsthal) 47
Doppelgänger 20, 22, 33
Dottore *see commedia dell'arte*
double 45, 52, 199, 200, 206, 217, 219
Double, The (Dostoevsky) 208
double bind (Bateson)
dream(s) 18, 19–21, 28, 47, 50, 70, 91, 97, 137, 138, 139, 170, 171, 173, 183, 197, 199, 201, 230, 237; American 95, 238; city of (Venice 50; Vienna 14); -like 52, 69, 135, 171
'Dream of Great Magic, A' (Hofmannsthal) 32
dualism vii, 7, 10, 11, 21, 22, 31, 77, 237
Duino Elegies (Rilke) 39

eagle *see* bird(s)
Ecce Homo (Nietzsche) 211
'Eclipse of Reality, The' (Voegelin) 199
economics 19
ecstasy 48, 55, 105, 139, 153
education 17, 25, 26, 34, 49, 50, 67, 126, 131, 151, 184; alchemic-hermetic 140, 143; mis- 25, 27, 36, 50, 51, 53, 67; modern 49; theatrical 26; *see also* learning to see
effect mechanism 21, 68, 75, 87
Egypt 130, 144
Ehrengard (Blixen) 163
Elf Scharfrichter 16
'Emancipation of Dissonance' (Schönberg) 11
empathy 33
empire 6; Carolingian 7; Chinese 7; Habsburg 5, 8–9, 64; Eastern (Austrian 1, 2; Byzantine 1, 7, 8, 203); Holy Roman 8, 9, 203; Ottoman 7; Persian 181; Roman 232
empiricism 18, 19
emptiness 86, 143, 168, 187; eyes 13, 215; *see also* void
enchantment(s) 27, 48, 51, 88, 238
end: of times 104; of world 6, 103, 113
Endgame (Beckett) 101
engineer(s) 170, 176, 178, 205
England 6, 8, 9
Enlightenment 8, 27, 34, 49, 53, 71, 72, 74, 106, 129, 140, 144, 146, 154; project 129, 234; radical 223, 234
entertainment 9, 11, 15, 20, 97, 131, 138, 145, 151, 211, 225
entrapment 27, 28, 148
entrepreneurship 138, 166, 169, 235, 238
envy 43
epiphany 51, 54, 56, 99, 133, 158; *see also* apparition
Epiphany (6 January) 21
episteme (Foucault): classical 169; modern 69

equation 74; absurd 70, 75; development of (Calasso) 70; mythic (Hughes) 70, 74, 75; theological dis- 74, 75; tragic (Hughes) 70, 75; tragicomic 70, 75;
Erinyes 161
'Ernst Mach Society' 18
Eros 11, 20, 111, 169
erotic 78, 131, 153; passion 48
error 90, 95, 99, 106, 165, 174
'Error, The' (Hamvas) 210
essence 36, 41, 42, 51, 54, 95, 103, 121, 131, 141, 163, 166, 168, 169, 226, 236
ethics 53, 216
Etruscan 91
etymology 7, 115, 119, 129, 150, 173, 188, 190, 193, 208, 237; English 141, 237–8; French 208; German 119; Greek 94, 104, 105, 121, 236, 238; Indo-European 193, 220; Italian 238; Hungarian 36, 130, 238; Latin 36, 115, 150, 237; Russian 188, 190, 193
Europe 2, 6, 7, 8, 13, 15, 16, 31, 35, 59, 95, 140, 152, 154, 155, 158, 172, 205, 239; Central 38, 59, 64; East 2, 71, 87, 180
evil 110, 111–18, 119, 147, 149, 159, 168, 171, 175, 177, 182; absolute (Citati) 116, 162
excess 20, 128, 144, 157, 163
exile 37, 82, 208
experience(s) 25, 27, 34, 53, 57, 58, 63, 68, 121, 128, 132, 133, 138, 141, 143, 152, 174, 195, 198, 200, 201, 219, 221, 230; childhood 41, 42, 54, 57, 114–15; carnival 146; cinema 145; communist 182; death 30, 128; epiphany 51, 54; formative 38, 47, 152; front 181, 217; of grace 32; of home 43; liminal 136, 137; modern 58; non- 128; participatory 31; strength 51; suffering 33; theatre 68; time 45; truth 33; unity 51, 238; virtue 51, war 184
experiential basis 140, 184, 201
expressionism 71
extreme(s) 11, 16, 18, 19, 20, 34, 46, 77, 99, 146, 150, 164, 177, 199; magic of (Voegelin) 11; Rilke and 42;
eye(s): demonic 228; empty 13, 215; terror in 227

Fackel, Der (Kraus) 24
failure to perceive (Doderer) 199, 200–1, 206–7

fair(s) 175, 176; world 211 (London 10; Vienna 10, 24)
fairground 104, 175, 211; barker 211, 212; capitalism 121, 203, 236
'Fairground Booth, The' (Meyerhold) 186
faith 27, 86, 95, 109, 112, 116, 218, 229, 232, 238; blind 93; *see also* believing
fake 81, 116, 117, 135, 138, 166, 168, 171, 175, 177, 191, 206, 211, 216
faking *see* fake
Fall 28, 29, 104, 105, 107, 108, 110, 116, 129, 157, 238, 239; modernity as second 104, 116, 239
fantasy 18, 50, 65, 81, 157, 199, 228, 230, 237
farce 173, 185, 215, 222
fascism 1
fashion 148, 198
Fasti (Ovidius) 233
Fatima 103, 121
Faust (Goethe) 37, 56, 112, 125, 132, 161, 181, 237
Faust myth 160
fear 77, 120, 187, 191
Fear and Trembling (Kierkegaard) 93
feast 132, 150, 155, 160, 211, 213–14, 229, 233
femme fatale 16, 133
Ferrara 8, 12
festivity *see* feast
finance 15, 105, 197, 198, 201, 204–5, 206; economy 2
finiteness 31, 80
'First Sorrow' (Kafka) 106
fixed idea 215, 228, 229
flâneur 42
Fledermaus (Vienna cabaret) 17
Fledermaus, Die (Strauss) 12
Florence 7, 8
fluidity *see* flux
flux 18, 76, 121, 128, 131, 176, 198, 207, 234, 236
Folie et déraison (Foucault) 129
folly *see* madness
fool(s) 188, 195, 200, 225, 228, 229; sacred 229, 230
force(s): external 237; imperceptible 76; inner 55, 56, 198; moving 223; obscure 77; vital 221
'forest of symbols' (Baudelaire) 165
formalism 8, 17, 19, 90
formlessness 10, 13, 168, 174
four horsemen *see* apocalypse

'Four Horsemen' (Dürer) 126
'Fragments for a Theory of the Novel' (Hamvas) 194, 222
France 8, 9, 160
Franceschina *see* commedia dell'arte
Franciscan(s) 54, 154
Frankfurt am Main 204
freedom vii, viii, 1, 28, 114, 120, 152, 178, 180, 203, 222, 223, 227, 232, 234, 236; value 198
Freemasonry 53, 65, 146
fundamentalism 164, 235
Furlani *see* Serious One, The

games 86, 88, 95, 157, 202, 211; masked 160; psychological 224; strategic 58, 161, 215
Garden of Eden *see* Paradise
Gay Science (Nietzsche) 6
gaze 51, 86, 112, 134, 136, 163
genealogy 36, 107; of modernity 2, 126
genius 24, 27, 36, 127, 192
genocide viii; 174
Germany 16, 22, 23, 38, 39, 40, 59, 63, 65, 119, 120; Weimar 16
Gestapo 159
gesture(s) 33, 44, 46, 66, 68, 80, 135, 139, 160, 186
ghost(s) 78, 233; *see also* phantasm
gift (relations) 1, 27, 108, 119, 121, 150, 191, 197, 217, 224, 235; divine 32, 178
given 119, 121, 196–7
glance 24, 127, 149, 215, 221
glaring 66, 68
glimpse *see* glance
globalisation 2, 172, 232, 234, 236
gnomic 85
Gnosticism 49, 84, 94, 176
goat(s) 22; -herd(s) 22, 182
Göbekli Tepe 190
God 45, 46, 60, 86, 90, 130, 148, 155, 157, 158, 162, 178, 179, 235
god(s) vii; Greek 100; alien 139; personal 108
golden age 104, 106, 108, 111, 182, 214, 219, 238, 239; Athens 7; Florence 7; myth 182; Vienna 7;
Good Soldier Švejk, The (Hašek) 22
Gorgon 215, 233
Gospel(s) 49, 186; John 85, 226, 231, 232; Luke 164; Mark 239; Matthew 239
grace 27, 32, 49, 54, 71, 88, 89, 90, 136, 138, 150, 154, 161, 179, 184, 191, 192, 224, 237

Grand Inquisitor 94, 101
Great War *see* war(s), First World
Great World Theatre (Hofmannsthal) 33
Greece 46, 56, 111, 115; classical 136, 218
Greek (language) 29, 51, 91, 98, 103, 105, 121, 185
'Green Cockatoo, The' (Schnitzler) 20
grotesque 16, 134, 135, 138, 181, 185, 199, 216
guillotine 156, 187
guilt 23, 67, 138, 168, 171

habitus 27
Hamburg 166
Hamlet (Shakespeare) 47, 152, 159, 161, 210, 219, 223, 229
happiness 98, 108
Hard Times (Dickens) 206
Harlequin *see* commedia dell'arte
Harlequin Sorcerer (Lun) 175
harmonia mundi 154, 157, 162, 165
harmony 27, 28, 45, 74, 90, 158, 162
hatred 20, 149, 201; self- 21
heart 27, 41, 43, 46, 49, 53, 54, 55, 90, 161, 231, 237–8; limitless 43, 46
heartbeat 237, 238; mother's 238
Heaven 19, 89
Heidelberg 239
Hell 19, 88, 190, 202
Hellenism 140, 190
Henoch 219, 233
Henry IV (Pirandello) 155
Hermann and Dorothea (Goethe) 65
Hermes 51, 87, 88, 98, 101, 133, 135, 140, 141, 146, 211
Hermes Trismegistos 140
hermit(s) 82, 209
Hermetism 49, 131, 140, 143
hesitation 119, 137, 161
hesychasm 39
hieroglyph 130
hilarity 138, 186, 210, 215, 222, 224, 226
Himalayas 218, 219
Hinduism 133, 232
Hippodrome: Clayton 97; Constantinople 97; Jerusalem 185; Moscow 185
hippopotamus 185, 190
Hitler and the Germans (Voegelin) 199
Hofmannsthal and His Time (Broch) 38
Hollywood 87, 97
Holocaust viii, 159
Holy Spirit 71, 72, 73, 232
home 43, 44, 170, 192, 219
Homunculus 25

262 *Subject index*

honour vii, 182
hope 21, 29, 75, 83, 89, 90, 91, 112, 129, 130, 149, 178, 180, 183, 203, 219, 222
horse 185, 193
humanism: Enlightenment 36; secular 235
humility 106, 138
humour-mysticism (Hamvas) 216, 221, 226, 230
Hungary 5, 35, 36, 194, 209, 210, 215, 221, 227, 232
hyper-democracy (Ortega) 1
Hyperion (Hölderlin) 1, 38, 40
hypermodernity 1, 2, 10, 19, 39, 40, 42, 47, 54, 56, 57, 58; its spirit 14
hypnosis 20
hypocrisy 202, 223, 230
hysteria 77, 175, 210, 215, 219

'I Live My Life in Expanding Rings' (Rilke) 37, 48, 59, 101
Iago *see Othello*
'ideal speech situation' (Habermas) 81
idealism 212
identification 26, 45, 78, 152, 153, 163, 169; self- 93, 103, 106
Idiot, The (Dostoevsky) 88, 155, 219, 220; Aglaia 220; Prince Myshkin 181, 219, 220
idiot(ic) 199, 216, 224, 227
idyll 16, 192, 219
illness 43, 127, 139, 146, 147, 149, 191, 192, 221, 227; anti- 127–30; epidemic 128, 137, 139, 145, 146, 147, 149; Kafka's 103; modern 196
illusion 6, 18, 30, 50, 53, 80, 81, 82, 117, 133, 145, 175, 230; infinite 82; theatrical 31
image(s) 6, 17, 20, 22, 28, 34, 41, 56, 64, 74, 77, 86, 88, 90, 96, 97, 104, 105, 115, 126–7, 130, 131, 136, 137, 141, 142, 145, 165, 185; archetypal 126; of God 178; magic 148, 149; vision- 109, 126
imagination 30, 44, 184, 199, 200, 229, 230, 237
imitation 30, 68, 103, 105, 117, 119, 121, 135, 138, 149, 166, 168, 169, 208
imitativity 5–6, 9
immorality 167, 174
immortality 108, 236
immunity (Shillabeer) 196, 213, 226
Imperial Court Theatre (Vienna) 20
'improbability factor' (Hamvas) 215

in-betweenness 31, 36, 80, 110, 111, 112, 117, 118, 129, 132, 165, 169; sleeping-waking 90, 98, 165, 171
Incarnation 238–9
incommensurable 39, 135
incubator 5, 10, 12, 25, 125, 140, 145
indecency 138, 198
indestructible 42, 46, 56, 99, 101, 104, 107–10, 115, 118, 120, 121, 127, 178–9, 219, 232, 236–9
individualism 19, 29, 31, 109, 129, 144, 148, 174, 175, 228, 237
infantilism 95, 96, 114–15, 137, 165, 195
infection *see* contagion
infinity 13, 31, 47, 55, 80, 91, 140, 141, 142, 153, 171, 176, 178
initiation 211, 212, 231; alchemic 140; archaic 143, 210; novel of 210; shamanistic 69, 77
innocence 95, 129, 156, 171, 213
'innocent fraud' (Galbraith) 179
insolence 69, 136, 137, 138, 204, 216
inspiration: external 40, 58, 64, 66, 69, 70, 74, 76, 79, 85, 91, 94, 106, 132, 140, 143, 183–4, 222
intactness *see* integrity
integrity 49, 89, 232; personal 14, 18, 174
intelligentsia *see* literati
intensity 65, 81, 134
interest(s) 150; 'passionate' (Latour) 129; public 131; self- 168; vested 235
International Political Anthropology (IPA) viii, 60
internet 82
Interpretation of Dreams (Freud) 20
intruder 90, 152, 156, 215, 221
intrusion 33, 80
invasion 76, 80, 119
Ion (Plato) 121, 132
Iphigenia 161
Ireland 59
Iron Age 182
irrationality 73, 118, 165, 177
Isaac 72
Isenheim Altarpiece (Grünewald) 126
Islam 8, 15, 39, 74, 86
Istanbul 15, 201
Italy 8, 39, 49, 126, 139, 162, 217

Jacobin(s) 156
Jane Eyre (Brontë) 164
Jaques *see As You Like It*
Java 144

Jerusalem 184, 185, 186
jester 105, 162
Jesuit(s) 146, 147
joke *see* joking
'Joker, The' (Mann) 132
joking 67, 78, 89, 90, 188, 189, 213, 216
Jonathan's Coffee-house (London) 15
Joseph and his Brothers (Mann) 92, 140
journalism 14, 24
Judaism 38, 64, 71, 73, 75, 89, 91, 175, 176; Ancient 92; Rabbinic 190
Juno 20
Judgement Day 149, 175, 183
Junker 166
Jupiter 20
justice 161, 162, 177, 182, 188, 191, 214, 231; popular 235; social 16

K. (Calasso) 77
Karamazov Brothers (Dostoevsky) 37, 221
Kenya 153
khóra (empty space) 81, 105
Kiev 180, 184
King Lear (Shakespeare) 80, 210, 229; Cordelia 80
'Knight, Death and Devil' (Dürer) 126, 182
Königsberg 188

labyrinth 79, 120, 211
'Lady and the Unicorn' (tapestry) 41, 44, 45
'Lady with a Unicorn' (Raphael) 59
ladybird 193
land surveyor 85, 90, 93–4, 100
language(s) 18, 21–2, 25, 30, 32, 80, 115; crisis of 25; minority (Kafka) 66
Last Supper 140, 186
Last Tales (Blixen) 162–3; Cardinal Salviati 153, 162; Orosmane 162–3; Pellegrina Leoni 162; Yorick 162–3
Latin (language) 36, 60, 201, 204, 23
Latin-America 217
laughter 11, 138, 215, 226, 230, 231
Law 73, 86, 89, 90, 92, 178
Laws (Plato) 132, 236
learning to see 42, 43, 131, 220, 230
Lemberg 67
lemur(s) 88, 211, 225, 233
leprosy 234
Les misérables (Hugo) 133
Les mots et les choses see *Order of Things*
letter(s) 40, 42, 43, 47, 54, 65, 66, 73, 75, 78–80, 81, 83, 86, 90, 119, 160, 161, 166, 202
Letter to the Corinthians, First (St Paul) 218

Leviathan 190
liberalism 11, 238; Manchester 9
Lido (Venice) 48, 147
Life is a Dream (Calderón) 22
life-conduct 216, 223
Lilith 142, 144, 148, 191, 192, 215
liminal authorities (Horvath) 112
liminality viii, 13, 20, 38, 42, 45, 63, 64, 67, 73–4, 102, 103, 110, 111, 112, 114, 117, 118, 126, 135, 136, 143, 152, 160, 165, 169, 188, 197, 205, 235, 236; forced 82, 236; permanent viii, 28, 33, 47, 57, 58, 63, 64, 74, 91, 99, 100, 121, 127, 129, 131, 195, 236–9; reflecting 63
limitlessness 20, 43 60, 74, 145, 146
links: appearance–reality 11, 13; art–life 104; art–reality 21, 179; art–science 130, 222; art–technology 179; Austria–China (Kafka) 7; charisma–trickster 174; Christianity–Platonism 49, 177, 178; circus–modernity 226; comedy–secularisation 232; concrete–Absolute 178; cosmos–chaos 111; death–sex 12, 14, 21, 147; divine–human 86; dog–prophecy 127; dream–reality 173; election–condemnation 91, 92; empowering–disempowering 143, 234; evil–world 111–18; formalism–sensualism 8, 19; good–evil 110, 112, 162, 173, 232; home–world 105; image–word 130; land surveyor–Messiah 85, 93–4, 100; language–reality 26; liberty–illness 146; life–death 46, 131, 153, 237; life–work 23, 222; life-writing 78, 222; liminality–desire 112; limit–unlimited 178; love–death 146, 147; love–hate 77, 79; loving–being loved 46; mask–reality 228; micro-micro–macro-macro 40, 196; modernity–poetry–novel 39; Muzak music–military parade 238; person–identity 228; personal–collective liminality 22; philosophy–spirituality 222; poets–prophets 40; power–knowledge (Foucault) 112, 217, 232; rationality–insanity 173, 176; rationality–irrationality 173, 174, 176, 178; reality–fantasy 50, 157, 173; reality–novel 50; reality–unreality 43, 81, 172, 174, 176–7; reason–imagination 229; religion–money 105; revolution–irrationality 177; saint–fool 219, 223, 231; sanity–insanity 181; sea–sky–snow 136–7, 140, 141, 144,

192; sleepwalking–travelling 170–1; sociology–literature 222; stock market–central committee 235; theatre–modernity 5; theatre–reality 30; theatricality–self-consciousness 29–35; truth–lies 10; zero–infinity 81–2, 86, 89, 96, 97, 121, 153, 226, 234
lion 191
liquidation *see* destruction
liquidity/liquefaction 13, 31, 236, 237
literati 16, 23, 36
Little Dorrit (Dickens) 204, 205; Mr Merdle 204, 205
Logic (Hegel) 212
Lola 215
Lolita (Nabokov) 215
London 5, 14, 15, 42, 69, 95
Louvre 152
love 41, 45–6, 48, 55, 56, 71, 79, 80, 81, 87, 115, 131, 146, 150, 153, 155, 159, 162, 169, 184, 191, 192, 207, 216, 217, 220, 221, 223, 226, 231; absurd 137; Divine 72, 150; as work 46
Lulu *see Out of Africa*

Macbeth (Shakespeare) 210
machine 8, 36, 90–1, 95, 97, 178, 203, 204, 222, 226; torture 82; world as 90–1
madness 58, 129, 216, 221, 224, 227, 229, 230, 231; divine 40, 230, 231, 232, 233; demonic 231
'Madonna di Foligno' (Raphael) 126
malevolence 149, 168
magic 32, 48, 52, 68, 131, 140, 176, 185, 186, 212, 219, 229
Magic Mountain (Mann) 2, 38, 47, 50, 52, 53, 55, 57, 59, 60, 125–6, 130, 131, 132, 133, 134, 138, 139–50, 164, 174, 179, 233; Behrens 131, 149; Chauchat 142, 144, 146, 147, 148; Hans Castorp 130, 131, 140–9, 179; Hippe 130; Joachim 142, 147, 179; Frau Landauer 144; Naphta 53, 140, 144, 146–7, 148, 149, 164; Pieperkorn 53, 144, 147–9; Settembrini 53, 60, 140, 142, 144, 146–7, 148, 149; Wiedemann 149
'magical accountability' (Calasso) 33
Malta 52
'Man and His Dog' (Mann) 121
man as measure (Protagoras) 147
Man Without Qualities (Musil) 18; Ulrich 18
manager(s) 137, 203, 204

marionette 88, 95, 132, 152, 157, 132, 175, 224
'Marionette theatre' (Kleist) 29, 157
market(s) 104, 234, 236
marriage 8, 12, 153, 155, 214, 220, 228–9
Martha and Mary 230, 233
Martin Chuzzlewit (Dickens) 57, 64
Marxism 85; anti- 182
maschera 44
mask(s) 6, 13, 17, 20, 36, 41, 42, 43, 44, 48, 49, 50, 53, 58, 103, 105, 117, 135, 137, 138, 146, 155, 156–8, 163, 171, 175, 177, 183, 186, 188, 195, 199, 204, 205, 210, 211, 213, 214, 215–16, 219, 220, 221, 224, 227–31, 233; play (Blixen 153; Kokoschka 17); will to be 77; world of 46
masque 189
Master and Margarita (Bulgakov) 77, 165, 180, 181, 182, 184–93, 233; Annushka-the-plague 187; Azazello 187, 190, 192; Behemoth 185, 186, 189, 192; Berlioz 187, 188; Hella, 187, 190; 'Homeless' 186, 187, 188, 193; Korov'ev 186, 189; Margarita 184–92 *passim*; Master 181, 184, 186, 191–2; Matthew Levi 184, 188, 192; Pilate 184, 185, 186; Praskovja Fjodorovna 187; Rimskij 186, 187; Varenusha 187–8, 191; Woland 186, 187, 188, 189, 192; Yeshua 181, 188
matriarchy 233
maturity 24, 47, 95, 165, 195
Maya (Goya) 133
meaning 7, 14, 19, 27, 42, 43, 44, 167, 197, 224
meaninglessness 91, 187, 217, 219, 222
mechanisation 91, 95, 96, 149, 160, 203, 215
media 118, 195, 234; mass 182, 236 *see also* press
Mediterranean 70, 72, 74
melancholy 11, 14, 126–31, 152, 155
'Melencolia I' (Dürer) 126–7, 130
memory 42, 54, 60, 104, 183, 196, 208, 238, 239; childhood 40, 41, 43, 130
Mephistopheles 88, 183
Merchant of Venice (Shakespeare) 154, 156; Shylock 154
Mercury *see* Hermes
mercy 161, 162
Merdle, Mr *see Little Dorrit*
Medusa the Gorgon 215
Merovingian(s) 197
Mesopotamia 191

Messiah 85, 93, 109, 115, 178, 179
Messianism 85, 94
metallurgy 190, 235
metamorphosis 2, 28, 33, 44, 48, 55, 56, 68, 128, 159, 175, 189, 207; permanent 224
'Metamorphosis' (Kafka) 38, 77, 88, 94
metaxy (Plato) 111
Methodenstreit 19
mice 119, 120
microcosm 32
microscope 131
Middle Ages 16, 22, 40, 41, 42, 74, 76, 92, 126, 145, 200, 201, 203
Midsummer 48, 70, 83, 141
Midsummer Night's Dream (Shakespeare) 210
mime(s) 67, 117, 118, 149, 168
mimesis *see* imitation
mimetic rivalry (Girard) 149, 150
Minoan Crete 153, 154, 191
miracle(s) 95, 219, 220
mirage 195, 228, 229, 230, 231
  see also illusion
misogyny 100, 133
Missing Person, The (Kafka) *see Amerika*
Möbius strip 2, 90
mocking 16, 136, 170, 211
modern world *see* modernity
modernism 1, 5, 59, 197, 201; Vienna 6, 7, 20, 193, 201, 202
modernity vii, viii, 1, 26, 42, 63, 64, 70, 71, 74, 91, 104, 106, 111, 116, 117, 118, 126, 131, 148, 160, 165, 174, 187, 196, 200, 203, 224, 226, 227, 228, 230, 231, 232, 234–9; ambivalence vii; diagnosis 43, 45, 130; endgame 2, 42; genesis/ genealogy 2, 126; global 173; 'horror' (Baudelaire) 39, 43; legitimacy 106; paradoxes 100; rise 5, 15; romantic apology 39; secret 19; self-understanding 43; transitionality 128; understanding 111; unreality 176–7
monasticism 82, 218
Mondo Novo (Tiepolo) 95, 101
monomania 148, 215, 216, 228, 229, 231
monotheism 72, 100, 176
monster 161, 185, 190, 230
Monte Verità (Ascona) 152
moon 18, 89; full 197
morality 29, 53, 130, 198, 204, 216, 218
morbidity 17
Morocco 145
Mosaic Law 71, 177

Moscow 181, 183, 184, 185, 186, 188, 189, 191, 201
Moses 92, 189
motley 186, 189
mountebank(s) 137
Munich 16, 38, 58, 134, 195
museum 41, 44, 45
music 17, 68, 153, 183, 211, 222, 238; Muzak 238; transformative 44
music hall 16
Muzot 39
mystery 15, 27, 131, 141, 158, 221, 229, 231
mysticism 40, 55, 86, 134, 230; Byzantine 102
myth 32, 157, 182, 223; modern 160, 237
mythology 39

narcissism 29, 76
natural place 33
Nature 51, 89, 235, 237
Nazism 158–9, 195, 207, 208, 226
Neanderthal 239
negativity 79, 106, 117, 149
neo-Kantianism 19, 29, 36, 49, 141, 142, 167, 172, 197, 198, 199
neo-liberalism 19, 179
neo-positivism 19
Netherlands 144
Neue Freie Press 14
New Testament 72, 74, 188, 191–2, 233
New York 42, 101
New York Film Critics Award 100
newsboy 211
night writing 68, 76, 78, 79, 82, 105, 106, 119, 182, 211
nihilism 7, 13, 26, 63, 95, 121, 129, 142, 144, 148, 156, 157, 168, 176, 177, 178, 238
9/11: Kafka 86; Rilke 40; Twin Towers 40
Nobel prize 37, 125, 132, 151
nobility 54, 182, 224
non-being 13, 90, 117
non-communicable 30, 52, 129, 207
non-place vii
non-reality *see* unreality
Nostalgia (Tarkovsky) 162
Notebooks of Malte Laurids Brigge (Rilke) 2, 37, 38, 39–46, 48, 49, 53, 55, 57, 59, 121; Abelone 41, 46; Malte 41–6, 57, Nikolai Kusmitch 45
nothingness 14, 23, 32, 35, 81, 82, 86, 101, 136, 145, 173, 178, 187, 218, 232

Novels and the Sociology of the Contemporary (Szakolczai) viii, 5, 125, 194
nudity 163, 190, 191
nulla see nothingness
nullity *see* nothingness
numbers 66, 83, 107–8, 110, 111, 113–14, 116, 117, 118, 120; forty 66, 82; hundred-and-three 102, 103, 107, 121; hundred-and-nine 107, 113–14; magical 60; nine 41, 60; seven 60, 142, 143, 145, 162, 210; ten 177; thirty-seven 133, 140; thousand-and-one 153; twelve 186

obituary 17
objectivity 143, 205, 223
obscenity 87
obsession 136, 166, 195, 196, 199, 207, 222
occult 39
Odyssey (Homer) 46
Old Testament 72, 74, 91, 92, 95, 98, 142, 183–91; Daniel 187; Isaiah 191; Job 189; Leviticus 190; Numbers 158, 189
omnipresence 10, 11, 37, 50, 176, 185, 201, 206; divine 86
'1 September 1939' (Auden) 120
opera 6, 9, 15, 21
operator (Foucault) 68, 72
operetta 6, 9, 11, 12, 36, 183
Order of Things (Foucault) 21
'Ördöngösök' (Hamvas) 194, 210
Orestes 161
original: 'disjoining' (Hamvas) 223; sin 23, 28, 44, 117
Oscar prize 151
Othello (Shakespeare) 156, 189; Iago 189
Out Of Africa (Blixen) 151, 153–4; Lulu 17, 153–4, 215
outcast(s) 43, 88, 97
outsider 20, 59, 93, 97, 167

pact with devil *see* devil: pact
painting(s) 13, 17, 126, 133, 163, 211
Palace of Justice (Vienna) 197, 206
Palaeolithic 72, 114, 143, 238; Heidelberg 239; homo antecessor 239; Neanderthal 239
panopticon 224
Pantalone 87, 189
pantomime 16, 33, 34, 96, 175
parable 57, 82; before the Law 89; of Prodigal Son 37, 46

Paradise 51, 104, 106–10, 111–21 *passim*; expulsion 107, 111, 112, 114, 117, 159
parasite: poet as 105–6
Paris 5, 6, 7, 10, 14, 15, 16, 24, 29, 39–46 *passim*, 57, 59, 144, 152, 189
Parliament 211
parody 131, 133, 164, 188, 189, 222, 228; self- 157
participation 35, 196
patience 106, 111, 121
peace 99, 192, 214, 217, 225, 234; treaty 234
'Penal Colony' (Kafka) 97
Pensées (Pascal) 102
people of god 93, 235
permanent: carnival 1, 165, 211, 219; comedy 236; festivities 14; flux 207; game of illusion 6; laws 207; liminality *see* liminality: permanent; liminoid: 59; mask-wearing 211; metamorphosis 224; revolution 235; transitoriness 34; terror 235
perpetual movement 18
person(ality) 18, 26, 29, 80, 144, 148, 149, 153, 219, 227, 230; loss of unity 53; non- 206
personal integrity 14, 17–18
Petroushka (Stravinsky) 153
Phaedo (Plato) 236
Phaedrus (Plato) 40, 50, 137, 139, 154, 221, 236
phantasm(s) 75, 76, 78, 79, 80, 81, 82, 83, 103, 104, 105, 106, 113, 219
phantasmagoria 173, 201, 208, 227
Philebus (Plato) 108, 111, 178, 221
philology 27
philosophy 17, 21, 64, 65, 100, 120, 165, 167, 172, 201; analytic 19; 'cacocentric' (Hamvas) 218; critical 13, 201; European 218; of history 85, 117; Kafka's 102, 103, 108; Kant's 141, 142, 172; logicism 19; political 126
phone calls 202
pied piper 119
Pierrot *see commedia dell'arte*
Pietism 39
pilgrimage 238; spiritual 53
pity 67, 68, 75, 162; self- 162
plague 70, 138, 139, 145, 150
playfulness 150, 157, 162, 212, 213, 223, 231
pleasure principle 225, 237

poiesis 32
Pola 134
Poland 8, 136, 138
polyphony (Bakhtin) 58
populism 16; anti- 182
pornography 11
positivism 17, 18, 19, 128, 167, 198
possession 77, 115; demonic 76, 77; religious 130; sexual 87; *see also* inspiration: external
'Potemkin City' (Loos) 10
Potnia 153, 191
powerlessness 135, 142, 143, 145
Prague 5, 8, 18, 22, 29, 38, 39, 41, 64, 66, 67, 71, 103, 121, 203
Prater (Vienna) 11, 151
precocity 21, 34, 39, 47
pre-existence (Hofmannsthal) 28, 29–31, 33
presence 16, 30, 31, 42, 52, 54, 70, 76, 80, 81, 128, 179, 197; divine 60; of mind 195
press 15, 16, 118, 166, 194, 198, 201, 202–4, 206
Prince (Machiavelli) 126
Prince Myshkin *see Idiot*
Privilegium Maius 8
problematisation 131, 146, 177; of self 18, of person 29
Process, The (Kafka) 52, 65, 76, 86, 88, 89, 90, 92, 97, 98, 115; Block 88; Huld 88; Joseph K. 52, 64, 88–92 *passim*, 98; sacristan 88, 89; Titorelli 52, 88
Prodigal Son *see* parable
profit-making 173, 174
progress 9, 43, 45, 109, 223, 235
Prometheus 106, 190
promiscuity 149
promised land 221; fake 94, 97
propaganda 2, 35
prophet(ess)/prophetic 40, 41, 91, 92
prophecy 91, 93, 127, 142, 177, 197, 214, 217; anti-prophetic 92, 93, 94, 218
proportionality 45, 74, 101, 115, 162
prostitution 16, 49, 87
Protestant Ethic (Weber) 130
Protestantism 9, 70, 74, 92, 175
Proteus 87, 157, 224
provisoriness 176
provocation 153, 167, 236
Prussia 8, 9, 19
psychopompos (guide of souls) 98, 101
public as judge 223

public sphere 15, 42, 43, 81, 101, 105, 176, 202, 205, 234, 236
Pulcinella *see commedia dell'arte*
Pulcinella (Ballets Russes) 155
Pulcinella (Tiepolo) 28, 103, 104
puppet(s) *see* marionettes
Pure America (Gothár) 100
Puritanism 2, 153, 157, 218, 223

quasi-novel 2, 37

Rand Corporation 208
Rape of Lucrece (Shakespeare) 70
ratio 73, 173, 178
rational choice 166, 237
rationalism 146, 148, 172, 175, 176, 177, 179, 199, 201, 208
rationality 173, 174, 205; calculative 58; individualistic 144; instrumental 118; irrational 205; Kantian 195; Puritan 144
raven *see* bird(s)
realism 71, 166
reality 29, 197, 228, 230; fake/falsified 167, 175, 203, 205, 206; no 221; second 195, 196, 197, 198, 199–200, 201–7, 208; sense of 195, 227; social 31; theatre as loss of 45, 175; truer 235; truth of (theatre 30; unreality 171); unreal 12, 172, 173, 176, 178
reason 54, 137, 143–4, 165, 229, 237
rebel 20, 72, 172, 190
recognition 46, 90, 170, 231
redemption 100, 112, 174
red-haired 17, 134, 137, 190, 191, 213, 217
Reflections on the Revolution in France (Burke) 94
reflexivity 32
Reformation 38, 126
refuge 114
regression 21, 223
reminiscence *see* memory
Renaissance 1, 8, 14, 32, 126, 154, 175, 176, 197
renunciation 33, 115
representation 21–2; theatrical 8
resentment 16–17, 20, 199
resignation 14, 17, 137, 187, 221, 239
responsibility 19, 168, 170, 222, 223, 227; irresponsibility 137, 171
Resurrection 1, 37, 109, 131, 162, 179, 233, 238–9
Resurrection (Tolstoy) 1, 37
revaluation of values 206–7, 216

268 Subject index

revelation 27, 28, 34, 60, 88, 103, 186, 197, 222
revenge 67, 161, 162, 168, 192
Revenge of Truth (Blixen) 152, 156
revolt *see* rebel
revolting 96, 213, 227
revolution(s) 1, 177, 178, 206, 208, 222, 231; American 63; Bolshevik 63, 74, 103, 180, 187, 222, 223; communist 38; conservative 35; French (1789) 9, 20, 22, 28, 49, 55, 63, 94, 156, 187, 234; from below 19; intellectual 20; permanent 235; rational 178
revolutionary(ies) 15, 19, 146, 167, 146, 201, 206–7; situation 20
rhythm 96, 107, 237, 238; cosmic 238
ridicule 179, 216
Rites of Passage (van Gennep) 36
rogue 213
Rolling Stones 193
Romanticism 77, 150, 151, 157, 166, 192, 217, 210
Rome 8, 20, 185, 232; foundation 20
Ronde, La (Schnitzler) 20
Rosenkavalier (Hofmannsthal) 7, 47, 48, 56, 60, 198; Faninal 60; Octavian 47
Rosicrucian 28
Rumania 144
Russia 13, 37, 39, 45, 73, 103, 136, 138, 152, 153, 180, 184, 189; Soviet 180, 181, 182, 184, 189, 191, 217

Sabbath 72
sacrifice 1, 2, 33–4, 90, 105, 139, 147, 153, 160, 171, 173, 190, 215; Abraham's 71, 72, 92, 93, 102; child 161; of Christ 34; human 93; of intellect 35; self- 207
sacrificial mechanism 1, 2, 33, 34, 226, 237, 238
salvation religions 119
San (Bushmen) 163
Sancho Panza 77, 182
Santo Domingo 160
Sanskrit 101
Satan 154, 184, 188
satire vii, 45, 185, 224; Menippean 180, 198
Sattelzeit (Koselleck) 63
scambio (mistake, exchange) 165
scandal(s) 13, 104, 212, 218
scapegoat 190, 215, 226; of mankind (Kafka) 78
Scheherazade (Ballets Russes) 152
Scheherazade 152, 153, 162, 163
schism 7, 11, 174, 198, 237

schismatic: mode of living/ being 77, 79: personality 47–8, 52, 53, 126, 157, 169, 200, 217, 219; society 13; spirit 8
schismogenesis vii, 146, 148, 150, 222, 235
schismotimia (Hamvas) 219
schizophrenia 77
Schwabing 133, 134, 152
science 43, 101, 128, 130, 178, 198, 214, 235; technologised 2, 13, 129, 236
'Science As A Vocation' (Weber) 103
Scientia Sacra (Hamvas) 159, 223
Scientific Conception of the World, The (Vienna Circle) 18
scientism 214, 221, 223, 233
Sea and the Mirror, The (Auden) 159
search for 225; 'better argument' 100; concrete 44 (Rilke); effects 173; excitement 11, 155; God 86, 92–3; indestructible (Kafka) 121; meaning 14, 120 (denied 19); new 21, 132; pleasure 30, 45, 87; reunification 49; for self 33, 49, 54, 213; truth 10, 18, 30; way 106, 120
Second Coming 6, 94
'Second Coming, The' (Yeats) 59, 101
secret police: Stalinist 97, 98
Secret Service 13
sect 231
secularism 72, 74, 75, 129, 187, 232
seduction 48, 112, 115, 116, 117, 153, 156, 163, 166, 169, 217
seismograph 6, 25, 130
self 54, 120; core 45, 46, 56, 121; deepest 49, 55; inner 42, 46, 53, 54, 56, 121; its power 51, 54; true 51, 54; unity 53, 54, 55
self-assertion 106
self-control 139, 146
self-contempt 55
self-divinisation 28, 32
self-debasement 213
self-denouncing 79, 82, 215
self-knowledge 117, 130
self-overcoming 129, 195, 196, 239
self-understanding 43, 105
sense of judgement 143, 146, 215, 229, 238
sensuality 60, 155
Serious One, The (Hofmannsthal) 28, 29, 36; Furlani 29; Hans Karl 35
Sermon on the Mount 217
serpent 111, 115, 117, 139, 158, 189; brass 158, 189

Seven Gothic Tales (Blixen) 151, 156
sexuality 11, 15, 18, 19–21, 74, 80, 87, 157, 194, 196, 199, 200, 202, 214, 215; ambivalence 47; immediate gratification 20, 87
'Sexuality and the Total State' (Doderer) 194
shadow 33, 56, 100; of dead 233
shaman(istic) 91–2, 93; confession (Calasso) 76; dream 69; experience 130; initiation 69, 77; prehistoric 238; trip 77
Ship of Fools (Brand/ Dürer) 126, 129
Siegfried 211, 212
silence 11, 12, 26, 42, 46, 80, 96, 106, 136, 145, 175, 215
simplicity 136, 167, 216
sin 44, 105, 116, 163, 174, 191; capital 106; original 23, 28, 44, 117
'Sistine Madonna' (Raphael) 126
sitting 127
slavery 15, 117, 152, 160, 183, 188, 214, 235
Sleepwalkers (Broch) 165–79; Bertrand 167–71, 173, 200, 204; Elisabeth 169, 170; Esch 166–77 *passim*; Huguenau 166, 167, 171–7 *passim*, 204; Joachim von Pasenow 166–70 *passim*, 174–5; Martin Geyring 166, 171; Ruzena 168, 169; Salvation Army girl 176, 179
sleepwalking 54, 58, 130, 165–7, 170, 171, 172, 176, 205, 225; institutionalised 173; life as 167
Slovakia 35
Small World Theatre (Hofmannsthal) 32
snake *see* serpent
snob 53, 223
sociability 48, 60
social theory 17, 18, 36, 66, 128
socialism 1, 11, 18, 153, 238
Society of Tower (Goethe) 89
sociology vii, 1, 2, 22, 50, 69, 70, 128, 203, 238
solitude 106, 129
somnolence *see* sleepwalking
Sonnets to Orpheus (Rilke) 39
Sophist (Plato) 117
Sophists 17, 18, 53, 147, 170, 188, 226
soul 32, 49, 54, 81, 82, 229, 230, 236, 237; Russian 210
Southern Star 164, 233
Spain 8, 52
spectatorship 30–3, 36, 45, 116, 199, 205
spider 199
split *see* schism

spectres vii, 83, 96
spiral 59, 65, 91, 100, 149, 161, 211
spirit(s) 77, 83, 105, 146, 147, 149, 203, 225, 233; Austrian 2, 7, 8, 18, 26; from bottle 73; Byzantine 7, 15, 17; cabalistic 15, 22; cabaret 17; carnival 146; evil 132; festive 150; irreverent 16; of nihilism 7; of revolt 72; of revolution 15; of times 21, 25; of world 105
spirituality 39, 115, 140, 147, 176, 205, 217, 219, 222, 223, 228
spiritism 14, 149
split personality *see* schismatic personality
spy 13
Stalinism 210
Statesman (Plato) 178
Stavrogin *see Demons* (Dostoevsky)
stigma 130
stimulant(s) 15
Stock Exchange (London) 15
stock market 15, 235; crash (1873) 10, 12, 24;
storm 39, 53, 83, 148, 149, 179, 181, 182, 183, 185, 191, 230, 237
'St Cecilia' (Raphael) 127
'St Jerome in His Cell' (Dürer) 126
St Petersburg 45, 74, 201
Strudlhofstiege, Die (Doderer) 195
struggle for survival 77, 223, 225
stupidity 195, 200, 205, 208, 228
sublime 17, 60
suffering viii, 33, 109, 115, 116, 118, 153, 191, 218, 228, 239
Sufi 15
suicide 19, 24, 37, 105, 151, 152, 168, 171, 182
surmodernité (Augé) 1
suspicion 137, 138, 149, 180, 224
swirling *see* spiral
Switzerland 39, 139
symbol 1, 6, 9, 10, 12, 19, 32, 33, 34, 36, 37, 38, 47, 94, 101, 165, 171, 185, 190, 197; resist 165
sympathy 33, 64, 75
'Sympathy with the Devil' (Rolling Stones) 193
Symposium (Plato) 40, 111, 154, 169
syphilis 12, 151, 154, 155
Syria 190
Szentendre 209

tabula rasa 94, 197
Tale of Two Cities (Dickens) 37

Subject index

Tasso (Goethe) 65, 100, 104
techniques of self (Foucault) 79
technology 29, 36, 95, 118, 131, 176, 205, 234, 235, 238; alchemic 236
telescope 131
Tel quel (Valéry) 205
tempest *see* storm
Tempest, The (Shakespeare) 21, 153, 189, 210
'Tempests' (Blixen) 153
temporariness 234
temptation 28, 44, 115, 163
terror 147; permanent 235
'Terzinen III' (Hofmannsthal) 21
thaumazein 51
theatre 2, 5, 6, 7, 9, 11, 13, 15, 25, 29–35, 36, 43, 48, 49, 50, 53, 58, 66–8, 70, 87, 88, 89, 97, 116, 149, 157, 166, 181, 183, 196, 199, 211, 229; as authentic 68; European 30; marionette 29; movie *see* cinema; reality of 30; re-birth 22; variety 16; Viennese 6; world- (Kafka) 66, 75; Yiddish 2, 66–8, 71, 72, 88 (Spiewakow Trupe 66; Yitzchak Lowy's group 66–8, 78)
Theatrical Novel (Bulgakov) 77, 180, 181, 182–4
theatricalisation 2, 21, 42, 51, 75, 77, 160, 176
theatricality 13, 17, 18, 26, 29–31, 51, 52, 66, 210
theology 64, 65–6, 70, 71, 72, 74–5, 85, 86, 89, 90, 92, 105, 106, 108, 111, 120, 205; anti- theological 2, 90, 91, 92, 100, 106
'Theses on the Philosophy of History' (Benjamin) 85
1001 Nights 60, 153, 154, 181, 212
thrownness (Heidegger) 111
Tibet 217, 218
tightrope walker 104, 171
Timaeus (Plato) 51, 105
time: freezing 212; out of joint 198, 223; reflections on 140, 141–4
Time Stands Still (Gothár) 100
Titan(ism) 34, 150, 161, 190, 191; anti- 106
Tivoli Gardens (Copenhagen) 151
'Tonio Kröger' (Mann) 132
total human fact 80
totalitarianism viii, 1, 2, 11, 97, 159, 176, 194, 195, 198, 205
Tower, The (Hofmannsthal) 34
tradition 1, 9, 27, 30, 49, 86, 91, 140, 166, 184, 188, 189, 190, 205, 211, 212, 235

traditionalism 72
Traffic (Tati) 96
tragedy 75, 210, 211, 226; domestic 71
trance 12, 171
transcendence 86, 176
transformation *see* metamorphosis
transience 35; cult of 13
transition 28, 33, 63, 73–4, 97, 110, 128, 131, 235–6
trapeze 105
travelling 39, 43, 132, 170–1, 176
Tree: of knowledge 110; of life 110;
trickster 21, 50, 51, 54, 58, 87, 88, 103, 135, 136, 137, 167, 193, 205, 211, 221
Trieste 59, 134
Trinity 71, 72, 238; 'new' 21
Troilus and Cressida (Shakespeare) 20
truthfulness 18, 21–2, 27, 30, 34, 35, 81, 153
Tristram Shandy (Sterne) 1, 36, 60, 219
'Two cities' (Augustine) 128

Ulysses (Homer) 46, 77, 88
Ulysses (Joyce) 2, 59, 125, 134
unconscious: collective 160
undifferentiation (Girard) 138, 142
unfinished (novels) 2, 18, 29, 38, 47, 49, 55, 56–7, 75, 92, 96, 98, 100, 151
Unheimlich (Kerényi) 211
unicorn 41, 59
United Nations Declaration of Human Rights 234
United States 175, 208
universalism 45, 93, 175
university 8; Vienna 19, 208
unlimited 36, 60, 64, 125, 131, 178, 192, 232, 236
unmasking 6, 30, 121, 155, 161, 186, 187, 211, 220, 221
unmoved mover 141
unpublished (novels) 52, 156, 163, 180, 194, 209, 222; *see also* unfinished
unreality 6, 76, 82, 90, 165, 167, 171, 176–7, 224, 227; absolute 44; modern 44; real 176; of theatre 43
Upanishads 236
Urnekloster 43
Use of Pleasures (Foucault) 68
Utopia (More) 126

vacuum *see* void
'Valse, La' (Ravel) 12
vampire 187, 190–1
vanguard *see* avant-garde

vanity 150, 227
Vedas 236
vengeance 20
Venice 14, 15, 41, 45, 48–54 *passim*, 57, 58, 59, 132–9, 147, 157, 186, 189, 192, 201, 211, 229
Venus and Adonis (Shakespeare) 70
'Verdict, The' (Kafka) 2, 38, 66, 68–75, 78, 86, 92, 94, 103; Georg Bendemann 69–75 *passim*; 'Russian friend' 69–76 *passim*
Verna 153
victim(hood) 88, 162, 169, 207, 215
Vienna 5–22, 38, 47, 48, 50, 130, 175, 193, 196, 197, 198, 201, 202; fin-de-siècle 5, 6, 11, 12–22, 19–21, 23, 26, 27, 34, 36, 37, 38, 201
Vienna School 18, 198
violence 33, 146, 173, 182; intrusive 33; taking as 33
virus 128
virtue 49, 130, 137, 182, 215
vision 68, 83, 97, 109, 126, 127, 132, 134, 137, 138–9, 144, 147, 157, 170, 183, 184, 197, 201, 214, 219, 233; of divine 176; of modernity (Dürer 126; Kafka 94–100); of power 234
Vita Nuova (Dante) 41, 220, 231
void 1, 2, 6, 7, 13, 26, 35, 42, 86, 99, 128, 129, 143, 150, 168, 169, 171, 212, 219, 234, 235, 236; inner 28; leap into 237; theatrical 26, 43; of values 6
voodoo 160
vulgarity 87, 200, 205
vulnerability 43, 191
vulture *see* bird(s)

Waiting for Godot (Beckett) 101
walking 46, 104, 125, 134, 144, 238
Walküres 211
waltz 12
'Waltz Dream, A' (Dörmann) 12
'Waltz Dream, A' (Straus) 12
Walpurgisnacht see Witches' Sabbath
wandering *see* walking
Waning of the Middle Ages (Huizinga) 60
war(s) 1, 172, 174, 177, 183, 214, 222, 223, 232, 234; civil (Russian) 181; colonial 225; of containment 225; Franco-Prussian 10; League of Cambrai 126; modern 226; Napoleonic 63; Thirty Years 38; Trojan 223; world viii, 2, 8, 160, 176, 187, 225 (First 10, 12, 13, 28, 34, 35, 38, 49, 59, 63, 64, 66, 71, 83, 103, 125, 132, 140, 148, 149–50, 151, 153, 158, 166, 175, 181, 195, 198, 205, 214, 217, 222; Second 29, 63, 147, 158, 159, 194, 195, 220; Third 221)
War Pilot (Saint Exupéry) 234
Wasteland (Eliot) 41
way 46, 55, 102, 104, 111, 114, 118–21, 150; of death 131; of life 46 (America 95; Christian 36); right 111, 113, 118–21, 143; true 106, 113
welfare state 238
White Guard (Bulgakov) 180, 183
Wilhelm Meister (Goethe) 53, 55, 57
Wilhelm Meister's Apprenticeship (Goethe) 65, 89, 100
Wilhelm Meister's Theatrical Mission (Goethe) 49
will-power 58, 133, 136, 137, 147 *see also* sleepwalking
will to power (Nietzsche) 54
Winter Tale, A (Shakespeare) 158
Winter's Tales (Blixen) 158
witch 152, 153, 157, 184; -hunt 200
Witches' Sabbath 145, 181, 184, 189
Wittgenstein's Vienna (Janik and Toulmin) 10, 11
Woman Without a Shadow (Hofmannsthal) 28, 33, 51, 55–6; Empress 33, 56
world 2, 6, 18, 25, 27, 30, 33, 42, 60, 89, 93, 95, 100, 104–5, 110, 111–18, 119; history 40, 43, 112, 229, 232; order 98; turned upside down 75, 79, 99, 160, 173, 216, 236; vision 39, 201 (Kafka's 89, 115; mechanical 90; Christian-Platonic 49, 177, 179; scientific 45, 101; technological-scientific 39, 49; theological 157; Thomist 207) understanding of 112
World Fair(s); London 10; Vienna 10, 24;

Yemen 15
Yesterday (Hofmannsthal) 47, 53
Yom Kippur 66, 68–9, 72, 78
'Young Vienna' circle 21, 22

Zarathustra (Nietzsche) 104
zero 81, 101, 114, 141, 143, 163, 168, 169
Zeus 48
Zodiac 233
zoo 213, 224
Zürau 83, 94, 102, 103, 112, 114
Zürau aphorisms *see* Zürau Notebooks
Zürau Notebooks (Kafka) 2, 56, 63, 82, 83, 85, 99, 100, 102–21
Zürich 16